The
Kristeva Reader

The
Kristeva Reader

Julia Kristeva

EDITED BY TORIL MOI

New York Columbia University Press

Library of Congress Cataloging-in-Publication Data
Kristeva, Julia, 1941–
    The Kristeva reader.

    Bibliography: p.
    Includes index.
    1. Semiotics. 2. Psychoanalysis. 3. Women.
    4. Political science. I. Moi, Toril. II. Title.
    P99.K687 1986   808'.00141   86–11706
    ISBN 0–231–06324–5
    ISBN 0–231–06325–3 (pbk.)

p 10 9 8
c 10 9 8 7 6 5 4 3 2

Contents

Preface

To think the unthinkable: from the outset this has been Julia Kristeva's project. Scanning with exceptional intensity the whole horizon of Western culture, her writing investigates the terrains of philosophy, theology, linguistics, literature, art, politics and, not least, psychoanalysis, which remains the crucial intellectual influence on her work. Always challenging, original, provocative, her work can lead to no easy consensus. However controversial, it is nevertheless far too important to be ignored. Speaking across the conventional disciplinary boundaries of the academic world, Kristeva raises the fundamental issues of human existence: language, truth, ethics, love. For me, as for many other women, the fact that this epochal *oeuvre* has been produced by a woman who often and explicitly chooses to focus on problems of femininity, motherhood and sexual difference is an added incentive to come to grips with her thought.

The Kristeva Reader is a comprehensive introduction to her work in English, containing a wide range of essays from all phases of Kristeva's career. The essays have been selected as representative of the three main areas of her writing: semiotics, psychoanalysis and politics. Given the conceptual and theoretical difficulty of her texts, each essay has been provided with a short introduction presenting the basic issues and explicating the central concepts of that specific text. The general introduction to the volume aims to provide an overview of Kristeva's intellectual development and a presentation of the main issues raised by her work. In order to avoid repetition of similar material, the general introduction does not, as a rule, repeat explanations provided elsewhere in this volume. Instead I have simply added a short, parenthetical reference to the relevant essay, to enable readers in doubt about specific definitions and ideas to turn to that particular text and its accompanying introduction for further information.

Offering at once enough editorial material to help those in search of a basic grounding in Kristeva's complex, disturbing theories, and a compact, convenient selection of important articles, some of them otherwise hard to come by, *The Kristeva Reader* is designed for beginners as well as for those already familiar with her work. The introductory presentations of her texts nevertheless presuppose some basic knowledge of psychoanalytic vocabulary, particularly as developed by Jacques Lacan, as well as some knowledge of Jacques Derrida's central ideas. Any current introduction to literary or psychoanalytic theory should provide the necessary background for the complete beginner (see for instance the works by Eagleton, Norris and Wright listed in the bibliography after the general introduction).

The Kristeva Reader presents the work of many different translators. Seán Hand's translations were commissioned specially for this volume. The other texts have been collected from a series of different sources, and apart from some minor stylistic changes they are reproduced as originally printed. Documentation style and terminology may therefore vary slightly from one essay to another. To intervene in other translators' already published work in order to systematize and streamline their efforts to reconstruct Kristeva's original French in English would seem to be both an insulting and a theoretically useless exercise: there can never be one, true translation of any text, let alone of a collection of thirteen different essays.

I would like to thank Julia Kristeva for her continuous support for this project. Her positive and encouraging responses to various queries have been a steady source of inspiration for my work. My editor at Basil Blackwell, Philip Carpenter, provided much practical help and remained perfectly calm when faced with unexpected obstacles and inexplicable delays. Seán Hand worked hard to produce the new translations required for this volume. Terence Cave, Terry Eagleton and Jacqueline Rose all provided help and advice on specific points. Needless to say, the responsibility for any remaining errors in the editorial material is mine.

Toril Moi

Acknowledgments

The editor and publishers would like to thank the following for permission to include the material collected in this edition: for 'The System and the Speaking Subject', the editor, *Times Literary Supplement*; for 'Word, Dialogue and Novel', Basil Blackwell Ltd; for 'From Symbol to Sign', Mouton Publishers (Division of Walter de Gruyter & Co.); for 'Semiotics: A Critical Science and/or a Critique of Science', 'Revolution in Poetic Language', 'The True-Real', 'Why the United States?' and 'A New Type of Intellectual: The Dissident', Editions du Seuil, Paris; for 'About Chinese Women', Marion Boyars Publishers, London and New York; for 'Revolution in Poetic Language', 'Stabat Mater' and 'Freud and Love: Treatment and Its Discontents', Columbia University Press; for 'Women's Time' and 'Psychology and the Polis', the University of Chicago Press.

Introduction

The semiotic project

In 1966 Paris witnessed not only the publication of Jacques Lacan's *Ecrits* and Michel Foucault's *Les Mots et les choses* (*The Order of Things*), but also the arrival of a young linguist from Bulgaria. At the age of 25, Julia Kristeva, equipped with a doctoral research fellowship, embarked on her intellectual encounter with the French capital. It would seem that she took the Left Bank by storm. By the spring of 1967 her articles were already appearing in its most prestigious reviews: *Critique*, *Langages* – and, not least, *Tel Quel*.[1] Kristeva's linguistic research was soon to lead to the publication of two important books, *Le Texte du roman* and *Séméiotiké*, and to culminate with the publication of her massive doctoral thesis, *La Révolution du langage poétique*, in 1974. This theoretical production earned her a chair in linguistics at the University of Paris VII.

In 1966, initially helped by her compatriot Tzvétan Todorov, Kristeva soon met and worked with the most important figures of the blossoming structuralist milieu in Paris. Although she started work as a research assistant to Lucien Goldmann, her most important teacher was – and always remained – Roland Barthes. Reviewing her first published book, *Séméiotiké*, in *La Quinzaine Littéraire*, Barthes wrote:

> I already owe her a lot and have done so right from the start. And now I have been made to feel again – and this time in its entirety – the force of her work. *Force* here means *displacement*. Julia Kristeva changes the order of things: she always destroys the latest preconception, the one we thought we could be comforted by, the one of which we could be proud: what she displaces is the *already-said*, that is to say, the insistence of the signified; what she subverts is the authority of monologic science and of filiation. (p. 19)

The reason why Kristeva right from the start of her career in Paris was in a position to inspire her own teachers is to be found in her unique intellectual background. Having equipped her not only with a solid grounding in Marxist theory but also with fluent Russian, her Eastern European training enabled her to gain first-hand knowledge of the Russian Formalists, and – more importantly – of the great Soviet theorist Mikhail Bakhtin, whose work she (along with Tzvétan Todorov) was instrumental in introducing to Western intellectuals (see 'Word, Dialogue and Novel'). This double heritage, at once Marxist and Formalist, enabled her to make the most of the structuralist impulses she met with in Paris, giving her the confidence and context necessary not only to learn from them but to appropriate and transform them for her own particular project. A third element, however, must be added to this picture: the philosophy of Hegel. In his excellent review of Kristeva's early work, Philip E. Lewis remarks on the importance of Hegel for *Revolution in Poetic Language*, while simultaneously stressing her independent appropriation of the Hegelian concept of negativity. 'Her relations to both Hegel and Marx', he warns, 'are exceedingly complex and never aquiescent, [and] certainly do not allow cursory characterization' (p. 29).

It was, then, this specific and relatively unusual intellectual background that enabled Kristeva to take up a *critical* position towards structuralism from the outset. Even her earliest work (from 1967–8) exhibits that dynamic, process-oriented view of the sign which in many ways still stands as the hallmark of her theoretical production. 'Semiotics: a Critical Science and/or a Critique of Science' demonstrates precisely her radical attack on the rigid, scientistic pretensions of a certain kind of structuralism, as well as on the subjectivist and empiricist categories of traditional humanism:

> No form of semiotics, therefore, can exist other than as a critique of semiotics. As the place where the sciences die, semiotics is both the knowledge of this death and the revival, *with* this knowledge, of the 'scientific'; less (or more) than a science, it marks instead the aggressivity and disillusionment that takes place within scientific discourse itself. We might argue that semiotics is that 'science of ideologies' suggested in revolutionary Russia, but it is also an ideology of sciences. (p. 78 below)

As Roland Barthes put it: Kristeva was always *foreign* to the theoretical scene she was in, radically subversive even of the new science of semiology (see 'L'Etrangère, pp. 19–20). In this sense, I think, she was never a structuralist at all, but rather (if labels are to be used) a kind of post-structuralist *avant la lettre*. In her preface to *Desire in Language*, she herself gives what is perhaps the best and most accessible summary of her own semiotic project, a summary which also reveals the intensity of her theoretical engagement:

> Next to structuralism, a critique of Hegelian, Heideggerian, Marxian or Freudian derivation jolted its occasionally simplistic elegance and carried theoretical thought to an intensity of white heat that set categories and concepts ablaze – sparing not even discourse itself. *Semanalysis*, as I tried to describe it and put it to work in Σημειωτικὴ, meets that requirement to describe the signifying phenomenon, or signifying phenomena, while analyzing, criticizing, and dissolving 'phenomenon', 'meaning' and 'signifier'. (p. vii)

Her own personal situation as a foreigner in Paris, and as a woman in an extremely male-dominated environment (with one or two exceptions, the *Tel Quel* group with which she soon became associated consisted of men), also helped to give shape and edge to her ambitious semiotic project. 'To work on language, to labour in the *materiality* of that which society regards as a means of contact and understanding, isn't that at one stroke to declare oneself a stranger/foreign [*étranger*] to language?' she asks defiantly in the first sentence of *Séméiotiké*. Ten yeas later, she stresses the fact of her femaleness as one of the determinants of her theoretical outlook: 'It was perhaps also necessary to be a *woman* to attempt to take up that exorbitant wager of carrying the rational project to the outer borders of the signifying venture of men...' (*Desire in Language*, p. x). It is, then, in her own exiled and marginalized position as an intellectual woman in Paris in the late sixties, as well as in her specific intellectual lineage, that we can locate the formative influences on Kristeva's early work.

Tel Quel: the politics of post-modernism?

From her earliest days in Paris, Kristeva's work was associated with the *Tel Quel* group headed by the novelist and theorist Philippe Sollers, who later became her husband. One of her very first articles to be published in France appeared in *Tel Quel* as early as the spring of 1967 ('Pour une sémiologie des paragrammes', *Tel Quel*, 29). By the summer of 1970 she had become a member of the editorial board, where she remained until 1983, when *Tel Quel* liquidated itself and the prestigious series of books published under its imprint, relinquishing its links with the Editions du Seuil, only to re-emerge from the ashes as the new journal *L'Infini*, now published by Denoël, who also published Kristeva's latest full-length book, *Histoires d'amour* (1983).

In the late sixties *Tel Quel* became a centre of gravitation for almost all of the younger generation of structuralist and emerging post-structuralist theorists in France. The *Théorie d'ensemble*, published as a collective work after the uprising of May 1968, has contributions from Roland Barthes, Michel Foucault, Jacques Derrida, Marcelin Pleynet and Jean Ricardou as well as Julia Kristeva, Philippe Sollers and a series of other avant-garde critics. Although *Tel Quel* never published any of Foucault's books, they did publish Barthes, Derrida, Genette, Todorov, Ricardou and, of course, Kristeva and Sollers, as well as many other works of an 'experimental' nature (whether 'theoretical' or 'creative').

What, then, was the hallmark of this group in the late sixties? If one were to summarize their project in one single concept, it would have to be, I think, the idea of a 'modernist theory' as distinct from a mere theory of modernism. Focusing, like structuralism, on *language* as the starting-point for a new kind of thought on politics and the subject, the group based its work on a new understanding of history as *text*; and of writing (*écriture*) as *production*, not representation. Within these parameters, they sought to elaborate new concepts for the description of this new vision of the social or signifying space (Kristeva, with her coinage of terms such as 'intertextuality', 'signifying practice' or 'signifiance', 'paragramme', 'genotext' and 'phenotext', was the main exponent of this specific trend); to produce a *plural history* of different kinds of writing situated in relation to their specific time and space; and, finally, to articulate a *politics* which would constitute the logical consequence of a non-representational understanding of writing.[2]

The *Tel Quel* group thus perceived itself and its own avant-garde activity as political, in a way which came increasingly to be identified with Maoism. Their political commitment in the late 1960s, however, can only be understood in the context of May 1968. Students and other intellectuals in the 1980s, struggling against a climate of unemployment, recession and increasingly savage cuts in the educational institutions, may have some trouble in understanding the exhilarating effect of the May revolt on students and intellectuals all over the world. It took everybody, including the Left, by surprise: 'The May Revolution in France was foreseen by nobody. It burst upon the world without warning. It did not fit any preconceived pattern', wrote the young editors of the British *New Left Review* in their investigation of the 'events' toward the end of that momentous year.[3] Here was what seemed an incipient revolution inspired and instigated by students and some of their teachers, supported and taken over by workers: at one time over ten million workers in France were on strike, in spite of active opposition from the French Communist Party (the PCF) and the communist-controlled sections of the trade union movement.

The May revolt was soon rolled back by the state. The parliamentary elections which followed the uprising produced an overwhelming victory for Gaullism, and the Left massively blamed the PCF for its defeat. For in May and June of 1968 the PCF went to great lengths to prevent the two potentially revolutionary forces – students and workers – from engaging with each other, locking factory gates and sending workers home in order to prevent sit-ins and occupations. Rejecting the unortho-dox methods (occupations, sit-ins, street fighting) of the revolutionary students and workers, the PCF opted decisively for parliamentary politics, thus aligning itself with the liberal democratic institutions of the bourgeois state. In spite of the defeat of the militancy, however, the French – and more generally the European – Left saw May 68 as a tremendous encouragement for their own political activism: the revolu-tion was still possible, Marxist theory was still relevant to contemporary political struggles in the Western world and, most importantly in our context, intellectuals did have a revolutionary role to play after all. 'The May events vindicated the fundamental socialist belief that the industrial proletariat is the revolutionary class of advanced capitalism', wrote the editors of *New Left Review*. 'It has at the same stroke, made indisputable the vital revolutionary role of intellectuals, of all generations. The combination of the two was precisely the chemical formula which produced the shattering explosion of May' (p. 7).

The reactionary role played by the PCF in this process put an end to the possibility of a meaningful dialogue between the French Left and the Communist Party, which was now perceived as nothing but the agent of the revisionist regime of the Soviet Union. Many committed left-wingers accordingly looked for other radical alternatives. The Soviet invasion in Czechoslovakia in August 1968 did nothing to endear the Soviet Union to Western intellectuals. At the same time, the steady escalation of the Vietnam war fuelled the anti-American tendencies of the French Left. It was in this context that the French *gauchistes* came to look to China, or to some kind of libertarian anarchism (or at times to a highly confusing mixture of both), for political inspiration.

For the *Tel Quel* group, China seemed to offer a radical perspective compatible with their own theoretical and artistic endeavours. In the late sixties their vision of The People's Republic, firmly rooted on the Left Bank as it was, seems to have constructed the Cultural Revolution as an effort towards the creation of a materialist practice bearing on the *sign*. Textual productivity, the desire to rewrite history as an open-ended text, the destruction of the monolithic institutions of the sign or the signifying space: all this seemed to euphoric, outside sympathizers to be taking place in Mao's China. The Red Brigades destroying the material institutions of traditional intellectual power seemed to point a way forward for the West. What *Tel Quel* did not know then, of course, was that behind the facade of smiling Chinese worker-intellectuals, happily tending pigs or spreading dung in order to increase their understanding of historical materialism, there was another, grimmer reality: the tortured, dead or dying Chinese, intellectuals and non-intellectuals alike, sacrificed to the greater glory of Chairman Mao.

The *Tel Quel* group's interest in China culminated in their three week long visit in April and May of 1974. Kristeva, having been brought up under an East European Communist regime, was probably never as uncritically enthusiastic about China as some other French intellectuals at the time. For her, China could not function as the absolute Other, in the way it obviously did for other members of *Tel Quel*. In this way, she also avoided suffering their disillusionment when the truth about the Cultural Revolution became generally known, and Mao turned out to have been a Stalinist wolf in Chinese clothing after all. In a conversation with Rosalind Coward at the Institute for Contemporary Art in London in 1983, Kristeva explained how the 'Chinese experience', coinciding as it did with her encounter with feminism and her own entry into psycho-analysis, made her re-evaluate her political positions and decide to settle for a more localized interest in the individual, thus in effect abandoning her previous interest in a more general, political engagement:[4]

In the meantime we went to China and for me it was more a cultural interest than a political one. There were both interests. But I wanted to see what can be done when Marxism is developed in a country that possessed a different cultural background, that doesn't have a monolithic religion, that thinks in a particular way, that speaks in a particular way because I think the Chinese character and language indicate not a particular mentality, which would be a racist position, but a different logic of organisation. I wanted to see what could be the difference of a society organised on the basis of the meeting of these two components. And what I saw was very problematic, particularly in the situation of women. Several positive things have been done and said but I couldn't notice any liberation of women in the sense of the Western movements, and of course in different fields, as well. So this was for me a point of re-evaluation of the whole problematic of political involvement. And personally from the point of view of my own development I thought that it would be more honest for me not to engage politically but to try to be helpful or useful in a narrow field, where the individual life is concerned, and where I can do something more objective and maybe more sharp, and more independent of different political pressures. (p. 25)

In 1974 Kristeva published her experience of the women of China in *Des Chinoises*, translated in 1977 as *About Chinese Women*. And in the period from about 1974 to 1977 her intellectual interests did undergo an obvious shift: away from the purely linguistic or semiotic work which culminated in *Revolution in Poetic Language*, and towards a more psychoanalytically oriented examination of the problems of femininity and motherhood, either as embodied in Western representations of women or mothers, or as an area posing new theoretical problems for the psychoanalyst. This shift is not unrelated to the fact that during this period she herself became a mother (her son was born in 1976), and completed her training as a psychoanalyst, starting her own psychoanalytic practice in 1979. In this volume, the excerpts from *About Chinese Women* (1974), 'Stabat Mater' (1977), 'The True-Real' (1979) and 'Women's Time' (1979) trace this development of her thought, a development that can be said to culminate in her ambitious study of love in the Western world, *Histoires d'amour* (1983).

Kristeva's 1977 article 'A New Type of Intellectual: the Dissident', which presents what one may call a politics of marginality, demonstrates at once her loss of belief in collective political action (she describes the politically active intellectual as someone hopelessly caught in the very logic of power he or she is seeking to undermine) and her continued commitment to a politicized analysis of intellectual activity. 'Why the United States?', also published in 1977, again demonstrates the *Tel Quel* group's tendency to project their own theoretical and aesthetic positions on to a conveniently distant Other – this time the USA. Since China turned out not to exemplify the revolution of the signifying space after all, *Tel Quel* looked to the States instead. Their presentation of the USA as a non-verbal culture which to some extent escapes the more repressive aspects of the Law of the Father has come in for harsh criticism from the Left.[5] However, it is important to notice that it is Kristeva herself who sounds a warning note against any such simplistic idealization of the States. In an illuminating presentation of her thought, Jacqueline Rose points out that Kristeva in this interview not only praises 'the "non-verbal" aspects of modern American culture which draw...on the realms of "gesture, colour and sound"', but [also asks] whether that same non-verbalisation might not also be the sign of a resistance, the almost psychotic hyper-activity of a violent and overproductive culture incessantly on the go'.[6]

In the 1980s it would seem that Kristeva, while not seeking to deny the relative importance of the political, refuses to accord it a general or primary status. Explicitly distancing herself from the slogan that 'everything is political', she argues for the need to elaborate a more complex understanding of the apparently non-political aspects of human life. For her, the fact that love or desire cannot be adequately understood by an exclusively political discourse becomes a crucial argument for the widening of the traditional horizons of the Left:

> The political discourse, the political causality which is dominant even in human sciences in universities and everywhere is too narrow and too feeble in comparison with St Bernard and St Thomas. If we stay with only a political explanation of human phenomena we will be overwhelmed by the so-called mystical crisis, or spiritual crisis – that happens, it's a reality. Every bourgeois family has a son or daughter who has a mystical crisis – it's understandable because of this very schematic explanation of such phenomena as

love or desire simply by politics. So my problem is: how, through psychoanalysis or something else like art, through such discourses can we try to elaborate a more complicated elaboration, discourse sublimation of these critical points of the human experience which cannot be reduced to a political causality. (ICA conversation, p. 25).[7]

Feminism and femininity

Kristeva's relationship to feminism has always been that of a somewhat critical fellow-traveller. This position appears more puzzling, perhaps, in a British or American context than it does in France. For at least some of Kristeva's more negative references to 'feminism' (often deliberately put in inverted commas) would seem to be directed against 'feminism' as defined in Paris by the Psych et Po group (who run the publishing house *des femmes*) – that is, as a reformist movement consisting of women seeking power within the existing framework of the bourgeois state. Such a position would be called 'bourgeois' or 'liberal' feminism in English-speaking countries, and as such is not at all representative of the politics of a great many feminist intellectuals on both sides of the Atlantic. At other times, however, her use of the word comes much closer to the more general English definition of it as a movement seeking to put an end to all forms of patriarchal or sexist power. At this general level, there is a sense in which Kristeva's texts, concerned as they are with the subversion and disruption of all monolithic power structures, can be taken to support such a goal. Yet the fact that she has apparently remained aloof from the call for explicitly feminist approaches to Western cultural tradition and her clearly stated disapproval of the feminist insistence on the need to politicize *all* human relationships would seem to indicate a curiously distant relationship to current feminist debates and to feminism in general.

In her essay 'From Ithaca to New York' ('D'Ithaca à New York'), first published in 1974 and reprinted in *Polylogue* (1977), Kristeva sets out the double bind of the feminist movement as she then perceived it. Characterizing it as a movement of hysterics (a term which in this context is to be taken as a descriptive, clinical term, much in the way it is used by Hélène Cixous in her discussion of Frued's *Dora* in *La Jeune née*, and not as a masculinist put-down), she argues that the hysteric split between non-verbal substance (defined as the body, the drives, *jouissance*) on the one hand, and the Law on the other, repeats itself in the demands and activities of the women's movement. The problem is that as soon as the insurgent 'substance' speaks, it is necessarily caught up in the kind of discourse allowed by and submitted to the Law:

> At the moment, this is all there is, and that's not bad. But will there be more? A different relationship of the subject to discourse, to power? Will the eternal frustration of the hysteric in relation to discourse oblige the latter to reconstruct itself? Will it give rise to unrest in everybody, male or female? Or will it remain a cry outside time, like the great mass movements that break up the old system, but have no problem in submitting to the demands of order, as long as it is a new order? (*Polylogue*, p. 511)

Capturing much of Kristeva's continuing unease with feminism, this passage also illuminates her consistent and fundamental project: the desire to produce a discourse which always confronts the *impasse* of language (as at once subject to and subversive of the rule of the Law), a discourse which in a final aporetic move dares to think language against itself, and in so doing knowingly situates itself in a place which is, quite literally, untenable.

In one sense, Kristeva's relatively distant attitude towards feminism stems from her fear that *any* kind of political idiom, be it liberal, socialist or feminist, will necessarily reveal itself as yet another master-discourse. Although this danger is real enough, I feel that she here underestimates the truly subversive potential of one of the most unsettling political discourses of our time. This is not to say that Kristeva is wrong to indict the distressing tendency of some contemporary forms of feminism towards simplistic, anti-intellectual analyses of women's position and struggle. It is, however, to argue that this is no reason to reject feminism *en bloc*.

Kristeva has repeatedly criticized liberal or bourgeois feminism for its lack of radicalism (see for instance 'Women's Time' in this volume), although she has reserved her most severe criticisms for French radical feminism or the kind of feminism which emphasizes women's intrinsic difference from men. In an article written for the *Nouvelle Revue de Psychanalyse* and published in 1979, she warns against a too rapid valorization of difference:

The desire to give voice to sexual difference, and particularly to the position of the woman-subject within meaning and signification, leads to a veritable insurrection against the homogenizing *signifier*. However, it is all too easy to pass from the search for *difference* to the denegation of the symbolic. The latter is the same as to remove the 'feminine' from the order of language (understood as dominated exclusively by the secondary process) and to inscribe it within the primary process alone, whether in the drive that calls out or simply the drive *tout court*. In this case, does not the struggle against the 'phallic sign' and against the whole mono-logic, monotheistic culture which supports itself on it, sink into an essentialist cult of *Woman*, into a hysterical obsession with the neutralizing cave, a fantasy arising precisely as the negative imprint of the maternal phallus?. . . In other words, if the feminine *exists*, it only exists in the order of signifiance or signifying process, and it is only in relation to meaning and signification, positioned as their excessive or transgressive other that it *exists, speaks, thinks* (itself) and *writes* (itself) for both sexes. ('Il n'y a pas de maître à langage', pp. 134–5)

Although primarily directed against the French 'feminism of difference' and various French theories of an *écriture féminine* (differently and divergently represented by the Psych et Po group, Hélène Cixous and Luce Irigaray),[8] this somewhat polemical passage highlights Kristeva's own position on the question of femininity: as different or other in relation to language and meaning, but nevertheless only thinkable within the symbolic, and therefore also necessarily subject to the Law. Maintaining such a finely balanced position is far from easy, and Kristeva herself has from time to time written about femininity in terms which would seem to equate the feminine with the 'semiotic' or the pre-Oedipal. While emphasizing these slippages in her discourse, Jacqueline Rose's critique of Kristeva convincingly sums up the difficulties of her project as it developed from a concentration on the semiotic (*Revolution in Poetic Language*) to an exploration of the hidden fantasies of violence and destruction linked to the pre-Oedipal mother (*Powers of Horror*):

Kristeva's work splits on a paradox, or rather a dilemma: the hideous moment when a theory arms itself with a concept of femininity as different, as something other to the culture as it is known, only to find itself face to face with, or even entrenched within, the most grotesque and fully cultural stereotypes of femininity itself. Unlike some of her most virulent detractors, Kristeva at least knows, however, that these images are not so easily dispatched. It is not by settling the question of their origins that we can necessarily dismantle their force.[9]

In *Histoires d'amour*, Kristeva takes a step further away from any tendencies towards an idealization of the pre-Oedipal mother, or the semiotic as an idealized feminine enclave, by introducing the concept of the 'father of personal prehistory' or pre-Oedipal father, understood as the mother's desire of the phallus, who intervenes crucially at the fourth month of the child's life in order to effectuate the first, preliminary split within the void of primary narcissism (see 'Freud and Love').[10]

Psychoanalysis and the subject

In the late sixties and early seventies Kristeva's linguistic theory came to be increasingly influenced by psychoanalysis, an influence which resulted in the psycho-linguistic understanding of language proposed in *Revolution in Poetic Language*.[11] These theories have in their turn become the starting-point for a series of discussions of the status of the subject and of the question of identity in psychoanalysis, an issue of central importance also to political theories such as feminism or Marxism.

Revolution in Poetic Language presents a theory of the processes which constitute language. These are centred on the speaking subject (see also 'The System and the Speaking Subject' in this volume). Setting out to understand the signifying process (*signifiance*), Kristeva transforms Lacan's distinction between the imaginary and the symbolic order into a distinction between the *semiotic* and the *symbolic*. The interaction between these two terms (which, it must be stressed, are processes, not static entities) then constitutes the signifying process. The semiotic is linked to the pre-Oedipal primary processes, the basic pulsions of which Kristeva sees as predominantly anal and oral, and as simultaneously dichotomous (life/death, expulsion/introjection) and heterogeneous. The endless flow of pulsions is gathered up in the *chora* (from the Greek word for enclosed space, womb). Kristeva appropriates and redefines this Platonic concept and concludes that the *chora* is neither a sign nor a position, but 'an essentially mobile and extremely provisional articulation constituted by movements and their emphemeral stases. . . Neither model nor copy, the *chora* precedes and underlies figuration and thus specularization, and is analogous only to vocal and kinetic rhythm' (pp. 93–4 below).

For Kristeva, *signifiance* is a question of positioning. The semiotic continuum must be split if signification is to be produced. This splitting (*coupure*) of the semiotic *chora* is the *thetic* phase (from *thesis*), enabling the subject to attribute differences and thus signification to what was the ceaseless heterogeneity of the *chora*. Following Lacan, Kristeva posits the mirror phase as the first step that permits 'the constitution of objects detached from the semiotic *chora*' (p. 100 below), and the Oedipal phase with its threat of castration as the moment in which the process of separation or splitting is fully achieved. Once the subject has entered into the symbolic order, the *chora* will be more or less successfully repressed and can be perceived only as pulsional *pressure* on or within symbolic language: as contradictions, meaninglessness, disruption, silences and absences. The *chora*, then, is a rhythmic pulsion rather than a new language. It constitutes the heterogeneous, disruptive dimension of language, that which can never be caught up in the closure of traditional linguistic theory.

Kristeva is acutely aware of the contradictions involved in trying to theorize the untheorizable *chora*, a contradiction located at the centre of the semiotic enterprise: 'Being, because of its explanatory meta-linguistic force, an agent of social cohesion, semiotics contributes to the formation of that reassuring image which every society offers itself when it understands everything, down to and including the practices which voluntarily expend it' ('The System and the Speaking Subject', p. 31 below). Semiotic theory is therefore always already caught up in a paradox, an aporia which is the same as that of the speaking subject: both find themselves in a position which is at once subversive of and dependent on the law. The Kristevan subject is a subject-in-process (*sujet en procès*), but a subject nevertheless. We find her carrying out once again a difficult balancing act between a position which would deconstruct subjectivity and identity altogether, and one that would try to capture these entities in an essentialist or humanist mould.

It is Kristeva's psychoanalytic practice that makes her put the case with such force for an unstable and always threatened, yet nevertheless real and necessary, form of subjectivity. The analyst is after all engaged in the task of healing her patients, and has therefore to provide them with some kind of 'identity' which will enable them to live in the world, that is to say, within the symbolic order dominated by the law. This is not to say that the analyst turns her patients into slavish conformists, but rather that without some kind of subject structure, meaningful, subversive or creative action is impossible. At the end of *Histoires d'amour*, Kristeva raises the question of the aim of psychoanalytic treatment. Is it really tenable to see the attempt to give the empty 'borderline case' (see the introduction to 'The True-Real') what might very well be yet another 'false self' as the end of the analysis? Arguing that it may be preferable to leave such patients their moments of emptiness, inauthenticity and absence, Kristeva nevertheless affirms that it is necessary first and foremost to help them to overcome the pain that made them seek psychoanalytic help in the first place. The modern, unstable and empty subject, she argues, ought not to be fixed and stabilized, but to be turned into a *work in progress*. This means that psychoanalytic patients must be left, at the end of analysis, in a position which enables them to express themselves. But expression requires subjectivity, and therefore the Law, which constructs speaking subjects in the first place. Perhaps, therefore, the speaking or writing one ought to seek out for such patients would be imaginative and imaginary, Kristeva argues, since this is the only kind of activity that can fill the narcissistic void without fixing it in a too rigid concept of 'self'.

In a recent interview, Kristeva explains this notion of the imaginary and the imagination as a support for identity:

> I think that in the imaginary, maternal continuity is what guarantees identity. One may imagine other social systems where it would be different... The imaginary of the work of art, that is really the most extraordinary and the most unsettling imitation of the mother–child dependence. [It is] its substitution and its displacement towards a limit which is fascinating because inhuman. The work of art is independence conquered through inhumanity. The work of art cuts off natural filiation, it is patricide and matricide, it is superbly solitary. But look back-stage, as does the analyst, and you will find a dependence, a secret mother on whom this sublimation is constructed. (*Les Cahiers du GRIF*, 32, p. 23)

The imaginary is the realm of the discourse of transference, which is love (see 'Freud and Love'). Love, for Kristeva, then becomes the indispensable element of the cure, the moment of structuring which intervenes in the imaginary chaos, an organizing force produced by the intervention of the 'father of personal prehistory' in the very first months of the child's life. The psychoanalytic situation is one in which such love (transference love) is allowed to establish itself, if only precariously and only in order to undo itself in the end. It is, then, this transference love which allows the patient tentatively to erect some kind of subjectivity, to become a subject-in-process in the symbolic order. The psychoanalytic interpretation, then, is precisely one that is poised in the space suspended between One Meaning and the deconstructive rejection of all truth, however tentative (see 'Psychoanalysis and the Polis'). A commitment to the concept of psychic identity, Jacqueline Rose argues, need not be politically reactionary or collude with the 'way that identity is paraded in the culture at large':

> Far from this involving a denial of the other psychic forces which have been at the centre of her writing, it could be seen as the only place from which they can be known...Nor do I think that Kristeva should be dismissed for her analysis of love as a strategy which allows individual subjects to negotiate the troubled psychic waters which she herself so graphically describes. To which we could add that this love does not have to be incompatible with politics.[12]

Indeed, one could argue that some concept of agency (of a *subject of action*) is essential to any political theory worthy of the name.

Ethics and truth: psychoanalysis, semiotics and deconstruction

Already in *Revolution in Poetic Language* Kristeva outlines her doubts about Derrida's theory of *différance*.[13] Seeing his grammatology essentially as a strategy drawing on Hegel's notion of negativity in order to construct a critique of phenomenology, Kristeva criticizes him for his *positivization* of this concept of negativity, which is suddenly 'drained of its potential for producing breaks...It holds itself back and appears as a delaying [*retardement*], it defers and thus becomes merely positive and affirmative' (*Revolution*, p. 141). While acknowledging that grammatology unsettles and disturbs logic and the subject of logic, it nevertheless fails in Kristeva's view to account for breaks, changes and transformations in the social structure, precisely because of its fundamental incapacity to account for the subject and the splitting (the *coupure* of the thetic) which produces it:

> Grammatology denounces the economy of the symbolic function and opens up a space that the latter cannot subsume. But in its desire to bar the thetic and put (logically or chronologically) previous energy transfers in its place, the grammatological deluge of meaning gives up on the subject and must remain ignorant not only of his functioning as social practice, but also of his chances for experiencing jouissance or being put to death. Neutral in the face of all positions, theses and structures, grammatology is, as a consequence, equally restrained when they break, burst or rupture: demonstrating disinterestedness toward (symbolic and/or social) structure, grammatology remains silent when faced with its destruction or renewal. (*Revolution*, p. 142)

In this critique of what has become known as deconstruction, we can see Kristeva's concern to safeguard a place for the subject, albeit a subject-in-process, simply because it is the instance which allows us to account for the various heterogeneous forces (drives, pulsions) which disrupt language. Kristeva's concern for a linguistics of the speaking subject and her view of language as *work* or *production* necessarily lead her to question the seemingly subjectless field of signifying play produced by deconstruction. While fully acknowledging deconstruction's subversive effects on transcendence, Kristeva points out that it also deconstructs every other thesis (material, natural, social, substantial or logical) and that it must do so 'in order to free itself from any dependence on the *Logos*' (*Revolution*, p. 143). Deconstruction thus falls into the trap of not being truly able to account for that which is heterogeneous to language and the symbolic space, precisely because such heterogeneous elements are *negative* (depending on splitting, scission, separation) in their mode of operation. This negativity situates them outside the space of the signifier which is the scene of *différance*. It is Kristeva's insistence on the *reality* of the drives of the imaginary which forces her to oppose Derrida's grammatological project, not so much because she disagrees with his analysis as because it doesn't go far enough, remaining as it does enclosed in the field of the signifier alone. Showing up the limited scope of a 'mere grammatology', semanalysis or semiotics, because of its emphasis on rejection (negativity, splitting), simply outflanks deconstruction:

> A heterogeneous energy discharge, whose very principle is that of scission and division, enters into contradiction with what has been traced [*le tracé*], but produces only flashes, ruptures and sudden displacements, which constitute preconditions for *new* symbolic productions in which the economy of *différance* will be able to find its place as well. But there is no guarantee that rejection will be able to maintain the scene of *différance*. Its expenditure could pierce and abolish it, and then all symbolic becoming would cease, thus opening the way to 'madness'. Similarly, without rejection, *différance* would be confined within a nonrenewable, non-productive redundancy, a mere precious variant within the symbolic enclosure: contemplation adrift. (*Revolution*, p. 145)

Kristeva's disparaging remark about philosophers who retain only the 'notion of analysis as *dissolution*, and write in a style similar to that of an outmoded *avant-garde* such as symbolism' ('A New Type of Intellectual: the Dissident', p. 300 below) alludes to this critique of Derrida, the implication being that if Derrida in the late 1970s writes like Mallarmé in 1890, his work is less subversive than some would have it. It also highlights Kristeva's belief that art or literature, precisely because it relies on the notion of the subject, is the privileged place of transformation or change: an abstract philosophy of the signifier can only repeat the formal gestures of its literary models.

As a practising psychoanalyst, Kristeva has increasingly come to emphasize the notions of truth and ethics as central to the analytic process. Relativizing all notions of truth, deconstruction cannot account for the experience of truth in analysis. This is not in any way an absolute concept, but a truth constructed in the here and now of the analytic session. The analyst, who is under the ethical obligation to try to cure her patients, is not free to say whatever she likes, to engage in the free play of the signifier. Instead there *is* a truth in analysis: a correct intervention or a mistaken one. That this 'truth' may change from day to day and is utterly dependent on its specific context does not prevent it from existing. The proof of this particular form of truth lies in the cure: if there is no truth in analysis, there will be no cure either. Kristeva's notion of truth, then, emphasizes its effects in the *real*: it is a dimension of reality, not only of the signifier.[14] In this sense it draws not only on Freudianism but also on Marxism, with its insistence on *praxis*. This is why the first epigraph of 'Psychoanalysis and the Polis' is the famous lines from Marx and Engels: 'Up until now philosophers have only interpreted the world. The point now is to change it.' More than just a motto for the psychoanalytic process, these lines also constitute a silent rebuff to Derrida.

The ethics of psychoanalysis, then, is to be found in the cure. For Kristeva, as we have seen, this means producing subjects who are free to construct imaginary fantasies (or works of art), to produce a new language, precisely because they are able to situate themselves in relation to the Law. In the end, however, the cure can only be effected through transference, and, as we have seen, transference for Kristeva means transference love: an imaginary process of identification with an archaic ideal ego (the 'father of personal prehistory'). The truth of analysis is therefore also the truth of love: 'When I am in love, there is palpitating, passionate, unique meaning, but only right here and now, a meaning that may be absurd in another conjunction' (*Histoires d'amour*, p. 259).

The ethics of psychoanalysis, then, is an ethics of love. It is in this specific sense that Kristeva aligns herself with the great Catholic theologians of love, St Bernard and St Thomas[15] – for them, as for her, the human subject *is* a subject of love. Exploring their analysis of love in *Histoires d'amour*, she emphasizes the structural parallels between their theory of the subject and her own. In her 1985 pamphlet *Au commencement était l'amour: psychanalyse et foi* ('In the beginning was love: psychoanalysis and faith') she explores these parallels further, concluding with the fundamental atheism of psychoanalysis. Her desire for a new ethics, one situated outside any concept of moralism or duty, is also evident in her work on maternity in art ('Motherhood according to Giovanni Bellini', *Desire in Language*) or as represented in the figure of the Holy Virgin ('Stabat Mater' in this volume). For Kristeva, motherhood represents a mode of love which, like transference love, is at once unconditional and directed towards the final separation of the two subjects caught up in the amorous relationship. This is not to say that such ideal love is an inevitable side-effect of motherhood:

the case histories of Kristeva's patients amply demonstrate the suffering caused by its absence (see 'The True-Real' and 'Freud and Love'). Indicating the need for further investigation of this specifically female access to love, Kristeva expresses her hope that it may lead to the discovery of an ethics based on a new psychoanalytic understanding of motherhood: a *herethics of love* ('Stabat Mater'). It is this herethical ethics she finds embodied in psychoanalytic practice: 'If the analyst doesn't love his patients he ought to give up trying to cure them' (Interview in *Les Cahiers du GRIF*, 32, 1985, p. 21). Sustained and produced by love, psychoanalytic practice is unthinkable without it.

NOTES

All translations from untranslated French texts are mine. Documentation in the text and in the notes has been limited to give only the amount needed to identify a work in the list of references.

1 For fuller information see the list of her first publications in Tel quel, *Théorie d'ensemble*, p. 413.
2 For a fuller presentation of the group's aims see 'Division de l'ensemble', in *Théorie d'ensemble*, p. 7–10.
3 For interesting discussions and analyses of the student movement in general and May 68 in particular, see A. Cockburn and R. Blackburn (eds), *Student Power*, and not least, *New Left Review*, 52 (Nov.–Dec. 1968), a special issue on May 68 with the title 'Festival of the Oppressed'. It contains articles by André Glucksmann, André Gorz, Ernest Mandel and J.-M. Vincent as well as the editors.
4 See also her 'Mémoire, *L'Infini*, 1 (1983), particularly p. 52.
5 See for instance Jennifer Stone's hostile view of Kristeva.
6 I am quoting from the manuscript version of this article, which is forthcoming in print (see bibliography), p. 17.
7 For some counter-arguments to Kristeva's points here, see the interventions from Jacqueline Rose, Rosalind Coward and others in the conversation printed in *Desire* (ICA Documents).
8 See Moi, *Sexual/Textual Politics* for a presentation and discussion of French feminist theory and the idea of an *écriture féminine*.
9 Manuscript, p. 23.
10 The feminist debate around Kristeva's theories of women, femininity, sexual identity and language has been intense. For further reading in this field, see my chapter on Kristeva in *Sexual/Textual Politics*, and the books and articles by Brown and Adams, Féral, Gallop, Jones, The Marxist-Feminist Literature Collective, Pajaczkowska, Rose, Spivak, Stanton, Stone and White listed in the bibliography.
11 For some general introductions to Kristeva's theories in this work, see Lewis, Roudiez, White and Coward and Ellis.
12 Manuscript, pp. 30–1.

13 For an introduction to Derrida see Norris and also Eagleton. An advanced presentation can be found in Leitch.
14 For a brief history of different notions of truth and of Kristeva's own position see 'The True-Real' in this volume.
15 The parallels between the Christian discourse of love and the psychoanalytic view lead her to emphasize her view of the ethics of love in the recent interview printed in *Les Cahiers du GRIF*, 32: 'For me, in a very Christian fashion, ethics merges with love, with is why ethics also merges with the psychoanalytic relationship' (p. 21).

BIBLIOGRAPHY

Works by Kristeva

Only works referred to in this volume are listed. Essays are not listed separately if they have been collected in *Séméiotiké, Polylogue* or *Desire in Language*. For a full bibliography of Kristeva's work up to and including 1982, see Elissa D. Gelfand and Virginia Thorndike Hules, *French Feminist Criticism: women, language, literature. An annotated bibliography* (New York: Garland Publishing, 1985).

1969 *Séméiotiké. Recherches pour une sémanalyse*. Paris: Seuil.
1970 *Le Texte du roman*. The Hague: Mouton.
1973 'The system and the speaking subject'. *Times Literary Supplement*, 12 October, pp. 1249–52. Reprinted in Thomas A. Sebeok (ed.), *The Tell-Tale Sign. A survey of semiotics*, Lisse, Netherlands: The Peter de Ridder Press, 1975, pp. 47–55.
1974 *La Révolution du langage poétique*. Paris: Seuil. Translated as *Revolution in Poetic Language* by Margaret Waller, Introduction by Léon S. Roudiez, New York: Columbia University Press, 1984.
1974 *Des Chinoises*. Paris: des femmes. Translated as *About Chinese Women* by Anita Barrows, London: Marion Boyars, 1977.
1977 *Polylogue*. Paris: Seuil.
1977 'Pourquoi les Etats-Unis?' (with Marcelin Pleynet and Philippe Sollers), *Tel Quel*, 71/73 (Autumn), pp. 3–19. Translated as 'The U.S. now: a conversation', *October*, (Fall 1978), pp. 3–17.
1977 'Un nouveau type d'intellectuel: le dissident'. *Tel Quel*, 74 (Winter), pp. 3–8.
1977 'Hérethique de l'amour'. *Tel Quel*, (Winter), pp. 30–49. Reprinted as 'Stabat Mater' in *Histoires d'amour* (1983).
1979 'Le vréel'. In *La Folle vérité. Vérité et vraisemblance du texte psychotique*, Séminaire dirigé par Julia Kristeva et édité par Jean-Michel Ribettes, Paris: Seuil, pp. 11–35.
1979 'Le temps des femmes'. *34/44: Cahiers de recherche de sciences des textes et documents*, 5 (Winter), pp. 5–19. Translated as 'Women's time' by Alice Jardine and Harry Blake, *Signs*, 7, no. 1 (1981), pp. 13–35.
1979 'Il n'y a pas de maître à langage'. *Nouvelle revue de psychanalyse*, 20 (Autumn), pp. 119–140.
1980 *Pouvoirs de l'horreur*. Paris: Seuil. Translated as *Powers of Horror* by Léon S. Roudiez, New York: Columbia University Press, 1982.

1980 *Desire in Language: a semiotic approach to literature and art*. Edited by Léon S. Roudiez, translated by Alice Jardine, Thomas A. Gora and Léon S. Roudiez. Oxford: Blackwell/New York: Columbia.

1982 'L'abjet d'amour'. *Tel Quel*, 91 (Spring), pp. 17–32.

1983 'Psychoanalysis and the polis'. Translated by Margaret Waller in W. J. T. Mitchell (ed.), *The Politics of Interpretation*, Chicago: Chicago University Press, pp. 83–98.

1983 'Mémoire', *L'infini*, 1, pp. 39–54.

1983 *Histoires d'amour*. Paris: Denoël.

1984 'Julia Kristeva in conversation with Rosalind Coward'. In Lisa Appignanesi (ed.), *Desire*, ICA Documents, pp. 22–7.

1985 *Au commencement était l'amour: psychanalyse et foi*. Paris: Hachette, Textes du XXe siècle.

1985 'Entretien avec Julia Kristeva, réalisé par Françoise Collin'. *Les Cahiers du GRIF*, 32, pp. 7–23.

Other works referred to in the introduction and notes

Barthes, Roland, 'L'étrangère'. *La Quinzaine Littéraire*, 94, 1–15 May (1970), pp. 19–20.

Brown, Beverly, and Adams, Parveen, 'The feminine body and feminist politics', *m/f*, 3 (1979), pp. 35–50.

Cixous, Hélène, and Clément, Catherine, *La Jeune née*. Paris: UGE, 10/18, 1975.

Cockburn, Alexander, and Blackburn, Robin (eds), *Student Power: problems, diagnosis, action*. Harmondsworth: Penguin, 1969.

Coward, Rosalind, and Ellis, John, *Language and Materialism*. London: Routledge & Kegan Paul, 1977.

Eagleton, Terry, *Literary Theory. An introduction*. Oxford: Blackwell, 1983.

Féral, Josette, 'Antigone or the irony of the tribe'. *Diacritics*, Fall (1978), pp. 2–14.

—— 'The powers of difference'. In Hester Eisenstein and Alice Jardine (eds), *The Future of Difference*, Boston, Mass.: G. K. Hall, 1980, pp. 88–94.

Gallop, Jane, *Feminism and Psychoanalysis: the daughter's seduction*. London: Macmillan, 1982.

Jones, Ann Rosalind, 'Julia Kristeva on femininity: the limits of a semiotic politics'. *Feminist Review*, 18, Winter (1984), pp. 56–73.

Leitch, Vincent B., *Deconstructive Criticism. An advanced introduction*. New York: Columbia University Press, 1983.

Lewis, Philip E., 'Revolutionary semiotics'. *Diacritics*, 4, no. 3, Fall (1974), pp. 28–32.

Marxist-Feminist Literature Collective, 'Women's writing: *Jane Eyre, Shirley, Villette, Aurora Leigh*'. *Ideology and Consciousness*, 1, no. 3, Spring (1978), pp. 27–48.

Moi, Toril, *Sexual/Textual Politics: feminist literary theory*. London: Methuen, 1985.

New Left Review, no. 52, Nov.–Dec. 'Festival of the oppressed'. Special Issue May 1968.

Norris, Christopher, *Deconstruction. Theory and practice*. London: Methuen, 1982.

Pajaczkowska, Claire, 'Introduction to Kristeva', *m/f*, 5 and 6 (1981), pp. 149–57.

Rose, Jacqueline, 'Julia Kristeva: take two'. In Jacqueline Rose, *Sexuality in the Field of Vision*, 1986, London: NLB/Verso. Also to be published in the papers of the

'Feminism/Theory/Politics' Conference held at the Pembroke Center for Teaching & Research on Women, Brown University, March 1985.

Roudiez, Léon S., 'Introduction'. In Julia Kristeva, *Desire in Language: a semiotic approach to literature and art*, Oxford: Blackwell, 1980, pp. 1–20.

—— 'Introduction'. In Julia Kristeva, *Revolution in Poetic Language*, New York: Columbia University Press, 1984, pp. 1–10.

Spivak, Gayatri Chakravorty, 'French feminism in an international frame'. *Yale French Studies*, 62 (1981), pp. 154–84.

Stanton, Domna C., 'Language and revolution: the Franco-American dis-Connection'. In Hester Eisenstein and Alice Jardine (eds), *The Future of Difference*, Boston, Mass.: G. K. Hall, 1980, pp. 73–87.

Stone, Jennifer, 'The horrors of power: a critique of Kristeva'. In Francis Barker et al. (eds), *The Politics of Theory. Proceedings of the Essex Conference on the Sociology of Literature July 1982*, Colchester: University of Essex, 1983, pp. 38–48.

Tel Quel, *Théorie d'ensemble*. Paris: Seuil, 1968.

White, Allon, *'L'Éclatement du sujet': the theoretical work of Julia Kristeva*. Birmingham: University of Birmingham Centre for Contemporary Studies, Stencilled Occasional Paper, no. 49 (1977).

Wright, Elizabeth, *Psychoanalytic Criticism: theory in practice*. London: Methuen, 1984.

PART I

Linguistics, Semiotics, Textuality

1

The System and the Speaking Subject

'The System and the Speaking Subject' first appeared in the *Times Literary Supplement* (12 October 1973, pp. 1249–52), and was reprinted in Thomas A. Sebeok (ed.), *The Tell-Tale Sign. A Survey of Semiotics* (Lisse, Netherlands: The Peter de Ridder Press, 1975). In the space of a few pages, this essay presents a challenging overview of the whole field of semiotics as Kristeva sees it. Distinguishing between 'semiology' or 'structuralism' on the one hand and 'semiotics' or 'semanalysis' on the other, Kristeva maintains that structuralism, by focusing on the 'thetic' or static phase of language, posits it as a homogeneous structure, whereas semiotics, by studying language as a discourse enunciated by a speaking subject, grasps its fundamentally heterogeneous nature. For semanalysis language is a *signifying process*, not simply a static system. In order to establish this new science of the sign, Kristeva draws heavily on Hegel, Marx and Freud. Linguistic practice, as she sees it, is at once system and transgression (negativity), a product of both the 'drive-governed basis of sound production' and the social space in which the enunciation takes place.

Insisting as it does on the heterogeneity of language, semiotics is caught in a paradox: being itself a metalanguage (language which speaks about language) it cannot but homogenize its object in its own discourse. In this sense, then, semiotics is structurally unable to practise what it preaches. For Kristeva, however, the paradoxical nature of the semiotic enterprise does not lead to paralysis but to renewed creativity, since the semiotician caught in this paradox is forced always to analyse her own discursive position, and thus to renew her connection with the heterogeneous forces of language which, according to Kristeva, is what makes language a *productive* structure in the first place.

In many ways this essay summarizes the main themes of Kristeva's major linguistic work, *La Révolution du langage poétique* (1974), translated by Margaret Waller as *Revolution in Poetic Language* (1984). In its preoccupation with the political or ethical nature of semanalysis as a mode of thought which subverts established beliefs in authority and order, 'The System and the Speaking Subject' should be read in the context of 'The Ethics of Linguistics', published in *Polylogue* (1977) and translated in *Desire in Language* (1980). Some of the central concepts left undefined in 'The System and the Speaking Subject' ('thetic', 'genotext', 'phenotext') are developed and defined in the excerpts from *Revolution* which appear in this volume as chapter 5. (See particularly the chapters entitled 'The Thetic: Rupture and/or Boundary' and 'Genotext and Phenotext'.)

The System and the Speaking Subject

However great the diversity, the irregularity, the disparity even of current research in semiotics, it is possible to speak of a specifically semiotic *discovery*. What semiotics has discovered in studying 'ideologies' (myths, rituals, moral codes, arts, etc.) as sign-systems is that the *law* governing, or, if one prefers, the *major constraint* affecting any social practice lies in the fact that it signifies; i.e., that it is articulated *like* a language. Every social practice, as well as being the object of external (economic, political, etc.) determinants, is also determined by a set of signifying rules, by virtue of the fact that there is present an order of language; that this language has a double articulation (signifier/signified); that this duality stands in an arbitrary relation to the referent; and that all social functioning is marked by the split between referent and symbolic and by the shift from signified to signifier coextensive with it.

One may say, then, that what semiotics had discovered is the fact that there is a general social law, that this law is the symbolic dimension which is given in language and that every social practice offers a specific expression of that law.

A discovery of this order cuts short the speculations characteristic of idealism, which throughout its history has claimed the domain of meaning as subordinate to itself, refusing to allow it both external determination and internal adjustment. But it is no less unkind to vulgar sociologism or those mechanistic assumptions which, under the ill-defined general term of 'ideology', define superstructures which are without exception externally determined. The semiological approach identifies itself, from Hjelmslev on, as an anti-humanism which outmodes those debates – still going on even now – between philosophers, where one side argues for a transcendence with an immanent 'human' causality while the other argues for an 'ideology' whose cause is external and therefore transcendent; but where neither shows any awareness of the linguistic and, at a more general level, semiotic logic of the sociality in which the (speaking, historical) subject is embedded.

And yet semiotics, by its attempts to set itself up as a theory of practices using language as its model, restricts the value of its discovery to the field of practices which do no more than subserve the principle of social cohesions, of the social contract. In other words, in so far as linguistics has established itself as the science of an object ('language', 'speech' or 'discourse') so obedient to the necessity for social communication as to be inseparable from sociality, any semiotics which adopts this linguistic model can speak only of those social practices (or those aspects of social practices) which subserve such social exchange: a semiotics that records the systematic, systematizing or informational aspect of signifying practices.

It is not difficult to see why its strong point should be the study of the rules of kinship and myths as examples of community knowledge. Nor is it difficult to see that it cannot simply go on following the linguistic model alone, or even the principle of systematicity if it aims also at tackling signifying practices which, although they do subserve social communications, are at the same time the privileged areas where this is put to non-utilitarian use, the areas of transgression and pleasure: one thinks of the specificity of 'art', of ritual, of certain aspects of myths, etc.

What is being called in question here, where the limitations of a familiar conception of semiotics are concerned, is not merely the theoretical presupposition on which that conception is based and which biases it towards discovering in every kind of field analogues of the system of language. Such rigidity has merely served to throw into relief a shortcoming of linguistics itself: established as a science in as much as it focuses on language as a social *code*, the science of linguistics has no way of apprehending anything in language which belongs not with the social contract but with play, pleasure or desire (or, if it does attempt to take account of these, it is forced to infringe its epistemological purity and call itself by such names as stylistics, rhetoric, poetics: aleatory forms of discourse which have no empirical status).

Thus we reach a crucial point in semiotic research: of its possible deployment as a critique of its own presuppositions. Semiotics must not be allowed to be a mere application to signifying practices of the linguistic model – or any other model, for that matter. Its *raison d'être*, if it is to have one, must consist in its identifying the systematic constraint within each signifying practice (using for that purpose borrowed or original 'models') but above all in going beyond that to specifying just what, within the practice, falls outside the system and characterizes the specificity of the practice as such.

One phase of semiology is now over: that which runs from Saussure and Peirce to the Prague School and structuralism, and has made possible the systematic description of the social and/or symbolic constraint within each signifying practice. To criticize this phase for its 'ideological bias' – whether phenomenological or more specifically phonological or linguistic – without recognizing the truth it has contributed by revealing and characterizing the immanent causality and/or the presence of a social-systematic constraint in each social functioning, leads to a rejection of the symbolic and/or social *thesis* (in Husserl's sense of the word) indispensable to every practice. This rejection is shared both by idealist philosophy, with its neglect of the historical socializing role of the symbolic, and by the various sociological dogmatisms, which suppress the specificity of the symbolic and its logic in their anxiety to reduce them to an 'external' determinant.

In my view, a critique of this 'semiology of systems' and of its phenomenological foundations is possible only if it starts from a theory of meaning which must necessarily be a theory of the speaking subject. It is common knowledge that the linguistic revival which goes by the name of Generative Grammar – whatever its variants and mutations – is based on the rehabilitation of the Cartesian conception of language as an *act* carried out by a *subject*. On close inspection, as certain linguists (from Jakobson to Kuroda) have shown in recent years, this 'speaking subject' turns out in fact to be that *transcendental ego* which, in Husserl's view, underlies any and every predicative synthesis, if we 'put in brackets' logical or linguistic externality. Generative Grammar, based firmly on this subject, not only expresses the truth of language which structuralism describes as a system – namely that it is the act of an *ego* which has momentarily broken off its connection with that externality, which may be social, natural or unconscious – but creates for itself the opportunity of describing, better than its predecessors, the logic of this thetic act, starting out from an infinity of predication which each national language subjects to strict systems of rules. Yet this transcendental subject is not the essential concern of the semiological revival, and if it bases itself on the conception of language proper to Generative Grammer, semiology will not get beyond the reduction – still commonly characteristic of it – of signifying *practices* to their systematic aspect.

In respect of the subject and of signifying, it is the Freudian revolution which seems to me to have achieved the definitive displacement of the Western *épistémé* from its presumed centrality. But although the effects of that revolution have been superbly and authoritatively worked out in the writings of Jacques Lacan in France, or, in a rather different way, in the English anti-psychiatry of R. D. Laing and David Cooper, it has by no means reached far enough yet to affect the semiotic conception of language and of practices. The theory of meaning now stands at a crossroad: either it will remain an attempt at formalizing meaning-systems by increasing sophistication of the logico-mathematical tools which enable it to formulate models on the basis of a conception (already rather dated) of meaning as the act of a *transcendental ego*, cut off from its body, its unconscious and also its history; or else it will attune itself to the theory of the speaking subject as a divided subject (conscious/unconscious) and go on to attempt to specify the types of operation characteristic of the two sides of this split, thereby exposing them to those forces extraneous to the logic of the systematic; exposing them, that is to say, on the one hand, to bio-physiological processes (themselves already inescapably part of signifying processes, what Freud labelled 'drives'); and, on the other hand, to social constraints (family structures, modes of production, etc.).

In following this latter path, semiology, or, as I have suggested calling it, *semanalysis*, conceives of meaning not as a sign-system but as a *signifying process*. Within this process one might see the release and subsequent articulation of the drives as constrained by the social code yet not reducible to the language system as a *genotext* and the signifying system as it presents itself to phenomenological intuition as a *phenotext*; describable in terms of structure, or of competence/performance, or according to other models. The presence of the *genotext* within the *phenotext* is indicated by what I have called a *semiotic disposition*. In the case, for example, of a signifying practice such as 'poetic language', the *semiotic disposition* will be the various deviations from the grammatical rules of the language: articulatory effects which shift the phonemative system back towards its articulatory, phonetic base and consequently towards the drive-governed bases of sound-production; the over-determination of a lexeme by multiple meanings which it does not carry in ordinary usage but which accrue to it as a result of its occurrence in other texts; syntactic irregularities such as ellipses, non-recoverable deletions, indefinite embeddings, etc,; the replacement of the relationship between the protagonists of any enunciation as they function in a locutory act – see here the work of J. L. Austin and John Searle – by a system of relations based on fantasy; and so forth.

These variations may be partly described by way of what are called the *primary* processes (displacement, condensation – or metonymy, metaphor), transversal to the logico-symbolic processes that function in the predicative synthesis towards establishing the language system. They had already been discovered by the structuralists, following Freud, at the 'lower', phonological, level of the linguistic synthesis. To them must be added the compulsion to repetition, but also 'operations' characteristic of topologies and capable of establishing *functions* between the signifying code and the fragmented body of the speaking subject as well as the bodies of his familial and social partners. All functions which suppose a *frontier* (in this case the fissure created by the act of naming and the logico-linguistic synthesis which it sets off) and the transgression of that frontier (the sudden appearance of new signifying chains) are relevant to any account of signifying *practice*, where practice is taken as meaning the acceptance of a symbolic law together with the transgression of that law for the purpose of renovating it.

The moment of transgression is the key moment in practice: we can speak of practice wherever there is a transgression of systematicity, i.e., a transgression of the unity proper to the *transcendental ego*. The subject of the practice cannot be the transcendental subject, who lacks the shift, the split in logical unity brought about by language which separates out, within the signifying body, the symbolic order from the workings of the libido (this last revealing itself by the *semiotic disposition*). Identifying the semiotic disposition means in fact identifying the shift in the speaking subject, his capacity for renewing the order in which he is inescapably caught up; and that capacity is, for the *subject*, the capacity for enjoyment.

It must, however, be remembered that although it can be described in terms of operations and concepts, this logic of shifts, splits and the infinitization of the symbolic limit leads us towards operations heterogeneous to meaning and its system. By that I mean that these 'operations' are *pre-meaning* and *pre-sign* (or *trans-meaning, trans-sign*), and that they bring us back to processes of division in the living matter of an organism subject to biological constraints as well as social norms. Here it seems indispensable that Melanie Klein's theory of drives should be refined and extended, together with the psycholinguistic study of the acquisition of language (provided that this study is conceived as something more than the mere reiteration of what is amply demonstrated in and by the linguistic system of the *transcendental ego*).

The point is not to replace the semiotics of signifying systems by considerations on the biological code appropriate to the nature of those employing them – a tautological exercise, after all, since the biological code has been modelled on the language system. It is rather to postulate the *heterogeneity* of biological operations in respect of signifying operations, and to study the dialectics of the former (that is, the fact that, though invariably subject to the signifying and/or social codes, they infringe the code in the direction of allowing the subject to get pleasure from it, renew it, even endanger it; where, that is, the processes are not blocked by him in repression or 'mental illness').

But since it is itself a metalanguage, semiotics can do no more than postulate this heterogeneity: as soon as it speaks about it, it homogenizes the phenomenon, links it with a system, loses hold of it. Its specificity can be preserved only in the signifying practices which set off the heterogeneity at issue: thus poetic language making free with the language code; music, dancing, painting, reordering the psychic drives which have not been harnessed by the dominant symbolization systems and thus renewing their own tradition; and (in a different mode) experiences with drugs – all seek out and make use of this heterogeneity and the ensuing fracture of a symbolic code which can no longer 'hold' its (speaking) subjects.

But if semiotics thus openly recognizes its inability to apprehend the heterogeneity of the signifying process other than by reducing it to a systematicity, does it thereby declare its own intellectual bankruptcy? Everything in current research that is solid and intellectually adequate impels those pursuing it to stress the limits of their own metalanguage in relation to the signifying process; their own metalanguage can apprehend only that part of the signifying process belonging to the domain of the general metalanguage to which their own efforts are tributary; the (vast) *remainder* has had, historically, to find a home in religion (notoriously, if more or less marginally, associated with semiotic reflection since the Stoics), moving up through medieval theories of the *modi significandi*, Leibniz's *Art of Combinations*, to phenomenology or positivism. It is only now, and only on the basis of a theory of the speaking subject as subject of a heterogeneous process, that semiotics can show that what lies outside its metalinguistic mode of operation – the 'remainder', the 'waste' – is what, in the process of the speaking subject, represents the moment in which it is set in action, put on trial, put to death: a heterogeneity with respect to system, operating within the practice and one which is liable, if not seen for what it is, to be reified into a transcendence.

We can now grasp all the ambiguities of *semanalysis*: on the one hand it demystifies the logic at work in the elaboration of every transcendental reduction and, for this purpose, requires the study of each signifying system as a practice. Thus intent on revealing the negativity which Hegel had seen at work beneath all rationality but which, by a masterly stroke, he subordinated to absolute knowledge, *semanalysis* can be thought of as the direct successor of the dialectical method; but the dialectic it continues will be one which will at last be genuinely materialist since it recognizes the *materiality – the heterogeneity* – of that negativity whose concrete base Hegel was unable to see and which mechanistic Marxists have reduced to a merely economic externality. Had not C. S. Peirce already been drawn by what dialectics seemed to promise, in writing 'my philosophy resuscitates Hegel, though in a strange costume'? To rediscover practice by way of the system, by rehabilitating what is heterogeneous to the system of meaning and what calls in question the transcendental subject: these, it seems to me, are the stakes for which semiotics is now playing.

And yet, by setting about this task, it brings the precarious or the enjoyable aspects of a practice into a system which, by this very fact, at once takes up its place within the dominant social code. Being, because of its explanatory metalinguistic force, an agent of social cohesion, semiotics contributes to the formation of that reassuring image which every society offers itself when it understands everything, down to and including the practices which voluntarily expend it.

If, in spite of everything, the semiotic venture can be justified, it is on the grounds of historical necessity. The present mutations of capitalism, the political and economic reawakening of ancient civilizations (India, China) have thrown into crisis the symbolic systems enclosed in which the Western subject, officially defined as a transcendental subject, has for two thousand years lived out its lifespan. Marxist theory, still a powerful tool for understanding the economic determinants of social relations, has little to say on the crisis in question: it is not a theory of meaning or of the subject. There *is* no subject in the economic rationality of Marxism; there is in Marxist revolution, but the 'founding fathers' have left us no thoughts about it, while the academic Marxologists of today can hardly wait to get rid both of meaning and of the subject in the name of some 'objective' process; or else they will fudge up a theory of the subject which turns out to be the subject of Hegel's view of Right, that is, the subject of bourgeois Right, and then invite us to conceive every signifying practice in its image. A far cry from revolution, from desire, and even from the Hegelian negative! Mechanistic Marxism is still paying its dues to Feuerbach and his humanistic standing of the dialectic on its head.

If, then, a gap can be seen in dialectical materialism in respect of signifying practices and their subject, semiotics may be the locus from which an attempt can be mounted to work out a new conception: semiotics, avoiding the twin pitfalls of imprisonment within the mechanism of psychoanalytic transference and of formalist description, can establish the heterogeneous logic of signifying practices, and locate them, finally and by way of their subject, in the historically determined relations of production. Semiotics can lead to a *historical typology of signifying practices* by the mere fact of recognizing the specific status within them of the speaking subject. In this way we arrive at the possibility of a new perspective on history, perhaps a new principle for dividing up historical time, since signifying temporality is not coextensive with that of the modes of production.

As 'classical' semiotics was already aware, discourse received its meaning from the person(s) to whom it is addressed. The semiotics of signifying practices is addressed to all those who, committed to a practice of challenge, innovation or personal experiment, are frequently tempted to abandon their discourse as a way of communicating the logic of that practice, since the dominant forms of discourse (from positivist grammar to sociologism) have no room for it, and to go into voluntary exile in what Mallarmé called an 'indicible qui ment', for the ultimate benefit of a practice that shall remain silent.

The semiology of signifying practices, by contrast, is ready to give a hearing to any or all of those efforts which, ever since the elaboration of a new position for the speaking subject, have been renewing and reshaping the status of meaning within social exchanges to a point where the very order of language is being renewed: Joyce, Burroughs, Sollers.

This is a moral gesture, inspired by a concern to make intelligible, and therefore socializable, what rocks the foundations of sociality. In this respect *semanalysis* carries on the semiotic discovery of which we spoke at the outset: it places itself at the service of the social law which requires systematization, communication, exchange. But if it is to do this, it must inevitably respect a further, more recent requirement – and one which neutralizes the phantom of 'pure science': the subject of the semiotic metalanguage must, however briefly, call himself in question, must emerge from the protective shell of a transcendental ego within a logical system, and so restore his connection with that negativity – drive-governed, but also social, political and historical – which rends and renews the social code.

2

Word, Dialogue and Novel

Written in 1966, shortly after Kristeva's arrival in France, this presentation and development of Mikhail Bakhtin's central ideas was published in *Séméiotiké* (1969) and translated in *Desire in Language* (1980). With her compatriot, Tzvétan Todorov, Kristeva was among the first to introduce Bakhtin's work to a Western audience. I have chosen to reprint the essay here both because of its intrinsic interest as a presentation of the great Russian theorist, and because it demonstrates how Kristeva's own linguistic and psycho-linguistic work in the late 1960s and early 1970s can be said to be produced as a result of her active dialogue with Bakhtin's texts.

'Word, Dialogue and Novel' is in many ways a divided text, uneasily poised on an unstable borderline between traditional 'high' structuralism with its yearnings for 'scientific' objectivity (as revealed by Kristeva's use of mathematics and set theory to illustrate her points) and a remarkably early form of 'post-structuralism' or the desire to show how the pristine structuralist categories always break down under the pressure of the *other* side of language: the irreverent, mocking and subversive tradition of carnival and Menippean satire as described by Bakhtin. In this context Kristeva's insistence on the importance of the speaking subject as the principal object for linguistic analysis would seem to have its roots in her own reading of Bakhtinian 'dialogism' as an open-ended play between the text of the subject and the text of the addressee, an analysis which also gives rise to the Kristevan concept of 'intertextuality'.

This fundamental essay also demonstrates how Bakhtin provides the starting-point for Kristeva's own work on modernist discourse in *Revolution in Poetic Language*. Working from Bakhtinian terms such as 'dialogism' and 'carnivalism', Kristeva turns them into allusions to the kind of textual play she was later to analyse through concepts such as 'the semiotic', 'the symbolic' and the 'chora' (see the excerpts from *Revolution* in this book). It is therefore not surprising to discover that her reading of carnivalism as a space where texts meet, contradict and relativize each other through extensive use of repetition, illogical constructions and non-exclusive opposition is illustrated not only with references to Rabelais or Swift (as in Bakhtin's own work), but also with allusions to authors such as Lautréamont, Joyce, Kafka, Bataille and Sollers, which were all to provide important examples of the practice of writing analysed not only in the *Revolution*, but also, from a different perspective, in *Powers of Horror* (1982). Testifying to her early interest in the aspects of language and the psyche which escape the dominant tradition of Aristotelian mono-logism, 'Word, Dialogue and Novel' follows Bakhtin in insisting on the subversive political effects of such language, and thus also comes to prefigure Kristeva's later analysis of the politics of marginality.

Word, Dialogue and Novel

If the efficacy of scientific approach in 'human' sciences has always been challenged, it is all the more striking that such a challenge should for the first time be issued on the very level of the structures being studied – structures supposedly answerable to a logic *other* than scientific.[1] What would be involved is the logic of language (and all the more so, of poetic language) that 'writing' has had the virtue of bringing to light. I have in mind that particular literary practice in which the elaboration of poetic meaning emerges as tangible, *dynamic gram*.[2] Confronted with this situation, then, literary semiotics can either abstain and remain silent, or persist in its efforts to elaborate a model that would be isomorphic to this other logic; that is, isomorphic to the elaboration of poetic meaning, a concern of primary importance to contemporary semiotics.

Russian Formalism, in which contemporary structural analysis claims to have its source, was itself faced with identical alternatives when reasons beyond literature and science halted its endeavors. Research was none the less carried on, recently coming to light in the work of Mikhail Bakhtin. His work represents one of that movement's most remarkable accomplishments, as well as one of the most powerful attempts to transcend its limitation. Bakhtin shuns the linguist's technical rigour, wielding an impulsive and at times even prophetic pen, while he takes on the fundamental problems presently confronting a structural analysis of narrative; this alone would give currency to essays written over forty years ago. Writer as well as 'scholar', Bakhtin was one of the first to replace the static hewing out of texts with a model where literary structure does not simply *exist* but is generated in relation to *another* structure. What allows a dynamic dimension to structuralism is his conception of the 'literary word' as an *intersection of textual surfaces* rather than a *point* (a fixed meaning), as a dialogue among several writings: that of the writer, the addressee (or the character) and the contemporary or earlier cultural context.

By introducing the *status of the word* as a minimal structural unit, Bakhtin situates the text within history and society, which are then seen as texts read by the writer, and into which he inserts himself by rewriting them. Diachrony is transformed into synchrony, and in light of this transformation, *linear* history appears as abstraction. The only way a writer can participate in history is by transgressing this abstraction through a process of reading-writing; that is, through the practice of a signifying structure in relation or opposition to another structure. History and morality are written and read within the infrastructure of texts. The poetic word, polyvalent and multi-determined, adheres to a logic exceeding that of codified discourse and fully comes into being only in the margins of recognized culture. Bakhtin was the first to study this logic, and he looked for its roots in *carnival*. Carnivalesque discourse breaks through the laws of a language censored by grammar and semantics and, at the same time, is a social and political protest. There is no equivalence, but rather, identity between challenging official linguistic codes and challenging official law.

The word within the space of texts

Defining the specific status of the word as signifier for different modes of (literary) intellection within different genres or texts put poetic analysis at the sensitive centre of contemporary 'human' sciences – at the intersection of *language* (the true practice of thought)[3] with *space* (the volume within which signification, through a joining of differences, articulates itself). To investigate the status of the word is to study its articulations (as semic complex) with other words in the sentence, and then to look for the same functions or relationships at the articulatory level of larger sequences. Confronted with this spatial conception of language's poetic operation, we must first define the three dimensions of textual space where various semic sets and poetic sequences function. These three dimensions or coordinates of dialogue are writing subject, addressee and exterior texts. The word's status is thus defined *horizontally* (the word in the text belongs to both writing subject and addressee) as well as *vertically* (the word in the text is oriented towards an anterior or synchronic literary corpus).[4]

The addressee, however, is included within a book's discursive universe only as discourse itself. He thus fuses with this other discourse, this other book, in relation to which the writer has written his own text. Hence horizontal axis (subject-addressee) and vertical axis (text-context) coincide, bringing to light an important fact: each word (text) is an intersection of word (texts) where at least one other word (text) can be read. In Bakhtin's work, these two axes, which he calls *dialogue* and *ambivalence*, are not clearly distinguished. Yet, what appears as a lack of rigour is in fact an insight first introduced into literary theory by Bakhtin: any text is constructed as a mosaic of quotations; any text is the absorption and transformation of another. The notion of *intertextuality*[5] replaces that of intersubjectivity, and poetic language is read as at least *double*.

The word as minimal textual unit thus turns out to occupy the status of *mediator*, linking structural models to cultural (historical) environment, as well as that of *regulator*, controlling mutations from diachrony to synchrony, i.e., to literary structure. The word is spatialized: through the very notion of status, it functions in three dimensions (subject-addressee-context) as a set of *dialogical*, semic elements or as a set of *ambivalent* elements. Consequently the task of literary semiotics is to discover other formalisms corresponding to different modalities of word-joining (sequences) within the dialogical space of texts.

Any description of a word's specific operation within different literary genres or texts thus requires a *translinguistic* procedure. First, we must think of literary genres as imperfect semiological systems 'signifying beneath the surface of language but never without it': and secondly, discover relations among larger narrative units such as sentences, questions-and-answers, dialogues, etc., not necessarily on the basis of linguistic models – justified by the principle of semantic expansion. We could thus posit and demonstrate the hypothesis that *any evolution of literary genres is an unconscious exteriorization of linguistic structures at their different levels*. The novel in particular exteriorizes linguistic dialogue.[6]

Word and dialogue

Russian Formalists were engrossed with the idea of 'linguistic dialogue'. They insisted on the dialogical character of linguistic communication[7] and considered the monologue, the 'embryonic form' of *common* language,[8] as subsequent to dialogue. Some of them distinguished between monological discourse (as 'equivalent to a psychic state')[9] and narrative (as 'artistic imitation of monological discourse').[10] Boris Eikhenbaum's famous study of Gogol's *The Overcoat* is based on such premises. Eikhenbaum notes that Gogol's text actively refers to an oral form of narration and to its linguistic characteristics (intonation, syntactic construction of oral discourse, pertinent vocabulary, and so on). He thus sets up two modes of narration, *indirect* and *direct*, studying the relationship between the two. Yet he seems to be unaware that before referring to an *oral* discourse, the writer of the narrative usually refers to the discourse of an *other* whose oral discourse is only secondary (since the other is the carrier of oral discourse).[11]

For Bakhtin, the dialogue-monologue distinction has a much larger significance than the concrete meaning accorded it by the Russian Formalists. It does not correspond to the *direct/indirect* (monologue/dialogue) distinction in narratives or plays. For Bakhtin, dialogue can be monological, and what is called monologue can be dialogical. With him, such terms refer to a linguistic infrastructure that must be studied through a *semiotics* of literary texts. This semiotics cannot be based on either linguistic methods or logical givens, but rather, must be elaborated from the point where they leave off.

> Linguistics studies 'language' and its specific logic in its *commonality* ('*obshchnost*') as that factor which makes dialogical intercourse *possible*, but it consistently refrains from studying those dialogical relationships themselves...Dialogical relationships are not reducible to logical or concrete semantic relationships, which are in and of *themselves* devoid of any dialogical aspect...Dialogical relationships are totally impossible without logical and concrete semantic relationships, but they are not reducible to them; they have their own specificity.[12]

While insisting on the difference between dialogical relationships and specifically linguistic ones, Bakhtin emphasizes that those structuring a narrative (for example, writer/character, to which we would add subject of enunciation/subject of utterance) are possible because dialogism is inherent in language itself. Without explaining exactly what makes up this double aspect of language, he none the less insists that 'dialogue is the only sphere possible for the life of language'. Today we can detect dialogical relationships on several levels of language: first, within the *combinative* dyad, langue/parole; and secondly, within the systems either of langue (as collective, monological contracts as well as systems of correlative value actualized in dialogue with the other) or of parole (as essentially 'combinative', not pure creation, but individual formation based on the exchange of signs).

On still another level (which could be compared to the novel's ambivalent space), this 'double character of language' has even been demonstrated as syntagmatic (made manifest through extension, presence and metonymy) and systematic (manifested through association, absence and metaphor). It would be important to analyse linguistically the dialogical exchanges between these two axes of language as basis of the novel's ambivalence. We should also note Jakobson's double structures and their overlappings within the code/message relationship,[13] which help to clarify Bakhtin's notion of dialogism as inherent in language.

Bakhtin foreshadows what Emile Benveniste has in mind when he speaks about *discourse*, that is 'language appropriated by the individual as a practice'. As Bakhtin himself writes, 'In order for dialogical relationships to arise among [logical or concrete semantic relationships], they must clothe themselves in the word, become utterances, and become the positions of various subjects, expressed in a word.'[14] Bakhtin, however, born of a revolutionary Russia that was preoccupied with social problems, does not see dialogue only as language assumed by a subject; he sees it, rather, as a *writing* where one reads the *other* (with no allusion to Freud). Bakhtinian dialogism identifies writing as both subjectivity and communication, or better, as intertextuality. Confronted with this dialogism, the notion of a 'person-subject of writing' becomes blurred, yielding to that of 'ambivalence of writing'.

Ambivalence

The term 'ambivalence' implies the insertion of history (society) into a text and of this text into history; for the writer, they are one and the same. When he speaks of 'two paths merging within the narrative', Bakhtin considers writing as a reading of the anterior literary corpus and the text as an absorption of and a reply to another text. He studies the polyphonic novel as an absorption of the carnival and the monological novel as a stifling of this literary structure, which he calls 'Menippean' because of its dialogism. In this perspective, a text cannot be grasped through linguistics alone. Bakhtin postulates the necessity for what he calls a *translinguistic* science, which, developed on the basis of language's dialogism, would enable us to understand intertextual *relationships*; relationships that the nineteenth century labelled 'social value' or literature's moral 'message'. Lautréamont wanted to write so that he could submit himself to a *high morality*. Within his practice, this morality is actualized as textual ambivalence: *The Songs of Maldoror* and the *Poems* are a constant dialogue with the preceding literary corpus, a perpetual challenge of past writing. Dialogue and ambivalence are borne out as the only approach that permits the writer to enter history by espousing an ambivalent ethics: negation as affirmation.

Dialogue and ambivalence lead me to conclude that, within the interior space of the text as well as within the space of *texts*, poetic language is a 'double'. Saussure's poetic *paragram* ('Anagrams') extends from *zero* to *two*: the unit 'one' (definition, 'truth') does not exist in this field. Consequently, the notions of definition, determination, the sign ' = ' and the very concept of sign, which presuppose a vertical (hierarchical) division between signifier and signified, cannot be applied to poetic language – by defining an infinity of pairings and combinations.

The notion of *sign* (Sr-Sd) is a product of scientific abstraction (identity-substance-cause-goal as structure of the Indo-European sentence), designating a vertically and hierarchically linear division. The notion of *double*, the result of thinking over poetic (not scientific) language, denotes 'spatialization' and correlation of the literary (linguistic) sequence. This implies that the minimal unit of poetic language is at least *double*, not in the sense of the signifier/signified dyad, but rather, in terms of *one and other*. It suggests that poetic language functions as a *tabular model*, where each 'unit' (this word can no longer be used without quotation marks, since every unit is double) acts as a multi-determined *peak*. The *double* would be the minimal sequence of a paragrammatic semiotics to be worked out starting from the work of Saussure (in the 'Anagrams') and Bakhtin.

Instead of carrying these thoughts to their conclusion we shall concentrate here on one of their consequences: the inability of any logical system based on a zero-one sequence (true-false, nothingness-notation) to account for the operation of poetic language.

Scientific procedures are indeed based upon a logical approach, itself founded on the Greek (Indo-European) sentence. Such a sentence begins as subject-predicate and grows by identification, determination and causality. Modern logic from Gottlob Frege and Giuseppe Peano to Jan Lukasiewicz, Robert Ackermann and Alonzo Church evolves out of a 0-1 sequence; George Boole, who begins with set theory, produces formulae that are more isomorphic with language – all of these are ineffective within the realm of poetic language, where 1 is not a limit.

It is therefore impossible to formalize poetic language according to existing logical (scientific) procedures without distorting it. A literary semiotics must be developed on the basis of a *poetic logic* where the concept of the *power of the continuum* would embody the 0-2 interval, a continuity where 0 denotes and 1 is implicitly transgressed.

Within this 'power of the continuum' from 0 to a specifically poetic double, the linguistic, psychic and social 'prohibition' is 1 (God, Law, Definition). The only linguistic practice to 'escape' this prohibition is poetic discourse. It is no accident that the shortcomings of Aristotelian logic when applied to language were pointed out by, on the one hand, twentieth-century Chinese philosopher Chang Tung-Sun (the product of a different linguistic heritage – ideograms – where, in place of God, there extends the Yin-Yang 'dialogue') and, on the other, Bakhtin (who attempted to go beyond the Formalists through a dynamic theorization accomplished in revolutionary society). With Bakhtin, who assimilates narrative discourse into epic discourse, narrative is a prohibition, a *monologism*, a subordination of the code to 1, to God. Hence, the epic is religious and theological; all 'realist' narrative obeying 0-1 logic is dogmatic. The realist novel, which Bakhtin calls monological (Tolstoy), tends to evolve within this space. Realist description, definition of 'personality', 'character' creation and 'subject' development – all are descriptive narrative elements belonging to the 0-1 interval and are thus *monological*. The only discourse integrally to achieve the 0-2 poetic logic is that of the carnival. By adopting a dream logic, it transgresses rules of linguistic code and social morality as well.

In fact, this 'transgression' of linguistic, logical and social codes within the carnivalesque only exists and succeeds, of course, because it accepts *another law*. Dialogism is not 'freedom to say everything', it is a *dramatic* 'banter' (Lautréamont), an *other* imperative than that of 0. We should particularly emphasize this specificity of dialogue as *transgression giving itself a law* so as radically and categorically to distinguish it from the pseudo-transgression evident in a certain modern 'erotic' and parodic literature. The latter, seeing itself as 'libertine' and 'relativizing', operates according to a principle of *law anticipating its own transgression*. It thus compensates for monologism, does not displace the 0-1 interval nor has anything to do with the architectonics of dialogism, which implies a categorical tearing from the norm and a relationship of non-exclusive opposites.

The novel incorporating carnivalesque structure is called *polyphonic*. Bakhtin's examples include Rabelais, Swift and Dostoevsky. We might also add the 'modern' novel of the twentieth century – Joyce, Proust, Kafka – while specifying that the modern polyphonic novel, although analogous in its status, where monologism is concerned, to dialogical novels of the past, is clearly marked off from them. A break occurred at the end of the nineteenth century: while dialogue in Rabelais, Swift and Dostoevsky remains at a representative, fictitious level, our century's polyphonic novel becomes 'unreadable' (Joyce) and interior to language (Proust, Kafka). Beginning with this break – not only literary but also social, political and philosophical in nature – the problem of inter-textuality (intertextual dialogue) appears as such. Bakhtin's theory itself (as well as that of Saussure's 'Anagrams') can be traced historically to this break: he was able to discover textual dialogism in the writings of Mayakovsky, Khlebnikov and Andrei Bely, to mention only a few of the Revolution's writers who made the outstanding imprints of this scriptural break. Bakhtin then extended his theory into literary history as a principle of all upheavals and defiant productivity.

Bakhtin's term *dialogism* as a semic complex thus implies the double, language, and another logic. Using that as point of departure, we can outline a new approach to poetic texts. Literary semiotics can accept the word 'dialogism'; the logic of *distance* and *relationship* between the different units of a sentence or narrative structure, indicating a *becoming* – in opposition to the level of continuity and substance, both of which obey the logic of being and are thus monological. Secondly, it is a logic of *analogy* and *non-exclusive opposition*, opposed to monological levels of causality and identifying determination. Finally, it is a logic of the 'transfinite', a concept borrowed from Georg Cantor, which, on the basis of poetic language's 'power of the continuum' (0-2), introduces a second principle of formation: a poetic sequence is a 'next-larger' (not causally deduced) to all preceding sequences of the Aristotelian chain (scientific, monological or narrative). The novel's ambivalent space thus can be seen as regulated by two formative principles: monological (each following sequence is determined by the preceding one), and dialogical (transfinite sequences that are next-larger to the preceding causal series).[18]

Dialogue appears most clearly in the structure of carnivalesque language, where symbolic relationships and analogy take precedence over substance-causality connections. The notion of *ambivalence* pertains to the permutation of the two spaces observed in novelistic structure: dialogical space and monological space.

From a conception of poetic language as dialogue and ambivalence, Bakhtin moves to a re-evaluation of the novel's structure. This investigation takes the form of a classification of words within the narrative – the classification being then linked to a typology of discourse.

Classification of words within the narrative

According to Bakhtin, there are three categories of words within the narrative.

First, the *direct* word, referring back to its object, expresses the last possible degree of signification by the subject of discourse within the limits of a given context. It is the annunciating, expressive word of the writer, the *denotative* word, which is supposed to provide him with direct, objective comprehension. It knows nothing but itself and its object, to which it attempts to be adequate (it is not 'conscious' of the influences of words foreign to it).

Second, the *object-oriented* word is the direct discourse of 'characters'. It has direct, objective meaning, but is not situated on the same level as the writer's discourse; thus, it is at some distance from the latter. It is both oriented towards its object and is itself the object of the writer's orientation. It is a foreign word, subordinate to the narrative word as object of the writer's comprehension. But the writer's orientation towards the word as object does not penetrate it but accepts it as a whole, changing neither meaning nor tonality; it subordinates that word to its own task, introducing no other signification. Consequently, the object-oriented word, having become the object of an another (denotative) word, is not 'conscious' of it. The object-oriented word, like the denotative word, is therefore univocal.

In the third instance, however, the writer can use another's word, giving it a new meaning while retaining the meaning it already had. The result is a word with two significations: it becomes *ambivalent*. This ambivalent word is therefore the result of a joining of two sign-systems. Within the evolution of genres, ambivalent words appear in Menippean and carnivalesque texts (I shall return to this point). The forming of two sign-systems relativizes the text. Stylizing effects establish a distance with regard to the word of another – contrary to *imitation* (Bakhtin, rather, has in mind *repetition*), which takes what is imitated (repeated) seriously, claiming and appropriating it without relativizing it. This category of ambivalent words is characterized by the writer's exploitation of another's speech – without running counter to its thought – for his own purposes; he follows its direction while relativizing it. A second category of ambivalent words, *parody* for instance, proves to be quite different. Here the writer introduces a signification opposed to that of the other's word. A third type of ambivalent word, of which the *hidden interior polemic* is an example, is characterized by the active (modifying) influence of another's word on the writer's word. It is the writer who 'speaks', but a foreign discourse is constantly present in the speech that it distorts. With this *active* kind of ambivalent word, the other's word is represented by the word of the narrator. Examples include autobiography, polemical confessions, questions-and-answers and hidden dialogue. The novel is the only genre in which ambivalent words appear; that is the specific characteristic of its structure.

The inherent dialogism of denotative or historical words

The notion of univocity or objectivity of monologue and of the epic to which it is assimilated, or of the denotative object-oriented word, cannot withstand psychoanalytic or semantic analysis of language. Dialogism is coextensive with the deep structures of discourse. Notwithstanding Bakhtin and Benveniste, dialogism appears on the level of the Bakhtinian denotative word as a principle of every enunciation, as well as on the level of the 'story' in Benveniste. The story, like Benveniste's concept of 'discourse' itself, presupposes an intervention by the speaker within the narrative as well as an orientation towards the other. In order to describe the dialogism inherent in the denotative or historical word, we would have to turn to the psychic aspect of writing as trace of a dialogue with oneself (with another), as a writer's distance from himself, as a splitting of the writer into subject of enunciation and subject of utterance.

By the very act of narrating, the subject of narration addresses an other; narration is structured in relation to this other. (On the strength of such a communication, Francis Ponge offers his own variation of 'I think therefore I am': 'I speak and you hear me, therefore we are.' He thus postulates a shift from subjectivism to ambivalence.) Consequently, we may consider narration (beyond the signifier/signified relationship) as a dialogue between the *subject* of narration (S) and the *addressee* (A) – the other. This addressee, quite simply the reading subject, represents a doubly oriented entity: signifier in his relation to the text and signified in the relation between the subject of narration and himself. This entity is thus a dyad (A_1 and A_2) whose two terms, communicating with each other, constitute a code-system. The subject of narration (S) is drawn in, and therefore reduced to a code, to a non-person, to an *anonymity* (as writer, subject of enunciation) mediated by a third person, the *he/she* character, the subject of utterance. The writer is thus the subject of narration transformed by his having included himself within the narrative system; he is neither nothingness nor anybody, but the possibility of permutation from S to A, from story to discourse and from discourse to story. He becomes an anonymity, an absence, a blank space, thus permitting the structure to exist as such. At the very origin of narration, at the very moment when the writer appears, we experience emptiness. We see the problems of death, birth and sex appear when literature touches upon this strategic point that writing becomes when it exteriorizes linguistic systems through narrative structure (genres). On the basis of this anonymity, this zero where the author is situated, the *he/she* of the character is born. At a later stage, it will become a *proper name* (N). Therefore, in a literary text, 0 does not exist; emptiness is quickly replaced by a 'one' (a *he/she*, or a *proper name*) that is really twofold, since it is subject and addressee. It is the addressee, the other, exteriority (whose object is the subject of narration and who is at the same time represented and representing) who transforms the subject into an *author*. That is, who has the S pass through this zero-stage of negation, of exclusion, constituted by the author. In this coming-and-going movement between subject and other, between writer (W) and reader, the author is structured as a signifier and the text as a dialogue of two discourses.

The constitution of characters (of 'personality') also permits a disjunction of S into S_r (subject of enunciation) and S_d (subject of utterance). A diagram of this mutation would appear as diagram 1. This diagram incorporates the structure of the pronominal system[16] that

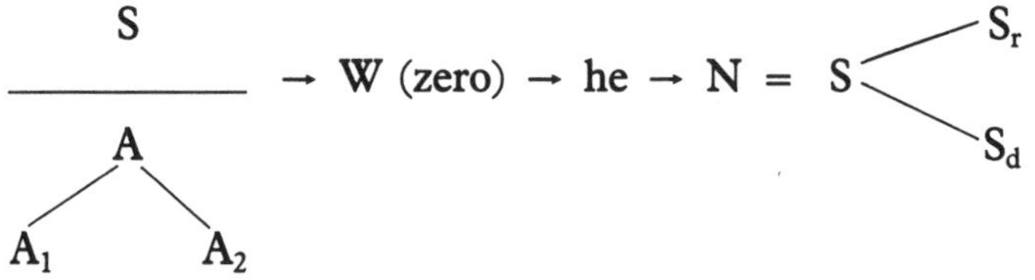

$$\frac{S}{\overset{A}{\underset{A_1 \quad A_2}{\wedge}}} \rightarrow W \text{ (zero)} \rightarrow he \rightarrow N = S \underset{S_d}{\overset{S_r}{\big<}}$$

Diagram 1

psychoanalysts repeatedly find in the discourse of the object of psychoanalysis (see diagram 2).

I	S
he_1	N
he_o	S_r
(some) one	S_d

Diagram 2

At the level of the text (of the signifier) – in the S_r-S_d relationship – we find this dialogue of the subject with the addressee around which every narration is structured. The subject of utterance, in relation to the subject of enunciation, plays the role of addressee with respect to the subject; it inserts the subject of enunciation within the writing system by making the latter pass through emptiness. Mallarmé called this operation 'elocutionary disappearance'.

The *subject of utterance* is both representative of the subject of enunciation and represented as object of the subject of enunciation. It is therefore commutable with the writer's anonymity. A *character* (a personality) is constituted by this generation of a double entity starting from zero. The subject of utterance is 'dialogical', both S and A are disguised within it.

The procedure I have just described in confronting narration and the novel now abolishes distinctions between signifier and signified. It renders these concepts ineffective for that literary practice operating uniquely within dialogical signifier(s). 'The signifier represents the subject for another signifier' (Lacan).

Narration, therefore, is always constituted as a dialogical matrix by the receiver to whom this narration refers. Any narration, including history and science, contains this dialogical dyad formed by the narrator in conjunction with the other. It is translated through the dialogical S_r/S_d relationship, with S_r and S_d filling the roles of signifier and signified in turns, but constituting merely a permutation of two signifiers.

It is, however, only through certain narrative structures that this dialogue – this hold on the sign as double, this ambivalence of writing – is exteriorized in the actual organization of poetic discourse on the level of textual literary occurrence.

Towards a typology of discourses

Bakhtin's radical undertaking – the dynamic analysis of texts resulting in a redistribution of genres – calls upon us to be just as radical in developing a typology of discourses.

As it is used by the Formalists, the term *'narrative'* is too ambiguous to cover all of the genres it supposedly designates. At least two different types of narrative can be isolated.

We have on the one hand *monological discourse*, including, first, the representative mode of description and narration (the epic); secondly, historical discourse; and thirdly, scientific discourse. In all three, the subject both assumes and submits to the rule of 1 (God). The dialogue inherent in all discourse is smothered by a *prohibition*, a censorship, such that this discourse refuses to turn back upon itself, to enter into dialogue with itself. To present the models of this censorship is to describe the nature of the differences between two types of discourse: the epic type (history and science) and the Menippean type (carnivalesque writings and novel), which transgresses prohibition. Monological discourse corresponds to Jakobson's systematic axis of language, and its analogous relationship to grammatical affirmation and negation has also been noted.

On the other hand, *dialogical discourse* includes carnivalesque and Menippean discourses as well as the polyphonic novel. In its structures, writing reads another writing, reads itself and constructs itself through a process of destructive genesis.

Epic monologism

The *epic*, structured at the limits of syncretism, illustrates the double value of words in their post-syncretic phase: the utterance of a subject

('I') inevitably penetrated by language as carrier of the concrete, universal, individual and collective. But in an epic, the speaker (subject of the epic) does not make use of another's speech. The dialogical play of language as correlation of signs – the dialogical permutation of two signifiers for one signified – takes place on the level of *narration* (through the denotative word, or through the inherency of the text). It does not exteriorize itself at the level of textual *manifestation* as in the structure of novels. This is the scheme at work within an epic, with no hint as yet of Bakhtin's problematic – the ambivalent word. The organizational principle of epic structure thus remains monological. The dialogue of language does not manifest itself except within a narrative infrastructure. There is no dialogue at the level of the apparent textual organization (historical enunciation/discursive enunciation); the two aspects of enunciation remain limited by the narrator's absolute point of view, which concides with the wholeness of a god or community. Within epic monologism, we detect the presence of the 'transcendental signified' and 'self presence' as highlighted by Jacques Derrida.

It is the systematic mode of language (similarity, according to Jakobson) that prevails within the epic space. Metonymic contiguity, specific to the syntagmatic axis of language, is rare. Of course, association and metonymy are there as rhetorical figures, but they are never a principle of structural organization. Epic logic pursues the general through the specific; it thus assumes a hierarchy within the structure of substance. Epic logic is therefore causal, that is, theological; it is a *belief* in the literal sense of the word.

The carnival: a homology between the body, dream, linguistic structure and structures of desire

Carnivalesque structure is like the residue of a cosmogony that ignored substance, causality or identity outside its link to the whole, *which exists only in or through relationship*. This carnivalesque cosmogony has persisted in the form of an anti-theological (but not anti-mystical) and deeply popular movement. It remains present as an often misunderstood and persecuted substratum of official Western culture throughout its entire history; it is most noticeable in folk games as well as in medieval theatre and prose (anecdotes, fables and the *Roman de Renart*). As composed of distances, relationships, analogies and non-exclusive oppositions, it is essentially dialogical. It is a spectacle, but without a stage; a game, but also a daily undertaking; a signifier, but also a signified. That is, two texts meet, contradict and relativize each other. A carnival participant is both actor and spectator; he loses his sense of individuality, passes through a zero point of carnivalesque activity and splits into a subject of the spectacle and an object of the game. Within the carnival, the subject is reduced to nothingness, while the structure of *the author* emerges as anonymity that creates and sees itself created as self and other, as man and mask. The cynicism of this carnivalesque scene, which destroys a god in order to impose its own dialogical laws, calls to mind Nietzsche's Dionysianism. The carnival first exteriorizes the structure of reflective literary productivity, then inevitably brings to light this structure's underlying unconscious: sexuality and death. Out of the dialogue that is established between them, the structural dyads of carnival appear: high and low, birth and agony, food and excrement, praise and curses, laughter and tears.

Figures germane to carnivalesque language, including repetition, 'inconsequent' statements (which are none the less 'connected' within an infinite context) and non-exclusive opposition, which function as empty sets or disjunctive additions, produce a more flagrant dialogism than any other discourse. Disputing the laws of language based on the 0-1 interval, the carnival challenges God, authority and social law; in so far as it is dialogical, it is rebellious. Because of its subversive discourse, the word 'carnival' has understandably acquired a strongly derogatory or narrowly burlesque meaning in our society.

The scene of the carnival, where there is no stage, no 'theatre', is thus both stage and life, game and dream, discourse and spectacle. By the same token, it is proffered as the only space in which language escapes linearity (law) to live as drama in three dimensions. At a deeper level, this also signifies the contrary: drama becomes located in language. A major principle thus emerges: all poetic discourse is dramatization, dramatic permutation (in a mathematical sense) of words. Within carnivalesque discourse, we can already adumbrate that 'as to mental condition, it is like the meanderings of drama' (Mallarmé). This scene, whose symptom is carnivalesque discourse, is the only dimension where 'theatre might be the reading of a book, its writing in operation'. In other words, such a scene is the only place where discourse attains its 'potential infinity' (to use David Hilbert's term), where prohibitions (representation, 'monologism') and their transgression (dream, body, 'dialogism') coexist. Carnivalesque tradition was absorbed into

Menippean discourse and put into practice by the polyphonic novel.

On the omnified stage of carnival, language parodies and relativizes itself, repudiating its role in representation; in so doing, it provokes laughter but remains incapable of detaching itself from representation. The syntagmatic axis of language becomes exteriorized in this space and, through dialogue with the systematic axis, constitutes the ambivalent structure bequeathed by carnival to the novel. Faulty (by which I mean ambivalent), both representative and anti-representative, the carnivalesque structure is anti-Christian and anti-rationalist. All of the most important polyphonic novels are inheritors of the Menippean, carnivalesque structure: those of Rabelais, Cervantes, Swift, Sade, Balzac, Lautréamont, Dostoevsky, Joyce and Kafka. Its history is the history of the struggle against Christianity and its representation; this means an exploration of language (of sexuality and death), a consecration of ambivalence and of 'vice'.

The word 'carnivalesque' lends itself to an ambiguity one must avoid. In contemporary society, it generally connotes parody, hence a strengthening of the law. There is a tendency to blot out the carnival's *dramatic* (murderous, cynical and revolutionary in the sense of *dialectical transformation*) aspects, which Bakhtin emphasized, and which he recognized in Menippean writings or in Dostoevsky. The laughter of the carnival is not simply parodic; it is no more comic than tragic; it is both at once, one might say that it is *serious*. This is the only way that it can avoid becoming either the scene of law or the scene of its parody, in order to become the scene of its *other*. Modern writing offers several striking examples of this omnified scene that is both *law* and *others* – where *laughter* is silenced because it is not parody but *murder* and *revolution* (Antonin Artaud).

The epic and the carnivalesque are the two currents that formed European narrative, one taking precedence over the other according to the times and the writer. The carnivalesque tradition of the people is still apparent in personal literature of late antiquity and has remained, to this day, the life source reanimating literary thought, orienting it towards new perspectives.

Classical humanism helped dissolve the epic monologism that speech welded together so well, and that orators, rhetoricians and politicians, on the one hand, tragedy and epic, on the other, implemented so effectively. Before another monologism could take root (with the triumph of formal logic, Christianity and Renaissance humanism),[17] late antiquity gave birth to two genres that reveal language's dialogism. Situated within the carnivalesque tradition, and constituting the yeast of the European novel, these two genres are *Socratic dialogue* and *Menippean discourse*.

Socratic dialogue: dialogism as a destruction of the person

Socratic dialogue was widespread in antiquity: Plato, Xenophon, Antisthenes, Aeschines, Phaedo, Euclid and others excelled in it, although only the dialogues of Plato and Xenophon have come down to us. Not as much rhetorical in genre as popular and carnivalesque, it was originally a kind of memoir (the recollections of Socrates' discussions with his students) that broke away from the constraints of history, retaining only the Socratic process of dialogically revealing truth, as well as the structure of a recorded dialogue framed by narrative. Nietzsche accused Plato of having ignored Dionysian tragedy, but Socratic dialogue had adopted the dialogical and defiant structure of the carnivalesque scene. According to Bakhtin, Socratic dialogues are characterized by opposition to any official monologism claiming to possess a ready-made truth. Socratic truth ('meaning') is the product of a dialogical relationship among speakers; it is correlational and its relativism appears by virtue of the observers' autonomous points of view. Its art is one of *articulation* of fantasy, *correlation* of signs. Two typical devices for triggering this linguistic network are syncrisis (confronting different discourses on the same topic) and anacrusis (one word prompting another). The subjects of discourse are non-persons, anonyms, hidden by the discourse constituting them. Bakhtin reminds us that the 'event' of Socratic dialogue is of the nature of discourse: a questioning and testing, through speech, of a definition. This speech practice is therefore organically linked to the man who created it (Socrates and his students), or better, speech *is* man and his activity. Here, one can speak of a practice possessing a synthetic character; the process separating the *word* as act, as apodeictic practice, as articulation of difference from the *image* as representation, as knowledge and as idea was not yet complete when Socratic dialogue took form. But there is an important 'detail' to Socratic dialogism; it is the exclusive position of a subject of discourse that provokes the dialogue. In the *Apology* of Plato, Socrates' trial and the period of awaiting judgement determine his discourse as the confessions of a man 'on the threshold'. The exclusive situation liberates the word from any univocal objectivity, from any representative function, opening it up to the symbolic sphere. Speech affronts death, measuring itself against another discourse; this dialogue counts the *person* out.

The resemblance between Socratic dialogue and the ambivalent word of the novel is obvious.

Socratic dialogue did not last long, but it gave birth to several dialogical genres, including *Menippean discourse*, whose origins also lie in carnivalesque folklore.

Menippean discourse: the text as social activity

1 Menippean discourse takes its name from Menippus of Gadara, a philosopher of the third century BC. His satires were lost, but we know of their existence through the writings of Diogenes Laertius. The term was used by the Romans to designate a genre of the first century BC (Marcus Terentius Varro's *Satirae Menippeae*).

Yet the genre actually appeared much earlier; its first representative was perhaps Antisthenes, a student of Socrates and one of the writers of Socratic dialogue. Heraclitus also wrote Menippean texts (according to Cicero, he created an analogous genre called *logistoricus*); Varro gave it definite stability. Other examples include Seneca the Younger's *Apocolocynthosis*, Petronius' *Satyricon*, Lucan's satires, Ovid's *Metamorphoses*, Hippocrates' *Novel*, various samples of Greek 'novels', classical utopian novels and Roman (Horatian) satire. Within the Menippean sphere there evolve diatribe, soliloquy and other minor genres of controversy. It greatly influenced Christian and Byzantine literature; in various forms, it survived through the Middle Ages, the Renaissance and the Reformation through to the present (the novels of Joyce, Kafka and Bataille). This carnivalesque genre – as pliant and variable as Proteus, capable of insinuating itself into other genres – had an enormous influence on the development of European literature and especially the formation of the novel.

Menippean discourse is both comic and tragic, or rather, it is *serious* in the same sense as is the carnivalesque; through the status of its words, it is politically and socially disturbing. It frees speech from historical constraints, and this entails a thorough boldness in philosophical and imaginative inventiveness. Bakhtin emphasizes that 'exclusive' situations increase freedom of language in Menippean discourse. Phantasmagoria and an often mystical symbolism fuse with macabre naturalism.

Adventures unfold in brothels, robbers' dens, taverns, fairgrounds and prisons, among erotic orgies and during sacred worship, and so forth. The word has no fear of incriminating itself. It becomes free from presupposed 'values'; without distinguishing between virtue and vice, and without distinguishing itself from them, the word considers them its private domain, as one of its creations. Academic problems are pushed aside in favour of the 'ultimate' problems of existence: this discourse orients liberated language towards philosophical universalism. Without distinguishing ontology from cosmogony, it unites them into a practical philosophy of life. Elements of the fantastic, which never appear in epic or tragic works, crop forth here. For example, an unusual perspective from above changes the scale of observation in Lucan's *Icaro-menippea*, Varro's *Endymion* and later in the works of Rabelais, Swift and Voltaire. Pathological states of the soul, such as madness, split personalities, daydreams, dreams and death, become part of the narrative (they affect the writing of Shakespeare and Calderón). According to Bakhtin, these elements have more structural than thematic significance; they destroy man's epic and tragic unity as well as his belief in identity and causality; they indicate that he has lost his totality and no longer coincides with himself. At the same time, they often appear as an exploration of language and writing: in Varro's *Bimarcus*, the two Marcuses discuss whether or not one should write in tropes. Menippean discourse tends towards the scandalous and eccentric in language. The 'inopportune' expression, with its cynical frankness, its desecration of the sacred and its attack on etiquette, is quite characteristic. This discourse is made up of contrasts: virtuous courtesans, generous bandits, wise men that are both free and enslaved, and so on. It uses abrupt transitions and changes; high and low, rise and fall, and misalliances of all kinds. Its language seems fascinated with the 'double' (with its own activity as graphic *trace*, doubling an 'outside') and with the logic of opposition replacing that of identity in defining terms. It is an all-inclusive genre, put together as a pavement of citations. It includes all genres (short stories, letters, speeches, mixtures of verse and prose) whose structural signification is to denote the writer's distance from his own and other texts. The multi-stylism and multi-tonality of this discourse and the dialogical status of its word explain why it has been impossible for classicism, or for any other authoritarian society, to express itself in a novel descended from Menippean discourse.

Put together as an exploration of the body, dreams and language, this writing grafts on to the topical: it is a kind of political journalism of its time. Its discourse exteriorizes political and ideological conflicts of the moment. The dialogism of its words *is* practical philosophy doing battle against idealism and religious metaphysics, against the epic. It constitutes the social and political thought of an era fighting against theology, against law.

2 Menippean discourse is thus structured as ambivalence, as the focus for two tendencies of Western literature: representation through language as staging, and exploration of language as a correlative system of signs. Language in the Menippean tradition is both representation of exterior space and 'an experience that produces its own space'. In this ambiguous genre appear, first, the *premises of realism* (a secondary activity in relation to what is lived, where man describes himself by making of himself an exhibition, finally creating 'characters' and 'personalities'); and secondly the *refusal to define* a psychic universe (an immediately present activity, characterized by images, gestures and word-gestures through which man lives his limits in the impersonal). This second aspect relates Menippean structure to the structure of dreams and hieroglyphic writing or, possibly, to the theatre of cruelty as conceived by Artaud. His words apply equally; Menippean discourse 'is not equal to individual life, to that individual aspect of life where characters triumph, but rather to a kind of liberated life that sweeps away human individuality and where man is no more than a reflected image.' Likewise, the Menippean experience is not cathartic; it is a festival of cruelty, but also a political act. It transmits no fixed message except that itself should be 'the eternal joy of becoming', and it exhausts itself in the act and in the present. Born after Socrates, Plato and the Sophists, it belongs to an age when thought ceases to be practice; the fact that it is considered as a *techne* shows that the *praxis-poiesis* separation has already taken place. Similarly, literature becoming 'thought' becomes conscious of itself as *sign*. Man, alienated from nature and society, becomes alienated from himself, discovering his 'interior' and 'reifying' this discovery in the ambivalence of Menippean writing. Such tokens are the harbingers of realist representation. Menippean discourse, however, knows nothing of a theological principle's monologism (or of the Renaissance man-God) that could have consolidated its representative aspect. The 'tyranny' it is subjected to is that of text (not speech as reflection of a pre-existing universe), or rather its own structure, constructing and understanding itself through itself. It constructs itself

as a *hieroglyph*, all the while remaining a spectacle. It bequeaths this ambivalence to the novel, above all to the polyphonic novel, which knows neither law nor hierarchy, since it is a plurality of linguistic elements in dialogical relationships. The conjunctive principle of the different parts of Menippean discourse is certainly *similitude* (resemblance, dependence and therefore 'realism'), but also contiguity (analogy, juxtaposition and therefore 'rhetoric' – not in Benedetto Croce's sense of ornament, but rather, as justification through and in language). Menippean ambivalence consists of communication between two spaces:[18] that of the scene and that of the hieroglyph, that of representation *by* language, and that of experience *in* language, system and phrase, metaphor and metonymy. This ambivalence is the novel's inheritance.

In other words, the dialogism of Menippean and carnivalesque discourses, translating a logic of relations and analogy rather than of substance and inference, stands against Aristotelian logic. From within the very interior of formal logic, even while skirting it, Menippean dialogism contradicts it and points it towards other forms of thought. Indeed, Menippean discourse develops in times of opposition against Aristotelianism, and writers of polyphonic novels seem to disapprove of the very structures of official thought founded on formal logic.

The subversive novel

1 In the Middle Ages, Menippean tendencies were held in check by the authority of the religious text; in the bourgeois era, they were contained by the absolutism of individuals and things. Only modernity – when freed of 'God' – releases the Menippean force of the novel.

Now that modern, bourgeois society has not only accepted, but claims to recognize itself in the novel,[18] such claim can only refer to the category of monological narratives, known as realistic, that censor all carnivalesque and Menippean elements, whose structures were assembled at the time of the Renaissance. On the contrary, the Menippean, dialogical novel, tending to refuse representation and the epic, has only been tolerated; that is, it has been declared unreadable, ignored or ridiculed. Today, it shares the same fate as the carnivalesque discourse practised by students during the Middle Ages outside the Church.

The novel, and especially the modern, polyphonic novel, incorporating Menippean elements, embodies the effort of European thought to break out of the framework of causally determined identical substances and head towards another modality of thought that proceeds through dialogue (a logic of distance, relativity, analogy, non-exclusive and transfinite opposition). It is therefore not surprising that the novel has been considered as an inferior genre (by neo-classicism and other similar regimes) or as subversive (I have in mind the major writers of polyphonic novels over many centuries – Rabelais, Swift, Sade, Lautréamont, Kafka and Bataille – to mention only those who have always been and still remain on the fringe of official culture). The way in which European thought transgresses its constituent characteristics appears clearly in the words and narrative structures of the twentieth-century novel. Identity, substance, causality and definition are transgressed so that others may be adopted: analogy, relation, opposition, and therefore dialogism and Menippean ambivalence.[20]

Although this entire historical inventory that Bakhtin has undertaken evokes the image of a museum or the task of an archivist, it is none the less rooted in our present concerns. Everything written today unveils either the possibility or impossibility of reading and rewriting history. This possibility is evident in the literature heralded by the writings of a new generation, where the text is elaborated as *theatre* and as *reading*. Mallarmé, one of the first to understand the Menippean qualities of the novel (let it be emphasized that Bakhtin's term has the advantage of situating a certain kind of writing within history), said that literature 'is nothing but the flash of what should have been produced previously or closer to the origin'.

2 I would now suggest two models for organizing narrative signification, based on two dialogical categories: (1) Subject (S) $\rightleftharpoons$ Addressee (A); and (2) Subject of enunciation $\rightleftharpoons$ Subject of utterance.

The first model implies a dialogical relationship, while the second presupposes modal relationships within this dialogical formation. The first model determines genre (epic poem, novel) while the second determines generic variants.

Within the polyphonic structure of a novel, the first dialogical model (S $\rightleftharpoons$ A) plays itself out entirely within the writing discourse; and it presents itself as perpetually challenging this discourse. The writer's interlocutor, then, is the writer himself, but as reader of another text. The one who writes is the same as the one who reads. Since his interlocutor is a text, he himself is no more than a text re-reading itself as it rewrites itself. The dialogical structure, therefore, appears only in the light of the text elaborating itself as ambivalent in relation to another text.

In the epic, on the other hand, A is an extra-textual, absolute entity (God or community) that relativizes dialogue to the point where it is cancelled out and reduced to monologue. With this in mind, it is easy to understand why not only the so-called 'traditional' novel of the nineteenth century, but also any novel with any ideological thesis whatsoever, tends towards an epic, thus constituting a deviation in the very structure of the novel; this is why Tolstoy's monologism is epic and Dostoevsky's dialogism novelistic.

Within the framework of the second model, several possibilities may be detected:

a The subject of utterance (S_d) coincides with the zero degree of the subject of enunciation (S_r), which can be designated either by the 'he/she' non-person pronoun or a proper name. This is the simplest technique found at the inception of the narrative.

b The subject of utterance (S_d) coincides with the subject of enunciation (S_r). This produces a first person narrative: 'I'.

c The subject of utterance (S_d) coincides with the addressee (A). This produces a second person narrative: 'you': as for example with Raskolnikov's object-oriented word in *Crime and Punishment*. Michel Butor insistently explored this technique in *A Change of Heart*.

d The subject of utterance (S_d) coincides both with the subject of enunciation (S_r) and the addressee (A). In such a case the novel becomes a questioning of writing and displays the staging of its dialogical structure. At the same time, the text becomes a reading (quotation and commentary) of an exterior literary corpus and is thus constructed as ambivalence. Through its use of personal pronouns and anonymous quotations, Philippe Sollers's *Drame* is an example of this fourth possibility.

A reading of Bakhtin therefore leads to the paradigm shown in figure 1.

I should finally like to insist on the importance of Bakhtin's concepts (on the status of the word, dialogue and ambivalence), as well as on the importance of certain new perspectives opened up through them.

By establishing the status of the word as *minimal unit* of the text, Bakhtin deals with structure at its deepest level, beyond the sentence

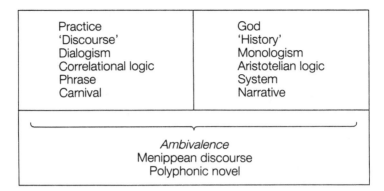

Figure 1

and rhetorical figures. The notion of *status* has added to the image of the text as a corpus of atoms that of a text made up of relationships, within which words function as quantum units. If there is a model for poetic language, it no longer involves lines or surfaces, but rather, *space* and *infinity* – concepts amenable to formalization through set theory and the new mathematics. Contemporary analysis of narrative structure has been refined to the point where it can delineate functions (cardinal or catalytic), and indices (as such or as information); it can describe the elaboration of a narrative according to particular logical or rhetorical patterns. Without gainsaying the undisputed value of this kind of research,[21] one might wonder whether the presuppositions of a metalanguage that sets up hierarchies or is heterogeneous to narrative do not weigh too heavily upon such studies. Perhaps Bakhtin's naïve procedure, centred on the word and its unlimited ability to generate dialogue (commentary of a quotation), is both simpler and more productive.

The notion of dialogism, which owed much to Hegel, must not be confused with Hegelian dialectics, based on a triad and thus on struggle and projection (a movement of transcendence), which does not transgress the Aristotelian tradition founded on substance and causality. Dialogism replaces these concepts by absorbing them within the concept of relation. It does not strive towards transcendence but rather toward harmony, all the while implying an idea of rupture (of opposition and analogy) as a modality of transformation.

Dialogism situates philosophical problems *within* language; more precisely, within language as a correlation of texts, as a reading-writing that falls in with non-Aristotelian, syntagmatic, correlational, 'carnival-esque' logic. Consequently, one of the fundamental problems facing contemporary semiotics is precisely to describe this 'other logic' without denaturing it.

The term 'ambivalence' lends itself perfectly to the current transitory stage of European literature – a coexistence (an ambivalence of 'the double of lived experience' (realism and the epic) and 'lived experience' itself (linguistic exploration and Menippean discourse) – a literature that will perhaps arrive at a form of thought similar to that of painting: the transmission of essence through form, and the configuration of (literary) space as revealing (literary) thought without 'realist' pre-tensions. This entails the study, through language, of the novel's space and of its transmutations, thereby establishing a close relationship between language and space, compelling us to analyse them as modes of thought. By examining the ambivalence of the spectacle (realist representation) and of lived experience (rhetoric), one might perceive the line where the rupture (or junction) between them takes place. That line could be seen as the graph of a motion through which our culture forsakes itself in order to go beyond itself.

The path charted between the two poles of dialogue radically abolishes problems of causality, finality, etc., from our philosophical arena. It suggests the importance of the dialogical principle for a space of thought much larger than that of the novel. More than binarism, dialogism may well become the basis of our time's intellectual structure. The predominance of the novel and other ambivalent literary structures; the communal, carnivalesque phenomena attracting young people; quantum exchanges; and current interest in the correlational symbolism of Chinese philosophy – to cite only a few striking elements of modern thought – all confirm this hypothesis.

NOTES

1 The point of departure for this essay lies in two books by Mikhail Bakhtin: *Rabelais and His World*. tr. Helene Iswolsky (Cambridge, Mass.:MIT Press, 1965), and *Problems of Dostoevsky's Poetics*, tr. R. W. Rotsel (Ann Arbor, Mich.: Ardis, 1973). Bakhtin died in 1975, the year of the publication of his collection of essays, *Voprosy literatury i estetiki* (Moscow), published in French as *Esthétique et théorie du roman* (Paris: Gallimard, 1978).

2 Derrida uses the word *gram* (from the Greek *gramma*, 'that which is written') to designate the irreducible material element of writing, as opposed to the vast amount

of extraneous connotations currently surrounding that word. See his *Of Grammatology*, tr. Gayatri Spivak (Baltimore, Md: Johns Hopkins University Press, 1976).

3 Language is as old as consciousness, language *is* practical consciousness that exists also for other men, and for that reason alone it really exists for me personally as well.' Karl Marx, *The German Ideology*, tr. S. Ryazanskaya, in *The Marx-Engels Reader*, ed. Robert C. Tucker (New York: Norton, 1972), p. 122. [The French translation quoted by Kristeva is less faithful to the German text, although, in the latter part of the sentence, the German word for 'genuine' does modify 'consciousness': '. . . auch für mich selbst echt existierende Bewußtsein;' The French version begins 'Le langage *est* la conscience réelle. . .'

4 I shall refer to only a few of Bakhtin's notions in so far as they are congruent with the conceptions of Ferdinand de Saussure as related to his 'anagrams' (see Jean Starobinski, *Les Mots sous les mots*, Paris: Gallimard, 1971) and suggest a new approach to literary texts.

5 See Julia Kristeva, *La Révolution du langage poétique* (Paris: Seuil, 1974), pp. 59–60.

6 'Indeed, when structural semantics refers to the linguistic foundations of discourse, it points out that 'an expanding sequence is recognized as the equivalent of a syntactically simpler communication' and defines 'expansion' as 'one of the most important aspects of the operation of natural languages'. A. J. Greimas, *Sémantique structurale* (Paris: Larousse, 1966), p. 72. I conceive of the notion of expansion as the theoretical principle authorizing me to study in the structure of genres an exteriorization (an expansion) of structures inherent to language.

7 E. F. Boudé, *K istorii velikoruskix govorov* (Towards a History of Russian Dialects) (Kazan: 1869).

8 L. V. Czerba, *Vostotchno-luzhickoe narechie* (The Eastern Loujiks' Dialect) (Petrograd: 1915).

9 V. V. Vinogradov, 'O dialogicheskoj rechi' (On dialogical discourse), in *Russkaja rech*, 1, p. 1440.

10 V. V. Vinogradov, *Poetika* (Moscow: Nauka, 1926), p. 33.

11 It seems that what is persistently being called 'interior monologue' is the most indomitable way in which an entire civilization conceives itself as identity, as organized chaos and finally, as transcendence. Yet this 'monologue' probably exists only in texts that pretend to reconstitute the so-called physical reality of 'verbal flux'. Western man's state of 'interiority' is thus a limited literary effect (confessional form, continuous psychological speech, automatic writing). In a way, then, Freud's 'Copernican' revolution (the discovery of the split within the subject) put an end to the fiction of an internal *voice* by positing the fundamental principles governing the subject's radical exteriority in relation to, and within, language.

12 Bakhtin, *Problems of Dostoevsky's Poetics*, pp. 151–2.

13 'Shifters, verbal categories and the Russian verb', in *Selected Writings II* (The Hague: Mouton, 1971), pp. 130–47.

14 Bakhtin, *Problems of Dostoevsky's Poetics*, p. 151.

15 I should emphasize that introducing notions of set theory into considerations on poetic language has only metaphorical value. It is legitimate to do so because one can draw an analogy between the Aristotelian logic/poetic logic relationship on the one hand, and the quantifiable/infinite relationship on the other.

16 See Luce Irigaray, 'Communication linguistique et communication speculaire', in *Cahiers pour l'Analyse*, 3, (May 1966), pp. 39–55.

17 I should like to stress the ambiguous role of Western individualism. Involving the concept of identity, it is linked to the substantialist, causal and atomist thought of Aristotelian Greece and has strengthened throughout centuries this activist, scientistic or theological aspect of Western culture. On the other hand, since it is founded on the principle of a difference between the 'self' and the 'world', it prompts a search for mediation between the two terms, or for stratifications within each of them, in order to allow the possibility of a correlative logic based on the very components of formal logic.

18 It was perhaps this phenomenon that Bakhtin had in mind when he wrote, 'The language of the novel can be located neither on a surface nor on a line. It is a system of surfaces that intersect. The author as creator of everything having to do with the novel cannot be located on any of these linguistic surfaces. Rather, he resides within the controlling centre constituted by the intersection of the surfaces. All these surfaces are located at varying distances from that authorial centre' ('Šlovo o romane', in *Voprosy literatury*, 8 (1965), pp. 84–90). Actually, the writer is nothing more than the *linking* of these centres. Attributing a single centre to him would be to constrain him within a monological, theological position.

19 This point of view is shared by all theorists of the novel: A. Thibaudet, *Réflexions sur le roman* (Thoughts on the Novel; Paris: Gallimard, 1938); Koskimies, 'Théorie des Romans' (Theory of the novel), in *Annales Academiae Scientarum Finnicae*, I, series B, 35 (1935), pp. 5–275. Georg Lukács, *Theory of the Novel* (Cambridge: MIT Press, 1971), and others.

An interesting perspective on the concept of the novel as dialogue is provided by Wayne Booth's *The Rhetoric of Fiction* (Chicago: University of Chicago Press, 1961). His ideas concerning the *reliable* and *unreliable writer* parallel some of Bakhtin's investigations into dialogism in the novel, although they do not posit any specific relationship between novelistic 'illusionism' and linguistic symbolism.

20 Such a mode shows up in modern physics as well as in ancient Chinese thought, as the two are equally anti-Aristotelian, anti-monological and dialogical. See S. I. Hayakawa, 'What is meant by Aristotelian structure in language', in *Language, Meaning and Maturity* (New York: Harper, 1959); Chang Tung-sun, 'A Chinese philosopher's theory of knowledge', in S. I. Hayakawa, (ed.), *Our Language and Our World* (New York: Harper, 1959); Joseph Needham, *Science and Civilization in China*, vol. II (Cambridge: Cambridge University Press, 1965).

21 See the important collection of studies on narrative structure in *Communications*, 8 (1966), which includes contributions by Roland Barthes, A. J. Greimas, Claude Bremond, Umberto Eco, Jules Gritti, Violette Morin, Christian Metz, Tzvetan Todorov and Gérard Genette.

Translated by Alice Jardine, Thomas Gora and Léon S. Roudiez

3

From Symbol to Sign

The essay is taken from Kristeva's first work in French, *Le Texte du roman: apprôche sémiologique d'une structure discursive transformationnelle* (The Hague: Mouton, 1970), written as a thesis in linguistics in 1966 and 1967, that is to say, shortly after her arrival in Paris in 1966. In this book Kristeva examines the prose work of Antoine de la Sale (*c.*1385 – after 1460) in order to show how the novel as a semiotic practice emerges in the late Middle Ages.

La Sale travelled widely in Europe, particularly in Italy, and became tutor to the Dukes of Burgundy. In 1442 he finished his first work, entitled *La Salade*, a collection of historical, geographical, juridical and ethical texts. The fourth part of this compilation is entitled *Le Paradis de la reine Sibylle* ('The Paradise of the Queen Sibyl') and this astonishing dream sequence is the implicit context of Kristeva's discussion of the various images of the Sibyl in medieval Europe (1.2.2). The same passage also mentions his *La Sale* (1451) which was a collection of moral anecdotes written for his three ducal pupils. As a whole, *Le Texte du roman* nevertheless concentrates on the linguistic study of the *Histoire et plaisante chronique du petit Jehan de Saintré et de la jeune dame des Belles Cousines* (1456) which, apart from being La Sale's best work, is also considered important in the development of French prose fiction.

In *Le Texte du roman* Kristeva shows that the emergence of the novel as a linguistic form is made possible by a fundamental change in the perception of the sign itself. It is this change which is examined and presented in 'From Symbol to Sign'. Briefly, her argument is that the general conception of the sign developed away from the idea of the sign as a transcendental closure and towards a linguistic practice which implied that it was an open-ended material structure. In order to develop this argument Kristeva borrows and redefines the term *ideologeme* from the Russian Formalist P. N. Medvedev. For Kristeva, the *ideologeme* is a term which enables her to grasp the inherent ideological value of the sign as *constitutive* of its meaning, and not simply as an 'ideological' addition to the linguistic analysis. In using this word, the point for Kristeva is to emphasize the fact that all forms of discourse are constructed by the social space in which they are enunciated (for further discussion of this term, see *Le Texte du roman*, pp. 12–13).

In her discussion of the symbol/sign distinction (1.1) Kristeva draws on C. S. Peirce's famous distinction between icon, index and symbol, but in this context she also uses the Peircean terms 'replica' and 'object'. According to Perice, the 'replica' is the 'embodiment of the word that is pronounced or written' ('Logic as semiotic: the theory of signs', in J. Buchler (ed.), *Philosophical Writings of Peirce*, New York: Dover Publications, 1955, p. 112), and we can therefore compare it to Saussure's well-known definition of the *signifier* as the material aspect of the sign. In the same way, Kristeva herself defines the 'object' as the *signified*.

From Symbol to Sign

> The articulation of cultures, as a function of the relations they entertain with the sign, will eventually permit a classification of cultures.
>
> J. Lotman, 'Problems of the typology of cultures',
> *Information sur les sciences sociales*, April–June 1967, p. 33

1.1 The symbol/sign distinction

We shall use the term novel to describe the kind of narrative that starts to emerge clearly at the end of the Middle Ages and the beginning of the Renaissance. The object of our analysis, *Jehan de Saintré* by Antoine de la Sale, is a perfect example of such a narrative. Similar efforts had already been observed towards the end of Greek antiquity, in 'Menippean' narrative structure.[1]

Despite their differences, what characterizes these two kinds of narrative (the novel and the Menippean form) is the way in which their structure indicates at once a disintegration of the epic system (the Greek republic or European feudalism) and a move to another way of thinking (late Greece after the fourth century BC and the Renaissance). We shall call this transition a passage from the *symbol* to the *sign* and postulate that the novel is a narrative structure revealing the ideologeme of the sign. This obliges us to define the *symbol/sign difference*.

We are familiar with Peirce's generally accepted classification of signs as icon, index and symbol.[2] The distinction is based on the relationship between the sign and its object. The symbol, which is the element that concerns us here, is defined as follows: it 'refers to the object that it denotes by virtue of a *law*, usually an association of general ideas'.

Our symbol/sign distinction, which acts both as a diachronic and as a synchronic classification of discursive (cultural) phenomena, involves Peirce's third category, where the symbol rests on a double criterion: (1) the relationship between the 'replica' (the signifying unit) and its 'object' (the interpretant, the idea, the signified); (2) the series in which these replicas can be placed.

This distinction is consequently more akin to the one made by Saussure, for in his terminology 'the symbol is characterized by its lack of total arbitrariness. It is not empty; it still betrays the rudiments of a natural link between signifier and signified.'[3] In other words, in the case of the symbol the signified object is *represented* by the signifying unit through a restrictive function-relation; while the sign, as we shall see, pretends not to assume this relation which in its case is weaker and therefore might be regarded as arbitrary.[4] But this Saussurian criterion of the symbol/sign distinction (which in fact is Hegelian) will be supplemented by a 'horizontal' criterion: the articulation of signifying units with one another.

1.2 Characteristics of the symbol

1.2.1

The second half of the Middle Ages (thirteenth to fifteenth centuries) was a period of transition for European culture: thought based on the sign replaced that based on the symbol.

The model of the symbol characterized European society until around the thirteenth century, as clearly shown in the literature and painting of the period. It is a cosmogonic semiotic practice where the elements (symbols) refer back to one or more unknowable and unrepresentable universal transcendence(s); univocal connections link the transcendences to the units evoking them; the symbol does not 'resemble' the object it symbolizes; the two spaces (symbolized-symbolizer) are separate and cannot communicate.

The symbol assumes that the symbolized (the universals) is irreducible to the symbolizer (the markings). Mythical thought operates within the sphere of the symbol (as in the epic, folk tales, *chansons de geste*, etc.), through symbolic units that are *units of restriction* in relation to the symbolized univerals ('heroism', 'courage', 'nobility', 'virtue', 'fear', 'treason', etc.). The symbol's function, in its vertical dimension (universals-markings), is thus one of restriction. In its horizontal dimension (the articulation of signifying units in relation to one another) the function of the symbol is one of escaping the paradox; one might say that the symbol is horizontally *anti-paradoxical*: within its 'logic' two opposing units are exclusive.

We are all familiar with the biblical and Augustinian dichotomy between 'the breath of life' and 'the dust of the earth'. In the field of the symbol, good and bad are incompatible, as are the raw and the cooked, honey and ashes, etc. The contradiction, once it appears, immediately demands a solution, and is thus hidden, 'resolved' and so put aside.[5]

The key to symbolic semiotic practice is given from the beginning of symbolic discourse: the course of semiotic development is a circle where the end is programmed, given in embryo, from the beginning (whose end *is* the beginning), since the function of the symbol (its ideologeme) exists prior to the actual symbolic statement. This evokes the general characteristics of symbolic semiotic practice: the quantitative limitation, repetition and general nature of symbols.

From the thirteenth to the fifteenth century, the symbol was challenged and weakened. This did not make it altogether disappear but it did assure its passage (assimilation) into the sign. The transcendental unity supporting the symbol – its other-worldly wrapping, its transmitting focus – was called into question. Thus, until the end of the fifteenth century, theatrical representations of the life of Christ were inspired by the canonical or apocryphal Gospels or the Golden Legend (see *The Mysteries* published by Jubinal and based on the manuscript at the Library of Sainte-Geneviève *c.* 1400). From the fifteenth century on, the theatre as well as art in general (as in the Cathedral at Evreux) was inundated by scenes depicting Christ's public life. The transcendental foundation evoked by the symbol seemed to capsize. This heralded a new signifying relation between two elements, both located in the 'real', 'concrete' world. In thirteenth-century art, the prophets were contrasted with the apostles; whereas in the fifteenth century, the four evangelists are no longer set against the four great prophets, but against the four fathers of the Latin Church (Saint Augustine, Saint Jerome, Saint Ambrose and Gregory the Great, as on the altar of Notre Dame of Avioth). Great literary and architectural compositions were no longer possible: the miniature replaced the cathedral, and the fifteenth century became the century of the miniaturists. The serenity of the symbol was replaced by the strained ambivalence of the *sign*'s connection, which presents the elements as similar and identical, despite the fact that it first postulates them as radically different. This is why one finds an obsessive insistence on the theme of *dialogue* between two *irreducible* but *similar* elements (a dialogue that generates the pathetic and the psychological) in this transitional period.

Thus, the fourteenth and fifteenth centuries abound in dialogues between God and the human soul: 'Dialogue of the Crucifix and the Pilgrim', 'Dialogue of the Sinful Soul and Christ', etc. Through this evolution the Bible became moralized (see the famous 'moralized Bible' of the Duke of Burgundy's library), and even replaced by pastiches that bracket and erase the transcendental basis of the symbol (the 'Bible of the Poor' and the 'Speculum humanae salvationis').[6]

1.2.2

Once the relation between the signifying unit and the idea had been weakened, the signifying unit became more and more 'material' until it forgot its 'origins'. Thus, up until 1350, it is the *Word*, in the guise of Jesus Christ, which creates the world. After this date, we see the appearance of 'an old man who measures the earth with a compass and throws the sun and the stars into the heavens'.[7] The Word, that is, 'the interpretant' (if one wishes to use modern terminology) becomes blurred and its replicas more visual and substantive, linked together in a horizontal chain firmly situated in this world. This is why it is no longer the Word (Christ as idea) which *retains the meaning*; instead it is the combination of 'markings' (images of the old man, the sky, the stars) which *produce* it.

In the gradual destruction of the symbol we can therefore see how the ideology of *creation* that had dominated Gothic art and given birth to its wonderful architectural compositions gave way to the ideology of *imitation*. The growing circulation of wood carvings, for example, expresses the change in aesthetic needs from those of the prevous age, which was dominated by the monumental constructions of Saint-Denis and Chartres. 'The chief merit of these naïve carvings', writes E. Mâle, 'is that they always coincided with themselves.' This transformation reveals a law wherein the signifying unit no longer refers back to the vast 'idea' behind it, but instead becomes opaque, 'materialized' and identifies with itself. Its vertical dimension begins to lose intensity, as its possible articulations with other signifying units are accentuated. This gives rise to the 'fragmentary' nature of works at the end of the Middle Ages: 'They are isolated chapters, never a whole narrative.'[8] This imitation and fragmentation can also be found in the novel by Antoine de la Sale, thus confirming the transition from symbol to sign we are here examining.

Since the signifying unit is capable of articulation either with itself (i.e., repetition) or with other, often opposing units, a monovalent (symbolic) structure is replaced with a heterovalent, broken, double structure. On the semantic level, this movement is made manifest in the replacement of the discourse preaching 'goodness, gentleness and love' (which dominated the thirteenth century) with a discourse centred on *suffering*, grief and death. Let us reserve the same *negative* for the lexemes 'suffering', 'grief' and 'death' and stress their introduction of *opposition*, destruction and annihilation within a homogeneous, positive unity. It is the introduction of this negativity which gives birth to psychology. Early signs of this change are to be found in the *Passions* dealing with Christ's sufferings ('De Planctu Mariae', attributed to Saint-Bernard; 'Dialogue of the Virgin and Saint Anselme' on the passion, etc.). Painting also comes to represent this split and negativity: images of the compassionate Christ start to appear (in 1374, on the seal of John, abbot of Anchin; some years later, in a book of Hours, from a manuscript dating from the end of the fourteenth century, to be found in the Bibliothèque Nationale).

The introduction of alterity or negativity into the signifying unit also shows up in those hybrid, double, ambiguous figures which we find in antiquity, but which also appear at the end of the Middle Ages. These hybrid figures introduce the fantastic and the supernatural into the 'real' world and retain only a highly tenuous relationship with the transcendental idea. Such, for example, is the image of the Sibyl which we find in Antoine de la Sale's *La Sale*. The thirteenth century is already familiar with these sibyls – Vincent de Beauvais names the sixteen sibyls listed by Varron – although in France only one is represented in art, the Erythraean Sibyl, the terrible prophetess of the last judgement.[9] In Italy, they are familiar with another sibyl, the Sibyl of Tivoli who met Augustus and announced to him the reign of God.

By the fifteenth century there are sibyls all over Europe. The first painted Sibyl is to be found in the missal of the Sainte Chapelle, illuminated at the close of the fifteenth century.

We might say that the image of the Sibyl is that of the infinitization of discourse, the figuralization of the word as it were liberated from its dependence on the symbol and enjoying the 'arbitrariness' of the sign. Belonging to this and not the other world, the Sibyl speaks all languages, possesses the future, reunites improbable elements both in and through the word. The unlimited possibilities of discourse, which the sign (novel) will try to represent, are symbolized in this transitory figure produced by the art of the late Middle Ages.

1.2.3

Nominalism marks a decisive stage in the passage from symbol to sign that takes place in the discourse of the Middle Ages. Its clearest expression is to be found in the doctrines of William of Occam, which were violently opposed to those of Duns Scotus and denounced the impossibility of using philosophy to lend support to dogma. Nominalism attacks the thought of the *symbol* in its *realist* mode (the Platonic doctrine represented by St Thomas and Duns Scotus which considered universals or abstract units to be independent of the intellect), as well as in its *conceptualist* mode (which held that universals exist but are the product of intelligence). We do not propose to offer a detailed analysis of the ideas of William of Occam.[10] Let us simply observe that such ideas (which were called *nominales* or *terministae* but also *moderni*) were widespread in the fourteenth century and lay at the heart of the philosophical debates that took place above all at the University of Paris and especially in the Faculty of Arts: on 25 September 1339 they were condemned; and on 29 December 1340 certain Occamist and nominalist theses were prohibited.[11] Let us recall for our purposes a few of the essential points of these theses.

First, they refuse to grant universals any real existence and so throw the symbolic system off-balance by depriving it of its support. It follows that whatever is singular cannot be universal, and consequently the accent is placed on the singularity of each thing ('term'), which was made independent of its transcendental background: 'It is not true that a thing is singular under one concept, and universal under another, for something in itself singular is never in any way or under any concept universal.' All reality is therefore singular, made up of independent terms free of any extrinsic clause. The universal lies only in the concept. Contrary to the logical conceptualism dominating Paris in the fourteenth century which taught that the universal was a separate genre of reality, an *esse obiectivum*, William of Occam taught a 'psychological conceptualism' that identified mental representation with the act of knowledge. As nominalism distinguishes between the *concept* and the *term*, valorizing the latter to the detriment of the former, it opens the way to a mode of thought that uses *terms* (*names*) as *signs* (and not symbols). It constructs reality as a combination [*combinatoire*] of terms (signs) and thus constitutes the *Arts* as a separate category (the majority of William of Occam's followers were found in the Faculties of Arts) by becoming the (unconscious) philosophy of the novel and its creation. Since God can only be reached through a nominal definition, the *series of nominal definitions* (also represented by the novel, as we shall see in Antoine de la Sale) were a matter for *real* science that was at once distinct from the science of concepts (philosophy) and the science of language (grammar, logic). In this way, the novel is conceived of as a *discourse*, that is, an accumulation of nominal definitions which, because it remains expressive, still remains theological. Its theology, however, differs from that of the symbol: the novel becomes an *expression* through its use of a series of 'names' ('things') 'independent' of any idea extrinsic to the order of their existence or their sequence.

1.2.4

This deconceptualization, which is a desymbolization of discursive structure, is clearly conveyed by the personification of the elements of symbolic discourse, such as the *virtues* and *vices* (to give only one example deliberately chosen from *Jehan de Saintré*). The Middle Ages recognized seven virtues: three theological (Faith, Hope and Charity) and four cardinal (Fortitude, Justice, Temperance, Prudence). Antoine de la Sale also retained seven, 'three of which are divine, and four moral: the three divine are Faith, Hope and Charity; the four moral are Prudence, Temperance, Fortitude and Justice'. The fifteenth century began to personify the virtues without giving them any special attributes. Gerson, in the prologue to his diatribe against the *Roman de la Rose*, Alain Chartier, in the *Consolation des trois vertus*, Georges Chastelain, in his *Temple de Boccace*, all make the Virtues speak and act, and even sometimes describe their costumes, but never speak of their attributes.[12] We find the same treatment of the vices. In *Jehan de Saintré* we find this discourse concerning the virtues and vices in the introductory remarks of the Lady who gives lessons in *savoir-vivre* to Saintré. The virtues and vices are not personified here, but are instead products of a mode of thought prior to the structure of the novel itself.

On the other hand, when these units (vices and virtues) are personified, that is to say, when they have become signs that signify in their own right, and do not have to rely on the idea they represent, or on the properties of meaning (attributes) which they might have had irrespective of the specific structure of meaning [*combinatoire*] or narrative in which they participate, then they are a striking example of the change in the dominant mode of thought which we have defined as being a passage from symbol to sign.

1.3   Characteristics of the sign

1.3.1

The sign which appears through these mutations retains the fundamental characteristic of the symbol: irreducibility of terms, that is, in the case of the sign, of the referent to the signified, of the signified to the signifier, and based on this, irreducibility of all the 'units' of the signifying structure itself. In its general make-up, the ideologeme of the sign is therefore similar to that of the symbol: the sign is dualist, hierarchical and hierarchizing. However, the difference between the sign and the symbol can be seen vertically as well as horizontally: within its vertical function, the sign refers back to entities of lesser dimensions that are more *concretized* than the symbol. These are reified universals, which have become objects in the strongest sense of the word. Placed in relationship within a sign-structure, however, the entity, phenomenon or person in question is at once transcendentalized and elevated to the level of theological unity. The semiotic practice of the sign thus assimilates the metaphysical strategy of the symbol and projects it on to the 'immediately perceptible'. The latter, thus valorized, is then transformed into an *objectivity*, which becomes the reigning law of discourse in the civilization of the sign.

Within their horizontal function, the units of the sign's semiotic practice are articulated as a *metonymic chain of deflections* [*écarts*] that signifies a *progressive creation of metaphors*.[13] Opposing terms, which are always exclusive, are caught up in a system of multiple and always possible deflections ('surprises' in narrative structures) giving the illusion of an *open* structure that is impossible to terminate, and which has an *arbitrary* ending. Therefore, in literary discourse, the semiotic practice of the sign first clearly appears during the European Renaissance in the adventure novel, which on the level of narrative structure is modelled on the unforeseeable and on surprise as a reification of the deflection [*écart*] characteristic of every practice of the sign. The course of this chain of deflections is practically infinite, which is why one has the impression that the end is arbitrary. This is an *illusory* impression that defines all 'literature' (all 'art'), since this course is programmed by the ideologeme constituting the sign. That is, it is programmed by a closed (finite), dyadic process which, first, institutes a referent-signified-signifier hierarchy, and secondly, interiorizes these opposing dyads in the very articulation of the terms, and thus, like the symbol, sets itself up as a *resolution of contradictions*. In a semiotic practice based on the symbol, contradiction was resolved by *exclusive disjunction* (non-equivalence) or non-conjunction (–/–); in a semiotic practice based on the sign contradiction is resolved by *non-disjunction* ($-\bar{v}-$).

1.3.2

The fact that the sign can create an open system of transformation and generation had already been indicated by Peirce when he spoke of the symbol which, for him, 'operates above all by virtue of an institution-alised and learnt contiguity between signifier and signified'. This concerns the expressiveness of the symbol which is akin to that of the sign as we have discussed it here. His judgements of the symbol are consequently valid for the sign: 'Every word is a symbol...The value of a symbol is that it serves to make thought and conduct rational and enables us to predict the future. Whatever is really general refers to the unspecified future, for the past is just a collection of specific acts that have been carried out. The past consists of pure facts. But a general law cannot be fully realized. It is a potentiality and its mode of being is *esse in futuro*.'[14] We can take this to mean that the ideologeme of the sign signifies an infinitization of discourse. Once the latter is more or less free from its dependence on the 'universal' (the concept, the idea in itself), it becomes a potential mutation, a constant transformation which despite being tied to one signified, is capable of many regenerations. The ideologeme of the sign can therefore suggest what is not, but *will be*, or rather *can be*. And this *future tense* is accepted by the sign not as something caused by extrinsic factors, but as a transformation produced by the possible combinations [*combinatoire*] within its own structure.

1.3.3

By way of summary, we can say that the sign, as the fundamental ideologeme of modern thought and the basic element of our (novelistic) discourse, possesses the following characteristics:

- It does not refer to a single unique reality, but *evokes* a collection of associated images and ideas. While remaining expressive, it none the less tends to distance itself from its supporting transcendental basis (it may be called 'arbitrary').
- It is part of a specific structure of meaning [*combinatoire*] and in that sense it is *correlative*: its meaning is the result of an interaction with other signs.
- It harbours a principle of *transformation*: within its field, new structures are forever generated and transformed.

NOTES

1 M. Bakhtin, *Problemi poetiki Dostoïevskovo* (Problems of Dostoevsky's Poetics) (Ann Arbor, Mich.: Ardis, 1973).
2 C. S. Peirce, in J. Buchler (ed.), *Philosophical Writings of Peirce* (New York: Dover Publications, 1955), p. 102.
3 F. de Saussure, *Cours de linguistique générale* (Paris: Payot 1960), p. 101 (*Course in General Linguistics*, London: Fontana/Collins, 1981, p. 68).
4 For a critique of the notion of the arbitrary nature of the sign, see E. Benveniste, *Problèmes de linguistique générale* (Paris: Gallimard, 1966), p. 49 (*Problems in General Linguistics*, Coral Gables, Fla: University of Miami Press, 1976).
5 In the history of Western scientific thought, three fundamental currents break away in succession from the symbol's domination, and move through the sign to the variable: these are Platonism, conceptualism and nominalism. See V. W. Quine, 'Reification of universals', in *From a Logical Point of View* (Cambridge, Mass.: Harvard University Press, 1953). I have borrowed from this study the differentiation between two meanings of the signifying unit: one within the space of the symbol, the other within that of the sign.
6 E. Mâle, *L'Art religieux de la fin du moyen âge en France* (Paris: A. Colin, 1925).
7 BN French 5, f. 5 and 6 *c.*1350; French 22912, f. 2v illuminated 1371–5; French 3, f. 5 et seq. end fourteenth century; French 9 f. 4 and 5, beginning fifteenth century; French 15393, f. 3 beginning fifteenth century; French 247, f. 3 beginning fifteenth century.

8 Mâle, *L'Art religieux*, p. 227.

9 Ibid., pp. 339ff.

10 See R. Gulluy, *Philosophie et théologie chez Guillaume d'Occam* (Louvain, 1947); C. Michalski, 'Les courants philosophiques à Oxford et à Paris pendant le XIVe siècle', *Bulletin de l'Académie polonaise des sciences et des lettres*, 1920, pp. 59–88; C. Michalski, *Les Sources du Christianisme et du scepticisme dans la philosophie du XIVe siècle* (Cracow, 1924).

11 See E. Gilson, *La Philosophie au moyen âge* (Paris: Payot, 1962), p. 657.

12 See Mâle, *L'Art religieux*.

13 'The novel is similar in form to the dream: both can be defined by one peculiar property: any deviation forms part of the whole' (Valéry).

14 C. S. Peirce, 'Existential graphs', in *Collected Papers*, ed. C. Hartshorne and P. Weiss, vol. IV, *The Simplest Mathematics* (Cambridge, Mass.: Harvard University Press, 1933), p. 361.

Translated by Seán Hand

4

Semiotics: A Critical Science and/or a Critique of Science

Written in 1968 and published in Σημειωτικὴ *[Séméiotiké]. Recherches pour une sémananalyse* (Paris: Seuil, 1969), this essay focuses on two main problems: (1) semiotics as a critical science and (2) the concept of *production* as the crucial connection between Marx, Freud and semiotics (or semanalysis). The importance of the article lies in its efforts to situate semiotics clearly within a double, Marxist and Freudian, intellectual space. Itself produced in a year of revolt, the essay presents semanalysis as a critical, political practice necessarily engaged in the subversion of the traditional order.

Discussing the critical impact of semiotics, Kristeva argues that it is not only a linguistic theory, but, crucially, a theory formation which necessarily theorizes its own production of theories: semiotics, in other words, can only exist as a critique of semiotics. The theoretical models of *any* science, including semiotics, are representations. It is because semiotics is the only science specifically concerned with the elaboration of a *theory* (i.e., a formalized representation) of representation, Kristeva argues, that it becomes inherently self-reflexive. Adopting models and terms from other sciences (preferably from the so-called 'hard' sciences which are not caught up in traditional, humanist and subjectivist categories), semanalysis nevertheless ceaselessly subverts and transforms the meaning of the terms it appropriates. Thus it also becomes a critique of other sciences, demonstrating how science is always constructed in and through ideology. In this way, semiotics can be said to continue the critical tradition first established by Marx. But Marx's critique of political economy also constitutes the prototype of 'classical' semiotics, in that Marx presents an economy or society (a signified) as a permutation of elements (signifiers).

Semiotics, however, goes further than Marx, who remained unable to analyse production other than from the perspective of the *products* (social value, circulation of goods and of money), in spite of the fact that his own theory of use value adumbrates a different mode of analysis: one that focuses on production seen 'from the inside'. This perspective, however, was never fully grasped by Marx and remained untheorized until Freud showed how dreams can be analysed as *work*, or in other words, as *processes*. Through its appropriation of Freud, semanalysis moves beyond the Marxist problematics, while still remaining faithful to its critical, anti-capitalist perspective. Thanks to Freud, semiotics is now able to analyse the *alterity* of its object: that 'other scene' where our desires are enacted *before* they become language, communication or product. The paradox of semiotics can here be seen to re-emerge (see 'From Symbol to Sign'): semiotics is established as a science which seeks to represent that which per definition cannot be represented: the unconscious.

Finally, Kristeva argues that although *literature* as a specific, highly valorized category cannot exist for semiotics (it simply becomes one among many forms of signifying practices), semiotics can and ought to learn from the modernist texts which since the late nineteenth century have perceived themselves as *production* rather than as *message* or *product*. The insights gained from work on such texts can then be used to analyse what Kristeva calls the *social text* as a series of transformations and/or productive processes.

Semiotics: A Critical Science and/or a Critique of Science

In a decisive move towards self-analysis, (scientific) discourse today has begun to re-examine languages in order to isolate their (its) models or patterns. In other words, since social practice (the economy, mores, 'art', etc.) is envisaged as a signifying system that is 'structured like a language', any practice can be scientifically studied as a secondary model in relation to natural language, modelled on this language and in turn becoming a model or pattern for it.[1] It is in this precise area that semiotics today is articulated or rather is searching for its identity.

We shall attempt to isolate a few of the characteristics which give semiotics a precise place in the history of knowledge and ideology, a place which makes this kind of discourse a clear register of the cultural subversion which our civilization is undergoing. These characteristics account for the barely disguised animosity of the bourgeois word (or 'conscience') in its various guises (ranging from esoteric aestheticism to scientific positivism, and from 'liberal' journalism to a restrictive sense of 'commitment') which calls this research 'obscure', 'gratuitous', 'schematic' or 'impoverishing', when it doesn't actually recuperate the lesser by-products of this inquiry by seeing it as a kind of harmless fringe activity.

Faced with the expansion (and the oppositional nature) of semiotics, we must formulate a theory of its evolution that will place it within the history of science and thought about science, and link up with the epistemological research at present being undertaken seriously only in the Marxist work written or inspired by Louis Althusser. The following notes are no more than an indication of this necessity. I shall therefore say less about the nature of semiotics than about its potential.

I Semiotics as the making of models

As soon as we try to define this new form of research, the complexity of the problem becomes apparent. For Saussure, who introduced the term (*Course in General Linguistics*, 1916), *semiology* designated an enormous science of signs of which linguistics was only a part. But it soon became clear that whatever semiology's sign-object happens to be (gesture, sound, image, etc.) it can only be known through language.[2] It follows that 'linguistics is not part of the general science of signs, not even a privileged part; rather, it is semiology which is part of linguistics, and specifically that part responsible for the large signifying units of speech'.[3] It is not possible here to discuss the advantages and disadvantages of this significant reversal which itself is destined to be modified precisely because of the new openings it has made possible.[4] Following the example of Jacques Derrida, we shall indicate the scientific and ideological limitations which the phonological model risks imposing on a science that aims to offer a model for translinguistic practice. But we shall none the less retain the fundamental gesture of semiotics: a formalization or production of models.[5] Thus, when we say semiotics, we mean the (as yet unrealized) development of *models*, that is, of formal systems whose structure is isomorphic or analogous to the structure of another system (the system under study).[6]

In other words, by borrowing its models from the formal sciences (such as mathematics or logic, which in this way are reduced to being a branch of the vast 'science' of language-models), semiotics could eventually become the axiomatization of signifying systems, without being hindered by its epistemological dependence on linguistics. The latter could then in turn renew itself by adopting these models.

In this sense, rather than speak of a semiotics, we prefer to talk of a semiotic level, which is that of the axiomatization, or formalization, of signifying systems.[7]

By defining semiotics as the production of models, however, we not only designate its object, but also touch on the characteristic that distinguishes it from the other 'sciences'.[8] The models elaborated by semiotics, like those of the exact sciences, are representations and, as such, are produced within spatio-temporal coordinates.[9] But this is where semiotics differs from the exact sciences, for the former is also the production of the theory of its own model-making, a theory which in principle can accommodate that which does not belong to the order of representation. Obviously, a theory is always implicit in the models of any science. But semiotics manifests this theory, or rather cannot be separated from the theory constituting it, that is, a theory which constitutes both its object (the semiotic level of the practice under study) and its instruments (the type of model corresponding to a certain semiotic structure designated by the theory). In each particular case of semiotic research, a theoretical reflection isolates the signifying function being axiomatized, which is then represented in a formal manner. (Note that this action is synchronic and dialectic, and is only called diachronic in order to ease representation.)

Semiotics is therefore a mode of thought where science sees itself as (is conscious of itself as) a theory. At every instant of its production, semiotics thinks of its object, its instruments and the relation between them, and in so doing thinks (of) itself: as a result of this reflection, it becomes the theory of the very science it constitutes. This means that semiotics is at once a re-evaluation of its object and/or of its models, a critique both of these models (and therefore of the sciences from which they are borrowed) and of itself (as a system of stable truths). As the meeting-point of the sciences and an endless theoretical process, semiotics cannot harden into *a* science let alone into *the* science, for it is an open form of research, a constant critique that turns back on itself and offers its own auto-critique. As it is its own theory, semiotics is the kind of thought which, without raising itself to the level of a system, is still capable of modelling (thinking) itself.

But this reflexive movement is not a circular one. Semiotic research remains a form of inquiry that ultimately uncovers its own ideological gesture, only in order to record and deny it before starting all over again. 'No key to no mystery', as Levi-Strauss said. It begins with a certain knowledge as its goal, and ends up discovering a *theory* which, since it is itself a signifying system, returns semiotic research to its point of departure, to the model of semiotics itself, which it criticizes or over-throws. This tells us that semiotics can only exist as a *critique of semiotics*, a critique which opens on to something other than semiotics, namely *ideology*. Through this method, which Marx was the first to practise, semiotics becomes the moment when the history of knowledge breaks with the tradition for and in which

> science exhibits itself as a *circle* returning upon itself, the end being wound back into the beginning, the simple ground, by the media-tion; this circle is moreover a *circle of circles*, for each individual member as ensouled by the method is reflected into itself, so that in returning into the beginning it is at the same time the beginning of a new member. Links of this chain are the individual sciences (of logic, nature and spirit), each of which has an *antecedent* and a *successor* – or, expressed more accurately, *has* only the *antecedent* and *indicates* its *successor* in its conclusion.[10]

Semiotic practice breaks with this teleological vision of a science that is subordinated to a philosophical *system* and consequently even destined itself to become a system.[11] Without becoming a system, the site of semiotics, where models and theories are developed, is a place of dispute and self-questioning, a 'circle' that remains open. Its 'end' does not rejoin its 'beginning', but, on the contrary, rejects and rocks it, opening up the way to another discourse, that is, another subject and another method; or rather, there is no more end than beginning, the end is a beginning and vice versa.

No form of semiotics, therefore, can exist other than as a critique of semiotics. As the place where the sciences die, semiotics is both the knowledge of this death and the revival, *with* this knowledge, of the 'scientific'; less (or more) than a science, it marks instead the aggressivity and disillusionment that takes place within scientific discourse itself. We might argue that semiotics is that 'science of ideologies' suggested in revolutionary Russia,[12] but it is also an ideology of sciences.

Such a conception of semiotics does not at all imply a relativism or agnostic scepticism. On the contrary, it unites with the scientific practice of Marx to the extent that it rejects an absolute system (including a scientific one), but retains a scientific approach, that is, a development of models doubled by the theory underlying the very same models. Created as it is by the constant movement between model and theory while at the same time being situated at a distance from them (thus taking up a position in relation to current social practice), this form of thought demonstrates the 'epistemological break' introduced by Marx.

The status here given to semiotics has consequences for: (1) the specific relation of semiotics to the other sciences and especially to linguistics, mathematics and logic from whom it borrows its models; and (2) the introduction of a new terminology and the subversion of the existing terminology.

The semiotics concerning us here uses linguistic, mathematical and logical models and *joins* them to the signifying practices it approaches. This junction is as theoretical as it is scientific, and therefore constitutes a profoundly ideological fact which demystifies the exactitude and 'purity' of the discourse of the so-called 'human' sciences. It subverts the exact premises of the scientific process, such that for semiotics, linguistics, logic and mathematics are 'subverted premises' which have little or nothing to do with their status outside semiotics. Far from being simply a stock of models on which semiotics can draw, these annexed sciences are also the object which semiotics *challenges* in order to make itself into an explicit critique. Mathematical terms such as 'theorem of existence' or 'axiom of choice'; terms from physics like 'isotrope'; linguistic ones such as 'competence', 'performance', 'generation' or 'anaphora'; terms from logic such as 'disjunction', 'ortho-complementary structure', etc. can acquire a different meaning when taken out of the conceptual field in which the retrospective terms were conceived and applied to a new ideological subject, such as that of contemporary semiotics. Playing on this 'novelty of non-novelty', or on the different meanings a term acquires in different theoretical contexts, semiotics reveals how science is born in ideology: 'The new object may well still retain some link with the old ideological object, *elements* may be found in it which belong to the old object, too: but the meaning of these elements changes with the new *structure*, which precisely confers to them their meaning. These apparent similarities in isolated elements may mislead a superficial glance unaware of the function of the structure in the constitution of the meaning of the elements of an object.'[13] Marx practised this subversion of the terms of a preceding science: to the mercantilists, 'surplus-value' 'arises out of the addition to the value of the product'. Marx gave the same word a new meaning: in so doing he brought to light 'the novelty of the non-novelty of a reality which appears in *two different discourses*, i.e., the question of the theoretical modality of this "reality" in two theoretical discourses'.[14] But if the semiotic approach provokes this displacement of meaning in terms, why use a terminology that already has a strict usage?

We know that any renewal of scientific thought is carried out by and through a renewal of terminology: there is only invention as such when a new term appears, be it oxygen or infinitesimal calculus. 'Every new aspect of a science involves a revolution in the technical terms (*Fachausdrucken*) of that science...Political economy has generally been content to take, just as they were, the terms of commercial and industrial life, and to operate with them, entirely failing to see that *by so doing, it confined itself within the narrow circle of ideas expressed by those terms...*'.[15] As semiotics today regards the capitalist system and its accompanying discourse as ephemeral phenomena, it uses terms different from those employed by previous discourses in the 'human sciences', when it articulates its signifying practices in the course of its critique. Semiotics therefore rejects a humanist and subjectivist terminology, and addresses itself to the vocabulary of the exact sciences. But, as we have indicated above, these terms have *another* meaning in the new ideological field which semiotic research *can* construct; an alterity to which we shall return. The use of terms from the exact sciences does not erase the possibility of introducing a completely new terminology, at the most crucial points of semiotic research.

II Semiotics and production

So far we have defined the subject of semiotics as a semiotic *level*, as a *section* through signifying practices where the signifier is taken as the model of the signified. This definition in itself suffices in order to designate the novelty of the semiotic process in relation to previous 'human sciences' and to science in general: a novelty by means of which semiotics allies itself to Marx's strategy when he presents an economy or society (a signified) as a permutation of elements (signifiers). If, sixty years after the appearance of the term, we can speak today of a 'classical' semiotics, it is precisely because its strategies fall under this definition. We none the less feel that we can place ourselves in the *opening afforded* by contemporary thought (Marx, Freud, Husserl) if we define the subject of semiotics in the following more subtle way.

It has already been frequently stressed that the great novelty of Marxist economy was to think of the social as being a particular *mode of production*. Work ceases to be a *subjectivity* or an *essence* of man: Marx replaces the concept of 'a supernatural creative power' (*Critique of the Gotha Programme*) with that of 'production' viewed in its double mode: as a work process, and as the social relations of production whose elements make up a *combinatoire* with its own specific logic. We might say that the possible combinations are the different kinds of semiotic *systems*. Marxist thought is therefore the first to *pose* the problematics of productive work as a major element in the definition of a semiotic system. This occurs, for example, when Marx explodes the concept of 'value' and speaks of it only as a crystallization of social work.[16] He even goes so far as to introduce concepts (surplus-value) which owe their existence to work that is unmeasurable and which themselves are measurable only through their effects (the circulation of merchandise, exchange).

But if Marx sees production as a problematics and a specific structure of meaning [*combinatoire*] that determines the social (or value), it is nevertheless studied only from the point of view of the social (value) and therefore only in terms of the distribution and circulation of goods, and not from the inside of production itself. Marx's work is therefore a study of capitalist society, of the laws of exchange and capital. Within this space and to this end, work is 'reified' into an object occupying a precise place (which, for Marx, is determining) in the process of exchange, but which is none the less examined from the angle of this exchange. In this way, Marx is led to study work as *value*, to adopt the distinction between use value and exchange value, and while still following the laws of capitalist society, to limit himself to a study of the latter. Marxist analysis rests on *exchange value*, that is, on the circulating *product* of work that enters the capitalist system as value ('a unit of work'), and it is in this way that Marx analyses its combinatory forces (workforce, workers, masters, object of production, instrument of production).

Therefore, when he tackles work itself and distinguishes between the different 'work' concepts, he does it from the point of view of circulation:

circulation of a utility (in which case work is *concrete*: 'expenditure of human force in such-and-such a productive form, determined by a particular fact, and consequently of a *concrete* and *useful* nature, producing exchange-values or utilities'[17]); or circulation of a value (in which case work is abstract: 'expenditure of human form in the psychological sense'). Let us stress in passing that Marx insists on the relativity and historicity of value and above all of exchange value. Therefore, when he tries to approach use value, in order to escape momentarily from this abstract process of (symbolic) circulation of exchange values in a bourgeois economy, Marx is content to indicate (and the terms used here are very significant) that it concerns a *body* and an *expenditure*. 'Use values, that is, the *body* of goods, are the result of a combination of two elements, matter and work...Work is not, then, the only source of the use values, or material riches it produces. It is the *father* and the earth is the *mother*.'[18] 'Quite apart from its usefulness, all productive activity is ultimately an *expenditure* of human force' (my emphasis).[19]

Marx states the problems clearly: from the point of view of distribution and social consumption, or, if you like, of *communication*, work is always a value, be it use value or exchange value. In other words: if, in communication, values are always a crystallized form of work, work *represents* nothing outside the value in which it is crystallized. This work-value can only be measured by its own value, that is, by the amount of social time taken to produce it.

Such a conception of work, taken out of its space of production, that is, a capitalist space, can lead to a valorization of production and provoke a pertinent critique from Heideggerian philosophy.

But Marx clearly outlines another possibility: another space where work can be apprehended without any consideration of value, that is, beyond any question of the circulation of merchandise. There, on a scene where work does not yet *represent* any value or *mean* anything, our concern is with the relation of a *body* to *expenditure*. Marx had neither the wish nor the means to tackle this notion of a productive labour prior to value or meaning. He gives only a *critical* description of political economy: a critique of the system of exchange of signs (values) that hides a work-value. When it is read as a critique, Marx's text on the circulation of money is one of the high-points achieved by a (communicative) discourse that can speak only of *measurable* communication, which exists against a background of production that is merely indicated. In this, Marx's critical reflections on the system of exchange resemble the contemporary critique of the sign and the circulation of meaning: moreover, the critical discourse on the sign acknowledges its similarity to the critical discourse on money. Thus, when Derrida opposes his theory of writing to the theory of the circulation of signs, he writes of Rousseau:

This movement of analytical abstraction in the circulation of arbitrary signs is quite parallel to that within which money is constituted. Money replaces things by their signs, not only within a society but from one culture to another, or from one economic organization to another. That is why the alphabet is commercial, a trader. It must be understood *within the monetary moment of economic rationality. The critical description of money is the faithful reflection of the discourse on writing* [my emphasis].[20]

It is the long development of the science of discourse, and of the laws of its permutations and annulments, as well as a long meditation on the principles and limits of the Logos as a model for the system of communication of meaning (value), which has enabled us to create this *concept* of a 'work' that 'means nothing', and of a silent production that marks and transforms while remaining prior to all circular 'speech', to communication, exchange or meaning. It is a concept that is formed by reading, for example, texts such as those by Derrida when he writes 'trace', 'gramma', '*différance*' or 'writing before the letter', while criticizing 'sign' and 'meaning'.

In this development, we must note the masterly contribution made by Husserl and Heidegger, but above all by Freud, who was the first to think of the work involved in the process of signification as anterior to the meaning produced and/or the representative discourse: in other words, the dream-process. The chapter-heading from *The Interpretation of Dreams*: 'The Dream-Work', shows how Freud revealed production itself to be a *process* not of exchange (or use) or meaning (value), but of playful permutation which provides the very model for production. Freud therefore opens up the problematics of *work as a particular semiotic system*, as distinct from that of exchange: this work exists within the communicative word but differs essentially from it. On the level of manifestation it is a *hieroglyph*, while on a latent level it is a *dream-thought*. 'Dream-work' becomes a theoretical concept that triggers off a new research, one that touches on pre-representative production, and the development of 'thinking' before *thought*. In this new inquiry a radical break separates the *dream-work* from the work of conscious thought and is 'for that reason not immediately comparable with it'. The dream-work 'does not think, calculate or judge in any way at all; it restricts itself to giving things a new form'.[21]

This seems to encapsulate the whole problem of contemporary semiotics: either it continues to formalize the semiotic systems from the point of view of communication (in the same way, to risk a brutal comparison, that Ricardo regarded surplus-value from the point of view of distribution and consumption), or else it opens up to the internal problematics of communication (inevitably offered by all social problematics) the 'other scene' of the production of meaning prior to meaning.

If we opt for this second route, two possibilities are offered: either we isolate a measurable and consequently representable aspect of the signifying system under study against the background of an unmeasurable concept (work, production, gramma, trace, *différance*); or else we try to construct a new scientific problematics (in the sense given above of a science that is also a theory) to which this new concept necessarily must give rise. In other words, the second case involves the construction of a new 'science' once a definition has been reached of a new subject: *work* as a different semiotic practice of exchange.

Several events in the current social and scientific environment justify, if not demand, such an endeavour. Irrupting on to the historical scene, the world of work claims its rights and protests against the system of exchange, demanding that 'knowledge' change its perspective so as to transform 'exchange based on production' into 'production regulated by exchange'.

Exact science itself is already tackling the problems of the unpresentable and the unmeasurable, as it tries to think of them not as 'deviations' from the observable world, but as a structure with special laws. We are no longer in the age of Laplace where one believed in a superior intelligence that was capable of embracing 'in the same formula the movements of the largest bodies and the lightest atoms in the universe: nothing would remain unknown to it, and both future and past would be present in its eyes'.[22] Quantum mechanics is aware that our discourse ('intelligence') needs to be 'fractured', and must change objects and structures in order to be able to tackle a problematics that can no longer be contained within the framework of classical reason. Consequently, one talks of the *unobserved object*[23] and searches for new logical and mathematical models of formalization. The semiotics of production has inherited this infiltration of the unrepresentable by scientific thought and will no doubt use these models elaborated by the exact sciences (polyvalent logic, topology). But since the semiotics of production is a science-theory of discourse and so of itself, and since it tends to emphasize the dynamics of production over the actual product, it consequently rebels against representation even as it uses representative models, and overthrows the very formalization that gives it substance with an unstable theory of the unrepresentable and the unmeasurable. This semiotics of production will therefore accentuate the *alterity* of its object in its relation with the representable and representative object of exchange examined by the exact sciences. At the same time it will accentuate the upheaval of (exact) scientific terminology by shifting it towards that other scene of work that exists prior to value and which can only be glimpsed today.

It is here that semiotic's difficulties lie, both for itself and for those who wish to come to understand it. It is virtually impossible to comprehend such a semiotics when it poses the problem of a production that is not that of communication but which at the same time is constituted through communication, unless one accepts the radical break which separates the problematics of exchange and work. Let us indicate just one of the many consequences entailed by such a semiotics: it replaces the concept of *linear historicity* with the necessity of establishing a typology of signifying practices from the particular models of the production of meaning which actually found them. This approach therefore differs from that of traditional historicism, which it replaced by a plurality of productions that cannot be reduced to one another and even less so to the thought of exchange. Let me stress that I do not wish to establish a list of the *modes* of production: Marx suggested this by limiting himself to the point of view of the circulation of goods. I rather wish to look at the difference between the *types* of signifying production prior to the product (value): oriental philosophies have attempted to tackle this from the point of view of work prior to communication.[24] These kinds of production will perhaps constitute what has been called a 'monumental history' to the extent that it literally becomes the foundation or background in relation to a 'cursive', figurative (teleological) history.[25]

III Semiotics and 'literature'

In the field thus defined of semiotics, does 'literary' practice occupy a privileged place?

Literature does not exist for semiotics. It does not exist as an utterance [*parole*] like others and even less as an aesthetic object. It is a *particular semiotic practice* which has the advantage of making more accessible than others the problematics of the production of meaning posed by a new semiotics, and consequently it is of interest only to the extent that it ('literature') is envisaged as irreducible to the level of an object for normative linguistics (which deals with the codified and denotative word [*parole*]). In this way we can adopt the term of *writing* when it concerns a text seen as a production, in order to distinguish it from the concepts of 'literature' and 'speech'. It then becomes apparent that it is thoughtless if not dishonest to write 'speech [*parole*] (or writing)', 'spoken (or written) language'.

Seen as a practice, the literary text

> is not assimilable to the historically determined concept of 'literature'. (It) implies the overthrow and complete revision of the place and effects of this concept. . .In other words, the specific problematics of writing isolates itself completely from myth and representation in order to think (of) itself in its own literality and space. The practice must be defined on the level of the 'text' to the extent that from now on this word refers to a function that writing does not 'express', but rather which it has at its *disposal*. A dramatic economy whose 'geometric place' cannot be represented (it is in play).[26]

Any 'literary' text may be envisaged as productivity. Literary history since the end of the nineteenth century has given us modern texts which, even structurally, perceive themselves as a production that cannot be reduced to representation (Joyce, Mallarmé, Lautréamont, Roussel). Therefore, a semiotics of production must tackle these texts precisely in order to join a scriptural practice concerned with its own production to a scientific thought in search of production. And it must do so in order to bring out all the consequences of such a confrontation, that is, the reciprocal upheavals which the two practices inflict on one another.

Developed from and in relation to these modern texts the new semiotic models then turn to the *social text*, to those social practices of which 'literature' is only one unvalorized variant, in order to conceive of them as so many ongoing transformations and/or productions.

NOTES

1 See 'Troudy po znadowym sisteman' (Work on signifying systems), vols I, II, III (Estonia: University of Tartu, 1965).

2 'Semiology, sooner or later, is bound to come up against ("true") language, not just as a model, but also as a component, relay or signified.' R. Barthes, 'Eléments de semiologie', *Communications* 4.

3 Loc. cit.

4 On this point, see the critique of J. Derrida, *De la grammatologie* (Paris: Minuit, 1967), p. 75 (*Of Grammatology*, tr. G. Spivak, Baltimore, Md: Johns Hopkins University Press, 1974, p. 57).

5 See A. Rosenbluth and W. Wiener, 'The role of models in science', *Philosophy of Sciences*, 12, no. 4 (1945), p. 314. Let us note, in passing, the etymology of the word 'model' in order to clarify the concept: lat. *modus* = measure, melody, mode, cadence, suitable limit, moderation, way, manner.

6 The notion of analogy, which seems to shock the purists, must be taken here in the serious sense which Mallarmé defined 'poetically' as follows: 'Herein lies the whole mystery: to pair things off and establish secret identities that gnaw at objects and wear them away in the name of a central purity.'

7 'We can say that the semiological is a sort of signifier which, under the control of some anagogical level, articulates the symbolic signified and constitutes it within a network of different significations.' A. J. Greimas, *Sémantique structurale* (Paris: Larousse, 1966), p. 60 (*Structural Semantics: an attempt at method*, Lincoln: Neb.: University of Nebraska Press, 1984).

8 The classical distinction between the natural and human sciences also considers the former to be more 'pure' than the latter.

9 'The model is always a representation. The problem is to know what is represented and how the function of representation appears.' G. Frey, 'Symbolische und ikonische Modelle', *Synthèse*, 12, no. 2–3 (1960), p. 213.

10 G. W. F. Hegel, *Science of Logic*, tr. A. V. Miller (London: Allen & Unwin, 1969), p. 842.

11 'It is here that the *content* of cognition as such first enters into the circle of consideration, since, as deduced, it now belongs to the method. The method itself by means of this moment expands itself into a *system*.' Ibid., p. 838.

12 'The Marxist science of ideologies raises two fundamental problems: 1) the problem of the characteristics and forms of the ideological material which is organized like a signifying material; 2) the problem of the characteristics and forms of the social communication that produces this signification.' P. N. Medvedev, *Formalnyi metod v literaturovedenci, Kriticheskoïe wedenie v sotsiologicheskuïu poetiku* (Leningrad, 1928) (*The Formal Method in Literary Scholarship*, tr. A. J. Wehrle,

Baltimore, Md: Johns Hopkins University Press, 1978). We shall return to the importance of this distinction.

13 L. Althusser, *Lire le Capital*, vol. II (Paris: Maspéro, 1966), p. 125 (*Reading Capital*, tr. B. Brewster, London: New Left Books, 1979, p. 157).

14 *Lire le Capital*, vol. II, pp. 114–15 (*Reading Capital*, pp. 149–50).

15 F. Engels, preface to the English edition of *Capital*, 1886, vol. I, pp. 4–6 (quoted by L. Althusser, *Lire le Capital*, vol. II, p. 112 (*Reading Capital*, p. 147)).

16 K. Marx, *A Contribution to the Critique of Political Economy* (London: Lawrence & Wishart, 1971), p. 38.

17 *Capital*.

18 Ibid.

19 Ibid.

20 J. Derrida, *De la grammatologie* (Paris: Minuit, 1967), p. 424 (*Of Grammatology*, tr. G. Spivak, Baltimore, Md: Johns Hopkins University Press, 1974, p. 300).

21 S. Freud, *The Interpretation of Dreams*, *Standard Edition*, vol. V (London: Hogarth Press, 1953), p. 507.

22 Laplace, *Essai philosophique sur les probabilités* (Paris: Gauthier-Villard, 1921), p. 3.

23 H. Reichenbach, *Philosophic Foundations of Quantum Mechanics* (Berkeley, Calif., and Los Angeles: University of California Press, 1944).

24 For a trial typology of signifying practices, see 'For a semiology of paragrams', in *Séméiotiké: recherches pour une sémanalyse* (Paris: Seuil, 1969), pp. 174–207, as well as 'Distance and antipresentation', *Tel Quel*, 32, pp. 49–53.

25 Ph. Sollers, 'Programme', *Tel Quel*, 31, reprinted in *Logiques* (Paris: Seuil, 1968).

26 Ibid.

Translated by Seán Hand

5

Revolution in Poetic Language

First published in 1974 as Kristeva's thesis for the French *Doctorat d'Etat*, *La Révolution du langage poétique* brings together and develops in a more systematic fashion many of the themes and concepts which had informed her linguistic work right from the first years in Paris. The book thus provides us with Kristeva's most fundamental and far-reaching theoretical examination of the possibilities of a linguistics focused on the speaking subject. The crucial 'new' impulse which distinguishes this epochal book from most of her earlier linguistic writings is the way in which Freudian and Lacanian psychoanalysis here is presented as the indispensable theoretical starting-point for her explorations of the signifying process.

The English-language edition, *Revolution in Poetic Language*, translated by Margaret Waller and published in 1984, contains only the first third of the original French edition and thus presents the reader with Kristeva's general linguistic or psycho-linguistic theory, but not with her meticulous exploration of the effects of this theory when applied to the textual practice of two early modernist poets, Lautréamont and Mallarmé. In the sections dealing with the poetry, Kristeva emphasizes the social, political and historical contexts which allowed these writers to let some of dynamic charge of the *chora* mark their language.

The chapters reproduced here (1, 2, 5, 6, 7, 8, 9, 10, 12) are all taken from the first section of the theoretical part of *Revolution* ('The Semiotic and the Symbolic'). Although this choice allows the reader to study the basic Kristevan theory of the acquisition of language and the signifying process in some detail, it means that her crucial explorations of the concepts of 'negativity' and 'rejection' contained in Margaret Waller's excellent translation have had to be left out. 'Rejection' inscribes negativity, difference and disruption in the modern text, and is characteristic of the mobile, unfixed, subversive writing subject (*le sujet-en-procès* – the subject in process/on trial) which re-presents itself in these texts. The analysis of negativity, linked to the Freudian and Kleinian hypothesis of the existence of a death drive, also provides an important point of departure for Kristeva's later work in psychoanalytic theory, as for instance in her presentation of 'abjection' in *The Powers of Horror* (1982).

In the selection which follows Kristeva focuses on the signifying process, that is to say that she is trying to answer not only the question of exactly *how* language comes to mean (signify), but also the equally important question of what it is that *resists* intelligibility and signification. In this context she develops and explores crucial terms such as 'the semiotic', 'the symbolic', the 'thetic', the 'chora', 'phenotext' and 'genotext'. There are by now many introductions to Kristeva's theories in this book. Philip E. Lewis's early review of the French edition of the *Revolution* remains one of the most helpful presentations of this complex text (see 'Revolutionary semiotics', *Diacritics*, 4 (Fall 1974), pp. 28–32). For further bibliographical information, see the general introduction to this volume.

Revolution in Poetic Language

I THE SEMIOTIC AND THE SYMBOLIC

1 THE PHENOMENOLOGICAL SUBJECT OF ENUNCIATION

We must specify, first and foremost, what we mean by the *signifying process* vis-à-vis general theories of meaning, theories of language and theories of the subject.

Despite their variations, all modern linguistic theories consider language a strictly 'formal' object – one that involves syntax or mathematicization. Wtihin this perspective, such theories generally accept the following notion of language. For Zellig Harris, language is defined by: (a) the arbitrary relation between signifier and signified, (2) the acceptance of the sign as a substitute for the extra-linguistic, (3) its discrete elements and (4) its denumerable, or even finite, nature.[1] But with the development of Chomskyan generative grammar and the logico-semantic research that was articulated around and in response to it, problems arose that were generally believed to fall within the province of 'semantics' or even 'pragmatics', and raised the awkward question of the *extra linguistic*. But language [*langage*] – modern linguistics' self-assigned object[2] – lacks a subject or tolerates one only as a *transcendental ego* (in Husserl's sense or in Benveniste's more specifically linguistic sense),[3] and defers any interrogation of its (always already dialectical because translinguistic) 'externality'.

Two trends in current linguistic research do attend to this 'externality' in the belief that failure to elucidate it will hinder the development of linguistic theory itself. Although such a lacuna poses problems (which we will later specify) for 'formal' linguistics, it has always been a particular problem for semiotics, which is concerned with specifying the functioning of signifying practices such as art, poetry and myth that are irreducible to the 'language' object.

1   The first of these two trends addresses the question of the so-called 'arbitrary' relation between signifier and signified by examining signifying systems in which this relation is presented as 'motivated'. It seeks the principle of this motivation in the Freudian notion of the unconscious in so far as the theories of drives [*pulsions*] and primary processes (displacement and condensation) can connect 'empty signifiers' to psychosomatic functionings, or can at least link them in a sequence of metaphors and metonymies; though undecidable, such a sequence replaces 'arbitrariness' with 'articulation'. The discourse of analysands, language 'pathologies' and artistic, particularly poetic, systems are especially suited to such an exploration.[4] Formal linguistic relations are thus connected to an 'externality' in the psychosomatic realm, which is ultimately reduced to a fragmented substance [*substance morcelée*] (the body divided into erogenous zones) and articulated by the developing ego's connections to the three points of the family triangle. Such a linguistic theory, clearly indebted to the positions of the psychoanalytic school of London and Melanie Klein in particular, restores to formal linguistic relations the dimensions (instinctual drives) and operations (displacement, condensation, vocalic and intonational differentiation) that formalistic theory excludes. Yet for want of a dialectical notion of the *signifying process* as a whole, in which signifiance puts the subject in process/on trial [*en procès*], such considerations, no matter how astute, fail to take into account the syntactico-semantic functioning of language. Although they rehabilitate the notion of the fragmented body – pre-Oedipal but always already invested with semiosis – these linguistic theories fail to articulate its transitional link to the post-Oedipal subject and his always symbolic and/or syntactic language. (We shall return to this point.)

2   The second trend, more recent and widespread, introduces within theory's own formalism a 'layer' of *semiosis*, which had been strictly relegated to pragmatics and semantics. By positing a *subject of enunciation* (in the sense of Benveniste, Culioli, etc.), this theory places logical modal

relations, relations of presupposition and other relations between interlocutors within the speech act, in a very deep 'deep structure'. This
subject of enunciation, which comes directly from Husserl and Benveniste
(see n. 3), introduces, through categorial intuition, both *semantic fields*
and *logical* – but also *intersubjective* – *relations*, which prove to be both
intra- and translinguistic.[5]

To the extent it is assumed by a subject who 'means' (*bedeuten*),
language has 'deep structures' that articulate *categories*. These categories
are semantic (as in the semantic fields introduced by recent developments
in generative grammar), logical (modality relations, etc.) and inter-
communicational (those which Searle called 'speech acts' seen as
bestowers of meaning).[6] But they may also be related to historical
linguistic changes, thereby joining diachrony with synchrony.[7] In this
way, through the subject who 'means', linguistics is opened up to all
possible categories and thus to philosophy, which linguistics had thought
it would be able to escape.

In a similar perspective, certain linguists, interested in explaining
semantic constraints, distinguish between different types of *styles*
depending on the speaking subject's position vis-à-vis the utterance.
Even when such research thereby introduces stylistics into semantics,
its aim is to study the workings of signification, taking into account
the subject of enunciation, which always proves to be the phenomenological subject.[8] Some linguistic research goes even further: starting
from the subject of enunciation/transcendental ego, and prompted by
the opening of linguistics on to semantics and logic, it views signification
as an ideological and therefore historical production.[9]

We shall not be able to discuss the various advantages and drawbacks
of this second trend in modern linguistics except to say that it is still
evolving, and that although its conclusions are only tentative, its
epistemological bases lead us to the heart of the debate on phenomenology which we can only touch on here – and only in so far as the specific
research we are presently undertaking allows.[10]

To summarize briefly what we shall elucidate later, the two trends
just mentioned designate *two modalities* of what is, for us, the same
signifying process. We shall call the first '*the semiotic*' and the second
'*the symbolic*'. These two modalities are inseparable within the *signifying
process* that constitutes language, and the dialectic between them determines the type of discourse (narrative, metalanguage, theory, poetry,
etc.) involved; in other words, so-called 'natural' language allows for

different modes of articulation of the semiotic and the symbolic. On the other hand, there are non-verbal signifying systems that are constructed exclusively on the basis of the semiotic (music, for example). But, as we shall see, this exclusivity is relative, precisely because of the necessary dialectic between the two modalities of the signifying process, which is constitutive of the subject. Because the subject is always *both* semiotic *and* symbolic, no signifying system he produces can be either 'exclusively' semiotic or 'exclusively' symbolic, and is instead necessarily marked by an indebtedness to both.

2   THE SEMIOTIC *CHORA* ORDERING THE DRIVES

We understand the term 'semiotic' in its Greek sense: $\sigma\eta\mu\tilde{\epsilon}\iota o\nu$ = distinctive mark, trace, index, precursory sign, proof, engraved or written sign, imprint, trace, figuration. This etymological reminder would be a mere archaeological embellishment (and an unconvincing one at that, since the term ultimately encompasses such disparate meanings) were it not for the fact that the preponderant etymological use of the word, the one that implies a *distinctiveness*, allows us to connect it to a precise modality in the signifying process. This modality is the one Freudian psychoanalysis points to in postulating not only the *facilitation* and the structuring *disposition* of drives, but also the so-called *primary processes* which displace and condense both energies and their inscription. Discrete quantities of energy move through the body of the subject who is not yet constituted as such and, in the course of his development, they are arranged according to the various constraints imposed on this body – always already involved in a semiotic process – by family and social structures. In this way the drives, which are 'energy' charges as well as 'psychical' marks, articulate what we call a *chora*: a non-expressive totality formed by the drives and their stases in a motility that is as full of movement as it is regulated.

We borrow the term *chora*[11] from Plato's *Timaeus* to denote an essentially mobile and extremely provisional articulation constituted by movements and their ephemeral stases. We differentiate this uncertain and indeterminate *articulation* from a *disposition* that already depends on representation, lends itself to phenomenological, spatial intuition and gives rise to a geometry. Although our theoretical description of the *chora* is itself part of the discourse of representation that offers it as evidence, the *chora*, as rupture and articulations (rhythm), precedes evidence, verisimilitude, spatiality and temporality. Our discourse – all discourse – moves with and against the *chora* in the sense that it simultaneously depends upon and refuses it. Although the *chora* can be designated and regulated, it can never be definitely posited: as a result, one can situate the *chora* and, if necessary, lend it a topology, but one can never give it axiomatic form.[12]

The *chora* is not yet a position that represents something for someone (i.e., it is not a sign); nor is it a *position* that represents someone for another position (i.e., it is not yet a signifier either); it is, however, generated in order to attain to this signifying position. Neither model nor copy, the *chora* precedes and underlies figuration and thus specularization, and is analogous only to vocal or kinetic rhythm. We must restore this motility's gestural and vocal play (to mention only the aspect relevant to language) on the level of the socialized body in order to remove motility from ontology and amorphousness[13] where Plato confines it in an apparent attempt to conceal it from Democritean rhythm. The theory of the subject proposed by the theory of the unconscious will allow us to read in this rhythmic space, which has no thesis and no position, the process by which signifiance is constituted. Plato himself leads us to such a process when he calls this receptacle or *chora* nourishing and maternal,[14] not yet unified in an ordered whole because deity is absent from it. Though deprived of unity, identity or deity, the *chora* is nevertheless subject to a regulating process [*réglementation*], which is different from that of symbolic law but nevertheless effectuates discontinuities by temporarily articulating them and then starting over, again and again.

The *chora* is a modality of signifiance in which the linguistic sign is not yet articulated as the absence of an object and as the distinction between real and symbolic. We emphasize the regulated aspect of the *chora*: its vocal and gestural organization is subject to what we shall call an objective *ordering* [*ordonnancement*], which is dictated by natural or socio-historical constraints such as the biological difference between the sexes or family structure. We may therefore posit that social organization, always already symbolic, imprints its constraint in a mediated form which organizes the *chora* not according to a *law* (a term we reserve for the symbolic) but through an *ordering*.[15] What is this mediation?

According to a number of psycholinguists, 'concrete operations' precede the acquisition of language, and organize pre-verbal semiotic space according to logical categories, which are thereby shown to precede or transcend language. From their research we shall retain not the principle of an operational state[16] but that of a pre-verbal functional state that governs the connections between the body (in the process of constituting itself as a body proper), objects and the protagonists of family structure.[17] But we shall distinguish this functioning from symbolic operations that depend on language as a sign system – whether the language [*langue*] is vocalized or gestural (as with deaf-mutes). The kinetic functional stage of the *semiotic* precedes the establishment of the sign; it is not, therefore, cognitive in the sense of being assumed by a knowing, already constituted subject. The genesis of the *functions*[18] organizing the semiotic process can be accurately elucidated only within a theory of the subject that does not reduce the subject to one of understanding, but instead opens up within the subject this other scene of pre-symbolic functions. The Kleinian theory expanding upon Freud's positions on the drives will momentarily serve as a guide.

Drives involve pre-Oedipal semiotic functions and energy discharges that connect and orient the body to the mother. We must emphasize that 'drives' are always already ambiguous, simultaneously assimilating and destructive; this dualism, which has been represented as a tetrad[19] or as a double helix, as in the configuration of the DNA and RNA molecule,[20] makes the semiotized body a place of permanent scission. The oral and anal drives, both of which are oriented and structured around the mother's body,[21] dominate this sensorimotor organization. The mother's body is therefore what mediates the symbolic law organizing social relations and becomes the ordering principle of the semiotic *chora*,[22] which is on the path of destruction, aggressivity and death. For although drives have been described as disunited or contradictory structures, simultaneously 'positive' and 'negative', this doubling is said to generate a dominant 'destructive wave' that is drive's most characteristic trait: Freud notes that the most instinctual drive is the death drive.[23] In this way, the term 'drive' denotes waves of attack against stases, which are themselves constituted by the repetition of these charges; together, charges and stases lead to no identity (not even that of the 'body proper') that could be seen as a result of their functioning. This is to say that the semiotic *chora* is no more than the place where the subject is both generated and negated, the place where his unity succumbs before the process of charges and stases that produce him. We shall call this process of charges and stases a *negativity* to distinguish it from negation, which is the act of a judging subject.

Checked by the constraints of biological and social structures, the drive charge thus undergoes stases. Drive facilitation, temporarily arrested, marks *discontinuities* in what may be called the various material supports [*matériaux*] susceptible to semiotization: voice, gesture, colours. Phonic (later phonemic), kinetic or chromatic units and differences are the marks of these stases in the drives. Connections or *functions* are thereby established between these discrete marks which are based on drives and articulated according to their resemblance or opposition, either by slippage or by condensation. Here we find the principles of metonymy and metaphor indissociable from the drive economy underlying them.

Although we recognize the vital role played by the processes of displacement and condensation in the organization of the semiotic, we must also add to these processes the relations (eventually representable as topological spaces) that connect the zones of the fragmented body to each other and also to 'external' 'objects' and 'subjects', which are not yet constituted as such. This type of relation makes it possible to specify the *semiotic* as a psychosomatic modality of the signifying process; in other words, not a symbolic modality but one articulating (in the largest sense of the word) a continuum: the connections between the (glottal and anal) sphincters in (rhythmic and intonational) vocal modulations, or those between the sphincters and family protagonists, for example.

All these various processes and relations, anterior to sign and syntax, have just been identified from a genetic perspective as previous and necessary to the acquisition of language, but not identical to language. Theory can 'situate' such processes and relations diachronically within the process of the constitution of the subject precisely because *they function synchronically within the signifying process of the subject himself*, i.e., the subject of *cogitatio*. Only in *dream* logic, however, have they attracted attention, and only in certain signifying practices, such as the *text*, do they dominate the signifying process.

It may be hypothesized that certain semiotic articulations are transmitted through the biological code or physiological 'memory' and thus form the inborn bases of the symbolic function. Indeed, one branch of generative linguistics asserts the principle of innate language universals. As it will become apparent in what follows, however, the *symbolic* – and therefore syntax and all linguistic categories – is a social effect of the relation to the other, established through the objective constraints of biological (including sexual) differences and concrete, historical family structures. Genetic programmings are necessarily semiotic: they include the primary processes such as displacement and condensation, absorption and repulsion, rejection and stasis, all of which function as innate preconditions, 'memorizable' by the species, for language acquisition.

Mallarmé calls attention to the semiotic rhythm within language when he speaks of 'The Mystery in Literature' ['Le Mystère dans les lettres']. Indifferent to language, enigmatic and feminine, this space underlying the written is rhythmic, unfettered, irreducible to its intelligible verbal translation; it is musical, anterior to judgement, but restrained by a single guarantee: syntax. As evidence, we could cite 'The Mystery in Literature' in its entirety.[24] For now, however, we shall quote only those passages that ally the functioning of that 'air or song beneath the text' with woman:

And the instrument of Darkness, whom they have designated, will not set down a word from then on except to deny that she must have been the enigma; lest she settle matters with a wisk of her skirts: 'I don't get it!'

– They [the critics] play their parts disinterestedly or for a minor gain: leaving our Lady and Patroness exposed to show her dehiscence or lacuna, with respect to certain dreams, as though this were the standard to which everything is reduced.[25]

To these passages we add others that point to the 'mysterious' functioning of literature as a rhythm made intelligible by syntax: 'Following the instinct for rhythms that has chosen him, the poet does not deny seeing a lack of proportion between the means let loose and the result.' 'I know that there are those who would restrict Mystery to Music's domain; when writing aspires to it.'[26]

What pivot is there, I mean within these contrasts, for intelligibility? a guarantee is needed –
Syntax –
...an extraordinary appropriation of structure, limpid, to the primitive lightning bolts of logic. A stammering, what the sentence seems, here repressed...

The debate – whether necessary average clarity deviates in a detail
– remains one for grammarians.[27]

Our positing of the semiotic is obviously inseparable from a theory
of the subject that takes into account the Freudian positing of the
unconscious. We view the subject in language as decentring the transcendental ego, cutting through it and opening it up to a dialectic in
which its syntactic and categorical understanding is merely the liminary
moment of the process, which is itself always acted upon by the relation
to the other dominated by the death drive and its productive reiteration of the 'signifier'. We will be attempting to formulate the distinction
between *semiotic* and *symbolic* within this perspective, which was introduced by Lacanian analysis, but also within the constraints of a practice
– the *text* – which is only of secondary interest to psychoanalysis.

5 THE THETIC: RUPTURE AND/OR BOUNDARY

We shall distinguish the semiotic (drives and their articulations) from
the realm of signification, which is always that of a proposition or
judgement, in other words, a realm of *positions*. This positionality, which
Husserlian phenomenology orchestrates through the concepts of *doxa*,
position and *thesis*, is structured as a break in the signifying process,
establishing the *identification* of the subject and its object as preconditions of propositionality. We shall call this break, which produces the
positing of signification, a *thetic* phase. All enunciation, whether of a
word or of a sentence, is thetic. It requires an identification; in other
words, the subject must separate from and through his image, from
and through his objects. This image and objects must first be posited
in a space that becomes symbolic because it connects the two separated
positions, recording them or redistributing them in an open combinatorial system.

The child's first so-called holophrastic enunciations include gesture,
the object and vocal emission. Because they are perhaps not yet sentences
(NP-VP), generative grammar is not readily equipped to account for
them. Nevertheless, they are already thetic in the sense that they separate
an object from the subject, and attribute to it a semiotic fragment, which
thereby becomes a signifier. That this attribution is either metaphoric or
metonymic ('woof-woof' says the dog, and all animals become 'woof-woof')

is logically secondary to the fact that it constitutes an *attribution*, which is to say, a positing of identity or difference, and that it represents the nucleus of judgement or proposition.

We shall say that the thetic phase of the signifying process is the 'deepest structure' of the possibility of enunciation, in other words, of signification and the proposition. Husserl theologizes this deep logic of signification by making it a productive *origin* of the 'free spontaneity' of the Ego:

> Its *free spontaneity and activity* consists in positing, positing on the strength of this or that, positing as an antecedent or a consequent, and so forth; it does not live within the theses as a passive indweller; the theses radiate from it as from a primary source of generation [*Erzeugungen*]. Every thesis begins with a *point of insertion* [*Einsatzpunkt*] with a point at which *the positing has its origin* [*Ursprungssetzung*]; so it is with the first thesis and with each further one in the synthetic nexus. This 'inserting' even belongs to the thesis as such, as a remarkable modus of original actuality. It somewhat resembles the *fiat*, the point of insertion of will and action.[28]

In this sense, *there exists only one signification*, that of the thetic phase, which contains the object as well as the proposition, and the complicity between them.[29] There is no sign that is not thetic and every sign is already the germ of a 'sentence' attributing a signifier to an object through a 'copula' that will function as a signified.[30] Stoic semiology, which was the first to formulate the matrix of the sign, had already established *this complicity between sign and sentence*, making them proofs of each other.

Modern philosophy recognizes that the right to represent the founding *thesis* of signification (sign and/or proposition) devolves upon the transcendental ego. But only since Freud have we been able to raise the question not of the origin of this thesis but rather of the process of its production. To brand the thetic as the foundation of metaphysics is to risk serving as an antechamber for metaphysics – unless, that is, we specify the way the thetic is produced in our view, the Freudian theory of the unconscious and its Lacanian development show, precisely, that thetic signification is a stage attained under certain precise conditions during the signifying process, and that it constitutes the subject without being reduced to his process precisely because it is the threshold of language. Such a standpoint constitutes neither a reduction of the subject to the transcendental ego, nor a denial [*dénégation*] of the thetic phase that establishes signification.

6   THE MIRROR AND CASTRATION POSITING THE SUBJECT AS ABSENT FROM THE SIGNIFIER

In the development of the subject, such as it has been reconstituted by the theory of the unconscious, we find the thetic phase of the signifying process, around which signification is organized, at two points: the mirror stage and the 'discovery' of castration.

The first, the mirror stage, produces the 'spatial intuition' which is found at the heart of the funtioning of signification – in signs and in sentences. From that point on, in order to capture his image unified in a mirror, the child must remain separate from it, his body agitated by the semiotic motility we discussed above, which fragments him more than it unifies him in a representation. According to Lacan, human physiological immaturity, which is due to premature birth, is thus what permits any permanent positing whatsoever and, first and foremost, that of the image itself, as separate, heterogeneous, dehiscent.[31] Captation of the image and the drive investment in this image, which institute primary narcissism, permit the constitution of objects detached from the semiotic *chora*. Lacan maintains, moreover, that the specular image is the 'prototype' for the 'world of objects'.[32] Positing the imaged ego leads to the positing of the object, which is, likewise, separate and signifiable.

Thus the two separations that prepare the way for the sign are set in place. The sign can be conceived as the voice that is projected from the agitated body (from the semiotic *chora*) on to the facing *imago* or on to the object, which simultaneously detach from the surrounding continuity. Indeed, a child's first holophrastic utterances occur at this time, within what are considered the boundaries of the mirror stage (six to eighteen months). On the basis of this positing, which constitutes a *break*, signification becomes established as a digital system with a double articulation combining discrete elements. Language-learning can therefore be thought of as an acute and dramatic confrontation between positing-separating-identifying and the motility of the semiotic *chora*. Separation from the mother's body, the *fort-da* game, anality and orality, all act as a permanent negativity that destroys the image and the isolated object even as it facilitates the articulation of the semiotic network, which will afterwards be necessary in the system of language where it will be more or less integrated as a *signifier*.

Castration puts the finished touches on the process of separation that posits the subject as signifiable, which is to say, separate, always confronted by an other: *imago* in the mirror (signified) and semiotic process (signifier). As the addressee of every demand, the mother occupies the place of alterity. Her replete body, the receptacle and guarantor of demands, takes the place of all narcissistic, hence imaginary, effects and gratifications; she is, in other words, the phallus. The discovery of castration, however, detaches the subject from his dependence on the mother, and the perception of this lack [*manque*] makes the phallic function a symbolic function – *the* symbolic function. This is a decisive moment fraught with consequences: the subject, finding his identity in the symbolic, *separates* from his fusion with the mother, *confines* his *jouissance* to the genital and transfers semiotic motility on to the symbolic order. Thus ends the formation of the thetic phase, which posits the gap between the signifier and the signified as an opening up towards every desire but also every act, including the very *jouissance* that exceeds them.[33]

At this point we would like to emphasize, without going into the details of Lacan's argument, that the phallus totalizes the effects of signifieds as having been produced by the signifier: the phallus is itself a signifier. In other words, the phallus is not given in the utterance but instead refers outside itself to a precondition that makes enunciation possible. For there to be enunciation, the *ego* must be posited in the signified, but it must do so as a function of the *subject* lacking in the signifier; a system of finite positions (signification) can only function when it is supported by a subject and on the condition that this subject is a want-to-be [*manque à être*].[34] Signification exists precisely because there is no subject in signification. The gap between the imaged ego and drive motility, between the mother and the demand made on her, is precisely the break that establishes what Lacan calls the place of the Other as the place of the 'signifier'. The subject is hidden 'by an ever purer signifier',[35] this want-to-be confers on an *other* the role of containing the possibility of signification; and this other, who is no longer the mother (from whom the child ultimately separates through the mirror stage and castration), presents itself as the place of the signifier that Lacan will call 'the Other'.

Is this to say, then, that such a theoretical undertaking transcendentalizes semiotic motility, setting it up as a transcendental signifier? In our view, this transformation of semiotic motility serves to remove it from its auto-erotic and maternal enclosure and, by introducing the signifier/signified break, allows it to produce signification. By the same token, signification itself appears as a stage of the signifying process – not so much its base as its boundary. Signification is placed 'under the sign of the pre-conscious'.[36] Ultimately, this signifier/signified transformation, constitutive of language, is seen as being indebted to, induced and imposed by the social realm. Dependence on the mother is severed, and transformed into a symbolic relation to an other, the constitution of the Other is indispensable for communicating with an other. In this way, the signifier/signified break is synonymous with social sanction: 'the first social censorship'.

Thus we view the thetic phase – the positing of the *imago*, castration and the positing of semiotic motility – as the place of the Other, as the precondition for signification, i.e., the precondition for the positing of language. The thetic phase marks a threshold between two heterogeneous realms: the semiotic and the symbolic. The second includes part of the first and their scission is thereafter marked by the break between signifier and signified. *Symbolic* would seem an appropriate term for this always split unification that is produced by a rupture and is impossible without it. Its etymology makes it particularly pertinent. The σύμβοχον is a sign of recognition: an 'object' split in two and the parts separated, but, as eyelids do, σύμβοχον brings together the two edges of that fissure. As a result, the 'symbol' is any joining, any bringing together that is a contract – one that either follows hostilities or presupposes them – and, finally, any exchange, including an exchange of hostility.

Not only is symbolic, thetic unity divided (into signifier and signified), but this division is itself the result of a break that put a heterogeneous functioning in the position of signifier. This functioning is the instinctual semiotic, preceding meaning and signification, mobile, amorphous, but already regulated, which we have attempted to represent through references to child psychoanalysis (particularly at the pre-Oedipal stage) and the theory of drives. In the speaking subject, fantasies articulate this irruption of drives within the realm of the signifier; they disrupt the signifier and shift the metonymy of desire, which acts within the place of the Other, on to a *jouissance* that divests the object and turns back towards the auto-erotic body. That language is a defensive construction reveals its ambiguity – the death drive underlying it. If language, constituted as symbolic through narcissistic, specular, imaginary investment, protects the body from the attack of drives by making it a place – the place of the signifier – in which the body can signify itself through positions; and if, therefore, language, in the service of the death drive, is a pocket of narcissism towards which this drive may be directed, then fantasies remind us, if we had ever forgotten, of the insistent presence of drive heterogeneity.[37]

All poetic 'distortions' of the signifying chain and the structure of signification may be considered in this light: they yield under the attack of the 'residues of first symbolizations' (Lacan), in other words, those drives that the thetic phase was not able to sublate [*relever, aufheben*] by linking them into signifier and signified. As a consequence, any disturbance of the 'social censorship' – that of the signifier/signified break – attests, perhaps first and foremost, to an influx of the death drive, which no signifier, no mirror, no other and no mother could ever contain. In 'artistic' practices the semiotic – the precondition of the symbolic – is revealed as that which also destroys the symbolic, and this revelation allows us to presume something about its functioning.

Psychoanalysts acknowledge that the pre-Oedipal stages Melanie Klein discusses are 'analytically unthinkable' but not inoperative, and, furthermore, that the relation of the subject to the signifier is established and language-learning is completed only in the pre-genital stages that are set in place by the retroaction of the Oedipus complex (which itself brings about initial genital maturation).[32] Thereafter, the supposedly characteristic functioning of the pre-Oedipal stages appears only in the complete, post-genital handling of language, which presupposes, as we have seen, a decisive imposition of the phallic. In other words, the subject must be firmly posited by castration so that drive attacks against the thetic will not give way to fantasy or to psychosis but will instead lead to a 'second-degree thetic', i.e., a resumption of the functioning characteristic of the semiotic *chora* within the signifying device of language. This is precisely what artistic practices, and notably poetic language, demonstrate.

Starting from and (logically and chronologically) after the phallic position and the castration that underlies it – in other words, after the Oedipus complex and especially after the regulation of genitality by the retroactive effect of the Oedipus complex in puberty – the semiotic *chora* can be read not as a failure of the thetic but instead as its very precondition. Neurotics and psychotics are defined as such by their relationship to what we are calling the thetic. We now see why, in treating them, psychoanalysis can only conceive of semiotic motility as a disturbance of language and/or of the order of the signifier. Conversely, the refusal of the thetic phase and an attempt to hypostasize semiotic motility as autonomous from the thetic – capable of doing without it or unaware of it – can be seen as a resistance to psychoanalysis. Some therefore even contend that one can find in poetry the unfolding of this refusal of the thetic, something like a direct transcription of the genetic code – as if practice were possible without the thetic and as if a text, in order to hold together as a text, did not require a completion [*finition*], a structuration, a kind of totalization of semiotic motility. This completion constitutes a synthesis that requires the thesis of language in order to come about, and the semiotic pulverizes it only to make it a new device – for us, this is precisely what distinguishes a text as *signifying practice* from the 'drifting-into-non-sense' [*dérive*] that characterizes neurotic discourse. The distinction cannot be erased unless one puts oneself outside 'monumental history' in a transcendence which often proves to be one of the reactionary forces combining that history's discrete blocks.[39]

In this way, only the subject, for whom the thetic is not a repression of the semiotic *chora* but instead a position either taken on or undergone, can call into question the thetic so that a new disposition may be articulated. Castration must have been a problem, a trauma, a drama, so that the semiotic can return through the symbolic position it brings about. This is the crux of the matter: both the completion of the Oedipus complex and its reactivation in puberty are needed for the *Aufhebung* of the semiotic in the symbolic to give rise to a signifying *practice* that has a socio-historical function (and is not just a self-analytical discourse, a substitute for the analyst's couch). At the same time, however, this completion of the Oedipal stage and the genitality it gives rise to should not repress the semiotic, for such a repression is what sets up metalanguage and the 'pure signifier'. No pure signifier can effect the *Aufhebung* (in the Hegelian sense) of the semiotic without leaving a remainder, and anyone who would believe this myth need only question his fascination or boredom with a given poem, painting or piece of music. As a traversable boundary, the thetic is completely different from an imaginary castration that must be evaded in order to return to the maternal *chora*. It is clearly distinct as well from a castration imposed once and for all, perpetuating the well-ordered signifier and positing it as sacred and unalterable within the enclosure of the Other.[40]

7 FREGE'S NOTION OF SIGNIFICATION: ENUNCIATION AND DENOTATION

What becomes of signification once the signifier has been posited?

We have seen that, according to Husserl, signification is a predication that necessitates the fundamental thesis of a Dasein, which is essentially that of the transcendental ego. Whether this predication, or more accurately, this judgement, is existential or attributive is – as Freud seemed to believe in his article on *Verneinung* – secondary to its being, first and foremost, a positing. But *what* does it posit, since the semiotic *chora* has been separated from the 'subject' – 'object' continuum? It posits an *object* or a *denotatum*. Frege calls the utterance of this *denotatum* a *Bedeutung* (signification), which in this case is denotation. But Frege's departure from Husserl is only apparent.

For Husserl, the isolation of an object as such is, as we have seen, the inseparable and concomitant precondition for the positing of the judging Ego, since that Ego's enunciation refers to an object. So much so that, as Frege shows, signs can be attributed the same signification by the same denotation. But Frege goes further: Doesn't the immense profusion of signs, even before denoting objects, imply the very *precondition of denotation*, which is the *positing of an object*, of the object, of objectness? In other words, denotation would be understood as the subject's ability to separate himself from the ecosystem into which he was fused, so that, as a result of this separation, he may designate it. Frege writes: 'If now the truth value of a sentence is its denotation, then on the one hand all true sentences have the same denotation and so, on the other hand, do all false sentences. *From this we see that in the denotation of the sentence all that is specific is obliterated.*'[41] According to Frege, sentences are able to have an object by virtue of their relation to 'concept' and to 'thought'; however, although he does not enter into this labyrinth, Frege maintains that the stated *predication* is the logical matrix of *Bedeutung*, which is nevertheless not identical to it. Judgement produces *Bedeutung* but does not enclose it, referring it instead elsewhere, to a heterogeneous domain, which is to say, within the existing object.[42]

By straddling these two 'levels', Frege's *Bedeutung*, in our view, designates, precisely, the break that simultaneously sets up the symbolic thesis and an object; as an externality within judgement, it has a truth value only by virtue of this scission. We may conclude, therefore, that *the thetic is the precondition for both enunciation and denotation.*[43] If the very possibility of such an internal externality is that which founds signification's truth capacity, we can understand why Frege suggests that there is in fact only one denotation.[44] But denotation is not equivalent to the Saussurean referent: Frege posits the existence of signs, 'artistic' signs, for example, that have no *denotation*, only *meaning*, because they do not refer to a real object. Therefore one should not be concerned with the denotation of a thought or a part of a thought taken as a work of art. Yet it must be supposed that the desire to do so exists, even with works of art, whenever they include thoughts in the form of propositions. The specific status of signification in art thus results from a constantly maintained ambiguity between the possibility of a *meaning* that amounts to grammaticality[45] and a *denotation* that is, likewise, given in the very structure of the judgement or proposition but is realized only under certain conditions – notably when predication achieved an existential value.[46] But under what conditions does predication cease being a copula that is indifferent to the existence of an object and obtain instead a denotative value referring to that object? Frege does not specify the economy of the signifying act that makes enunciation a denotation; but when he speaks of the 'same denotation' for all true propositions, he lets us see that the subject's ability to separate from the semiotic *chora* and to designate an object as real lies in the thetic function of symbolism.

The thetic posits the signifiable object: it posits signification as both a *denotation* (of an object) and an *enunciation* (of a displaced subject, absent from the signified and signifying position). From then on, the thetic prepares and contains within itself the very possibility of making this division explicit through an opposition and a juxtaposition of syntagms: the proposition, and judgement as well – to the extent that the latter is coexistensive with the proposition – unfold or *linearize* (by concatenation or application) the signification (enunciation + denotation) opened up by the thetic. Even if it is presented as a simple act of naming, we maintain that the thetic is already *propositional* (or syntactic) and that syntax is the ex-position of the thetic. The subject and predicate represent the division inherent in the thetic; they make it plain and actual. But if theory persists in regarding them as independent entities, notions of the subject and predicate may end up obscuring not only the link between (thetic) signification and syntactic structure, but also the complicity and opposition between denotation (given in the subject) and enunciation (given in the predicate).

Therefore we could consider that which has been relegated to the terms 'subject' and 'predicate' or, more narrowly, 'noun' and 'verb', as two modalities of the thetic, representing the posited and positing, linked and linking elements – denotation and enunciation – that are indissociable from the thetic process and, consequently, permutable or reversible. The positing, linking, assertive, cohesive element, the one that completes the utterance and makes it finite (a sentence), in short, the element in which the spatio-temporal and communicational positing of the speaking subject is marked, is the element with the predicative *function*. It may be, but is not necessarily, what morphology identifies as a 'verb'. But at the same time, as Benveniste shows, variable predication itself is the 'seat of an invariant' which simultaneously posits an extra-linguistic reality [*réel*] and phrastic completion and ensures the relation between the two orders. This is, in fact, what we have called a thetic function, demonstrating that assertion and intra-syntactic completion are inseparable.

Conceiving the signifying process as a thetic negativity thus leads us to relativize the classic terms 'subject' and 'predicate' and see them as mere 'subsets' (characteristic of certain languages or linguistic theories) of a more general relation which is actually in play between two indissociable modalities of the thetic (posited-positing, linked-linking, modified-modifier, etc.) The relations between Kurylowicz's 'modifier' and 'modified', Strawson's 'feature concepts' or 'feature-placing statements' or Shauryman's 'applicational generative model'[47] on a technical linguistic level would also seem to corroborate the inseparability of the thetic and syntax. Their indivisibility implies that signification (*Bedeutung*) is a process in which opposable 'terms' are posited as phenomena but can be identified as the two faces (denotation-enunciation) of the thetic break.[48]

Syntax registers the thetic break as an opposition of discrete and permutable elements but whose concrete position nevertheless indicates that each one has a definite signification. Syntax displaces and represents, within the homogeneous element of language, the thetic break separating the signifier from what was heterogeneous to it. The *transformation* [from drive to signifier] produced by the thetic is registered only as an inter-syntactical *division* (modified-modifier, 'feature-placing' or subject-predicate). This transformation, which produced the speaking subject, comes about only if it leaves that subject out, within the heterogeneous. Indeed, although he is the bearer of syntax, the speaking subject is absent from it.

But when this subject re-emerges, when the semiotic *chora* disturbs the thetic position by redistributing the signifying order, we note that the denoted object and the syntactic relation are disturbed as well. The denoted object proliferates in a series of connoted objects produced by the *transposition* of the semiotic *chora*[49] and the syntactic division (modified-modifier, NP-VP or the placement of semantic features) is disrupted. In the latter aspect of the signifying process – syntax – we note that the division of the grammatical sequence (which we have called the transposition of the thetic break into a homogeneous sign-system) is maintained; this means that syntactic categories, which ensure the possibility of both verisimilar denotation and communication, are also preserved. But the *completion* of the grammatical sequence does not take place because the division is not completely rejoined in a NP-VP, modified-modifier, etc. whole. This ellipsis or syntactic *non-completion* can be interpreted as the thetic break's inability to remain simply intra-syntactic – a division within a signifying homogeneity. A heterogeneous division, an irruption of the semiotic *chora*, marks each 'category' of the syntactic sequence and prevents the 'other' from being posited as an identifiable syntactic term (subject or predicate, modified or modifier, etc.). In this realization of the signifier, particularly as it is seen in poetic texts, alterity is maintained within the pure signifier and/or in the simply syntactic element only with difficulty. For the Other has become heterogeneous and will not remain fixed in place: it negativizes all terms, all posited elements and thus syntax, threatening them with possible dissolution.

It should be understood that the path completed by the *text* is not a simple return, as in the Hegelian dialectic, from the 'predicate' to the 'subject', from the 'general' to the 'particular'; it does not con-stitute a Hegelian synthesis operating in judgement and realized in the syllogism. Instead it involves both shattering and maintaining *position* within the heterogeneous *process*: the proof can be found in the phonetic, lexical and syntactic disturbance visible in the *semiotic device* of the text.[50] The disturbance of sentential completion or syntactic ellipsis lead to an infinitization of logical (syntactic) applications. Terms are linked together but, as a consequence of non-recoverable deletion,[51] they are linked *ad infinitum*. The sentence is not suppressed, it is infinitized. Similarly, the denoted object does not disappear, it proliferates in mimetic, fictional, connoted objects.

8 BREACHING[52] THE THETIC: MIMESIS

Signification in literature implies the possibility of denotation. But instead of following denotative sequences, which would lead, from one judgement to another, to the knowledge of a real object, literary signification tends towards the exploration of grammaticality and/or towards enunciation. *Mimesis* is, precisely, the construction of an object, not according to truth but to *verisimilitude*, to the extent that the object is posited as such (hence separate, noted but not denoted); it is, however, internally dependent on a subject of enunciation who is unlike the transcendental ego in that he does not suppress the semiotic *chora* but instead raises the *chora* to the status of a signifier, which may or may not obey the norms of grammatical locution. Such is the *connoted* mimetic object.

Although mimesis partakes of the symbolic order, it does so only to re-produce some of its constitutive rules, in other words, grammaticality. By the same token, it must posit an object, but this 'object' is merely a result of the drive economy of enunciation; its true position is inconsequential.[53] What is more when poetic language – especially modern poetic language – transgresses grammatical rules, the *positing* of the symbolic (which mimesis has always explored) finds itself subverted, not only in its possibilities of *Bedeutung* or denotation (which mimesis has always contested), but also as a possessor of *meaning* (which is always grammatical, indeed more precisely, syntactic). In imitating the constitution of the symbolic as *meaning*, poetic mimesis is led to dissolve not only the denotative function but also the specifically thetic function of *positing* the subject. In this respect modern poetic language goes further than any classical mimesis – whether theatrical or novelistic – because it attacks not only denotation (the positing of the object) but meaning (the positing of the enunciating subject) as well.

In thus eroding the verisimilitude that inevitably underlaid classical mimesis and, more importantly, the very position of enunciation (i.e., the positing of the subject as absent from the signifier), poetic language puts the subject in process/on trial through a network of marks and semiotic facilitations. But the moment it stops being mere instinctual glossolalia and becomes part of the linguistic order, poetry meets up with denotation and enunciation – verisimilitude and the subject – and, through them, the social.

We now understand how the thetic conditions the possibilities of truth specific to language: all transgressions of the thetic are a crossing of the boundary between true and false – maintained, inevitably, whenever signification is maintained, and shaken, irremediably, by the flow of the semiotic into the symbolic. Mimesis, in our view, is a transgression of the thetic when truth is no longer a reference to an object that is identifiable outside language; it refers instead to an object that can be constructed through the semiotic network but is nevertheless posited in the symbolic and is, from then on, always verisimilar.

Mimetic verisimilitude does not, therefore, eliminate the unique break Frege saw presiding over signification. Instead it maintains that break because it preserves meaning and, with it, a certain object. But neither true nor false, the very status of this verisimilar object throws into question the absoluteness of the break that establishes truth. Mimesis does not actually call into question the unicity of the thetic; indeed it could not, since mimetic discourse takes on the structure of language and, through narrative sentences, posits a signified and signifying object. Mimesis and the poetic language inseparable from it tend, rather, to prevent the thetic from becoming theological; in other words, they prevent the imposition of the thetic from hiding the semiotic process that produces it, and they bar it from inducing the subject, reified as a transcendental ego, to function solely within the systems of science and monotheistic religion.

To note that there can be no language without a thetic phase that establishes the possibility of truth, and to draw consequences from this discovery, is quite a different matter from insisting that every signifying practice operate uniquely out of the thetic phase. For this would mean that the thetic, as origin and transcendence, could only produce (in the Husserlian sense) a tautological discourse, which, having originated in a thesis, can only be a synthesis of theses. We maintain therefore that science and theological dogma are doxic. By repressing the *production* of doxy, they make the thetic a belief from which the quest for truth departs; but the path thus programmed is circular and merely returns to its thetic point of departure.[54] If mimesis, by contrast, pluralizes denotation, and if poetic language undermines meaning, by what specific operations are these corruptions of the symbolic carried out?

As we know, Freud specifies two fundamental 'processes' in the work of the unconscious: *displacement* and *condensation*. Kruszewski and Jakobson[55] introduced them, in a different way, during the early stages of structural linguistics, through the concepts of *metonymy* and *metaphor*, which have since been interpreted in light of psychoanalysis.[56]

To these we must add a third 'process' – the *passage from one sign-system to another*. To be sure, this process comes about through a combination of displacement and condensation, but this does not account for its total operation. It also involves an altering of the thetic *position* – the destruction of the old position and the formation of a new one. The new signifying system may be produced with the same signifying material; in language, for example, the passage may be made from narrative to text. Or it may be borrowed from different signifying materials: the transposition from a carnival scene to the written text, for instance. In this connection we examined the formation of a specific signifying system – the novel – as the result of a redistribution of several different sign-systems: carnival, courtly poetry, scholastic discourse[57]. The term *intertextuality* denotes this transposition of one (or several) sign-system(s) into another; but since this term has often been understood in the banal sense of 'study of sources', we prefer the term *transposition* because it specifies that the passage from one signifying system to another demands a new articulation of the thetic – of enunciative and denotative positionality. If one grants that every signifying practice is a field of transpositions of various signifying systems (an intertextuality), one then understands that its 'place' of enunciation and its denoted 'object' are never single, complete and identical to themselves, but always plural, shattered, capable of being tabulated. In this way polysemy can also be seen as the result of a semiotic polyvalence – an adherence to different sign-systems.

Along with condensation (*Verdichtung*) and displacement (*Verschiebung*), Freud also speaks of *considerations of representability* (*die Rücksicht auf Darstellbarkeit*), which are essential to dream-work (*die Traumarbeit*). Representability comes about through a process, closely related to displacement but appreciably different from it, that Freud calls 'ein Vertauschung des sprachlichen Ausdruckes'. We shall call *transposition* the signifying process' ability to pass from one sign-system to another, to exchange and permutate them, and *representability* the specific articulation of the semiotic and the thetic for a sign-system. Transposition plays an essential role here inasmuch as it implies the abandonment of a former sign-system, the passage to a second via an instinctual intermediary common to the two systems and the articulation of the new system with its new representability.[58]

Poetic mimesis maintains and transgresses thetic unicity by making it undergo a kind of anamnesis, by introducing into the thetic position the stream of semiotic drives and making it signify.[59] This telescoping of the symbolic and the semiotic pluralizes signification or denotation: it pluralizes the thetic doxy. Mimesis and poetic language do not therefore disavow the thetic, instead they go through its truth (signification, denotation) to tell the 'truth' about it. To be sure, the latter use of the term 'truth' is inappropriate, since it no longer refers to denotative truth in Frege's sense. This 'second truth' reproduces the path which was cleared by the first truth (that of *Bedeutung*) in order to posit itself. Both mimesis and poetic language with its connotations assume the right to enter into the social debate, which is an ideological debate, on the strength of their confrontation with *Bedeutung* (signification and denotation) but also with all meaning, and hence all enunciation produced by a posited subject.

But mimesis and poetic language do more than engage in an intra-ideological debate; they question the very principle of the ideological because they unfold the *unicity* of the thetic (the precondition for meaning and signification) and prevent its theologization. As the place of production for a subject who transgresses the thetic by using it as a necessary boundary – but not as an absolute or as an origin – poetic language, and the mimesis from which it is inseparable, are profoundly a-theological. They are not critics of theology but rather the enemy within and without, recognizing both its necessity and its pretensions. In other words, poetic language and mimesis may appear as an argument complicitous with dogma – we are familiar with religion's use of them – but they may also set in motion what dogma represses. In so doing, they no longer act as instinctual floodgates within the enclosure of the sacred and become instead protestors against its posturing. And thus, its complexity unfolded by its practices, the signifying process joins social revolution.

9   THE UNSTABLE SYMBOLIC.
SUBSTITUTIONS IN THE SYMBOLIC: FETISHISM

The thetic permits the constitution of the symbolic with its vertical stratification (referent, signified, signifier) and all the subsequent modalities of logico-semantic articulation. The thetic originates in the 'mirror stage' and is completed, through the phallic stage, by the re-activation of the Oedipus complex in puberty; no signifying practice can be without it. Though absolutely necessary, the thetic is not exclusive: the semiotic, which also precedes it, constantly tears it open, and this transgression brings about all the various transformations of the signifying practice that are called 'creation'. Whether in the realm of metalanguage (mathematics, for example) or literature, what remodels the symbolic order is always the influx of the semiotic. This is particularly evident in poetic language since, for there to be a transgression of the symbolic, there must be an irruption of the drives in the universal signifying order, that of 'natural' language which binds together the social unit. That the subject does not vanish into psychosis when this transgression takes place poses a problem for metaphysics, both the kind that sets up the signifier as an untransgressable law and the kind for which there exists no thetic and therefore no subject.

The semiotic's breach of the symbolic in so-called poetic practice can probably be ascribed to the very unstable yet forceful positing of the thetic. In our view, the analysis of texts shows that thetic liability is ultimately a problem with imaginary captation (disorders in the mirror stage that become marked scopophilia, the need for a mirror or an identifying addressee, etc.) and a resistance to the discovery of castration (thereby maintaining the phallic mother who usurps the place of the Other). These problems and resistances obstruct the thetic phase of the signifying process. When they fail to prevent the constitution of the symbolic (which would result in psychosis), they return in and through its position. In so doing, they give rise to 'fantasies'; more importantly, they attempt to dissolve the first social censorship – the bar between signifier and signified – and, simultaneously, the first guarantee of the subject's position – signification, then meaning (the sentence and its syntax). Language thus tends to be drawn out of its symbolic function (sign-syntax) and is opened out within a semiotic articulation; with a material support such as the voice, this semiotic network gives 'music' to literature.

But the irruption of the semiotic within the symbolic is only relative. Though permeable, the thetic continues to ensure the position of the subject put in process/on trial. As a consequence, musicality is not without signification; indeed it is deployed within it. Logical synthesis and all ideologies are present, but they are pulverized within their own logic before being displaced towards something that is no longer within the realm of the idea, sign, syntax and thus Logos, but is instead simply semiotic functioning. The precondition for such a heterogeneity that alone posits and removes historical meaning is the thetic phase: we cannot overemphasize this point.

Without the completion of the thetic phase, we repeat, no signifying practice is possible; the negation/denial [*dénégation*] of this phase leads the subject to shift the thetic, even though he is determined by it, on to one of the places that the signifying process must cross on its way to fulfilment. Negating or denying the symbolic, without which he would be incapable of doing anything, the subject may imagine the thetic at the place of an object or a partner. This is a fetishist mechanism, which consists in denying the mother's castration, but perhaps goes back even further to a problem in separating an image of the ego in the mirror from the bodily organs invested with semiotic motility. Negation-as-denial (*Verneinung*) or disavowal (*Verleugnung*) in perversion, which may go so far as the foreclosure (*Verwerfung*) of the thetic phase, represent different modalities capable of obscuring castration and the sexual difference underlying it as well as genital sexuality. Further on we shall see how a marked investment in anal eroticism leads to this rejection of the thetic because it allows a questioning of the symbolic order; but by this very process it shifts the *thesis* onto *objects*. The prototype of such objects is excrement since it is midway between an auto-erotic body, which is not yet autonomous from its eroticized sphincters, and the pleasure the mother's body or her supposed phallus would procure – a belief that is disclaimed but maintained, behind, as a compromise.

Since there can be no signifying practice without a thetic phase, the thetic that does not manage to posit itself in the symbolic order necessarily places itself in the objects surrounding the body and instinctually linked to it. Fetishism is a compromise with the thetic; although erased from the symbolic and displaced on to the drives, a 'thesis' is nevertheless maintained so that signifying practice can take place. Therefore we shall contend that it is the thetic, and not fetishism, that is inherent in every cultural production, because fetishism is a displacement of thetic on to the realm of drives. The instinctual *chora* articulates facilitations and stases, but fetishism is a telescoping of the symbolic's characteristic thetic moment and of one of those instinctually invested stases (bodies, parts of bodies, orifices, containing objects, and so forth). This stasis thus becomes the ersatz of the sign. Fetishism is a stasis that acts as a thesis.

We might then wonder whether the semiotic's dismantling of the symbolic in poetry necessarily implies that the thetic phase is shifted towards the stases of the semiotic *chora*. Doesn't poetry lead to the establishment of an object as a substitute for the symbolic order under attack, an object that is never clearly *posited* but always 'in perspective'?[60] The object may be either the body proper or the apparatuses erotized during vocal utterance (the glottis, the lungs), objects that are either linked to the addressee of desire or to the very material of language as the predominant object of pleasure. Moreover, since the symbolic is corrupted so that an object – the book, the work – will result, isn't this object a substitute for the thetic phase? Doesn't it take the thetic's place by making its symbolicity opaque, by filling the thetic with its presence whose pretension to universality is matched only by its very finite limits? In short, isn't art the fetish *par excellence*, one that badly camouflages its archaeology? At its base, isn't there a belief, ultimately maintained, that the mother is phallic, that the ego – never precisely identified – will never separate from her, and that no symbol is strong enough to sever this dependence? In this symbiosis with the supposedly phallic mother, what can the subject do but occupy her place, thus navigating the path from fetishism to auto-eroticism? That indeed is the question.

In order to keep the process signifying, to avoid foundering in an 'unsayable' without limits, and thus posit the subject of a practice, the subject of poetic language clings to the help fetishism offers. And so, according to psychoanalysis, poets as individuals fall under the category of fetishism; the very practice of art necessitates reinvesting the maternal *chora* so that it transgresses the symbolic order; and, as a result, this practice easily lends itself to so-called perverse subjective structures. For all these reasons, the poetic function therefore converges with fetishism; it is not, however, identical to it. What distinguishes the poetic function from the fetishist mechanism is that it maintains a *signification* (*Bedeutung*). All its paths into, indeed valorizations of, pre-symbolic semiotic stases not only require the ensured maintenance of this signification but also serve signification, even when they dislocate it. No text, no matter how 'musicalized', is devoid of meaning or signification; on the contrary, musicalization pluralizes meanings. We may say therefore that the text is not a fetish. It is, moreover, just like 'natural' language in this regard, if the abstract word is thought of as a correlate for the fetish in primitive societies. The text is completely different from a fetish because it *signifies*; in other words, it is not a *substitute* but a *sign* (signifier/signified), and its semantics is unfurled in sentences.[61] The text signifies the un-signifying: it assumes [*relève*] within a signifying practice this functioning (the semiotic), which ignores meaning and operates before meaning or despite it. Therefore it cannot be said that everything signifies, nor that everything is 'mechanistic'. In opposition to such dichotomies, whether 'materialist' or 'metaphysical', the text offers itself as the dialectic of two heterogeneous operations that are, reciprocally and inseparable, preconditions for each other.[62]

We understand, then, that this heterogeneity between the semiotic and the symbolic cannot be reduced to computer theory's well-known distinction between 'analog' and 'digital'.[63] An analog computer is defined as any device that "computes" by means of an analog between real, physical, *continuous* quantities and some other set of variables', whereas the digital computer presupposes '*discrete* elements and discontinuous scales'.[64] Certain linguists have wanted to transpose this distinction – which arose with the development of computers and perhaps applies to 'natural' codes (nerve cell codes or animal communication, for example) – on to the functioning of language. But in making this transposition, one quickly forgets not only that language is simultaneously 'analog' and 'digital' but that it is, above all, a doubly articulated system (signifier and signified), which is precisely what distinguishes it from *codes*. We therefore maintain that what we call the semiotic can be described as both analog and digital: the functioning of the semiotic *chora* is made up of continuities that are segmented in order to organize a digital system as the *chora*'s guarantee of survival (just as digitality is the means of survival both for the living cell and society);[65] the stases marked by the facilitation of the drives are the discrete elements in this digital system, indispensable for maintaining the semiotic *chora*.

Yet this description (which itself is possible only on the basis of a highly developed symbolic system) does not account for what produces the *qualitative leap* between a code and a double articulation.[66] But this essential phase is precisely what we are examining when we distinguish between the semiotic and the symbolic, and when we assign the thetic phase the role of boundary between the two heterogeneous domains. Because of the human being's prematurity, his semiotic 'code' is cut off from any possible identification unless it is assumed by the other (first the mother, then the symbolic and/or the social group). Making the analog digital is thus not enough to ensure our bodily survival because it cannot check the drives' endless facilitations. An *alteration* must be made, making the *other* the regulator between the semiotic *chora* and the totality called the *ecosystem*. This alteration makes it possible to gather together the analog and digital 'code' and, through a break prepared by the mirror stage posit it as unified, mastered, dominated and in another space – imaginary, representational, symbolic. Through this alteration, the 'code' leaves the place of the body and the eco-system and, freed from their constraints, acquires the variability characteristic of a system of 'arbitrary' signs – human language – the later development of which forms the immense edifice of signifying practices.

The *semiotic* (analog and digital) thereby assumes the role of a linguistic signifier signifying an *object* for an *ego*, thus constituting them both as thetic. Through its thetic, altering aspect, the signifier *represents* the subject – not the thetic ego but the very process by which it is posited. A signifier indebted in this manner to semiotic functioning tends to return to it. In all its various vacillations, the thetic is displaced towards the stages previous to its positing or within the very stases of the semiotic – in a particular element of the digital code or in a particular continuous portion of the analog code. These movements, which can be designated as fetishism, show (human) language's characteristic tendency to return to the (animal) code, thereby breaching what Freud calls a 'primal repression'. The thetic – that crucial place on the basis of which the human being constitutes himself as signifying and/or social – is the very place textual experience aims towards. In this sense, textual experience represents one of the most daring explorations the subject can allow himself, one that delves into his constitutive process. But at the same time and as a result, textual experience reaches the very foundation of the social – that which is exploited by sociality but which elaborates and can go beyond it, either destroying or trans-forming it.

10 THE SIGNIFYING PROCESS

Once the break instituting the symbolic has been established, what we have called the semiotic *chora* acquires a more precise status. Although originally a precondition of the symbolic, the semiotic functions within signifying practices as the result of a transgression of the symbolic. Therefore the semiotic that 'precedes' symbolization is only a *theoretical supposition* justified by the need for description. It exists in practice only within the symbolic and requires the symbolic break to obtain the complex articulation we associate with it in musical and poetic practices. In other words, symbolization makes possible the complexity of this semiotic combinatorial system, which only theory can isolate as 'preliminary' in order to specify its functioning. Nevertheless, the semiotic is not solely an abstract object produced for the needs of theory.

As a precondition of the symbolic, semiotic functioning is a fairly rudimentary combinatorial system, which will become more complex only after the break in the symbolic. It is, however, already put in place by a biological set-up and is always already social and therefore historical. This semiotic functioning is discernible before the mirror stage, before the first suggestion of the thetic. But the semiotic we find in signifying practices always comes to us after the symbolic thesis, after the symbolic break, and can be analysed in psychoanalytic discourse as well as in so-called 'artistic' practice. One could not, then, limit oneself to representing this semiotic functioning as simply 'analog' or 'digital' or as a mere scattering of traces. The thetic gathers up these facilitations and instinctual semiotic stases within the positing of signifiers, then opens them out in the three-part cluster of referent, signified and signifier, which alone makes the enunciation of a truth possible. In taking the thetic into account, we shall have to represent the semiotic (which is produced recursively on the basis of that break) as a 'second' return of instinctual functioning within the symbolic, as a negativity introduced into the symbolic order and as the transgression of that order.

This transgression appears as a breach [*effraction*] subsequent to the thetic phase, which makes that phase negative and tends to fuse the layers of signifier/signified/referent into a network of traces, following the facilitation of the drives. Such a breach does not constitute a positing. It is not at all thetic, nor is it an *Aufhebung* of 'original doxy' through a synthesizing spiral movement and within the pursuit of the exhaustion of truth undertaken by Hegelian absolute knowledge. On the contrary, the transgression breaks up the thetic, splits it, fills it with empty spaces and uses its device only to remove the 'residues of first symbolizations' and make them 'reason' ['*raisonner*'] within the symbolic chain. This explosion of the semiotic in the symbolic is far from a negation of negation, an *Aufhebung* that would suppress the contradiction generated by the thetic and establish in its place an ideal positivity, the restorer of pre-symbolic immediacy.[67] It is, instead, a *transgression* of position, a reversed reactivation of the contradiction that instituted this very position.

The proof is that this negativity has a tendency to suppress the thetic phase, to de-syn-thesize it. In the extreme, negativity aims to foreclose the thetic phase, which, after a period of explosive semiotic motility, may result in the loss of the symbolic function, as seen in schizophrenia.

'Art', on the other hand, by definition, does not relinquish the thetic even while pulverizing it through the negativity of transgression. Indeed, this is the only means of transgressing the thetic, and the difficulty of maintaining the symbolic function under the assault of negativity indicates the risk that textual practice represents for the subject. What had seemed to be a process of fetishizing inherent in the way the text functions now seems a structurally necessary protection, one that serves to check negativity, confine it within stases and prevent it from sweeping away the symbolic position.

The regulation of the semiotic in the symbolic through the thetic break, which is inherent in the operation of language, is also found on the various levels of a society's signifying edifice. In all known archaic societies, this founding break of the symbolic order is represented by murder – the killing of a man, a slave, a prisoner, an animal. Freud reveals this founding break and generalizes from it when he emphasizes that society is founded on a complicity in the common crime.[68] We indicated earlier how language, already as a semiotic *chora* but above all as a symbolic system, is at the service of the death drive, diverts it and confines it as if within an isolated pocket of narcissism. The social order, for its part, reveals this confinement of the death drive, whose endless course conditions and moves through every stasis and thus every structure, in an act of murder. Religions, as we know, have set themselves up as specialists on the discourse concerning this radical, unique, thetic event.

Opposite religion or alongside it, 'art' takes on murder and moves through it. It assumes murder in so far as artistic practice considers death the inner boundary of the signifying process. Crossing that boundary is precisely what constitutes 'art'. In other words, it is as if death becomes interiorized by the subject of such a practice; in order to function, he must make himself the bearer of death. In this sense, the artist is comparable to all other figures of the 'scapegoat'. But he is not just a scapegoat; in fact, what makes him an artist radically distinguishes him from all other sacrificial murderers and victims.[69]

In returning, through the event of death, towards that which produces its break; in exporting semiotic motility across the border on which the symbolic is established, the artist sketches out a kind of second birth. Subject to death but also to rebirth, his function becomes harnessed, immobilized, represented and idealized by religious systems (most explicitly by Christianity), which shelter him in their temples, pagodas, mosques and churches. Through themes, ideologies and social meanings, the artist introduces into the symbolic order an asocial drive, one not yet harnessed by the thetic. When this practice, challenging any stoppage, comes up, in its turn, against the produced object, it sets itself up as a substitute for the initially contested thetic, thus giving rise to the aesthetic fetishism and narcissism supplanting theology.

12 GENOTEXT AND PHENOTEXT

In light of the distinction we have made between the semiotic *chora* and the symbolic, we may now examine the way texts function. What we shall call a *genotext* will include semiotic processes but also the advent of the symbolic. The former includes drives, their disposition and their division of the body, plus the ecological and social system surrounding the body, such as objects and pre-Oedipal relations with parents. The latter encompasses the emergence of object and subject, and the constitution of nuclei of meaning involving categories: semantic and categorial fields. Designating the genotext in a text requires pointing out the transfers of drive energy that can be detected in phonematic devices (such as the accumulation and repetition of phonemes or rhyme) and melodic devices (such as intonation or rhythm), in the way semantic and categorial fields are set out in syntactic and logical features, or in the economy of mimesis (fantasy, the deferment of denotation, narrative, etc.). The genotext is thus the only transfer of drive energies that organizes a space in which the subject is not *yet* a split unity that will become blurred, giving rise to the symbolic. Instead, the space it organizes is one in which the subject will be *generated* as such by a process of facilitations and marks within the constraints of the biological and social structure.

In other words, even though it can be seen in language, the genotext is not linguistic (in the sense understood by structural or generative linguistics). It is, rather, a *process*, which tends to articulate structures that are ephemeral (unstable, threatened by drive charges, 'quanta', rather than 'marks') and non-signifying (devices that do not have a double articulation). It forms these structures out of: (a) instinctual dyads, (b) the corporeal and ecological continuum, (c) the social organism and family structures, which convey the constraints imposed by the mode of production, and (d) matrices of enunciation, which give rise to discursive 'genres' (according to literary history), 'psychic structures' (according to psychiatry and psychoanalysis) or various arrangements of 'the participants in the speech event' (in Jakobson's notion of the linguistics of discourse).[70] We may posit that the matrices of enunciation are the result of the repetition of drive charges (a) within biological, ecological and socio-familial constraints (b and c), and the stabilization of their facilitation into stases whose surrounding structure accommodates and leaves its mark on symbolization.

The genotext can thus be seen as language's underlying foundation. We shall use the term *phenotext* to denote language that serves to communicate, which linguistics describes in terms of 'competence' and 'performance'. The phenotext is constantly split up and divided, and is irreducible to the semiotic process that works through the genotext. The phenotext is a structure (which can be generated, in generative grammar's sense); it obeys rules of communication and presupposes a subject of enunciation and an addressee. The genotext, on the other hand, is a process; it moves through zones that have relative and transitory borders and constitutes a *path* that is not restricted to the two poles of univocal information between two fully fledged subjects. If these two terms – genotext and phenotext – could be translated into a metalanguage that would convey the difference between them, one might say that the genotext is a matter of topology, whereas the phenotext is one of algebra. This distinction may be illustrated by a particular signifying system: written and spoken Chinese, particularly classical Chinese. Writing represents-articulates the signifying process into specific networks or spaces; *speech* (which may correspond to that writing) restores the diacritical elements necessary for an exchange of meaning between two subjects (temporality, aspect, specification of the pro- tagonists, morpho-semantic identifiers, and so forth).[71]

The signifying process therefore includes both the genotext and the phenotext; indeed it could not do otherwise. For it is in language that all signifying operations are realized (even when linguistic material is not used), and it is on the basis of language that a theoretical approach may attempt to perceive that operation.

In our view, the process we have just described accounts for the way all signifying practices are generated.[72] But every signifying practice does not encompass the infinite totality of that process. Multiple con- straints – which are ultimately socio-political – stop the signifying process at one or another of the theses that it traverses; they knot it and lock it into a given surface or structure; they discard *practice* under fixed, fragmentary, symbolic *matrices*, the tracings of various social constraints that obliterate the infinity of the process: the phenotext is what conveys these obliterations. Among the capitalist mode of production's numerous signifying practices, only certain literary texts of the avant-garde (Mallarmé, Joyce) manage to cover the infinity of the process, that is, reach the semiotic *chora*, which modifies linguistic structures. It must be emphasized, however, that this total exploration of the signifying process generally leaves in abeyance the theses that are characteristic of the social organism, its structures and their political transformation: the text has a tendency to dispense with political and social signifieds.

It has only been in very recent years or in revolutionary periods that signifying practice has inscribed within the phenotext the plural, heterogeneous and contradictory process of signification encompassing the flow of drives, material discontinuity, political struggle and the pulverization of language.

Lacan has delineated four types of discourse in our society: that of the hysteric, the academic, the master and the analyst.[73] Within the perspective just set forth, we shall posit a different classification, which in certain respects, intersects these four Lacanian categories, and in others, adds to them. We shall distinguish between the following signi- fying practices: narrative, metalanguage, contemplation and text- practice.

Let us state from the outset that this distinction is only provisional and schematic, and that although it corresponds to actual practices, it interests us primarily as a didactic implement [*outil*] – one that will allow us to specify some of the modalities of signifying dispositions. The latter interest us to the extent that they give rise to different practices and are, as a consequence, more or less coded in modes of production. Of course narrative and contemplation could also be seen as devices stemming from (hysterical and obsessional) transference neurosis; and metalanguage and the text as practices allied with psychotic (paranoid and schizoid) economies.

NOTES

1 See Zellig Harris, *Mathematical Structures of Language* (New York: Interscience Publishers, 1968). See also Maurice Gross and André Lentin, *Introduction to Formal Grammars*, tr. M. Salkoff (Berlin: Springer-Verlag, 1970); M.-C. Barbault and J.-P. Desclés, *Transformations formelles et théories linguistiques*, Documents de linguistique quantitative, no. 11 (Paris: Dunod, 1972).

2 On this 'object' see *Langages*, 24 (Dec. 1971), and, for a didactic, popularized account, see Julia Kristeva, *Le Langage cet inconnu* (Paris: Seuil 1981).

3 Edmund Husserl, in *Ideas: General Introduction to Pure Phenomenology*, tr. W. R. Boyce Gibson (London: Allen & Unwin, 1969), posits this subject as a subject of intuition, sure of this universally valid unity (of consciousness), a unity that is provided in *categories* itself, since transcendence is precisely the immanence of this 'Ego', which is an expansion of the Cartesian *cogito*. 'We shall consider conscious experiences'. Husserl writes, '*in the concrete fullness and entirety* with which they figure in their concrete context – the *stream of experience* – and to which they are closely attached through their own proper essence. It then becomes evident that every experience in the stream which our reflexion can lay hold on has *its own essence open to intuition*, a "content" which can be considered in its *singularity in and for itself*. We shall be concerned to grasp this individual content of the *cogitatio* in its *pure* singularity, and to describe it in its general features, excluding everything which is not to be found in the *cogitatio* as it is in itself. We must likewise describe the *unity of consciousness* which is demanded *by the intrinsic nature of the cogitationes*, and so necessarily demanded that they could not be without this unity' (p. 116). From a similar perspective, Benveniste emphasizes language's dialogical character, as well as its role in Freud's discovery. Discussing the I/you polarity, he writes: 'This polarity does not mean either equality or symmetry: "ego" always has a position of transcendence with regard to *you*.' in Benveniste, 'Subjectivity in language', *Problems in General Linguistics*, Miami Linguistics Series, no. 8, tr. Mary Elizabeth Meek (Coral Gables, Fla: University of Miami Press, 1971), p. 225. In Chomsky, the subject-bearer of syntactic synthesis is clearly shown to stem from the Cartesian *cogito*. See his *Cartesian Linguistics: a chapter in the history of rationalist thought* (New York: Harper & Row, 1966). Despite the difference between this Cartesian-Chomskyan subject and the transcendental ego outlined by Benveniste and others in a more clearly phenomenological sense, both these notions of the act of

understanding (or the linguistic act) rest on a common metaphysical foundation: consciousness as a synthesizing unity and the sole guarantee of Being. Moreover, several scholars – without renouncing the Cartesian principles that governed the first syntactic descriptions – have recently pointed out that Husserlian phenomenology is a more explicit and more rigorously detailed basis for such description than the Cartesian method. See Roman Jakobson, who recalls Husserl's role in the establishment of modern linguistics, 'Linguistics in relation to other sciences', in *Selected Writings* (2 vols, The Hague: Mouton, 1971), vol. II, pp. 655–96; and S.-Y. Kuroda, 'The categorical and the thetic judgement: evidence from Japanese syntax', *Foundations of Language* (Nov. 1972), 9, no. 2, pp. 153–85.

4 See the work of Ivan Fónagy, particularly 'Bases pulsionnelles de la phonation'. *Revue Française de Psychanalyse*, 34, no. 1 (January 1970), pp. 101–36, and 35, no. 4 (July 1971), pp. 543–91.

5 On the 'subject of enunciation', see Tzvetan Todorov, spec. ed. *Langages*, 17 (March 1970). Formulated in linguistics by Benveniste ('The correlations of tense in the French verb' and 'Subjectivity in language', in *Problems*, pp. 205–16 and 223–30), the notion is used by many linguists, notably Antoine Culioli, 'A propos d'opérations intervenant dans le traitement formel des langues naturelles', *Mathématiques et Sciences Humaines*, 9, no. 34 (Summer 1971), pp. 7–15; and Oswald Ducrot, 'Les indéfinis et l'énonciation'. *Langages*, 5, no. 17 (March 1970), pp. 91–111. Chomsky's 'extended standard theory' makes use of categorial intuition but does not refer to the subject of enunciation, even though the latter has been implicit in his theory ever since *Cartesian Linguistics* (1966); see his *Studies on Semantics in Generative Grammar*, Janua Linguarum, series minor, no. 107 (The Hague: Mouton, 1972).

6 See John R. Searle, *Speech Acts: an essay on the philosophy of language* (London: Cambridge University Press, 1969).

7 See Robert D. King, *Historical Linguistics and Generative Grammar* (Englewood Cliffs, NJ: Prentice-Hall, 1969); Paul Kiparsky, 'Linguistic universals and linguistic change', in *Universals of Linguistic Theory*, ed. Emmon Bach and Robert T. Harms (New York: Holt, Rinehart & Winston, 1968), pp. 170–292; and Kiparsky, 'How abstract is phonology?', mimeograph reproduced by Indiana University Linguistics Club, Oct. 1968.

8 S.-Y. Kuroda distinguishes between two styles, 'reportive' and 'non-reportive', 'Reportive' includes first-person narratives as well as those in the second and third person in which the narrator is 'effaced'; 'non-reportive' involves an omniscient narrator or 'multi-consciousness'. This distinction explains certain anomalies in the distribution of the adjective and verb of sensation in Japanese. (Common usage requires that the adjective be used with the first person but it can also refer to the third person. When it does, this agrammaticality signals another 'grammatical style': an omniscient narrator is speaking in the name of a character, or the utterance expresses a character's point of view.) No matter what its subject of enunciation, the utterance, Muroda writes, is described as representing that subject's *'Erlebnis'* ('experience'), in the sense Husserl uses the term in *ideas*. See Kuroda, 'Where epistemology, style, and grammar meet', mimeographed, University of California, San Diego, 1971.

9 Even the categories of dialectical materialism introduced to designate a discourse's conditions of production as essential bestowers of its signification are based on a 'subject-bearer' whose logical positing is no different from that found in Husserl (see above, n. 3). For example, Cl. Haroche, P. Henry and Michel Pêcheux stress 'the importance of linguistic studies on the relation between utterance and enunciation, by which the "speaking subject" situates himself with respect to the representations he *bears* – representations that are put together by means of the linguistically analyzable 'pre-constructed'''. They conclude that 'it is undoubtedly on this point – together with that of the syntagmatization of the characteristic substitutions of a discursive formation – that the contribution of the theory of discourse to the study of ideological formation (and the theory of ideologies) can now be most fruitfully developed'. 'La Sémantique et la coupure saussurienne: langue, langage, discours', *Langages*, 24 (Dec. 1971), p. 106. This notion of the subject as always already there on the basis of a 'pre-constructed' language (but how is it constructed? and what about the subject *who constructs* before *bearing* what has been constructed?') has even been preserved under a Freudian cover. As a case in point, Michel Tort questions the relation between psychoanalysis and historical materialism by placing a subject-bearer between 'ideological agency' and 'unconscious formations'. He defines this subject-bearer as 'the biological specificity of individuals (individuality as a biological concept), inasmuch as it is the material basis upon which individuals are called to function by social relations'. 'La psychanalyse dans le matérialisme historique'. *Nouvelle Revue de Psychanalyse*, 2 (Spring 1970), p. 154. But this theory provides only a hazy view of how this subject-bearer is produced through the unconscious and within the 'ideological' signifier, and does not allow us to see this production's investment in ideological representations themselves. From this perspective, the only thing one can say about 'arts' or 'religions', for example, is that they are 'relics'. On language and history, see also Jean-Claude Chevalier, 'Langage et histoire', *Langue Française*, 15 (Sept. 1972), pp. 3–17.

10 On the phenomenological bases of modern linguistics, see Kristeva, 'Les épistémologies de la linguistique', *Langages*, 24 (December 1971), p. 11; and especially: Jacques Derrida, 'The supplement of copula: philosophy before linguistics', in *Textual Strategies*, ed. and tr. Josué v. Harari (Ithaca, NY: Cornell University Press, 1979), pp. 82–120; *Of Grammatology*, tr. Gayatri Chakravorty Spivak (Baltimore, Md: Johns Hopkins University Press, 1976), pp. 27–73; and *Speech and Phenomena, and Other Essays on Husserl's Theory of Signs*, introd. and tr. David B. Allison (Evanston, Ill.: Northwestern University Press, 1973).

11 The term *'chora'* has recently been criticized for its ontological essence by Jacques Derrida: *Positions*. annot. and tr. Alan Bass (Chicago: University of Chicago Press, 1981), pp. 75 and 106, n. 39.

12 Plato emphasizes that the receptacle ($\dot{v}\pi o\delta o\chi\epsilon\tilde{\iota}ov$), which is also called space ($\chi\tilde{\omega}\varrho\alpha$) vis-à-vis reason, is necessary – but not divine since it is unstable, uncertain, ever changing and becoming; it is even unnameable, improbable, bastard: 'Space, which is everlasting, not admitting destruction; providing a situation for all things that come into being but itself apprehended without the senses by a sort of bastard reasoning, and hardly an object of belief. This, indeed, is that which we look upon

as in a dream and say that anything that is must needs be in some place and occupy some room...' (*Timaeus*, tr. Francis M. Cornford, 52a–52b). Is the receptacle a 'thing' or a mode of language? Plato's hesitation between the two gives the receptacle an even more uncertain status. It is one of the elements that antedate not only the *universe* but also *names* and even *syllables*. 'We speak...positing them as original principles, elements (as it were, letters) of the universe; whereas one who has ever so little intelligence should not rank them in this analogy even so low as syllables' (ibid., 48b). 'It is hard to say, with respect to any one of these, which we ought to call really water rather than fire, or indeed which we should call by any given name rather than by all the names together or by each severally, so as to use language in a sound and trustworthy way...Since, then, in this way no one of these things ever makes its appearance as the *same* thing, which of them can we steadfastly affirm to be *this* – whatever it may be – and not something else, without blushing for ourselves? It cannot be done' (ibid., 49b–d).

13 There is a fundamental ambiguity: on the one hand, the receptacle is mobile and even contradictory, without unity, separable and divisible: pre-syllable, pre-word. Yet, on the other hand, because this separability and divisibility antecede numbers and forms, the space or receptacle is called *amorphous*: thus its suggested rhythmicity will in a certain sense be erased, for how can one think an articulation of what is not yet singular but is nevertheless necessary? All we may say of it, then, to make it intelligible, is that it is amorphous but that it 'is of such and such a quality', not even an index or something in particular ('this' or 'that'). Once named, it immediately becomes a container that takes the place of infinitely repeatable separability. This amounts to saying that this repeated separability is 'ontologized' the moment a *name* or a *word* replaces it, making it intelligible. 'Are we talking idly whenever we say that there is such a thing as an intelligible Form of anything? Is this nothing more than a word?' (ibid., 51c). Is the Platonic *chora* the 'nominability' of rhythm (of repeated separation)?

Why then borrow an ontologized term in order to designate an articulation that antecedes positing? First, the Platonic term makes explicit an insurmountable problem for discourse: once it has been named, that functioning, even if it is pre-symbolic, is brought back into a symbolic position. All discourse can do is differentiate, by means of a 'bastard reasoning', the receptacle from the motility, which, by contrast, is not posited as being 'a *certain* something' ['une *telle*']. Secondly, this motility is the precondition for symbolicity, heterogeneous to it, yet indispensable. Therefore what needs to be done is to try to differentiate, always through a 'bastard reasoning', the specific arrangements of this motility, without seeing them as recipients of accidental singularities, or a *Being* always posited in itself, or a projection of the *One*. Moreover, Plato invites us to differentiate in this fashion when he describes this motility, while gathering it into the receiving membrane. 'But because it was filled with powers that were neither alike nor evenly balanced, there was no equipoise in any region of it, but it was everywhere swayed unevenly and shaken by these things and by its motion shook them in turn. And they, being thus moved, were perpetually being separated and carried in different directions, just as when things are shaken and winnowed by means of winnowing baskets and other instruments for cleaning corn...it separated the most unlike kinds farthest apart from one another, and thrust the most alike closest together: whereby the different kinds came to have different regions, even before the ordered whole consisting of them came to be...but were altogether in such a condition as we should expect for anything when deity is absent from it' (ibid., 52d–53b). Indefinite 'conjunctions' and 'disjunctions' (functioning, devoid of Meaning), the *chora* is governed by a necessity that is not God's law.

14 The Platonic space or receptacle is a mother and wet nurse: 'Indeed we may fittingly compare the Recipient to a mother, the model to a father, and the nature that arises between them to their offspring' (ibid., 50d); 'Now the wet nurse of Becoming was made watery and fiery, received the characters of earth and air, and was qualified by all the other affections that go with these...'ibid., 52d; translation modified.

15 'Law', which derives etymologically from *lex*, necessarily implies the act of judgement whose role in safeguarding society was first developed by the Roman law courts. 'Ordering', on the other hand, is closer to the series 'rule', 'norm' (from the Greek $\gamma\nu\omega\mu\omega\nu$, meaning 'discerning' [adj.], 'carpenter's square' [noun]), etc., which implies a numerical or geometrical necessity. On normativity in linguistics, see Alain Rey, 'Usages, jugements et prescriptions linguistiques', *Langue Française*, 16 (Dec. 1972), p. 5. But the temporary ordering of the *chora* is not yet even a *rule*: the arsenal of geometry is posterior to the *chora*'s motility; it fixes the *chora* in place and reduces it.

16 Operations are, rather, an act of the subject of understanding. [Hans G. Furth, in *Piaget and Knowledge: theoretical foundations* (Englewood Cliffs, NJ; Prentice-Hall, 1969), offers the following definition of 'concrete operations': 'Characteristic of the first stage of operational intelligence. A concrete operation implies underlying general systems or "groupings" such as classification, seriation, number. Its applicability is limited to objects considered as real (concrete)' (p. 260) – Tr.]

17 Piaget stresses that the roots of sensorimotor operations precede language and that the acquisition of thought is due to the symbolic function, which, for him, is a notion separate from that of language *per se*. See Jean Piaget, 'Language and symbolic operations', in *Piaget and Knowledge*, pp. 121–30.

18 By 'function' we mean a dependent variable determined each time the independent variables with which it is associated are determined. For our purposes, a function is what links stases within the process of semiotic facilitation.

19 Such a position has been formulated by Lipot Szondi, *Experimental Diagnostic of Drives*, tr. Gertrude Aull (New York: Grune & Stratton, 1952).

20 See James D. Watson, *The Double Helix: a personal account of the discovery of the structure of DNA* (London: Weidenfeld & Nicolson, 1968).

21 Throughout her writings, Melanie Klein emphasizes the 'pre-Oedipal' phase, i.e., a period of the subject's development that precedes the 'discovery' of castration and the positing of the superego, which itself is a subject to (paternal) Law. The processes she describes for this phase correspond, *but on a genetic level*, to what we call the semiotic, as opposed to the symbolic, which underlies and conditions the semiotic. Significantly, these pre-Oedipal processes are organized through projection on to the mother's body, for girls as well as for boys: 'at this stage of development children of both sexes believe that it is the body of their mother which contains all that is desirable, especially their father's penis'', *The Psycho-analysis*

of Children, tr. Alix Strachey (London: Hogarth Press, 1932), p. 269. Our own view of this stage is as follows: Without 'believing' or 'desiring' any 'object' whatsoever, the subject is in the process of constituting himself vis-à-vis a non-object. He is in the process of separating from this non-object so as to make that non-object 'one' and posit himself as 'other': the mother's body is the not-yet-one that the believing and desiring subject will image as a 'receptacle'.

22 As for what situates the mother in symbolic space, we find the phallus again (see Jacques Lacan, 'La relation d'objet et les structures freudiennes', *Bulletin de Psychologie*, April 1957, pp. 426–30), represented by the mother's father, i.e., the subject's maternal grandfather (see Marie-Claire Boons, 'Le meurtre du Père chez Freud', *L'Inconscient*, 5, Jan.–March 1968, pp. 101–29.

23 Though disputed and inconsistent, the Freudian theory of drives is of interest here because of the predominance Freud gives to the death drive in both 'living matter' and the 'human being'. The death drive is transversal to identity and tends to disperse 'narcissisms' whose constitution ensures the link between structures and, by extension, life. But at the same time and conversely, narcissism and pleasure are only temporary positions from which the death drive blazes new paths [*se fraye de nouveaux passages*]. Narcissism and pleasure are therefore inveiglings and realizations of the death drive. The semiotic *chora*, converting drive discharges into stases, can be thought of both as a delaying of the death drive and as a possible realization of this drive, which tends to return to a homeostatic state. This hypothesis is consistent with the following remark: 'at the beginning of mental life', writes Freud, 'the struggle for pleasure was far more intense than later but not so unrestricted: it had to submit to frequent interruptions,' *Beyond the Pleasure Principle*, in *The Standard Edition of the Works of Sigmund Freud*, ed. James Strachey (London: Hogarth Press and the Institute of Psychoanalysis, 1953), vol. XVIII, p. 63.

24 Mallarmé, *OEuvres complètes* (Paris: Gallimard, 1945), pp. 382–87.

25 Ibid., p. 383.

26 Ibid., pp. 383 and 385.

27 Ibid., pp. 385–86.

28 Husserl, *Ideas*, p. 342.

29 In *Ideas*, posited meaning is 'the unity of meaning and thetic character'. 'The concept of proposition (*Satz*)', Husserl writes, 'is certainly extended thereby in an exceptional way that may alienate sympathy, yet it remains within the limits of an important unity of essence. We must constantly bear in mind that for us the concepts of meaning (*Sinn*) and posited meaning (or position) (*Satz*) contain nothing of the nature of expression and conceptual meaning, but on the other hand include all explicit propositions and all propositional meanings' (*Ideas*, p. 369). Further on, the inseparability of posited meaning, meaning and the object is even more clearly indicated: 'According to our analyses these concepts indicate an abstract stratum belonging to the *full tissue of all noemata* [emphasis added]. To grasp this stratum in its all-enveloping generality, and thus to realize that it is represented in *all act-spheres*, has a wide bearing on our way of knowledge. Even in the plain and simple *intuitions* the concepts meaning (*Sinn*) and posited meaning (*Satz*) which belong inseparably to the concept of object (*Gegenstand*) have their necessary application... (pp. 369–70).

30 On the matrix of the sign as the structure of a logical proof, see Emile Bréhier, *La Théorie des incorporels dans l'ancien stoicisme* (Paris: J. Vrin, 1970).

31 The fact is that the total form of the body by which the subject anticipates in a mirage the maturation of his power is given to him only as *Gestalt*, that is to say, in an exteriority in which this form is certainly more constituent than constituted, but in which it appears to him above all in a contrasting size (*un relief de stature*) that fixes it and in a symmetry that inverts it, in contrast with the turbulent movements that the subject feels are animating him.' Lacan, 'The mirror stage as formative of the function of the I', in *Ecrits: a selection*, tr. Alan Sheridan (New York: Norton, 1977), p. 2.

32 'The subversion of the subject and the dialectic of desire in the Freudian unconscious', *Ecrits: a selection*, p. 319.

33 In Lacan's terminology, castration and the phallus are defined as 'position', 'localization' and 'presence': 'We know that the unconscious castration complex has the function of a knot:...(2) in a regulation of the development that gives its *ratio* to this first role: namely, the *installation* in the subject of an unconscious *position* without which he would be unable to identify himself with the ideal type of his sex...' ('The signification of the phallus', *Ecrits: a selection*, p. 281; emphasis added). 'We know that in this term Freud specifies the first genital maturation: on the one hand, it would seem to be characterized by the imaginary dominance of the phallic attribute and by masturbatory *jouissance* and, on the other, it *localizes* this *jouissance* for the woman in the clitoris, which is thus raised to the function of the phallus' (p. 282; emphasis added). '[The phallus] is the signifier intended to *designate* as a whole the effects of the signified, in that the signifier conditions them by its *presence* as a signifier' (p. 285; emphasis added).

34 Lacan himself has suggested the term 'want-to-be' for his neologism (*manque à être*). Other proposed translations include 'want-of-being' (Leon S. Roudiez, personal communication) and 'constitutive lack' (Jeffrey Mehlman, 'The "floating signifier": from Lévi-Strauss to Lacan', *Yale French Studies*, 48, 1972, p. 37). – Tr.

35 *Ecrits: a selection*, p. 299.

36 Loc. cit.

37 Our definition of language as deriving from the death drive finds confirmation in Lacan: 'From the approach that we have indicated, the reader should recognize in the metaphor of the return to the inanimate (which Freud attaches to every living body) that margin beyond life that language gives to the human being by virtue of the fact that he speaks, and which is precisely that in which such a being places in the position of a signifier, not only those parts of his body that are exchangeable, but this body itself' ('The subversion of the subject and the dialectic of desire in the Freudian unconscious', *Ecrits: a selection*, p. 301). We would add that the symbolism of magic is based on language's capacity to store up the death drive by taking it out of the body. Lévi-Strauss suggests this when he writes that 'the relationship between monster and disease is internal to [the patient's] mind, whether conscious or unconscious: It is a relationship between symbol and thing symbolized, or, to use the terminology of linguists, between signifier and signified. The shaman provides the sick woman with a *language*, by means of which unexpressed and otherwise inexpressible psychic states can be immediately expressed. And it is the

transition to this verbal expression – at the same time making it possible to undergo in an ordered and intelligible form a real experience that would otherwise be chaotic and inexpressible – which induces the release of the physiological process, that is, the reorganization, in a favorable direction, of the process to which the sick woman is subjected.' 'The effectiveness of symbols', in *Structural Anthropology*, 1, pp. 197–8; translation modified.

38 See Lacan, 'On a question preliminary to any possible treatment of psychosis', in *Ecrits: a selection*, p. 197.

39 'The theory of textual writing's history may be termed "monumental history" in so far as it serves as a "ground" ['*fait fond*'] in a literal way, in relation to a "cursive", figural (teleological) history which has served at once to constitute and dissimulate a written/exterior space...Writing "that recognizes the rupture" is therefore irreducible to the classical (representational) concept of "written text": what it writes is never more than one part of itself. It makes the rupture the intersection of two sets (two irreconcilable states of language)', Philippe Sollers writes, 'Program', in *Writing and the Experience of Limits*, ed. David Hayman, tr. Philip Barnard and David Hayman (New York: Columbia University Press, 1983), p. 7. Our reading of Lautréamont and Mallarmé will attempt to follow these principles, see *La Révolution du langage poétique* (Paris: Seuil, 1974), pp. 361–609. [This is the first of many references to the latter portion of *La Révolution du langage poétique*, which has not been translated – tr.]

40 Indeed, even Lacanian theory, although it establishes the signifier as absolute master, makes a distinction between two modalities of the signifier represented by the two levels of the 'completed graph'(*Ecrits: a selection*, p. 314). On the one hand, the *signifier* as 'signifier's treasure', as distinct from the *code*, 'for it is not that the univocal correspondence of a sign with something is preserved in it, but that the signifier is constituted only from a synchronic and enumerable collection of elements in which each is sustained only by the principle of its opposition to each of the others' (p. 304). Drives function within this 'treasure of the signifiers' (p. 314), which is also called a signifying 'battery'. But from that level on, and even beforehand, the subject submits to the signifier, which is also shown as a 'punctuation in which the signification is constituted as finished product' (p. 304). In this way the path from the treasure to punctuation forms a 'previous site of the pure subject of the signifier', which is not yet, however, the true place [*lieu*] of the Other. On that level, the psychotic 'dance' unfolds, the 'pretence' [*feinte*] that 'is satisfied with that previous Other', accounted for by game theory. The fact remains that this *previous site* does not exhaust the question of signification because the subject is not constituted from the code that lies in the Other, but rather from the message emitted by the Other. Only when the Other is distinguished from all other partners, unfolding as signifier and signified – and, as a result, articulating himself within an always already sentential signification and thus transmitting messages – only then are the preconditions for language ('speech') present.

At this second stage, the signifier is not just a 'treasure' or a 'battery' but a *place* [lieu]: 'But it is clear that Speech begins only with the passage from "pretence" to the order of the signifier, and that the signifier requires another locus – the locus of the Other, the Other witness, the witness Other than any of the partners – for the Speech that it supports to be capable of lying, that is to say, of presenting itself as Truth' (p. 305). Only from this point will the ego start to take on varous configurations. What seems problematic about this arrangement, or in any case what we believe needs further development, is the way in which the 'battery', the 'treasure' of the signifier, functions. In our opinion, game theory cannot completely account for this functioning, nor can a signification be articulated until an alterity is *distinctly posited* as such. One cannot speak of the 'signifier' before the positing or the thesis of the Other, the articulation of which begins only with the mirror stage. But what of the previous processes that are not yet 'a site', but a *functioning*? The thetic phase will establish this functioning, as a signifying *order* (though it will not stop it) and will return in this order.

41 'On sense and reference', tr. Max Black, in *Translations from the Philosophical Writings of Gottlob Frege*, ed. Peter Geach and Max Black (New York: Philosophical Library, 1952), p. 65; emphasis added; translation modified. [To maintain consistency with Kristeva's terminology and with the French translations of Frege she cites, I have changed 'sense' to 'meaning' (*sens*) and 'reference' to 'denotation' (*dénotation*) throughout – Tr.] Indeed, analogous remarks can be found in Husserl: 'Every synthetically unitary consciousness, however many special theses and syntheses it may involve, possesses the *total object* which belongs to it as a synthetically *unitary* consciousness. We call it a total object in contrast with the objects which belong intentionally to the lower or higher grade members of the synthesis . . .' '[These] noetic experiences [have] a quite determinate essential content, over which, despite the endlessness, a proper oversight can still be kept, all the experiences agreeing in this that they are a consciousness of "the same" object. This *unanimity* is evidenced in the sphere of consciousness itself. . .' (*Ideas*, pp. 335 and 375; emphasis added).

42 'By combining subject and predicate, one reaches only a thought, never passes from meaning to denotation, never from a thought to its truth value. One moves at the same level but never advances from one level to the next. A truth value cannot be a part of a thought, any more than, say, the sun can, for it is not a meaning but an object.' Frege, 'On sense and reference', p. 64; translation modified.

43 Brentano, Venn, Bayn and Russell, among others, have argued the possibility of converting existential assertions into predicative assertions. Existence in this case is understood as the existence of a subject that has a predicate and not simply as an existence of the predicate within the subject. Frege clearly distinguishes the two levels: denotation as the existence of the logical subject as denoted object, meaning as the existence of a predicate for a subject (ibid., pp. 64–5).

44 'If now the truth value of a sentence is its denotation, then on the one hand all true sentences have the same denotation and so, on the other hand, do all false sentences.' Ibid., p. 65; translation modified.

45 'It may perhaps be granted that every grammatically well-formed expression representing a proper name always has a meaning.' Ibid., p. 58; translation modified.

46 The functioning of the verb 'to be' in several non-Indo European languages shows the course the signifying process follows before it posits an existence. In this respect, these languages are different from Greek and Indo-European languages in general, which unhesitatingly posit existence and thereby tend to make it a metaphysical category. (Heidegger and Benveniste, to name only two, thought they had proved the

complicity between the category of being and the verb 'to be'.) These languages lead us to identify semiotic *stages* or *modalities* that precede or take place within the thetic, but are distinct from existence: designation, accentuation, reminders of the unicity or the accuracy of the act of enunciating, and so forth. Thus, in modern Chinese, the 'illogical' functioning of *shi* ('to be') in its position as copula is resolved by supposing that, in most of these 'illogical' cases, 'to be' is simply a substitute for the verbal function *per se* and is called a 'pro-verb'. See Anne Yue Hashimoto, 'The Verb "To Be" in Modern Chinese', in *The Verb 'Be' and Its Synonyms: philosophical and grammatical studies*, ed. John W. M. Verhaar (Dordrecht, Holland: D. Reidel, 1969), pt 4, pp. 90ff. Since, as it could be shown, *shi* assumes the function of pro-verb in several cases other than those indicated by Hashimoto, we could say that its function is to indicate the logical moment of enunciation and denotation, to mark the *positing* of the act of enunciation-denotation and the relational *possibilities* deriving from it (before there is any affirmation of the existence of the subject or denoted object and their modalities). In our view, the *emphatic* function of *shi*, which is common in Chinese, as well as its semantic functions, such as those indicating the *accuracy* or the truth of the utterance, confirm this interpretation. We might add that *shi* was not used as a verb in classical Chinese until the second century. Before that time it was used solely as a *demonstrative*; only its negative form had a verbal function.

On the other hand, in Arabic, there is no verb 'to be'. Its function is filled – as translations from Arabic into Indo-European languages and vice versa show – by a series of morphemes. These include: the verb *kana* (with its two meanings, 'to exist' and 'to be such and such'), which indicates a genetic process and not something already in existence; the assertive particle, *inna* which means 'indeed'; the incomplete verb *laysa*, which is a negative copula; the third-person pronoun, *huwa*, which refers to an extra-allocutory moment but nevertheless ensures the unity of the discursive act and is, according to standard metaphysical intepretation, God; and finally, the verbal root *wjd*, which means 'to find', a localization that, by extension, indicates truth. See Fadlou Shedadi, 'Arabic and "To Be"', ibid., pp. 112–25.

In summary, semantically as well as syntactically, explicitly in these languages but implicitly in others (Indo-European languages, for example), 'to be' condenses the different modalities of the predicative function. The most fundamental of these modalities seems to be *position* (the thetic) or localization, from which the others – the enunciation of an existence, a truth, a spatio-temporal differentiation effected by the subject of enunciation, and so forth – derive. See John Lyons, 'A note on possessive, existential and locative sentences', *Foundations of Language*, 3 (1967), pp. 390–6; Charles H. Kahn, *The Verb 'Be' in Ancient Greek*, in *The Verb 'Be' and Its Synonyms*, suppl. series, vol. XVI, ed. John W. M. Verhaar (Dordrecht, Holland: D. Reidel, 1973).

47 On the predicative function as the foundation of a complete utterance, see Jerzy Kuryłowicz, *Esquisses linguistiques* (Wroclaw, Cracow: Zakład Narodowy Imienia Ossolinskich, Wydawnictwo Polskej Akademii Nauk, 1960), pp. 35ff.; S. K. Shaumyan and P. A. Soboleva, *Osnovanija porozdajuščej grammatiki ruskovo jazyka* [Foundations of generative grammar in Russian] (Moscow: Nauka, 1968). On this

same problem with respect to the utterance's relation to what is extra-linguistic, see Benveniste. 'The nominal sentence', in *Problems*, pp. 131–44; P. F. Strawson, *Individuals: an essay in descriptive metaphysics* (Garden City, New York: Doubleday, 1959; 1963).

48 Comparative linguistics generally used to consider the *verb* as the predominant element of language and as the one from which the *noun* derived. Generative linguistics revalorizes the *noun* by making it an essential component of deep structure, while including the *verb* in another no less essential component, the *predicate*. Some linguists tend to give the *noun* a determining role because it particularizes the utterance by giving it a concrete referent. From this point of view, predication is determinative only for the act of enunciation and only if it is completed by the *noun*. See Lyons, 'A note on possessive, existential and locative sentences'; Strawson, *Individuals*; and so forth. For others, the noun always appears under the 'nexus of the predicate', which follows the assertion of certain logicians (Russell, Quine) that every 'particular' is replaced by a variable linked to existential quantification.

We thus see that predication is defined as being coextensive with every act of naming. What we call a *thetic* function is none other than the speaking subject's positing of enunciation through a syntagm or proposition: the distinctions between noun and verb, etc., are posterior to this function and concern only the surface structure of certain languages. But we would emphasize that (logically) even *before* this distinction, enunciation is thetic, no matter what the morphology of the syntagms used, and that it is 'predicative' in the sense that it situates the act of the subject of enunciation with respect to the Other, in a space and time preceding any other particularization. This thetic (predicative) act is the *presupposition* of every simple nominal utterance, which, in its turn, will select a specific predicative morpheme. See C.-E. Bazell, 'Syntactic relations and linguistic typology', *Cahiers Ferdinand de Saussure* (1949), vol. VIII, pp. 5–20. On a genetic level, Benveniste observes a 'pre-inflectional period' of Indo-European in which the noun and the verb, 'set up on a common basis', are not differentiated. *Origines de la formation des noms en indo-européen* (Paris: Maisonneuve, 1935).

49 On the traumatizing object which hinders the positing of the thetic, see 'La transposition, le déplacement, la condensation', *La Révolution du langage poétique*, pp. 230–9.

50 See 'Le dispositif sémiotique du texte', ibid., pp. 209–358.

51 See 'Instances du discours et altération du sujet', ibid., pp. 315–35, where we establish that it is a non-recoverable deletion.

52 '*Effraction*', in French, is the juridical term for 'breaking and entering'; in Kristeva's sense it also means a 'breaking into' or 'breaking through'. I have translated it as 'breach'; the act or result of breaking and, more significantly, an infraction or violation as of a law – Tr.

53 It has recently been emphasized that *mimesis* is not an imitation of an object but a reproduction of the trajectory of enunciation; in other words, *mimesis* departs from denotation (in Frege's sense) and confines itself to meaning. Roland Barthes makes this explicit: 'The function of narrative is not to "represent", it is to constitute a spectacle still very enigmatic for us...Logic has here an emancipatory value – and with it the entire narrative. it may be that men ceaselessly re-inject into narrative what they have known, what they have experienced; but if they do, at least it is

in a form which has vanquished repetition and instituted the model of a process of becoming. Narrative does not show, does not imitate; the passion which may excite us in reading a novel is not that of a "vision" (in actual fact, we do not "see" anything). Rather it is that of meaning...; "what happens" is language alone, the adventure of language, the unceasing celebration of its coming.' Barthes, 'Introduction to the structuralist analysis of narratives', in *Image, Music, Text*, tr. Stephen Heath (New York: Hill & Wang, 1977), pp. 123–4. This is also what Goethe means when he writes: 'In your own mode of rhyme my feet I'll find./ The repetitions of pleasures shall incite:/ At first the sense and then the words I'll find [*Erst werd ich Sinn, sodann auch Worte finden*]. No sound a second time will I indite/ Unless thereby the meaning is refined/ As you, with peerless gifts, have shown aright!' But this analysis of meaning through sounds must result in a new device that is not just a new meaning but also a new 'form': 'Measured rhythms are indeed delightful./ And therein a pleasing talent basks;/ But how quickly they can taste so frightful./ There's no blood nor sense in hollow masks [*Hohle Masken ohne Blut und Sinn*]./ Even wit must shudder at such tasks/ If it can't, with new form occupied/ Put an end at last to form that's died.' 'Imitation' [*Nachbildung*], *West-Eastern Divan/West-Oestlicher Divan*. tr. J. Whaley (London: Oswald Wolff, 1974), pp. 34–7.

54 This is why Lacan stated in his spring 1972 seminar that the expression '*Die Bedeutung des Phallus*' is a tautology.

55 See Jakobson, 'L'importanza di Kruszewski per lo sviluppo della linguistica generale'. *Ricerche Slavistiche* (1967), 14, pp. 1–20.

56 See Lacan, *Ecrits: a selection*, pp. 156–7 and passim.

57 See Kristeva, *Le Texte du roman: approche sémiologique d'une structure discursive transformationnelle* (The Hague: Mouton, 1970).

58 'We have not yet referred to any other sort of displacement [*Verschiebung*]. Analyses show us, however, that another sort exists and that it reveals itself in a change in the *verbal expression* of the thoughts concerned... One element is replaced by another [*ein Element seine Wortfassung gegen eine andere vertauscht*]... Any one thought, whose form of expression may happen to be fixed for other reasons, will operate in a determinant and selective manner on the possible forms of expression allotted to the other thoughts, and it may do so, perhaps, from the very start – as is the case in writing a poem [*Der eine Gedanke, dessen Ausdruck etwa aus anderen Gründen feststeht, wird dabei verteilend und auswählend auf die Ausdrucksmöglichkeiten des anderen einwirken, und dies vielleicht von vorneherein, ähnlich wie bei der Arbeit des Dichters*].' *The Interpretation of Dreams*. *Standard Edition*, vol. V, pp. 339–40; *Gesammelte Werke* (London: Imago, 1942), vol. II–III, pp. 344–5. See 'La transposition, le déplacement, la condensation', *La Révolution du langage poetique*, pp. 230–9.

59 Goethe speaks of this when, describing the Arabic tradition, he calls to mind the poet whose role is to express 'Undeniable truth indelibly:/ But there are some small points here and there/ Which exceed the limits of the law [*Ausgemachte Wahreit unauslöschlich:/ Aber hie und da auch Kleinigkeiten/ Ausserhalb der Grenze des Gesetzes*].' 'Fetwa', *West-Eastern Divan*, pp. 30–3.

60 'Yet this "object of perspective" may be handled in different ways. In fetishism (and, in my view, in art works), it pushes itself into the great ambiguous realm of disavowal, and materializes... As a result, we see... that all scientific or esthetic

observation or activity has a part to play in the fate reserved for the "perspective object"', writes Guy Rosolato, 'Le fétishisme dont se "dérobe" l'objet', *Nouvelle Revue de Psychanalyse*, 2 (Autumn 1970), p. 39. [For a more complete account of this concept in English, see Rosolato, 'Symbol formation', *International Journal of Psychanalysis*, 59, 1978, pp. 303–13 – Tr.]

61 As Jean Pouillon remarks, 'if words were merely fetishes, Semantics would be reduced to phonology', 'Fétiches sans fétichisme', *Nouvelle Revue de Psychanalyse*, 2 (Autumn 1970), p. 147.

62 By contrast, discourse in Molière's 'Femmes savantes' is an exemplary case of the fetishizing process since it focuses exclusively on the signifier. 'It is indeed the sign that becomes an erotic object and not the "erotic" signified of discourse, as is usual in simple cases of repression (obscene talk or graffiti). It is not obsession but perversion.' Josette Rey-Debove, 'L'orgie langagière', *Poétique*, 12 (1972), p. 579.

63 See John von Neumann, *The Computer and the Brain* (New Haven; Conn.: Yale University Press, 1958).

64 Anthony Wilden, 'Analog and digital communication', *Semiotica*, 6, no. 1 (1972), pp. 50–1. [Kristeva gives a loose translation of these passages in French. I have restored the original English quotation. Wilden, it should be noted, uses 'computer' in the broad sense, whether the device actually computes in the strict sense or not – Tr.]

65 Ibid., p. 55.

66 Benveniste has taught us not to confuse these two operations, but rather to call something a language only when it has a double articulation; the distinction between phonemes devoid of meaning and morphemes as elements – for which no code is pertinent – is a *social*, specifically human occurrence. See 'Animal communication and human language', *Problems*, pp. 49–54.

67 This is what Hegel believes. At the end of the 'Larger logic', describing negativity as that which constructs absolute knowledge, he writes: 'This negativity, as self-transcending contradiction, is the *reconstitution of the first immediacy*, of simple universality; for, immediately, the Other of the Other and the negative of the negative is the *positive, identical,* and *universal.*' Hegel's *Science of Logic*, tr. W. H. Johnston and L. G. Struthers (2 vols, London: Allen & Unwin, 1929; 1966), vol. II, p. 478; emphasis added.

68 *Moses and Monotheism, Standard Edition*, vol. XXIII, pp. 7–137.

69 The two roles have often merged, as Georges Dumézil reminds us in *Mitra-Varuna* (Paris: Gallimard, 1948). See 'Deux conceptions de la souveraineté', *La Révolution du langage poétique*, pp. 545–52.

70 See 'Shifters. Verbal categories, and the Russian verb', in Jakobson, *Selected Writings*, vol. II, pp. 130–47.

71 See Joseph Needham, *Science and Civilisation in China*, (4 vols, Cambridge: Cambridge University Press, 1960), vol. I.

72 From a similar perspective, Edgar Morin writes: 'We can think of magic, mythologies, and ideologies both as mixed systems, making affectivity rational and rationality affective, and as outcomes of combining: a) fundamental drives, b) the chancy play of fantasy, and c) logico-constructive systems. (To our mind, the theory of myth must be based on triunic syncretism rather than unilateral logic.)' He adds,

in a note, that 'myth does not have a single logic but a synthesis of three kinds of logic'. 'Le paradigme perdu: la nature humaine', paper presented at the 'Invariants biologiques et universaux culturels' Colloquium, Royaumont, 6–9 Sept. 1972.

73 Lacan presented this typology of discourse at his 1969 and 1970 seminars.

Translated by Margaret Waller

PART II

Women, Psychoanalysis, Politics

6

About Chinese Women

Published in 1974, *Des Chinoises* (Paris: des femmes) is a small collection of notes and impressions from Kristeva's three weeks in China in April and May of that year. The book is divided into two parts: one short section entitled 'On This Side', which examines the position of the speaker, that is to say, of a Western woman observing China, and the main bulk of the book, entitled 'Women of China', which deals with Kristeva's impressions from her trip. Her perspective on China has been criticized as ethnocentric. In her essay 'French Feminism in an International Frame' (*Yale French Studies*, 62, 1981, pp. 154–85), Gayatri Chakravorty Spivak, for instance, argues that Kristeva's approach is not only cavalier but also sometimes condescending towards Chinese culture and society. For this volume I have selected the four short chapters (2, 3, 4 and 5) constituting Kristeva's analysis of the Judaeo-Christian tradition which shapes the Western understanding of femininity and sexual difference. These chapters are translated specially for this volume by Seán Hand. The whole text of *Des Chinoises* has been translated by Anita Barrows and was published in 1977 under the title *About Chinese Women* (London: Marion Boyars).

In the selection reproduced here, Kristeva first analyses the development of Judaism as the victory of patriarchal monotheism over an earlier, maternal and fertility-oriented religion. While stressing the negative consequences of patriarchal monotheism for women, who find themselves reduced to the role of the silent Other of the symbolic order, she also emphasizes the necessity of upholding the Law and sexual difference as long as one remains within the framework of patrilinear, class-structured capitalist society. While continuing the Judaic, monotheist tradition, Christianity nevertheless also adds its own particular insistence on female virginity and martyrdom. In Christian ideology, Kristeva argues, motherhood is perceived as a conspicuous sign of the *jouissance* of the female (or maternal) body, a pleasure that must at all costs be repressed: the function of procreation must be kept strictly subordinated to the rule of the Father's Name. As with Judaism, woman's only access to the symbolic order goes through the father. In this way, woman is presented with a clear-cut choice: either she remains identified with the mother, thus ensuring her own exclusion from and marginality in relation to patriarchal society or, repressing the body of the mother, she identifies with the father, thus raising herself to his symbolic heights. Such an identification, however, not only deprives the woman of the maternal body, but also of her own. For Kristeva, the frigid figure of Electra, the daughter who kills her mother in order to avenge her father (the mother, Clytemnestra, having committed the unforgivable sin of taking a lover, thus exposing her female *jouissance* to the world), represents the father-identified woman who cannot tolerate the *jouissance* of the mother. But is she also, as Kristeva claims, the emblem of any woman who wants to escape her condition?

In the chapter dealing with time, Kristeva presents us with a series of reflections on femininity and its time, a theme she develops further in her influential essay 'Women's Time', also reprinted in this volume. Here she argues that the Judaeo-Christian culture represents woman as the unconscious of the symbolic order, as a timeless, drive-related *jouissance*, which through its very marginality threatens to break the symbolic chain. But again we face the same double bind: if women refuse this role as the unconscious 'truth' of patriarchy, they are forced instead to identify with the father, thus turning themselves into supporters of the very same patriarchal order. Kristeva argues for a refusal of this dilemma: women must neither refuse to insert themselves into the symbolic order, nor embrace the masculine model for femininity (the 'homologous' woman) which is offered her there. Recognizing that such a task may well be impossible in the present situation, Kristeva finally turns to an examination of female suicide, notably that of female writers, workers of the word, such as Virginia Woolf, Maria Tsvetaeva and Sylvia Plath.

About Chinese Women

I ON THIS SIDE

2 THE WAR BETWEEN THE SEXES

Yahweh Elohim created the world and concluded alliances by *dividing* (*karath*) light from darkness, the waters of the heavens from the waters of the earth, the earth from the seas, the creatures of the water from the creatures of the air, the animals each according to their kind and man (in His own image) from himself. It's also by division that He places them opposite each other: man and woman. Not without hesitation, though, for it is said at first that 'male and female created He them'. But this first version is quickly corrected by the story of Adam's rib. Later, the first female creature, due to the hesitation wherein man and woman are not all that separate, makes an ephemeral appearance in the form of the diabolical Lilith, an emanation of Sodom and Gomorrah (Isaiah xxxiv, 14), who crops up in several more or less heterodox exegeses, but not in the Bible itself.

Divided from man, made of that very thing which is lacking in him, the biblical woman will be wife, daughter or sister, or all of them at once, but she will rarely have a name. Her function is to assure pro- creation – the propagation of the race. But she has no direct relation with the law of the community and its political and religious unity: God generally speaks only to men. Which is not to say that woman doesn't know more about Him; indeed, she is the one who knows the material conditions, as it were, of the body, sex and procreation, which permit the existence of the community, its permanence and thus man's very dialogue with his God. Besides, is the entire community not the *bride* of God? But woman's knowledge is corporal, aspiring to pleasure rather than tribal unity (the forbidden fruit seduces Eve's senses of *sight* and *taste*). It is an informulable knowledge, an ironic common sense (Sarah, pregnant at 90, laughs at this divine news); or else, when it serves social necessity, it's often in a roundabout way, after having violated the most ancient of taboos, that of incest (Sarah declared the sister of Abraham; Lot's daughters sleeping with their father).

Long before the establishment of the people of Israel, the Northern Semites worshipped maternal divinities. Even while such worship continued, though, these farmers and shepherds had already begun to isolate the principle of a male, paternal divinity and a pantheon in the image of the family (father-mother-son). But Judaism was founded through and beyond this tradition, when, around 2000 BC, Egyptian refugees, nomads, brigands and insurgent peasants banded together, it seems, without any coherent ethnic origin, without land or State, seeking at first merely to survive as a wandering community. Jewish monotheism is undoubtedly rooted in this will to create a community in the face of all the unfavourable concrete circumstances: an abstract, nominal, symbolic community beyond individuals and their beliefs, but beyond their political organization as well. In fact, the Kingdom of David survived only a short while after its foundation in 1000 BC, preceded by wars, and followed by discord, before becoming the vassal, and eventually the victim, of Babylonia. Devised to create a community, monotheism does not, however, accommodate itself to the political community that is the State; initially it doesn't even help it. Monotheism does survive the State, however, and determine the direction the latter will take, even much later, through Christianity up to the various forms of modern technocracies, both religious and secular. But this is not the problem that concerns us here. Let us note that by establishing itself as the principle of a symbolic, paternal community in the grip of the superego, beyond all ethnic considerations, beliefs or social loyalties, monotheism represses, along with paganism, the greater part of agrarian civilizations and their ideologies, women and mothers. The Syrian goddess who was worshipped up until the beginning of the Christian era in the Armenian city of Hieropolis-Menbidj, or the numerous sacrifices to Ishtar, survive the biblical expurgation only in the shape of Deborah, the inspired warrior who accompanied the soldiers and celebrated their deeds, or else in the mouths of prophets who deplore idolatry, such as Jeremiah, the last of the pre-exile prophets, who denounced the cult of the 'Queen of the Heavens'.

Consequently, no other civilization seems to have made the principle of sexual difference so crystal clear: between the two sexes a cleavage or abyss opens up. This gap is marked by their different relationship to the law (both religious and political), a difference which is in turn the very condition of their alliance. Monotheistic unity is sustained by a radical separation of the sexes: indeed, it is this very separation which is its prerequisite. For without this gap between the sexes, without this localization of the polymorphic, orgasmic body, desiring and laughing, in the *other* sex, it would have been impossible, in the *symbolic realm*, to isolate the principle of One Law – the One, Sublimating, Transcendent Guarantor of the ideal interests of the community. In the sphere of *reproductive relations*, at that time inseparably linked to relations of production, it would have been impossible to ensure the propagation of the species simply by turning it into the highest premium of pleasure.

There is one unity: an increasingly purified community discipline, that is isolated as a transcendent principle and which thereby ensures the survival of the group. This *unity* which is represented by the God of monotheism is sustained by a *desire* that pervades the community, a desire which is at once stirring and threatening. Remove this threatening desire, the dangerous support of cohesion, from man; place it beside him and create a supplement for what is lacking in this man who speaks to his God; and you have woman, who has no access to the word, but who appears as the pure desire to seize it, or as that which ensures the permanence of the divine paternal function for all humans: that is, the desire to continue the species.

This people of shepherds and nomads settled only temporarily to found their community by means of the only durable bond in the steppes and the desert: the word. The shepherd (Abel, for example) will therefore be sacrificed so that a lowly farmer can initiate the narrative of tribal wanderings. Invasions and exiles ensue: a sixth century BC of exodus, and a fifth century of temporary return to the land, with the invaders displaying a relative degree of tolerance. The word of the community will consequently oscillate between prophecy and legislation, but it will always be a word that aims to gather together this society which history is bent on dispersing. We must not employ some vulgar form of sociology in order to attribute to climatic or socio-historic conditions the privilege granted to the word and the monotheistic transcendence that represents its agency in the southern Mediterranean basin. But the discovery, by one of the peoples of this region, of the specific form of religiosity known as monotheism (which had failed in Egypt after the attempts of Amen-Hotep *IV*) on the one hand corresponds to the function of human symbolism, which is to provide an agency of communication and cohesion despite the fact that it works through interdiction and division (thing/word, body/speech, pleasure/law, incest/procreation...); while on the other hand it simultaneously represents the paternal function: patrilinear descent with transmission of the name of the father centralizes eroticism, giving it the single goal of procreation. It is thus caught in the grip of an abstract symbolic authority which refuses to recognise the growth of the child in the mother's body, something a matrilinear system of descent kept alive in the minds by leaving open certain possibilities of polymorphism, if not incest. If, with these two keys, one can consolidate a social group and make it resistant to any test of internal or external dissolution, one begins to understand that the monotheistic community acquires a vitality that allows it not only to survive geographic or historical threats, but to ensure an otherwise impossible development of productive forces by an infinite perfecting of goods and of means of production. This control ensures a productivist teleology: even if the threats of the prophets disturb this teleology and keep it from degenerating into profiteering and the enjoyment of wealth, this does not in any way preclude the advantage that the property-owning classes derive from it for the perfecting of their economic and political power.

The economy of this system requires that women be excluded from the single true and legislating principle, namely the Word, as well as from the (always paternal) element that gives procreation a social value: they are excluded from knowledge and power. The myth of the relationship between Eve and the serpent is the best summary of this exclusion. The serpent stands for the opposite of God, since he tempts Eve to transgress His prohibition. But he is also Adam's repressed desire to transgress, that which he dares not carry out, and which is his shame. The sexual symbolism helps us understand that the serpent is that which, in God or Adam, remains beyond or outside the sublimation of the Word. Eve has no relationship other than with that, and even then because she is its very opposite, the 'other race'.

When Yahweh says to the serpent, 'I will put enmity between thee and woman, and between they seed (*zera*) and her seed (*zera*): it shall bruise thy head, and thou shalt bruise (*teshufenu*) its heel (*akev*)', He established the divergence – of race or 'seed' – between God and man on the one hand and woman on the other. Furthermore, in the second part of the sentence, woman disappears completely into seed: generation. But, even more essentially, Yahweh formulates the code of eroticism between the two seeds as though it were a code of war. An endless war, where *he* will lose his head (or his gland?), and *she* her trace, her limit, her succession (the threat, perhaps, to deprive her of descendants, if she takes herself to be all-powerful, and phallic?). It is a strange goal at all events, to follow on the heels of women, and one to be borne in mind when one is confronted with the bound feet of Chinese women, crushed in a way that is infinitely less decisive, but more painful and much more certain.

St Augustine returns to this function of the serpent and offers a definition when he points out that it represents the 'sense of the body' but 'belongs to the reason of science' and 'is dependent on cognition'; and when he thinks (must we believe that this is a consequence of the double nature of the 'sense of the body'?) that sexual difference, far from being a question of distinguishing between two individuals, 'can be discerned in a single human being':

For this reason I have thought that the sense of the body should not be taken for the woman, since we see that it is common to us and beasts, and have preferred to take something which the beasts do not have, and have believed that it is more appropriate for the serpent to be understood as the sense of the body...for these are the senses of the rational nature and pertain to the intelligence, but that five-fold sense of the body by which the corporeal species and movement are perceived, not only by us but also by the beasts...Whenever that carnal or animal sense, therefore, introduces into this purpose of the mind, which uses the living force of reason in temporal and corporeal things for the purpose of carrying out its functions some inducement to *enjoy itself*, that is, to enjoy itself as a kind of *private* and *personal* good and not as a *public* and *common* good which is an *unchangeable good*, then the serpent, as it were, addresses the woman. But to consent to this inducement is to eat of the forbidden tree.[1]

If what woman desires is the very opposite of the sublimating Word and paternal legislation, she neither *has* nor *is* that opposite. All that remains for her is to pit herself constantly against that opposite in the very movement by which she desires it, to kill it repeatedly and then suffer endlessly: a radiant perspective on masochism, a masochism that is the price she must pay in order to be Queen. In a symbolic economy of production and reproduction centred on the paternal Word (the phallus, if you like), one can make a woman believe that she *is* (the phallus) even if she doesn't have it (the serpent, the penis): doesn't she have the child? In this way, social harmony is preserved: the structure functions, produces and reproduces. Without it, the very foundation of this society is endangered.

We must stress that this last point, for its importance is overlooked. At best one is guilty of naïvety if one considers our modern societies as simply patrilinear, or class-structured, or capitalist-monopolist, and omits the fact that they are at the same time (and never one without the other) governed by a monotheism whose essence is best expressed in the Bible: the 'paternal Word' sustained by a fight to the death between the two races (men/women). In this naïvety, one forgets that whatever attacks this radical location of sexual difference, while still remaining *within the framework of our patrilinear, class-structured, capitalist societies*, is above all also attacking a fundamental discovery of Judaism that lies in the separation of the sexes and in their incompatibility: in castration, if you like – the support of monotheism and the source of its eroticism. To wish to deny this separation and yet remain within the framework of patrilinear capitalist society and its monotheistic ideology (even when disguised as humanism) necessarily plunges one back into the petty perversion of fetishism. And we know the role that the pervert, with his invincible belief in the maternal phallus and his obstinate refusal to recognize the existence of the other sex, has been able to play in anti-semitism and the totalitarian movements that embrace it. Let us recall the fascist or social-fascist homosexual community (and all homosexual communities for whom there is no 'other race'), and the fact that it is inevitably flanked by a community of viragos who have forgotten the war of the sexes and identify with the paternal Word or its serpent. The feminist movements are equally capable of a similar perverse denial of biblical teaching. We must recognize this and be on our guard.

On the other hand, there are analysts who do recognize this and, faithful to Freudian pessimism, accept the abyss between the two races; yet they go on to preach the impossibility of communication between the two, the 'lack of relation'. Here it is no longer a question of the war between the sexes: doesn't every psychiatrist have as a companion a 'dead woman', an aphasic mother, an inaudible haven of procreation, that ensures and reassures the 'analytic word'?.

The solution? To go on waging the war beteen the two races without respite, without a perverse denial of the abyss that marks sexual difference or a disillusioned mortification of the division. In the meantime, some other economy of the sexes installs itself, but not before it has transformed our entire logic of production (class) and reproduction (family). China will just be one more horizon, which we will be able to read once this transformation is complete. Before it has happened, however, that country is susceptible of functioning as just another perversion, another mortification (for example: the blindness of the left-winger who believes in Chinese chastity – the final discovery of a happiness that can be opposed to 'bourgeois morality').

3 THE VIRGIN OF THE WORD

Universalist as it is, Christianity does associate women with the symbolic community, but only provided they keep their *virginity*. Failing that, they can atone for their carnal *jouissance* with their martyrdom. Between these two extremes, the mother participates in the community of the Christian Word not by giving birth to her children, but merely by preparing them for baptism.

St Augustine once again offers a fairly cynical explanation for the basically economic reasons for this association of women with the Christian Word, which is secured at the price of the virginity represented by Mary and imitated by the female monastic orders. Quite simply, by the time of Augustine, the survival of the European community no longer depended on the accelerated propagation of the species, but rather on the participation by all men and women in the symbolic efforts (technical as well as ideological) to perfect the means and relations of production:

> But it would be very foolish, for the sake of enjoying marriage even at the present time, when the coming of Christ is not served through carnal generation by the very begetting of children, to take upon oneself the burden of this tribulation of the flesh which the Apostle predicts for those who marry – unless those who cannot remain continent feared that under the temptation of Satan they would fall into sins leading to damnation.[2]

Between this historical constraint and the myth of the Virgin impregnated by the Word there is still a certain distance, which will be bridged by two psychoanalytical processes, one relating to the role of the mother, the other to the workings of language.

The first consists in ceasing to repress the fact that the mother is *other*, has no penis, but experiences *jouissance* and bears children. But this is acknowledged only at the pre-conscious level: just enough to imagine that she bears children, while censuring the fact that she has experienced *jouissance* in an act of coitus, that there was a 'primal scene'. Once more, the vagina and the *jouissance* of the mother are disregarded, and immediately replaced by that which puts the mother on the side of the socio-symbolic community: childbearing and procreation in the name of the father. This operation of false recognition – mis-recognition – of maternal *jouissance* is accomplished by a process whose origins Ernest Jones was the first to understand. Too hastily categorized simply as the biographer of Freud, Jones in fact deserves credit not only for having proposed one of the most interesting concepts of female sexuality, but for having been the first to attempt an analysis of the sexual economy of the great Christian myths. So, in the Word and Breath celebrated by many religions of which Christianity is the chief, the psychoanalyst sees an emanation not of the glottal but of the anal sphincter. This sacrilegious theory, confirmed by the fantasies of analysands, tends to prove that impregnation by the fart (hiding behind its sublimation into Word) corresponds to the fantasy of anal pregnancy, of penetration or auto-penetration by an anal penis, and, in any case, of a confusion of anus and vagina: in short, to a denial of sexual difference. Such a scenario is probably more frequent among male subjects, and represents the way in which the small boy usurps the role of the mother, by denying his difference in order to submit himself in her place and as a woman to the father. In this homosexual economy, we can see that what Christianity recognizes in a woman, what it demands of her in order to include her within its symbolic order, is that by living or thinking of herself as a virgin impregnated by the Word, she should live and think of herself as a male homosexual. If, on the other hand, this identification with the homosexual does not succeed, if a woman is not a virgin, a nun, and chaste, but has orgasms and gives birth, her only means of gaining access to the symbolic paternal order is by engaging in an endless struggle between the orgasmic maternal body and the symbolic prohibition – a struggle that will take the form of guilt and mortification, and culminate in masochistic *jouissance*. For a woman who has not easily repressed her relationship with her mother, participation in the symbolic paternal order as Christianity defines it can only be masochistic. As St Augustine again so marvellously puts it: 'No-one, however, to my way of thinking, would ever prefer virginity to martyrdom' ('Holy Virginity', XLVII, 47). The *ecstatic* and the *melancholic*, two great female archetypes of Christianity, exemplify two ways in which a woman may participate in this symbolic Christian order.

In the first discourse, the maternal traits are attributed to the symbolic father, the mother is denied by this displacement of her attributes and the woman then submits herself to a sexually undifferentiated androgynous being:

But when this most wealthy Spouse desires to enrich and comfort the Bride still more, He draws her so closely to Him that she is like one who swoons from excess of pleasure and joy and seems to be suspended in those Divine arms and drawn near to that sacred side and to those Divine breasts. Sustained by that Divine milk with which her Spouse continually nourishes her and growing in grace so that she may be enabled to receive His comforts, she can do nothing but rejoice. Awakening from that sleep and heavenly inebriation, she is like one amazed and stupefied; well, I think, may her sacred folly wring these words from her: 'Thy breasts are better than wine'.[3]

At the same time, in the second discourse, submission to the father is experienced as punishment, pain and suffering inflicted upon the heterogeneous body. Such a confrontation provokes a melancholic *jouissance* whose most emotive eulogy is perhaps to be found in Catherine of Siena's treatise on the sensuality of tears.

What is there in the psycho-sexual development of a little girl in monotheistic capitalist society that prepares her for this economy of which the *ecstatic* and the *melancholic* represent the two extremes of the attempt to gain access to the social order (to symbolism, power, knowledge)?

There is increasing insistence on the importance of pre-Oedipal phases, oral and anal, in the subsequent development of both boy and girl. The child is bound to the mother's body without the latter being, as yet, a 'separate object'. Instead, the mother's body acts with the child's as a sort of socio-natural continuum. This period is dominated by the oral and anal drives of incorporation and aggressive rejection: hence the pleasure is auto-erotic as well as inseparable from the mother's body. Through language, the Oedipal phase introduces the symbolic agency, the prohibition of auto-eroticism and the recognition of the paternal function. As Jones once again points out, the boy as well as the girl must renounce his or her own pleasure in order to find an object of the opposite sex, or renounce his or her own sex in order to find a homogeneous pleasure that has no *other* as its object. But if such is the rule, it is realized differently in boys and in girls. When the boy does not identify with his mother to submit like a woman to his father, he becomes his father's rival for the mother's love, and the castration he experiences is rather a fear of 'aphanisis': fear of not being able to satisfy both *her* and *himself*. The girl also finds herself faced with a choice: either she identifies with the mother, or she raises herself to the symbolic stature of the father. In the first case, the pre-Oedipal stages (oral and anal eroticism) are intensified. By giving herself a male object (a substitute for the father), she desires and appropriates him for herself through that which her mother has bequeathed her during the 'female' pre-Oedipal phase – i.e., through the oral-sadistic veil that accompanies the vaginal *jouissance* of heterosexual woman. If we perceive a sort of fundamental female 'homosexuality' in this identification with the pre-Oedipal mother, we perceive at the same time that this has nothing whatever to do with male homosexuality, and is not superseded by the 'female heterosexual'. In the second case, identification with the father, the girl represses the oral-sadistic stage, and at the same time represses the vagina and the possibility of finding someone else as her partner. (This situation can come about, for instance, by refusing the male partner, by feminizing the male partner or by assuming either a male or a female role in a relationship with a female partner.) The sadistic component of such an economy is so violent as to obliterate the vagina. In her imagination, the girl obtains a real or imaginary penis for herself; the imaginary acquisition of the male organ seems here to be less important than the access she gains to the symbolic mastery which is necessary to censor the pre-Oedipal stage and wipe out all trace of dependence on the mother's body. Obliteration of the pre-Oedipal stage, identification with the father, and then: 'I'm looking, as a man would, for a woman'; or else, 'I submit myself, as if I were a man who thought he was a woman, to a woman who thinks she is a man'. Such are the double or triple twists of what is commonly called female homosexuality, or lesbianism. The oral-sadistic dependence on the mother has been so strong that it now represents not simply a veil over the vagina, but a veritable blockade. Thus the lesbian never discovers the vagina, but creates from this restitution of pre-Oedipal drives (oral/anal, absorption/ rejection) a powerful mechanism of symbolization. Intellectual or artist, she wages a vigilant war against her pre-Oedipal dependence on her mother, which keeps her from discovering her own body as other, different, possessing a vagina. Melancholy – fear of aphanisis – punctuated by sudden bursts of energy marks the loss of the maternal body, this immediate investment of sadism in the symbolic.

It is interesting to note that, on the level of speech, the pre-Oedipal stage corresponds to an intense echolalia, first in rhythm and then in intonation, before a phonologico-syntactic structure is imposed on the sentence. This latter is only totally achieved at the end of the Oedipal phase. It is obvious, then, that a reactivation of the pre-Oedipal phase in a man (by homosexuality or imaginary incest) creates in his pre-sentence speech an explosion of rhythm, intonation and nonsense: nonsense invades sense, and creates laughter. When he flees the symbolic paternal order (through fear of castration, Freud would say, through fear of aphanisis, Jones would say), man can laugh. But the daughter, on the other hand, is rewarded by the symbolic order when she identifies with the father: only here is she recognized not as herself but in opposition to her rival, the mother with a vagina who experiences *jouissance*. Thus, at the price of censuring herself as a woman, she will be able to triumph in her henceforth sublimated sadistic attacks on the mother whom she has repressed and with whom she will always fight, either (as a heterosexual) by identifying with her, or (as a homosexual) by pursuing her erotically. Therefore the invasion of her speech by these unphrased, nonsensical, maternal rhythms, far from soothing her, or making her laugh, destroys her symbolic armour and makes her ecstatic, nostalgic or mad. Nietzsche would not have known how to be a woman. A woman has nothing to laugh about when the symbolic order collapses. She can take pleasure in it if, by identifying with the mother, the vaginal body, she imagines she is the sublime, repressed forces which return through the fissures of the order. But she can just as easily die from this upheaval, as a victim or a militant, if she has been deprived of a successful maternal identification and has found in the symbolic paternal order her one superficial, belated and easily severed link with life.

Faithful to a certain biblical tradition, Freud saw the fear of castration as the essential moment in the formation of any psyche, male or female. Closer to Christianity, but also to the post-Romantic psychology which defines all characters according to the amorous relations, Jones proposed to find the determining element in psychic structure in aphanisis (the fear of losing the possibility of *jouissance*), rather than in castration. Perhaps it would not merely be a resurgence of Greek or logico-phenomenological thought to suggest locating this fundamental event neither in castration nor in aphanisis (both of which would be only its fantasmic derivatives), but rather in *the process of learning the symbolic function* to which the human animal is subjected from the pre-Oedipal phase onward. By symbolic function we mean a system of signs (first, rhythmic and intonational difference, then signifier/signified) which are organized into logico-syntactic structures whose aim is to accredit social communication as exchange purified of pleasure. From the beginning, then, we are dealing with a training process, an inhibition, which already begins with the first echolalias, but fully asserts itself with language-learning. If the pre-Oedipal phase of this inhibition is still full of pleasure and not yet detached from the mother/child continuum, it already entails certain prohibitions: notably the training of the glottal and anal sphincters. And it is on the foundation of these prohibitions that the superego will be built.

The symbolic order functions in our monotheistic West by means of a *system of kinship* that involves transmission of the name of the father and a rigorous prohibition of incest, and a *system of speech* that involves an increasingly logical, simple, positive and 'scientific' form of communication, that is stripped of all stylistic, rhythmic and 'poetic' ambiguities. Such an order brings this *inhibition constitutive of the speaking animal* to a height never before attained, one logically assumed by the role of the father. The role of the 'mother' (the repressed element) includes not only the drives (of which the most basic is that of aggressive rejection) but also, through the education of the sphincters, the first training of these drives in the oral/anal phase, marked by rhythms, intonations and gestures which as yet have no significance.

Daughter of the father? Or daughter of the mother?

As the Sophoclean chorus says, 'Never was a daughter more her father's daughter' than Electra. Not only does she incite vengeance; she is also the principal agent in the murder of her mother, more so than Orestes himself, for in the murder scene, is it not the voices of the daughter and the mother we hear while the son remains silent? It is a delusion to think that Orestes, an anti-Oedipus, has killed his mother to wrest himself thus from the family and move into a new community that is supra-familial and political: the *city* whose cult was already becoming an economic and political necessity in Greece. Faced with this murder, thought-out and spoken by Electra, of which Orestes is only the agent, one wonders if anti-Oedipal man is not a fiction, or, at all events, if he is not always appended to the *jouissance* of a wife-sister. There would be no unavenged dead father – no Resurrection of the Father – if that father did not have a (virgin) daughter. A daughter does not put up with the murder of a father. That the father is made a symbolic power – that is, that he is dead, and thus elevated to the rank of a Name – is what gives meaning to her life, which will henceforth be an eternal vendetta. Not that this fixation does not drive her mad: in vain Electra says that 'Only a madman could forget a father killed so heartlessly'; in vain does she accuse poor Chrysothemis, 'her mother's daughter', of being demented, of forgetting her father; she cannot stop herself from being driven mad by her own activity. But her own madness, contrary to Chrysothemis' passive clinging to her mother, is what the leader of the chorus will call, at the end, an 'effort that crowns history', for without it, there would be no 'freedom', and no 'history' for the city from which, as woman, she is none the less alienated. For, in fact, this pursuit of the father's cause has a darker side to it: hatred of the mother, or, more precisely, hatred of her *jouissance*. Electra wants Clytemnestra dead, not because she is a mother who kills the father, but because she is a mistress (of Aegisthus). Let *jouissance* be forbidden to the mother: this is the demand of the father's daughter, fascinated by the mother's *jouissance*. And one can imagine how the city will depend on these fathers' daughters (given that a man can fulfil the office of daughter) in order to cover up the fact that the mother's *jouissance* is nourished by the war of the sexes and ends in the murder of the father. The Electras – 'deprived forever of their hymens' – militants in the cause of the father, frigid with exaltation – are they then dramatic figures emerging at the point where the social consensus corners any woman who wants to escape her condition: nuns, 'revolutionaries', even 'feminists'?

It takes a Mozart to make a comedy out of this fidelity of the daughter to the father. The dead father is retained in the guise of the Commander. Orestes is cut out and replaced with poor Ottavio. Aegisthus and Clytemnestra have no reason to exist: power and *jouissance*, following one upon the other in a radiant musical infinity, will be represented by Don Giovanni. So the heroic Electra becomes the pitiful, unhappy Donna Anna: the ill-treated hysteric, passionately in love with the death of her father, commemorating his murder – but without hope of revenge – in a hallucinatory monologue of bitterness and jubilation. Since history repeats itself only as farce, Donna Anna is a comic Electra: still a slave to her father, but to a father whose political and moral law are crumbling enough, by the eighteenth century, to allow Mozart not to treat it as tragedy.

4 WITHOUT TIME

The symbolic order – the order of verbal communication, the paternal order of genealogy – is a temporal order. For the speaking animal, it is the clock of objective time: it provides the reference point, and, consequently, all possibilities of measurement, by distinguishing between a before, a now and an after. If *I* don't exist except in the speech I address to another, *I* am only *present* in the moment of that communication. In relation to this present of my being, there is that which precedes and that which follows. My family lineage will also be placed in this before and after: the number of ancestors and future generations. Within these coordinates I shall project myself: a journey on the axis centred by the moment of my speech, exemplified by its most intimate phenomenon, my own family tree. This projection will not be a mere displacement of my present on to the future or on to someone else: it may also overthrow the well-oiled order of communication (and thus of society) or of descent (and thus of the family), if I project not the moment of my fixed, governed word, ruled by a series of inhibitions and prohibitions (ranging from rules to sexual taboos and economic, political and ideological constraints), but rather the underlying causality that shapes it, which I repress in order that I may enter the socio-symbolic order, and which is capable of blowing up the whole construct.

'Underlying causality' – a figure of speech that alludes to the social contradictions that a given society can provisionally subdue in order to constitute itself as such. But a figure of speech that is also used to designate that 'other scene': the unconscious, drive-related and transverbal scene whose eruptions determine not only my speech or my interpersonal relationships, but even the complex relations of production and reproduction which we so frequently see only as dependent on, rather than shaping, the economy.

No reference point in the unconscious; I still don't speak there. No now, no before, no after. No true or false either. It [*ça*] displaces, condenses, distributes. It retains everything repressed by the word: by sign, by sense, by communication, by the symbolic order, in whatever is legislating, paternal and restrictive.

There is no time without speech. Therefore, there is no time without the father. That, incidentally, is what the Father is: sign and time. It is understandable, then, that what the father doesn't say about the unconscious, what sign and time repress in the drives, appears as their *truth* (if there is no 'absolute', what is truth, if not the unspoken of the spoken?) and that this truth can be imagined only as a *woman*.

A curious truth: outside time, with neither a before nor an after, neither true nor false; subterranean, it neither judges nor postulates, but refuses, displaces and breaks the symbolic order before it can re-establish itself.

If a woman cannot be part of the temporal symbolic order except by identifying with the father, it is clear that as soon as she shows any sign of that which, in herself, escapes such identification and acts differently, resembling the dream or the maternal body, she evolves into this 'truth' in question. It is thus that female specificity defines itself in patrilinear society: woman is a specialist in the unconscious, a witch, a baccanalian, taking her *jouissance* in an anti-Apollonian, Dionysian orgy.

A *jouissance* which breaks the symbolic chain, the taboo, the mastery. A *marginal discourse*, with regard to the science, religion and philosophy of the *polis* (witch, child, underdeveloped, not even a poet, at best his accomplice). A *pregnancy*: an escape from the temporality of day-to-day social obligations, an interruption of the regular monthly cycles, where the surfaces – skin, sight – are abandoned in favour of a descent into the depths of the body, where one hears, tastes and smells the infinitesimal life of the cells. Perhaps the notion that the period of gestation approaches *another temporality*, more cosmic and 'objective' than human and 'subjective', is just another myth designed to restore time (even if different) at the very moment when time breaks up, before its product (the child) emerges. The child: sole evidence, for the symbolic order, of *jouissance* and pregnancy, thanks to whom the woman will be coded in the chain of production and thus perceived as a temporalized parent. *Jouissance*, pregnancy, marginal discourse: this is the way in which this 'truth', hidden and cloaked [*dérobent et enrobent*] by the truth of the symbolic order and its time, functions through women.

The artist (that imaginary committer of incest) suspects that it is from the mother's side that the unverifiable atemporal 'truth' of the symbolic order and its time springs out and explodes. The Western artist (that fetishist), then, raises this 'truth' to the skies by finding its symbol in the female body. Let us not even speak about the endless 'Madonnas with Child'. Let us take something less evangelical: Tiepolo's *Time Disrobing Truth* (Museum of Fine Arts at Boston, Massachusetts) for example. A scene of abduction, or of coitus? The enigma is emphasized by the anomaly of the design. Truth has a right leg where her left should be, and this leg is thrust forward, between herself and the genitals of Time. But his pain and her air of majesty do not deceive: their gaze is caught by two others who do not speak: the infant and the parrot. The arrows (of love?) and a mask are there to indicate the borrowed and indirect means by which 'truth', so armed, can not only trample the globe underfoot, but steal Time's scythe [*faux*] and transform the latter into a fallen master, an angry servant. But in this fantasy, where a woman, intended to represent Truth, takes the place of the phallus (notably in Tiepolo's painting), she ceases to act as an atemporal, unconscious force, splitting, defying and breaking the symbolic and temporal order, and instead substitutes herself for it as solar mistress, a priestess of the absolute. Once it is disrobed in order to be presented in itself, 'truth' is lost 'in itself'; for in fact it has no self, it emerges only in the gaps of an identity. Once it is represented, even by the form of a woman, the 'truth' of the unconscious passes into the symbolic order, and even overshadows it, as fundamental fetish, phallus-substitute, support for all transcendental divinity. A crude but enormously effective trap for 'feminism': to acknowledge us, to turn us into the Truth of the temporal order, so as to keep us from functioning as its unconscious 'truth', an unrepresentable form beyond true and false, and beyond present-past-future.

Until now this trap has always worked in the West. It seems to me, however, that far from being simply the affair of 'others' stubbornly refusing the specificity of women, the dilemma arises from a very profound structural mechanism concerning the casting of sexual difference and even of discourse in the West. A woman finds herself caught here, and can't do much about it. But a few concrete results of this implacable structure can be noted.

We cannot gain access to the temporal scene, that is, to the political and historical affairs of our society, except by identifying with the values considered to be masculine (mastery, superego, the sanctioning communicative word that institutes stable social exchange). From Louise Michel to Alexandra Kollontai, to cite only two fairly recent examples – not to speak of the suffragettes or their contemporary Anglo-Saxon sisters, some of whom are more threatening than the father of the primitive horde – we have been able to serve or overthrow the socio-historic order by playing at being supermen. A few enjoy it: the most active, the most effective, the 'homosexual' women (whether they know it or not). Others, more bound to the mother, and more tuned in to their unconscious drives, refuse this role and sullenly hold back, neither speaking nor writing, in a permanent state of expectation, occasionally punctuated by some kind of outburst: a cry, a refusal, 'hysterical symptoms'. These two extremes condemn us either to being the most passionate servants of the temporal order and its apparatus of consolidation (the new wave: women ministers), or of subversion (the other new wave, always a little behind the first: the promotion of women in left-wing parties). Or else we will forever remain in a sulk in the face of history, politics and social affairs: symptoms of their failure, but symptoms destined for marginality or for a new mysticism.

Let us refuse both these extremes. Let us know that an ostensibly masculine, paternal identification, because it supports symbol and time, is necessary in order to have a voice in the chapter of politics and history. Let us achieve this identification in order to escape a smug poly-morphism where it is so easy and comfortable for a woman to remain; and let us in this way gain entry to social practice. Let us right away be wary of the premium on narcissism that such an integration can carry: let us reject the development of a 'homologous' woman, who is finally capable and virile; and let us rather act on the socio-politico-historical stage as her negative: that is, act first with all those who refuse and 'swim against the tide' – all who rebel against the existing relations of production and reproduction. But let us not take the role of Revolu-tionary either, whether male or female: let us on the contrary refuse all roles to summon this 'truth' situated outside time, a truth that is neither true nor false, that cannot be fitted in to the order of speech and social symbolism, that is an echo of our *jouissance*, of our mad words, of our pregnancies. But how can we do this? By listening; by recognizing the unspoken in all discourse, however Revolutionary, by emphasizing at each point whatever remains unsatisfied, repressed, new, eccentric, incomprehensible, that which disturbs the mutual understanding of the established powers.

A constant alternation between time and its 'truth', identity and its loss, history and that which produces it: that which remains extra-phenomenal, outside the sign, beyond time. An impossible dialectic of two terms, a permanent alternation: never the one without the other. It is not certain that anyone here and now is capable of this. An analyst conscious of history and politics? A politician tuned into the un-conscious? Or, perhaps, a woman...

5 I WHO WANT NOT TO BE

For a woman, the call of the mother is not only a call from beyond time, or beyond the socio-political battle. With family and history at an impasse, this call troubles the word: it generates hallucinations, voices, 'madness'. After the superego, the ego founders and sinks. It is a fragile envelope, incapable of staving off the irruption of this conflict, of this love which had bound the little girl to her mother, and which then, like black lava, had lain in wait for her all along the path of her desperate attempts to identify with the symbolic paternal order. Once the moorings of the word, the ego, the superego, begin to slip, life itself can't hang on: death quietly moves in. Suicide without a cause, or sacrifice without fuss for an apparent cause which, in our age, is usually political: a woman can carry off such things without tragedy, even without drama, without the feeling that she is fleeing a well-fortified front, but rather as though it were simply a matter of making an inevitable, irresistible and self-evident transition.

I think of Virginia Woolf, who sank wordlessly into the river, her pockets weighed down with stones. Haunted by voices, waves, lights, in love with colours – blue, green – and seized by a strange gaiety that would bring on the fits of strangled, screeching laughter recalled by Miss Brown. Or I think of the dark corner of the deserted farmhouse in the Russian countryside whee, a few months later in that same year of 1941, Maria Tsvetaeva, fleeing the war, hanged herself: the most rhythmic of Russian poets, whose drumbeats went further back in the memory of the Russian language than those of Mayakovsky, and who wrote: 'My problem (in writing verse, and my reader's problem in understanding it) consists in the impossibility of my task: for example, to express the sigh a-a-a- with words (that is, meaning). With words/meanings to say the sound. Such that all that remains in the ear is a-a-a.'

Or Sylvia Plath, another of those women disillusioned with meanings and words, who took refuge in lights, rhythms and sounds: a refuge that already announces, for those who know how to read her, her silent departure from life:

> *Axes*
> *After whose stroke the wood rings*
> *And the echoes!*
> *Echoes travelling*
> *Off from the centre like horses.*

Words dry and riderless,
the indefatigable hoof-taps.
While
From the bottom of the pool fixed stars
Govern a life.[4]

When Dostoevsky's Kirilov commits suicide, it's to prove that his will is stronger than God's. By proving thus that the human ego possesses supreme power, he believes he is emancipating Man by putting him in the place of God. ('If I kill myself I become God' – 'God is necessary and therefore He must exist').

Something entirely different is at stake in Tsvetaeva's suicide: not *to be*, that is, in the final instance, *to be God*; but to dissolve being itself, to free it of the word, of the self, of God. 'I don't want to die. I want not to be', she writes in her notes.

In an analogous situation a man can imagine an all-powerful, though always insignificant, mother in order to 'legitimize' himself: to make himself known, to lean on her and be guided by her through the social labyrinth, though not without his own occasional ironic commentary. Méry-Laurent for Mallarmé, Madame Straus for 'little Marcel', Miss Weaver for Joyce, the series of fiancées taken and rejected by Kafka . . . For a woman, as soon as the father is not calling the tune and language is being torn apart by rhythm, no mother can serve as an axis for the sacred or for farce. If she tries to provide it herself, the result is so-called female homosexuality, identification with virility, or a tight rein on the least pre-Oedipal pleasure. And if no paternal legitimation comes along to dam up the inexhaustible non-symbolized drive, she collapses into psychosis or suicide.

The triumph of narcissism? But that would be the most primal form of narcissism: the most archaic death-drive, that which precedes and therefore surpasses any identity, sign, order or belief. As a motive for revolutionary action, this drive, if it is strangled in the throat of history, can destroy the body itself. For Tsvetaeva, the failure of the Revolution, Soviet bureaucracy and the war are all features to be considered. But without faith – without testament.

When, striving for access to the word and to time, she identifies with the father, she becomes a support for transcendence. But when she is inspired by that which the symbolic order represses, isn't a woman also the most radical atheist, the most committed anarchist? In the eyes of this society, such a posture casts her as a victim. But elsewhere?

NOTES

1 St Augustine, *The Trinity*, tr. S. McKenna (Washington, DC: The Catholic University of America Press, 1963), p. 362 and pp. 359–60. My emphasis.

2 St Augustine, 'Holy Virginity', in *Treatises on Marriage and Other Subjects*, tr. J. McQuade (New York: Fathers of the Church, 1955), p. 159.

3 St Teresa of Jesus, 'Conceptions of the love of God', in *The Complete Works*, tr. and ed. E. Allison Peers (London: Sheed & Ward, 1946), vol. II, p. 384.

4 S. Plath, *Ariel* (London: Faber, 1968), p. 86.

Translated by Seán Hand

In reply to her own question, she points to the need for a new understanding of the mother's body; the physical and psychological suffering of childbirth and of the need to raise the child in accordance with the Law; the mother-daughter relationship; and finally, the female foreclosure of masculinity. There is, then, an urgent need for a 'post-virginal' discourse on maternity, one which ultimately would provide both women and men with a new ethics: a 'herethics' encompassing both reproduction and death.

Opening up a fascinating field of investigation, this essay is of particular interest to feminists. So far, Kristeva herself has not really followed up her own 'programme' for research into maternity, although *Histoires d'amour* as a whole does contain many valuable observations on the topic.

Stabat Mater

The paradox: mother or primary narcissism

If it is not possible to say of a *woman* what she *is* (without running the risk of abolishing her difference), would it perhaps be different concerning the *mother*, since that is the only function of the 'other sex' to which we can definitely attribute existence? And yet, there too, we are caught in a paradox. First, we live in a civilization where the *consecrated* (religious or secular) representation of femininity is absorbed by motherhood. If, however, one looks at it more closely, this motherhood is the *fantasy* that is nurtured by the adult, man or woman, of a lost territory; what is more, it involves less an idealized archaic mother than the idealization of the *relationship* that binds us to her, one that cannot be localized – an idealization of primary narcissism. Now, when feminism demands a new representation of femininity, it seems to identify motherhood with that idealized misconception and, because it rejects the image and its misuse, feminism circumvents the real experience that fantasy overshadows. The result? – A negation or rejection of motherhood by some avant-garde feminist groups. Or else an acceptance – conscious or not – of its traditional representations by the great mass of people, women and men.

Christianity is doubtless the most refined symbolic construct in which femininity, to the extent that it transpires through it – and it does so incessantly – is focused on *Maternality*.[1] Let us call 'maternal' the

FLASH – instant of time or of dream without time; inordinately swollen atoms of a bond, a vision, a shiver, a yet formless, unnameable embryo. Epiphanies. Photos of what is not yet visible and that language necessarily skims over from afar, allusively. Words that are always too distant, too abstract for this underground swarming of seconds, folding in unimaginable spaces. Writing them down is an ordeal of discourse, like love. What is loving, for a woman, the same thing as writing. Laugh. Impossible. Flash on the unnameable, weavings of abstractions to be torn. Let a body venture at last out of its shelter, take a chance with meaning under a veil of words. WORD FLESH. From one to the other, eternally, broken up visions, metaphors of the invisible.

ambivalent principle that is bound to the species, on the one hand, and on the other stems from an identity catastrophe that causes the Name to topple over into the unnameable that one imagines as femininity, non-language or body. Thus Christ, the Son of man, when all is said and done is 'human' only through his mother – as if Christly or Christian humanism could only be a materialism (this is, besides, what some secularizing trends within its orbit do not cease claiming in their esotericism). And yet, the humanity of the Virgin mother is not always obvious, and we shall see how, in her being cleared of sin, for instance, Mary distinguishes herself from mankind. But at the same time the most intense revelation of God, which occurs in mysticism, is given only to a person who assumes himself as 'maternal'. Augustine, Bernard of Clairvaux, Meister Eckhart, to mention but a few, played the part of the Father's virgin spouses, or even, like

Bernard, received drops of virginal milk directly on their lips. Freedom with respect to the maternal territory then becomes the pedestal upon which love of God is erected. As a consequence, mystics, those 'happy Schrebers' (Sollers) throw a bizarre light on the psychotic sore of modernity: it appears as the incapability of contemporary codes to tame the maternal, that is, primary narcissism. Uncommon and 'literary', their present-day counterparts are always somewhat oriental, if not tragical – Henry Miller who says he is pregnant, Artaud who sees himself as 'his daughters' or 'his mother'. . . It is the orthodox constituent of Christianity, through John Chrysostom's golden mouth, among others, that sanctioned the transitional function of the Maternal by calling the Virgin a 'bond', a 'middle' or an 'interval', thus opening the door to more or less heretical identifications with the Holy Ghost.

This resorption of femininity within the Maternal is specific to many civilizations, but Christianity, in its own fashion, brings it to its peak. Could it be that such a reduction represents no more than a masculine appropriation of the Maternal, which, in line with our hypothesis, is only a fantasy masking primary narcissism? Or else, might one detect in it, in other respects, the workings of enigmatic sublimation? These are perhaps the workings of masculine sublimation, a sublimation just the same, if it be true that for Freud picturing Da Vinci, and even for Da Vinci himself, the taming of that economy (of the Maternal or of primary narcissism) is a requirement for artistic, literary or painterly accomplishment?

Within that perspective, however, there are two questions, among others, that remain unanswered. What is there, in the portrayal of the Maternal in general and particularly in its Christian, virginal, one, that reduces social anguish and gratifies a male being; what is there that also satisfies a woman so that a commonality of the sexes is set up, beyond and in spite of their glaring incompatibility and permanent warfare? Beyond social and political demands, this takes the well-known 'discontents' of our civilization to a level where Freud would not follow – the discontents of the species.

A triumph of the unconscious in monotheism

It would seem that the 'virgin' attribute for Mary is a translation error, the translator having substituted for the Semitic term that indicates the socio-legal status of a young unmarried woman the Greek word *parthenos*, which on the other hand specifies a physiological and psychological condition: virginity. One might read into this the Indo-European fascination (which Dumezil analysed)[2] with the virgin daughter as guardian of paternal power; one might also detect an ambivalent conspiracy, through excessive spiritualization, of the mother-goddess and the underlying matriarchy with which Greek culture and Jewish monotheism kept struggling. The fact remains that Western Christianity has organized that 'translation error', projected its own fantasies into it and produced one of the most powerful imaginary constructs known in the history of civilizations.

The story of the virginal cult in Christianity amounts in fact to the imposition of pagan-rooted beliefs on, and often against, dogmas of the official Church. It is true that the Gospels already posit Mary's existence. But they suggest only very discreetly the immaculate conception of Christ's mother, they say nothing concerning Mary's own background and speak of her only seldom at the side of her son or during crucifixion. Thus Matthew 1.20 ('...the angel of the Lord appeared to him in a dream and said, "Joseph, son of David, do not be afraid to take Mary home as your wife, because she has conceived what is in her by the Holy Spirit"'), and Luke 1.34 ('Mary said to the angel, "But how can this come about since I do not know man?"'), open a door, a narrow opening for all that, but one that would soon widen thanks to apocryphal additions, on impregnation without sexuality; according to this notion a woman, preserved from masculine intervention, conceives alone with a 'third party', a non-person, the Spirit. In the rare instances when the Mother of Jesus appears in the Gospels, she is informed that filial relationship rests not with the flesh but with the name or, in other words, that any possible matrilinearism is to be repudiated and the symbolic link alone is to last. We thus have Luke 2.48–9 ('...his mother said to him, "My child, why have you done this to us? See how worried your father and I have been, looking for you." "Why were you looking for me?" he replied. "Did you not know that I must be busy with my father's affairs?"'), and also John 2.3–5 ('...the mother of Jesus said to him, "They have no wine." Jesus said, "Woman, why turn to me?[3] My hour has not come yet."') and 19.26–7 ('Seeing his mother and the disciple he loved standing near her, Jesus said to his mother, "Woman, this is your son." Then to the disciple he said, "This is your mother." And from that moment the disciple made a place for her in his home.').

Starting from this programmatic material, rather skimpy nevertheless, a compelling imaginary construct proliferated in essentially three directions. In the first place, there was the matter of drawing a parallel between Mother and Son by expanding the theme of the immaculate conception, inventing a biography of Mary similar to that of Jesus and, by depriving her of sin, to deprive her of death: Mary leaves by way of Dormition or Assumption. Next, she needed letters patent of nobility, a power that, even though exercised in the beyond, is none the less political, since Mary was to be proclaimed queen, given the attributes and paraphernalia of royalty and, in parallel fashion, declared Mother of the divine institution on earth, the Church. Finally, the relationship with Mary and from Mary was to be revealed as the prototype of love relationships and followed two fundamental aspects of Western love: courtly love and child love, thus fitting the entire range that goes from sublimation to asceticism and masochism.

Neither sex nor death

Mary's life, devised on the model of the life of Jesus, seems to be the fruit of apocryphal literature. The story of her own miraculous conception, called 'immaculate conception', by Anne and Joachim, after a long, barren marriage, together with her biography as a pious maiden, show up in apocryphal sources as early as the end of the first century. Their entirety may be found in the *Secret Book of James* and also in one of pseudo-epigrapha, the Gospel according to the Hebrews (which inspired Giotto's frescos, for instance). Those 'facts' were quoted by Clement or Alexandria and Origen but not officially accepted; even though the Eastern Church tolerated them readily, they were translated into Latin only in the sixteenth century. Yet the West was not long before glorifying the life of Mary on its own but always under orthodox guidance. The first Latin poem, 'Maria', on the birth of Mary was written by the nun Hrotswith von Gandersheim (who died before 1002), a playwright and poet.

Fourth-century asceticism, developed by the Fathers of the Church, was grafted on that apocryphal shoot in order to bring out and rationalize the immaculate conception postulate. The demonstration was based on a simple logical relation: the intertwining of sexuality and death. Since they are mutually implicated with each other, one cannot avoid the one without fleeing the other. This asceticism, applicable to both sexes, was vigorously expressed by John Chrysostom (*On Virginity*: 'For where there is death there is also sexual copulation, and where there is no death there is no sexual copulation either'); even though he was attacked by Augustine and Aquinas, he none the less fuelled Christian doctrine. Thus, Augustine condemned 'concupiscence' (*epithumia*) and posited that Mary's virginity is in fact only a logical precondition of Christ's chastity. The Orthodox Church, heir no doubt to a matriarchy that was more intense in Eastern European societies, emphasized Mary's virginity more boldly. Mary was contrasted with Eve, life with death (Jerome, *Letter 22*, 'Death came through Eve but life came through Mary';

Irenaeus, 'Through Mary the snake becomes a dove and we are freed from the chains of death'). People even got involved in tortuous arguments in order to demonstrate that Mary remained a virgin after childbirth (thus the second Constantinople council, in 381, under Arianistic influence, emphasized the Virgin's role in comparison to official dogma and asserted Mary's perpetual virginity; the 451 council called her *Aeiparthenos* – ever virgin). Once this was established, Mary, instead of being referred to as Mother of man or Mother of Christ, would be proclaimed Mother of God: *Theotokos*. Nestorius, patriarch of Constantinople, refused to go along; Nestorianism, however, for all practical purposes died with the patriarch's own death in 451, and the path that would lead to Mary's deification was then clear.

Head reclining, nape finally relaxed, skin, blood, nerves warmed up, luminous flow: stream of hair made of ebony, of nectar, smooth darkness through her fingers, gleaming honey under the wings of bees, sparkling strands burning bright... silk, mercury, ductile copper: frozen light warmed under fingers. Mane of beast – squirrel, horse, and the happiness of a faceless head, Narcissus-like touching without eyes, slight dissolving in muscles, hair, deep, smooth, peaceful colours. Mamma: anamnesis.

Taut eardrum, tearing sound out of muted silence. Wind among grasses, a seagull's faraway call, echoes of waves, auto horns, voices, or nothing? Or his own tears, my newborn,

Very soon, within the complex relationship between Christ and his Mother where relations of God to mankind, man to woman, son to mother, etc. are hatched, the problematics of *time* similar to that of cause loomed up. If Mary preceded Christ and he originated in her if only from the standpoint of his humanity, should not the conception of Mary herself have been immaculate? For, if that were not the case, how could a being conceived in sin and harbouring it in herself produce a God? Some apocryphal writers had not hesitated, without too much caution, to suggest such an absence of sin in Mary's conception, but the Fathers of the Church were more careful. Bernard of Clairvaux is reluctant to extol the conception of Mary by Anne, and thus he tries to check the homologation of Mary with Christ. But it fell upon Duns Scotus to change the hesitation over the promotion of a mother spasm of syncopated void. I no longer hear anything, but the eardrum keeps transmitting this resonant vertigo to my skull, the hair. My body is no longer mine, it doubles up, suffers, bleeds, catches cold, puts its teeth in, slobbers, coughs, is covered with pimples, and it laughs. And yet, when its own joy, my child's, returns, its smile washes only my eyes. But the pain, its pain – it comes from inside, never remains apart, other, it inflames me at once, without a second's respite. As if that was what I had given birth to and, not willing to part from me, insisted on coming back, dwelled in me permanently. One does not give birth in pain, one gives birth to pain: the child represents it and henceforth it settles in, it is continuous. Obviously you may close your eyes, cover up your ears, teach courses, run errands, tidy up the house, think about objects, subjects. But a mother is always branded by pain, she yields to it. 'And a sword will pierce your own soul too...'

Dream without glow, without sound, dream of brawn. Dark twisting, pain in the back, the arms, the thighs – pincers

goddess within Christianity into a logical problem, thus saving them both, the Great Mother as well as logic. He viewed Mary's birth as a *praeredemptio*, as a matter of congruency: if it be true that Christ alone saves us through his redemption on the cross, the Virgin who bore him can but be preserved from sin in 'recursive' fashion, from the time of her own conception up to that redemption.

For or against, with dogma or logical shrewdness, the battle around the Virgin intensified between Jesuits and Dominicans, but the Counter-Reformation, as is well known, finally ended the resistance: henceforth, Catholics venerated Mary in herself. The Society of Jesus succeeded in completing a process of popular pressure distilled by patristic asceticism, and in reducing, with neither explicit hostility nor brutal rejection, the share of the Maternal (in the sense given above) useful to a certain balance between the two sexes. Curiously and necessarily, when that balance began to be seriously threatened in the nineteenth century, the Catholic Church – more dialectical and subtle here than the Protestants who were already spawning the first suffragettes – raised the Immaculate Conception to dogma status in 1854. It is often suggested that the blossoming of feminism turned into fibres, infernos bursting veins, stones breaking bones: grinders of volumes, expanses, spaces, lines, points. All those words, now, ever visible things to register the roar of a silence that hurts all over. As if a geometry ghost could suffer when collapsing in a noiseless tumult... Yet the eye picked up nothing, the ear remained deaf. But everything swarmed, and crumbled, and twisted, and broke – the grinding continued... Then, slowly, a shadowy shape gathered, became detached, darkened, stood out: seen from what must be the true place of my head, it was the right side of my pelvis. Just bony, sleek, yellow, misshapen, a piece of my body jutting out unnaturally, unsymmetrically, but slit: severed scaly surface, revealing under this disproportionate pointed limb the fibres of a marrow... Frozen placenta, live limb of a skeleton, monstrous graft of life on myself, a living dead. Life...death...undecidable. During delivery it went to the left with the afterbirth...My removed marrow, which nevertheless acts as a graft, which wounds but increases me. Paradox: deprivation and benefit of childbirth. But calm

in Protestant countries is due, among other things, to the greater initiative allowed women on the social and ritual plane. One might wonder if, in addition, such a flowering is not the result of a *lack* in the Protestant religious structure with respect to the Maternal, which, on the contrary, was elaborated within Catholicism with a refinement to which the Jesuits gave the final touch, and which still makes Catholicism very difficult to analyse.

The fulfilment, under the name of Mary, of a totality made of woman and God is finally accomplished through the avoidance of death. The Virgin Mary experiences a fate more radiant than her son's: she undergoes no Calvary, she has no tomb, she doesn't die and hence has no need to rise from the dead. Mary doesn't die but, as if to echo oriental beliefs, Taoist among others, according to which human bodies pass from one place to another in an eternal flow that constitutes a carbon copy of the maternal receptacle – she is transported.

Her transition is more passive in the Eastern Church: it is a Dormition (*Koimesis*) during which, according to a number of iconographic representations, Mary can be seen changed into a little girl in the arms of her son who henceforth becomes her father; she thus finally hovers over pain, over the terror of this dried branch that comes back to life, cut off, wounded, deprived of its sparkling bark. The calm of another life, the life of that other who wends his way while I remain henceforth like a framework. Still life. There is him, however, his own flesh, which was mine yesterday. Death, then, how could I yield to it?

reverses her role as Mother into a Daughter's role for the greater pleasure of those who enjoy Freud's 'Theme of the Three Caskets'.

Indeed, *mother* of her son and his *daughter* as well, Mary is also, and besides, his *wife*: she therefore actualizes the threefold metamorphosis of a woman in the tightest parenthood structure. From 1135 on, transposing the Song of Songs, Bernard of Clairvaux glorifies Mary in her role of beloved and wife. But Catherine of Alexandria (said to have been martyred in 307) already pictured herself as receiving the wedding ring from Christ, with the Virgin's help, while Catherine of Siena (1347–80) goes through a mystical wedding with him. Is it the impact of Mary's function as Christ's beloved and wife that is responsible for the blossoming out of the Marian cult in the West after Bernard and thanks to the Cistercians? '*Vergine Madre, figlia del tuo Figlio*', Dante exclaims, thus probably best condensing the gathering of the three feminine functions (daughter-wife-mother) within a totality where they vanish as specific corporealities while retaining their psychological functions. Their bond makes up the basis of unchanging and timeless spirituality; 'the set time limit of an eternal design' [*Termine fisso d'eterno consiglio*], as Dante masterfully points out in his *Divine Comedy*.

The transition is more active in the West, with Mary rising body and soul towards the other world in an *Assumption*. That feast, honoured in Byzantium as early as the fourth century, reaches Gaul in the seventh under the influence of the Eastern Church; but the earliest Western visions of the Virgin's assumption, women's visions (particularly that of Elizabeth von Schonau who died in 1164), date only from the twelfth century. For the Vatican, the Assumption became dogma only in 1950. What death anguish was it intended to soothe after the conclusion of the deadliest of wars?

Image of power

On the side of 'power', *Maria Regina* appears in imagery as early as the sixth century in the church of Santa Maria Antiqua in Rome. Interestingly enough, it is she, woman and mother, who is called upon to represent supreme earthly power. Christ is king but neither he nor his father are pictured wearing crowns, diadems, costly paraphernalia and other external signs of abundant material goods. That opulent infringement to Christian idealism is centred on the Virgin Mother. Later, when she assumed the title of *Our Lady*, this will also be in analogy to the earthly power of the noble feudal lady of medieval courts. Mary's function as guardian of power, later checked when the Church became wary of it, nevertheless persisted in popular and pictural representation, witness Piero della Francesca's impressive painting, *Madonna della Misericordia*, which was disavowed by Catholic authorities at the time. And yet, not only did the papacy revere more and more the Christly mother as the Vatican's power over cities and municipalities was strengthened, it also openly identified its own institution with the Virgin: Mary was officially proclaimed Queen by Pius XII in 1954 and *Mater Ecclesiae* in 1964.

Eia Mater, fons amoris!

Fundamental aspects of Western love finally converged on Mary. In a first step, it indeed appears that the Marian cult homologizing Mary with Jesus and carrying asceticism to the extreme was opposed to courtly love for the noble lady, which, while representing social transgression, was not at all a physical or moral sin. And yet, at the very dawn of a 'courtliness' that was still very carnal, Mary and the Lady shared one common trait: they are the focal point of men's desires and aspirations. Moreover, because they were unique and thus excluded all other women, both the Lady and the Virgin embodied an absolute authority the more attractive as it appeared removed from paternal sternness. This feminine power must have been experienced as denied power, more pleasant to seize because it was both archaic and secondary, a kind of substitute for effective power in the family and the city but no less authoritarian, the underhand double of explicit phallic power. As early as the thirteenth century, thanks to the implantation of ascetic Christianity and especially, as early as 1328, to the promulgation of Salic laws, which excluded daughters from the inheritance and thus made the loved one very vulnerable and coloured one's love for her with all the hues of the impossible, the Marian and courtly streams came together. Around Blanche of Castile (who died in 1252) the Virgin explicitly became the focus of courtly love, thus gathering the attributes of the desired woman and of the holy mother in a totality as accomplished as it was inaccessible. Enough to make any woman suffer, any man dream. One finds indeed in a *Miracle de Notre Dame* the story of a young man who abandons his fiancée for the Virgin: the latter came to him in a dream and reproached him for having left her for an 'earthly woman'.

Nevertheless, besides that ideal totality that no individual woman could possibly embody, the Virgin also became the fulcrum of the humanization of the West in general and of love in particular. It is again about the thirteenth century, with Francis of Assisi, that this tendency takes shape with the representation of Mary as poor, modest and humble – madonna of humility at the same time as a devoted, fond mother. The famous nativity of Piero della Francesca in London, in which Simone de Beauvoir too hastily saw a feminine defeat because the mother kneeled before her barely born son, in fact consolidates the new cult of humanistic sensitivity. It replaces the high spirituality that assimilated the Virgin to Christ with an earthly conception of a wholly human mother. As a source for the most popularized pious images, such maternal humility comes closer to 'lived' feminine experience than the earlier representations did. Beyond this, however, it is true that it integrates a

Scent of milk, dewed greenery, acid and clear, recall of wind, air, seaweed (as if a body lived without waste): it slides under the skin, does not remain in the mouth or nose but fondles the veins, detaches skin from bones, inflates me like an ozone balloon, and I hover with feet firmly planted on the ground in order to carry him, sure, stable, ineradicable, while he dances in my neck, flutters with my hair, seeks a smooth shoulder on the right, on the left, slips on the breast, swingles, silver vivid blossom of my belly, and finally flies away on my navel in his dream carried by my hands. My son.

Nights of wakefulness, scattered sleep, sweetness of the child, warm mercury in my

arms, cajolery, affection, defenceless body, his or mine, sheltered, protected. A wave swells again, when he goes to sleep, under my skin – tummy, thighs, legs: sleep of the muscles, not of the brain, sleep of the flesh. The wakeful tongue quietly remembers another withdrawal, mine: a blossoming heaviness in the middle of the bed, of a hollow, of the sea...Recovered childhood, dreamed peace restored, in sparks, flash of cells, instants of laughter, smiles in the blackness of dreams, at night, opaque joy that roots me in her bed, my mother's, and projects him, a son, a butterfly soaking up dew from her hand, there, nearby, in the night. Alone: she, I and he.

He returns from the depths of the nose, the vocal chords, the lungs, the ears, pierces their smothering stopping sickness swab, and awakens in his eyes. Gentleness of the sleeping face, contours of pinkish jade – forehead, eyebrows, nostrils, cheeks, parted features of the mouth, delicate, hard, pointed chin. Without fold or shadow, neither being nor unborn, neither present nor absent, but real, real inaccessible

certain feminine masochism but also displays its counterpart in gratification and *jouissance*. The truth of it is that the lowered head of the mother before her son is accompanied by the immeasurable pride of the one who knows she is also his wife and daughter. She knows she is destined to that eternity (of the spirit or of the species), of which every mother is unconsciously aware, and with regard to which maternal devotion or even sacrifice is but an insignificant price to pay. A price that is borne all the more easily since, contrasted with the love that binds a mother to her son, all other 'human relationships' burst like blatant shams. The Franciscan representation of the Mother conveys many essential aspects of maternal psychology, thus leading up to an influx of common people to the churches and also a tremendous increase in the Marian cult – witness the building of many churches dedicated to her ('Notre Dame'). Such a humanization of Christianity through the cult of the mother also lead to an interest in the humanity of the father-man: the celebration of 'family life' showed Joseph to advantage as early as the fifteenth century.

What body?

We are entitled only to the ear of the virginal body, the tears and the innocence, engaging weight and seraphic lightness. A child? – An angel, a glow on an Italian painting, impassive, peaceful dream – dragnet of Mediterranean fishermen. And then, the mother-of-pearl bead awakens: quicksilver. Shiver of the eyelashes, imperceptible twitch of the eyebrows, quivering skin, anxious reflections, seeking, knowing, casting their knowledge aside in the face of my non-knowledge: fleeting irony of childhood gentleness that awakens to meaning, surpasses it, goes past it, causes me to soar in music, in dance. Impossible refinement, subtle rape of inherited genes: before what has been learned comes to pelt him, harden him, ripen him. Hard, mischievous gentleness of the first ailment overcome, innocent wisdom of the first ordeal undergone, yet hopeful blame on account of the suffering I put you through, by calling for you, desiring, creating...Gentleness, wisdom, blame: your face is already human, sickness has caused you to join our species, you speak without words but your throat no longer gurgles – it harkens with me to the silence of your born meaning that draws my tears toward a smile.

breast. With the female sexual organ changed into an innocent shell, holder of sound, there arises a possible tendency to eroticize hearing, voice or even understanding. By the same token, however, sexuality is brought down to the level of innuendo. Feminine sexual experience is thus rooted in the universality of sound, since it is distributed *equally* among all men, all women. A woman will only have the choice to live her life either *hyper-abstractly* ('immediately universal', Hegel said) in order thus to earn divine grace and homologation with symbolic order; or merely *different*, other, fallen ('immediately particular', Hegel said). But she will not be able to accede to the complexity of being divided, of heterogeneity, of the catastrophic-fold-of-'being' ('never singular', Hegel said).

Under a full blue dress, the maternal, virginal body allowed only the breast to show, while the face, with the stiffness of Byzantine icons gradually softened, was covered with tears. Milk and tears became the privileged signs of the *Mater Dolorosa* who invaded the west beginning with the eleventh century, reaching the peak of its influx in the fourteenth. But it never ceased to fill the Marian visions of those, men or women (often children), who were racked by the anguish of a maternal

The lover gone, forgetfulness comes, but the pleasure of the sexes remains, and there is nothing lacking. No representation, sensation or recall. Inferno of vice. Later, forgetfulness returns but this time as a fall – leaden – grey, dull, opaque. Forgetfulness: blinding, smothering foam, but on the quiet. Like the fog that devours the park, wolfs down the branches, erases the green, rusty ground and mists up my eyes.

Absence, inferno, forgetfulness. Rhythm of our loves.

A hunger remains, in place of the heart. A spasm that spreads, runs through the blood vessels to the tips of the breasts, to the tips of the fingers. It throbs, pierces the void, erases it and gradually settles in. My heart: a tremendous pounding wound. A thirst.

Anguished, guilty. Freud's *Vaterkomplex* on the Acropolis? The impossibility of being without repeated legitimation (without books, man, family). Impossibility – depressing possibility – of 'transgression'.

Either repression in which I hand the other what I want from others.

Or this squalling of the void, open wound in my heart,

frustration. Even though orality – threshold of infantile regression – is displayed in the area of the breast, while the spasm at the slipping away of eroticism is translated into tears, this should not conceal what milk and tears have in common: they are the metaphors of non-speech, of a 'semiotics' that linguistic communication does not account for. The Mother and her attributes, evoking sorrowful humanity, thus become representatives of a 'return of the repressed' in monotheism. They re-establish what is non-verbal and show up as the receptacle of a signifying disposition that is closer to so-called primary processes. Without them the complexity of the Holy Ghost would have been mutilated. On the other hand, as they return by way of the Virgin Mother, they find their outlet in the arts – painting and music – of which the Virgin necessarily becomes both patron saint and privileged object.

The function of this 'Virginal Maternal' may thus be seen taking shape in the Western symbolic economy. Starting with the high Christly sublimation for which it yearns and occasionally exceeds, and extending to the extra-linguistic regions of the unnameable, the Virgin Mother occupied the tremendous territory hither and yon of the parenthesis of which allows me to be only in purgatory.

I yearn for the Law. And since it is not made for me alone, I venture to desire outside the law. Then, narcissism thus awakened – the narcissism that wants to be sex – roams, astonished. In sensual rapture I am distraught. Nothing reassures, for only the law sets anything down. Who calls such a suffering *jouissance*? It is the pleasure of the damned.

language. She adds to the Christian trinity and to the Word that delineates their coherence the heterogeneity they salvage.

The ordering of the maternal libido reached its apotheosis when centred in the theme of death. The *Mater Dolorosa* knows no masculine body save that of her dead son, and her only pathos (which contrasts with the somewhat vacant, gentle serenity of the nursing Madonnas) is her shedding tears over a corpse. Since resurrection there is, and, as Mother of God, she must know this, nothing justifies Mary's outburst of pain at the foot of the cross, unless it be the desire to experience within her own body the death of a human being, which her feminine fate of being the source of life spares her. Could it be that the love, as puzzling as it is ancient, of mourners for corpses relates to the same longing of a woman whom nothing fulfills – the longing to experience the wholly masculine pain of a man who expires at every moment on account of *jouissance* due to obsession with his own death? And yet, Marian pain is in no way connected with tragic outburst: joy and even a kind of triumph follow upon tears, as if the conviction that death does not exist were an irrational but unshakeable maternal certainty, on which the principle of resurrection had to rest. The brilliant illustration of the wrenching between desire for the masculine corpse and negation of death, a wrenching whose paranoid logic cannot be overlooked, is masterfully presented by the famous *Stabat Mater*. It is likely that all beliefs in resurrections are rooted in mythologies marked by the strong dominance of a mother goddess. Christianity, it is true, finds its calling in the displacement of that bio-maternal determinism through the postulate that immortality is mainly that of the name of the Father. But it does not succeed in

Belief in the mother is rooted in fear, fascinated with a weakness – the weakness of language. If language is powerless to locate myself for and state myself to the other, I assume – I want to believe – that there is someone who makes up for that weakness. Someone, of either sex, *before* the id speaks, before language, who might make me be by means of borders, separations, vertigos. In asserting that 'in the beginning was the Word', Christians must have found such a postulate sufficiently hard to believe and, for whatever it was worth, they added its compensation, its permanent lining: the maternal receptacle, purified as it might be by the virginal fantasy. Archaic maternal love would be an incorporation of my suffering that is unfailing, unlike what often happens with the lacunary network of signs. In that sense, any belief, anguished by definition, is upheld by the fascinated fear of language's impotence. Every God, even including the God of the Word, relies on a mother Goddess. Christianity is perhaps also the last of the religions to have displayed in broad daylight the bipolar structure of belief: on the one hand, the difficult experience of the Word – a passion; on the other, the reassuring wrapping in the proverbial mirage of the mother – a love. For

imposing *its* symbolic revolution without relying on the feminine representation of an immortal biology. Mary defying death is the theme that has been conveyed to us by the numerous variations of the *Stabat Mater*, which, in the text attributed to Jacopone da Todi, enthralls us today through the music of Palestrina, Pergolesi, Haydn and Rossini.

Let us listen to the baroque style of the young Pergolesi (1710–36) who was dying of tuberculosis when he wrote his immortal *Stabat Mater*. His musical inventiveness, which, through Haydn, later reverberated in the work of Mozart, probably constitutes his one and only claim to immortality. But when this cry burst forth, referring to Mary facing her son's death, '*Eia Mater, fons amoris!*' ('Hail mother, source of love!') – was it merely a remnant of the period? Man overcomes the unthinkable of death by postulating maternal love in its place – in the place and stead of death and thought. This love, of which divine love is merely a not always convincing derivation, psychologically is perhaps a recall, on the near side of early identifications, of the primal shelter that ensured the survival of the newborn. Such a love is in fact, logically speaking, a surge of anguish at the very moment when the identity of thought and living that reason, it seems to me that there is only one way to go through the religion of the Word, or its counterpart, the more or less discreet cult of the Mother; it is the 'artists'' way, those who make up for the vertigo of language weakness with the oversaturation of sign-systems. By this token, all art is a kind of counter-reformation, an accepted baroqueness. For is it not true that if the Jesuits finally did persuade the official Church to accept the cult of the Virgin, following the puritanical wave of the Reformation, that dogma was in fact no more than a pretext, and its efficacy lay elsewhere? It did not become the opposite of the cult of the mother but its inversion through expenditure in the wealth of signs that constitutes the baroque. The latter renders belief in the Mother useless by overwhelming the symbolic weakness where she takes refuge, withdrawn from history, with an overabundance of discourse.

The immeasurable, unconfinable maternal body.

First there is the separation, previous to pregnancy, but which pregnancy brings to body collapses. The possibilities of communication having been swept away, only the subtle gamut of sound, touch and visual traces, older than language and newly worked out, are preserved as an ultimate shield against death. It is only 'normal' for a maternal representation to set itself up at the place of this subdued anguish called love. No one escapes it. Except perhaps the saint, the mystic or the writer who, through the power of language, nevertheless succeeds in doing no better than to take apart the fiction of the mother as mainstay of love, and to identify with love itself and what he is in fact – *a fire of tongues*, an exit from representation. Might not modern art then be, for the few who are attached to it, the implementation of that maternal love – a veil of death, in death's very site and with full knowledge of the facts? A sublimated celebration of incest...

Alone of her sex

Freud collected, among other objects of art and archaeology, countless statuettes representing mother goddesses. And yet his interest in them comes to light only in discreet fashion in his work. It shows up when Freud examines artistic creation and homosexuality in connection with Leonardo da light and imposes without remedy.

On the one hand – the pelvis: centre of gravity, unchanging ground, solid pedestal, heaviness and weight to which the thighs adhere, with no promise of agility on that score. On the other – the torso, arms, neck, head, face, calves, feet: unbounded liveliness, rhythm and mask, which furiously attempt to compensate for the immutability of the central tree. We live on that border, crossroads beings, crucified beings. A woman is neither nomadic nor a male body that considers itself earthly only in erotic passion. A mother is a continuous separation, a division of the very flesh. And consequently a division of language – and it has always been so.

Then there is this other abyss that opens up between the body and what had been its inside: there is the abyss between the mother and the child. What connection is there between myself, or even more unassumingly between my body and this internal graft and fold, which, once the umbilical cord has been severed, is an inaccessible other? My body and...him. No connection. Nothing to do

Vinci and deciphers there the ascendency of an archaic mother, seen therefore from the standpoint of her effects on man and particularly on this strange function of his sometimes to change languages. Moreover, when Freud analyses the advent and transformations of monotheism, he emphasizes that Christianity comes closer to pagan myths by integrating, through and against Judaic rigour, a pre-conscious acknowledgement of a maternal feminine. And yet, among the patients analysed by Freud, one seeks in vain for mothers and their problems. One might be led to think that motherhood was a solution to neurosis and, by its very nature, ruled out psychoanalysis as a possible other solution. Or might psychoanalysis, at this point, make way for religion? In simplified fashion, the only thing Freud tells us concerning motherhood is that the desire for a child is a transformation of either penis envy or anal drive, and this allows her to discover the neurotic equation child-penis-faeces. We are thus enlightened concerning an essential aspect of male phantasmatics with respect to childbirth, and female phantasmatics as well to the extent that it embraces, in large part and in its hysterical labyrinths, the male one. The fact remains, as far as the complexities with it. And this, as early as the first gestures, cries, steps, long before *its* personality has become my opponent. The child, whether *he* or *she* is irremediably an other. To say that there are no sexual relationships constitutes a skimpy assertion when confronting the flash that bedazzles me when I confront the abyss between what was mine and is henceforth but irreparably alien. Trying to think through that abyss: staggering vertigo. No identity holds up. A mother's identity is maintained only through the well-known closure of consciousness within the indolence of habit, when a woman protects herself from the borderline that severs her body and expatriates it from her child. Lucidity, on the contrary, would restore her as cut in half, alien to its other – and a ground favourable to delirium. But also and for that very reason, motherhood destines us to a demented *jouissance* that is answered, by chance, by the nursling's laughter in the sunny waters of the ocean. What connection is there between it and myself? No connection, except for that overflowing laughter where one senses the collapse of some ringing, subtle, fluid identity or

and pitfalls of maternal experience are involved, that Freud offers only a massive *nothing*, which, for those who might care to analyse it, is punctuated with this or that remark on the part of Freud's mother, proving to him in the kitchen that his own body is anything but immortal and will crumble away like dough; or the sour photograph of Marthe Freud, the wife, a whole mute story... There thus remained for his followers an entire continent to explore, a black one indeed, where Jung was the first to rush in, getting all his esoteric fingers burnt, but not without calling attention to some sore points of the imagination with regard to motherhood, points that are still resisting analytical rationality.[4]

There might doubtless be a way to approach the dark area that motherhood constitutes for a woman; one needs to listen, more carefully than ever, to what mothers are saying today, through their economic difficulties and, beyond the guilt that a too existentialist feminism handed down, through their discomforts, insomnias, joys, angers, desires, pains and pleasures...One might, in similar fashion, try better to understand the incredible construct of the Maternal that the West elaborated by means of the Virgin, and of which I have just other, softly buoyed by the waves.

Concerning that stage of my childhood, scented, warm and soft to the touch, I have only a spatial memory. No time at all. Fragrance of honey, roundness of forms, silk and velvet under my fingers, on my cheeks. Mummy. Almost no sight – a shadow that darkens, soaks me up or vanishes amid flashes. Almost no voice in her placid presence. Except, perhaps, and more belatedly, the echo of quarrels: her exasperation, her being fed up, her hatred. Never straight-forward, always held back, as if, although the unmanageable child deserved it, the daughter could not accept the mother's hatred – it was not meant for her. A hatred without recipient or rather whose recipient was no 'I' and which, perturbed by such a lack of recipience, was toned down into irony or collapsed into remorse before reaching its destination. With others, this maternal aversion may be worked up to a spasm that is held like a delayed orgasm. Women doubtless reproduce among themselves the strange gamut of forgotten body relationships with their mothers. Complicity in the

mentioned a few episodes in a never-ending history.

What is it then in this maternal representation that, alone of her sex, goes against both of the two sexes,[5] and was able to attract women's wishes for identification as well as the very precise inter-position of those who assumed to keep watch over the symbolic and social order?

Let me suggest, by way of hypo-thesis, that the virginal maternal is a way (not among the less effective ones) of dealing with feminine paranoia.

– The Virgin assumes her feminine denial of the other sex (of man) but overcomes him by setting up a third person: *I* do not conceive with *you* but with *Him*. The result is an immaculate con-ception (therefore with neither man nor sex), conception of a God with whose existence a woman has indeed something to do, on condi-tion that she acknowledge being subjected to it.

– The Virgin assumes the paranoid lust for power by chang-ing a woman into a Queen in heaven and a Mother of the earthly institutions (of the Church). But she succeeds in stifling that megalomania by putting it on its knees before the child-god.

– The Virgin obstructs the desire for murder or devoration by means of a strong oral cathexis (the unspoken, connivance of the inexpressible, of a wink, a tone of voice, a gesture, a tinge, a scent. We are in it, set free of our identification papers and names, on an ocean of preciseness, a computerization of the unnameable. No communication between individuals but connections between atoms, molecules, wisps of words, droplets of sentences. The community of women is a community of dolphins. Conversely, when the other woman posits herself as such, that is, as singular and inevitably in opposition, 'I' am startled, so much that 'I' no longer know what is going on. There are then two paths left open to the rejection that bespeaks the recognition of the other woman as such. Either, not wanting to experience her, I ignore her and, 'alone of my sex', I turn my back on her in friendly fashion. It is a hatred that, lacking a recipient worthy enough of its power, changes to unconcerned complacency. Or else, outraged by her own stubbornness, by that other's belief that she is singular, I unrelentingly let go at her claim to address me and find respite only in the eternal return of power strokes, bursts of hatred – blind and dull but

breast), valorization of pain (the sob) and incitement to replace the sexed body with the ear of understanding.

– The Virgin assumes the paranoid fantasy of being excluded from time and death through the very flattering representation of Dormition or Assumption.

– The Virgin especially agrees with the repudiation of the other woman (which doubtless amounts basically to a repudiation of the woman's mother) by suggesting the image of A Unique Woman: alone among women, alone among mothers, alone among humans since she is without sin. But the acknowledgement of a longing for uniqueness is immediately checked by the postulate according to which uniqueness is attained only through an exacerbated masochism: a concrete woman, worthy of the feminine ideal embodied by the Virgin as an inaccessible goal, could only be a nun, a martyr or, if she is married, one who leads a life that would remove her from the 'earthly' condition and dedicate her to the highest sublimation alien to her body. A bonus, however: the promised *jouissance*.

A skilful balance of concessions and constraints involving feminine paranoia, the representation of virgin motherhood appears to crown the efforts of a society to reconcile the social remnants of obstinate. I do not see her as herself but beyond her I aim at the claim to singularity, the unacceptable ambition to be something other than a child or a fold in the plasma that constitutes us, an echo of the cosmos that unifies us. What an inconceivable ambition it is to aspire to singularity, it is not natural, hence it is inhuman; the mania smitten with Oneness ('There is only One woman') can only impugn it by condemning it as 'masculine'...Within this strange feminine see-saw that makes 'me' swing from the unnameable community of women over to the war of individual singularities, it is unsettling to say 'I'. The languages of the great formerly matriarchal civilizations must avoid, do avoid, personal pronouns: they leave to the context the burden of distinguishing protagonists and take refuge in tones to recover an underwater, trans-verbal communication between bodies. It is a music from which so-called oriental civility tears away suddenly through violence, murder, blood baths. A woman's discourse, would that be it? Did not Christianity attempt, among other things, to freeze that see-saw? To

matrilinearism and the unconscious needs of primary narcissism on the one hand, and on the other the requirements of a new society based on exchange and before long on increased production, which require the contribution of the superego and rely on the symbolic paternal agency.

While that clever balanced architecture today appears to be crumbling, one is led to ask the following: what are the aspects of the feminine psyche for which that representation of motherhood does not provide a solution or else provides one that is felt as too coercive by twentieth-century women?

The unspoken doubtless weighs first on the maternal body: as no signifier can uplift it without leaving a remainder, for the signifier is always meaning, communication or structure, whereas a woman as mother would be, instead, a strange fold that changes culture into nature, the speaking into biology. Although it concerns every woman's body, the heterogeneity that cannot be subsumed in the signifier nevertheless explodes violently with pregnancy (the threshold of culture and nature) and the child's arrival (which extracts woman out of her oneness and gives her the possibility – but not the certainty – of reaching out to the other, the ethical). Those particularities of stop it, tear women away from its rhythm, settle them permanently in the spirit? Too permanently... the maternal body compose woman into a being of folds, a catastrophe of being that the dialectics of the trinity and its supplements would be unable to subsume.

Silence weighs heavily none the less on the corporeal and psychological suffering of childbirth and especially the self-sacrifice involved in becoming anonymous in order to pass on the social norm, which one might repudiate for one's own sake but within which *one must* include the child in order to educate it along the chain of generations. A suffering lined with jubilation – ambivalence of masochism – on account of which a woman, rather refractory to perversion, in fact allows herself a coded, fundamental, perverse behaviour, ultimate guarantee of society, without which society will not reproduce and will not maintain a constancy of standardized household. Feminine perversion does not reside in the parcelling or the Don Juan-like multiplying of objects of desire; it is at once legalized, if not rendered paranoid, through the agency of masochism: all sexual 'dissoluteness' will be accepted and hence become insignificant, provided a child seals up such outpours. Feminine perversion [*père-version*] is coiled up in the desire for law as desire for reproduction and continuity, it promotes feminine masochism to the rank of structure stabilizer (against its deviations); by assuring the mother that she may thus enter into an order that is above that of human will it gives her her reward of pleasure. Such coded perversion, such close combat between maternal masochism and the law have been utilized by totalitarian powers of all times to bring women to their side, and, of course, they succeed easily. And yet, it is not enough to 'declaim against' the reactionary role of mothers in the service of 'male dominating power'. One would need to examine to what extent that role corresponds to the bio-symbolic latencies of motherhood and, on that basis, to try to understand, since the myth of the Virgin does not subsume them, or no longer does, how their surge lays women open to the most fearsome manipulations, not to mention blinding, or pure and simple rejection by progressive activists who refuse to take a close look.

Among things left out of the virginal myth there is the war between mother and daughter, a war masterfully but too quickly settled by promoting Mary as universal and particular, but never singular – as 'alone of her sex'. The relation to the other woman has presented our culture, in massive fashion during the past century, with the necessity to reformulate its representations of love and hatred – inherited from Plato's *Symposium*, the troubadours or Our Lady. On that level, too, motherhood opens out a vista: a woman seldom (although not necessarily) experiences her passion (love and hatred) for another woman without having taken her own mother's place – without having herself become a mother, and especially without slowly learning to differentiate between same beings – as being face to face with her daughter forces her to do.

Finally, repudiation of the other sex (the masculine) no longer seems possible under the aegis of the third person, hypostatized in the child as go-between: 'neither me, nor you, but him, the child, the third person, the non-person, God, which I still am in the final analysis...' Since there is repudiation, and if the feminine being that struggles within it is to remain there, it henceforth calls for, not the deification of the third party, but counter-cathexes in strong values, in strong *equivalents of power*. Feminine psychosis today is sustained and absorbed through passion for politics, science, art... The variant that accompanies motherhood might be analysed perhaps more readily than the others from the standpoint of the rejection of the other sex that it compromises. To allow what? Surely not some understanding or other on the part of 'sexual partners' within the pre-established harmony of primal androgyny. Rather, to lead to an acknowledgement of what is irreducible, of the irreconcilable interest of both sexes in asserting their differences, in the quest of each one – and of women, after all – for an appropriate fulfilment.

The love of God and for God resides in a gap: the broken space made explicit by sin on the one side, the beyond on the other. Discontinuity, lack and arbitrariness: topography of the sign, of the symbolic relation that posits my otherness as impossible. Love, here, is only for the impossible.

For a mother, on the other hand, strangely so, the other as arbitrary (the child) is taken for granted. As far as she is concerned – impossible, that is just the way it is: it is reduced to the implacable. The other is

These, then, are a few questions among others concerning a motherhood that today remains, after the Virgin, without a discourse. They suggest, all in all, the need of an ethics for this 'second' sex, which, inevitable, she seems to say, turn it into a God if you wish, it is nevertheless natural, for such an other has come out of myself, which is yet not myself but a flow of unending germinations, an eternal cosmos. The other goes much without saying and without my saying that, at the limit, it does not exist for itself. The 'just the same' of motherly peace of mind, more persistent than philosophical doubt, gnaws, on account of its basic disbelief, at the symbolic's allmightiness. It bypasses perverse negation ('I know, but just the same') and constitutes the basis of the social bond in its generality, in the sense of 'resembling others and eventually the species'. Such an attitude is frightening when one imagines that it can crush everything the other (the child) has that is specifically irreducible: rooted in that disposition of motherly love, besides, we find the leaden strap it can become, smothering any different individuality. But it is there, too, that the speaking being finds a refuge when his/her symbolic shell cracks and a crest emerges where speech causes biology to show through: I am thinking of the time of illness, of sexual-intellectual-physical passion, of death...

as one asserts it, is reawakening.

Nothing, however, suggests that a feminine ethics is possible, and Spinoza excluded women from his (along with children and the insane). Now, if a contemporary ethics is no longer seen as being the same as morality; if ethics amounts to not avoiding the embarrassing and inevitable problematics of the law but giving it flesh, language and *jouissance* – in that case its reformulation demands the contribution of women. Of women who harbour the desire to reproduce (to have stability). Of women who are available so that our speaking species, which knows it is moral, might withstand death. Of mothers. For an heretical ethics separated from morality, an *herethics*, is perhaps no more than that which in life makes bonds, thoughts, and therefore the thought of death, bearable: herethics is undeath [*a-mort*], love...*Eia Mater, fons amoris*...So let us again listen to the *Stabat Mater*, and the music, all the music...it swallows up the goddesses and removes their necessity.

NOTES

1 Between the lines of this section one should be able to detect the presence of Marina Warner, *Alone of All Her Sex. The Myth and Cult of the Virgin Mary* (New York: Knopf, 1976) and Ilse Barande, *Le Maternel singulier* (Paris: Aubier-Montaigne, 1977), which underlay my reflections.

2 Georges Dumezil, *La Religion romaine archaïque* (Paris: Payot, 1974).

3 [The French version quoted by Kristeva ('Woman, what is there in common between you and me?') is even stronger than the King James' translation, 'Woman, what have I to do with thee?' – trans.]

4 Jung thus noted the 'hierogamous' relationship between Mary and Christ as well as the over-protection given the Virgin with respect to original sin, which places her on the margin of mankind; finally, he insisted very much on the Vatican's adoption of the Assumption as dogma, seeing it as one of the considerable merits of Catholicism as opposed to Protestantism (C. J. Jung, *Answer to Job*, Princeton: Princeton University Press, 1969).

5 As Caelius Sedulius wrote, 'She...had no peer/ Either in our first mother or in all women/ Who were to come. But alone of all her sex/ She pleased the Lord' ('Paschalis Carminis', Book II, ll. 68ff. of *Opera Omnia*, Vienna, 1885). Epigraph to Marina Warner, *Alone of All Her Sex*.

Translated by León S. Roudiez

8

Women's Time

First published as 'Le temps des femmes' in *33/44: Cahiers de recherche de sciences des textes et documents*, 5 (Winter 1979), pp. 5–19, this essay was translated in *Signs*, 7, no.1 (Autumn 1981), pp. 13–35, and reprinted in N. O. Keohane, M. Z. Rosaldo and B. C. Gelpi (eds), *Feminist Theory: a critique of ideology* (Chicago: University of Chicago Press, 1982). From a feminist perspective, this is one of Kristeva's most important essays, not least because she here explicitly addresses the question of feminism and its relations to femininity on the one hand, and the symbolic order on the other. According to Kristeva, female subjectivity would seem to be linked both to *cyclical* time (repetition) and to *monumental* time (eternity), at least in so far as both are ways of conceptualizing time from the perspective of motherhood and reproduction. The time of history, however, can be characterized as *linear* time: time as project, teleology, departure, progression and arrival. This linear time is also that of language considered as the enunciation of a *sequence* of words.

In 'Women's Time', Kristeva's explicit aim is to emphasize the *multiplicity* of female expressions and preoccupations so as not to homogenize 'woman', while at the same time insisting on the necessary recognition of sexual difference as psychoanalysis sees it. Stressing that for her, the word 'generation' emphasizes less a chronology than a signifying space, Kristeva distinguishes between two generations of feminists: the first wave of egalitarian feminists demanding equal rights with men or, in other words, their right to a place in linear time, and the second generation, emerging after 1968, which emphasized women's radical difference from men and demanded women's right to remain *outside* the linear time of history and politics. After an examination of the role of socialism and Freudianism in relation to the demands of the women's movement, Kristeva focuses on the problems of the second position, perceived as a 'counter-ideology' which risks degenerating into an inverted form of sexism.

A new generation of feminists is now emerging, however, a generation which will have to confront the task of reconciling maternal time (motherhood) with linear (political and historical) time. Unless we manage to theorize women's continued desire to have children, Kristeva argues, we leave the door wide open to religion and mysticism. The new generation, or more accurately, the corporeal and desiring mental space now available to women is one that advocates the parallel existence or the intermingling of all three approaches to feminism, all three concepts of time within the same historical moment. Presupposing as it does the deconstruction of the concept of 'identity', this demand opens up a space where individual difference is allowed free play. Anarchy will be avoided through the 'interiorization of the founding separation of the socio-symbolic contract' or, in other words, by the acceptance and integration of castration and sexual difference as the original, founding moment of civilization.

Women's Time

The nation – dream and reality of the nineteenth century – seems to have reached both its apogee and its limits when the 1929 crash and the National-Socialist apocalypse demolished the pillars that, according to Marx, were its essence: economic homogeneity, historical tradition and linguistic unity. It could indeed be demonstrated that the Second World War, though fought in the name of national values (in the above sense of the term), brought an end to the nation as a reality: it was turned into a mere illusion which, from that point forward, would be preserved only for ideological or strictly political purposes, its social and philosophical coherence having collapsed. To move quickly towards the specific problematic that will occupy us in this article, let us say that the chimera of economic *homogeneity* gave way to *interdependence* (when not submission to the economic superpowers), while *historical* tradition and *linguistic* unity were recast as a broader and deeper determinant: what might be called a *symbolic denominator*, defined as the cultural and religious memory forged by the interweaving of history and geography. The variants of this memory produce social territories which then redistribute the cutting up into political parties which is still in use but losing strength. At the same time, this memory or symbolic denominator, common to them all, reveals beyond economic globalization and/or uniformization certain characteristics transcending the nation that sometimes embrace an entire continent. A new social ensemble superior to the nation has thus been constituted, within which the nation, far from losing its own traits, rediscovers and accentuates them in a strange temporality, in a kind of 'future perfect', where the most deeply repressed past gives a distinctive character to a logical and sociological distribution of the most modern type. For this memory or symbolic common denominator concerns the response that human groupings, united in space and time, have given not to the problems of the *production* of material goods (i.e., the domain of the economy and of the human relationships it implies, politics, etc.) but, rather, to those of *reproduction*, survival of the species, life and death, the body, sex and symbol. If it is true, for example, that Europe is representative of such a socio-cultural ensemble, it seems to me that its existence is based more on this 'symbolic denomination', which its art, philosophy and religions manifest, than on its economic profile, which is certainly interwoven with collective memory but whose traits change rather rapidly under pressure from its partners.

It is clear that a social ensemble thus constituted possesses both a *solidity* rooted in a particular mode of reproduction and its representations through which the biological species is connected to its humanity, which is a tributary of time: as well as a certain *fragility* as a result of the fact that, through its universality, the symbolic common denominator is necessarily echoed in the corresponding symbolic denominator of another socio-cultural ensemble. Thus, barely constituted as such, Europe finds itself being asked to compare itself with, or even to recognize itself in, the cultural, artistic, philosophical and religious constructions belonging to other supra-national socio-cultural ensembles. This seems natural when the entities involved were linked by history (e.g., Europe and North America, or Europe and Latin America), but the phenomenon also occurs when the universality of this denominator we have called symbolic juxtaposes modes of production and reproduction apparently opposed in both the past and the present (e.g., Europe and India, or Europe and China). In short, with socio-cultural ensembles of the European type, we are constantly faced with a double problematic: that of their *identity* constituted by historical sedimentation, and that of their *loss of identity* which is produced by this connection of memories which escape from history only to encounter anthropology. In other words, we confront two temporal dimensions: the time of linear history, or *cursive time* (as Nietzsche called it), and the time of another history, thus another time, *monumental time* (again according to Nietzsche), which englobes these supra-national, socio-cultural ensembles within even larger entities.

I should like to draw attention to certain formations which seem to me to summarize the dynamics of a socio-cultural organism of this type. The question is one of socio-cultural groups, that is, groups defined according to their place in production, but especially according to their role in the mode of reproduction and its representations, which, while bearing the specific socio-cultural traits of the formation in question, are *diagonal* to it and connect it to other socio-cultural formations. I am thinking in particular of socio-cultural groups which are usually defined as age groups (e.g., 'young people in Europe'), as sexual divisions (e.g., 'European women'), and so forth. While it is obvious that 'young people' or 'women' in Europe have their own particularity, it is none the less just as obvious that what defines them as 'young people' or as 'women' places them in a diagonal relationship to their European 'origin' and links them to similar categories in North America or in China, among others. That is, in so far as they also belong to 'monumental history', they will not be only European 'young people' or 'women' of Europe but will echo in a most specific way the universal traits of their structural place in reproduction and its representations.

Consequently, the reader will find in the following pages, first, an attempt to situate the problematic of women in Europe within an inquiry on time: that time which the feminist movement both inherits and modifies. Secondly, I will attempt to distinguish two phases or two generations of women which, while immediately universalist and cosmopolitan in their demands, can none the less be differentiated by the fact that the first generation is more determined by the implications of a national problematic (in the sense suggested above), while the second, more determined by its place within the 'symbolic denominator', is European *and* trans-European. Finally, I will try, both through the problems approached and through the type of analysis I propose, to present what I consider a viable stance for a European – or at least a European woman – within a domain which is henceforth worldwide in scope.

Which time?

'Father's time, mother's species', as Joyce put it; and indeed, when evoking the name and destiny of women, one thinks more of the *space* generating and forming the human species than of *time*, becoming or history. The modern sciences of subjectivity, of its genealogy and accidents, confirm in their own way this intuition, which is perhaps itself the result of a socio-historical conjuncture. Freud, listening to the dreams and fantasies of his patients, thought that 'hysteria was linked to place'.[1] Subsequent studies on the acquisition of the symbolic function by children show that the permanence and quality of maternal love condition the appearance of the first spatial references which induce the child's laugh and then induce the entire range of symbolic manifestations which lead eventually to sign and syntax.[2] Moreover, anti-psychiatry and psychoanalysis as applied to the treatment of psychoses, before attributing the capacity for transference and communication to the patient, proceed to the arrangement of new places, gratifying substitutes that repair old deficiencies in the maternal space. I could go on giving examples. But they all converge on the problematic of space, which innumerable religions of matriarchal (re)appearance attribute to 'woman', and which Plato, recapitulating in his own system the atomists of antiquity, designated by the aporia of the *chora*, matrix space, nourishing, unnameable, anterior to the One, to God and, consequently, defying metaphysics.[3]

As for time, female[4] subjectivity would seem to provide a specific measure that essentially retains *repetition* and *eternity* from among the multiple modalities of time known through the history of civilizations. On the one hand, there are cycles, gestation, the eternal recurrence of a biological rhythm which conforms to that of nature and imposes a temporality whose stereotyping may shock, but whose regularity and unison with what is experienced as extra-subjective time, cosmic time, occasion vertiginous visions and unnameable *jouissance*.[5] On the other hand, and perhaps as a consequence, there is the massive presence of a monumental temporality, without cleavage or escape, which has so little to do with linear time (which passes) that the very word 'temporality' hardly fits: all-encompassing and infinite like imaginary space, this temporality reminds one of Kronos in Hesiod's mythology, the incestuous son whose massive presence covered all of Gea in order to separate her from Ouranos, the father.[6] Or one is reminded of the various myths of resurrection which, in all religious beliefs, perpetuate the vestige of an anterior or concomitant maternal cult, right up to its most recent elaboration, Christianity, in which the body of the Virgin Mother does not die but moves from one spatiality to another within the same time via dormition (according to the Orthodox faith) or via assumption (the Catholic faith).[7]

The fact that these two types of temporality (cyclical and monumental) are traditionally linked to female subjectivity in so far as the latter is thought of as necessarily maternal should not make us forget that this repetition and this eternity are found to be the fundamental, if not the sole, conceptions of time in numerous civilizations and experiences, particularly mystical ones.[8] The fact that certain currents of modern feminism recognize themselves here does not render them fundamentally incompatible with 'masculine' values.

In return, female subjectivity as it gives itself up to intuition becomes a problem with respect to a certain conception of time: time as project, teleology, linear and prospective unfolding: time as departure, progression and arrival – in other words, the time of history. It has already been abundantly demonstrated that this kind of temporality is inherent in the logical and ontological values of any given civilization, that this temporality renders explicit a rupture, an expectation or an anguish which other temporalities work to conceal. It might also be added that this linear time is that of language considered as the enunciation of sentences (noun + verb; topic-comment; beginning-ending), and that this time rests on its own stumbling block, which is also the stumbling block of that enunciation – death. A psychoanalyst would call this 'obsessional time', recognizing in the mastery of time the true structure of the slave. The hysteric (either male or female) who suffers from reminiscences would, rather, recognize his or her self in the anterior temporal modalities: cyclical or monumental. This antimony, one perhaps embedded in psychic structures, becomes, none the less, within a given civilization, an antimony among social groups and ideologies in which the radical positions of certain feminists would rejoin the discourse of marginal groups of spiritual or mystical inspiration and, strangely enough, rejoin recent scientific preoccupations. Is it not true that the problematic of a time indissociable from space, of a space-time in infinite expansion, or rhythmed by accidents or catastrophes, preoccupies both space science and genetics? And, at another level, is it not true that the contemporary media revolution, which is manifest in the storage and reproduction of information, implies an idea of time as frozen or exploding according to the vagaries of demand, returning to its source but uncontrollable, utterly bypassing its subject and leaving only two preoccupations to those who approve of it: Who is to have power over the origin (the programming) and over the end (the use)?

It is for two precise reasons, within the framework of this article, that I have allowed myself this rapid excursion into a problematic of unheard-of complexity. The reader will undoubtedly have been struck by a fluctuation in the term of reference: mother, woman, hysteric...I think that the apparent coherence which the term 'woman' assumes in contemporary ideology, apart from its 'mass' or 'shock' effect for activist purposes, essentially has the negative effect of effacing the differences among the diverse functions or structures which operate beneath this word. Indeed, the time has perhaps come to emphasize the multiplicity of female expressions and preoccupations so that from the intersection of these differences there might arise, more precisely, less commercially and more truthfully, the real *fundamental difference* between the two sexes: a difference that feminism has had the enormous merit of rendering painful, that is, productive of surprises and of symbolic life in a civilization which, outside the stock exchange and wars, is bored to death.

It is obvious, moreover, that one cannot speak of Europe or of 'women in Europe' without suggesting the time in which this socio-cultural distribution is situated. If it is true that a female sensibility emerged a century ago, the chances are great that by introducing *its own* notion of time, this sensibilty is not in agreement with the idea of an 'eternal Europe' and perhaps not even with that of a 'modern Europe'. Rather, through and with the European past and present, as through and with the ensemble of 'Europe', which is the repository of memory, this sensibility seeks its own trans-European temporality. There are, in any case, three attitudes on the part of European feminist movements towards this conception of linear temporality, which is readily labelled masculine and which is at once both civilizational and obsessional.

Two generations

In its beginnings, the women's movement, as the struggle of suffragists and of existential feminists, aspired to gain a place in linear time as the time of project and history. In this sense, the movement, while immediately universalist, is also deeply rooted in the socio-political life of nations. The political demands of women; the struggles for equal pay for equal work, for taking power in social institutions on an equal footing with men; the rejection, when necessary, of the attributes traditionally considered feminine or maternal in so far as they are deemed incompatible with insertion in that history – all are part of the *logic of identification*[9] with certain values: not with the ideological (these are combated, and rightly so, as reactionary) but, rather, with the logical and ontological values of a rationality dominant in the nation-state. Here it is unnecessary to enumerate the benefits which this logic of identification and the ensuing struggle have achieved and continue to achieve for women (abortion, contraception, equal pay, professional recognition, etc.); these have already had or will soon have effects even more important than those of the Industrial Revolution. Universalist in its approach, this current in feminism *globalizes* the problems of women of different milieux, ages, civilizations or simply of varying psychic structures, under the label 'Universal Woman'. A consideration of *generations* of women can only be conceived of in this global way as a succession, as a progression in the accomplishment of the initial programme mapped out by its founders.

In a second phase, linked, on the one hand, to the younger women who came to feminism after May 1968 and, on the other, to women who had an aesthetic or psychoanalytic experience, linear temporality has been almost totally refused, and as a consequence there has arisen an exacerbated distrust of the entire political dimension. If it is true that this more recent current of feminism refers to its predecessors and that the struggle for socio-cultural recognition of women is necessarily its main concern, this current seems to think of itself as belonging to another generation – qualitatively different from the first one – in its conception of its own identity and, consequently, of temporality as such. Essentially interested in the specificity of female psychology and its symbolic realizations, these women seek to give a language to the intra-subjective and corporeal experiences left mute by culture in the past. Either as artists or writers, they have undertaken a veritable exploration of the *dynamic of signs*, an exploration which relates this tendency, at least at the level of its aspirations, to all major projects of aesthetic and religious upheaval. Ascribing this experience to a new generation does not only mean that other, more subtle problems have been added to the demands for socio-political identification made in the beginning. It also means that, by demanding recognition of an irreducible identity, without equal in the opposite sex and, as such, exploded, plural, fluid, in a certain way non-identical, this feminism situates itself outside the linear time of identities which communicate through projection and revindication. Such a feminism rejoins, on the one hand, the archaic (mythical) memory and, on the other, the cyclical or monumental temporality of marginal movements. It is certainly not by chance that the European and trans-European problematic has been poised as such at the same time as this new phase of feminism.

Finally, it is the mixture of the two attitudes – *insertion* into history and the radical *refusal* of the subjective limitations imposed by this history's time on an experiment carried out in the name of the irreducible difference – that seems to have broken loose over the past few years in European feminist movements, particularly in France and in Italy.

If we accept this meaning of the expression 'a new generation of women', two kinds of questions might then be posed. What socio-political processes or events have provoked this mutation? What are its problems: its contributions as well as dangers?

Socialism and Freudianism

One could hypothesize that if this new generation of women shows itself to be more diffuse and perhaps less conscious in the United States and more massive in Western Europe, this is because of a veritable split in social relations and mentalities, a split produced by socialism and Freudianism. I mean by *socialism* that egalitarian doctrine which is increasingly broadly disseminated and accepted as based on common sense, as well as that social practice adopted by governments and political parties in democratic regimes which are forced to extend the zone of egalitarianism to include the distribution of goods as well as access to culture. By *Freudianism* I mean that lever, inside this egalitarian and socializing field, which once again poses the question of sexual difference and of the difference among subjects who themselves are not reducible one to the other.

Western socialism, shaken in its very beginnings by the egalitarian or differential demands of its women (e.g., Flora Tristan), quickly got rid of those women who aspired to recognition of a specificity of the female role in society and culture, only retaining from them, in the egalitarian and universalistic spirit of Enlightenment Humanism, the idea of a necessary identification between the two sexes as the only and unique means for liberating the 'second sex'. I shall not develop here the fact that this 'ideal' is far from being applied in practice by these socialist-inspired movements and parties and that it was in part from the revolt against this situation that the new generation of women in Western Europe was born after May 1968. Let us just say that in theory, and as put into practice in Eastern Europe, socialist ideology, based on a conception of the human being as determined by its place in *production* and the *relations of production*, did not take into consideration this same human being according to its place in *reproduction*, on the one hand, or in the *symbolic order*, on the other. Consequently, the specific character of women could only appear as non-essential or even non-existent to the totalizing and even totalitarian spirit of this ideology.[10] We begin to see that this same egalitarian and in fact censuring treatment has been imposed, from Enlightenment Humanism through socialism, on religious specificities and, in particular, on Jews.[11]

What has been achieved by this attitude remains none the less of capital importance for women, and I shall take as an example the change in the destiny of women in the socialist countries of Eastern Europe. It could be said, with only slight exaggeration, that the demands of the suffragists and existential feminists have, to a great extent, been met in these countries, since three of the main egalitarian demands of early feminism have been or are now being implemented despite vagaries and blunders: economic, political and professional equality. The fourth, sexual equality, which implies permissiveness in sexual relations (including homosexual relations), abortions and contraception, remains stricken by taboo in Marxian ethics as well as for reasons of state. It is, then, this fourth equality which is the problem and which therefore appears *essential* in the struggle of a new generation. But simultaneously and as a consequence of these socialist accomplishments – which are in fact a total deception – the struggle is no longer concerned with the quest for equality but, rather, with difference and specificity. It is precisely at this point that the new generation encounters what might be called the *symbolic* question.[12] Sexual difference – which is at once biological, physiological and relative to reproduction – is translated by and translates a difference in the relationship of subjects to the symbolic contract which *is* the social contract: a difference, then, in the relationship to power, language and meaning. The sharpest and most subtle point of feminist subversion brought about by the new generation will henceforth be situated on the terrain of the inseparable conjunction of the sexual and the symbolic, in order to try to discover, first, the specificity of the female, and then, in the end, that of each individual woman.

A certain saturation of socialist ideology, a certain exhaustion of its potential as a programme for a new social contract (it is obvious that the effective realization of this programme is far from being accomplished, and I am here treating only its system of thought) makes way for...Freudianism. I am, of course, aware that this term and this practice are somewhat shocking to the American intellectual consciousness (which rightly reacts to a muddled and normatizing form of psychoanalysis) and, above all, to the feminist consciousness. To restrict my remarks to the latter: Is it not true that Freud has been seen only as a denigrator or even an exploiter of women? as an irritating phallocrat in a Vienna which was at once puritan and decadent – a man who fantasized women as sub-men, castrated men?

Castrated and/or subject to language

Before going beyond Freud to propose a more just or more modern vision of women, let us try, first, to understand his notion of castration. It is, first of all, a question of an *anguish* or *fear* of castration, or of correlative penis *envy*; a question, therefore, of *imaginary* formations readily perceivable in the *discourse* of neurotics of both sexes, men and women. But, above all, a careful reading of Freud, going beyond his biologism and his mechanism, both characteristic of his time, brings out two things. First, as presupposition for the 'primal scene', the castration fantasy and its correlative (penis envy) are hypotheses, a priori suppositions intrinsic to the theory itself, in the sense that these are not the ideological fantasies of their inventor but, rather, logical necessities to be placed at the 'origin' in order to explain what unceasingly functions in neurotic discourse. In other words, neurotic discourse, in man and woman, can only be understood in terms of its own logic when its fundamental causes are admitted as the fantasies of the primal scene and castration, even if (as may be the case) nothing renders them present in reality itself. Stated in still other terms, the reality of castration is no more real than the hypothesis of an explosion which, according to modern astrophysics, is at the origin of the universe: nothing proves it, in a sense it is an article of faith, the only difference being that numerous phenomena of life in this 'big-bang' universe are explicable only through this initial hypothesis. But one is infinitely more jolted when this kind of intellectual method concerns inanimate matter than when it is applied to our own subjectivity and thus, perhaps, to the fundamental mechanism of our epistemophilic thought.

Moreover, certain texts written by Freud (*The Interpretation of Dreams*, but especially those of the second topology, in particular the *Metapsychology*) and their recent extensions (notably by Lacan),[13] imply that castration is, in sum, the imaginary construction of a radical operation which constitutes the symbolic field and all beings inscribed therein. This operation constitutes signs and syntax; that is, language, as a *separation* from a presumed state of nature, of pleasure fused with nature so that the introduction of an articulated network of differences, which refers to objects henceforth and only in this way separated from a subject, may constitute *meaning*. This logical operation of separation (confirmed by all psycho-linguistic and child psychology) which preconditions the binding of language which is already syntactical, is therefore the common destiny of the two sexes, men and women. That certain biofamilial conditions and relationships cause women (and notably hysterics) to deny this separation and the language which ensues from it, whereas men (notably obsessionals) magnify both and, terrified, attempt to master them – this is what Freud's discovery has to tell us on this issue.

The analytic situation indeed shows that it is the penis which, becoming the major referent in this operation of separation, gives full meaning to the *lack* or to the *desire* which constitutes the subject during his or her insertion into the order of language. I should only like to indicate here that, in order for this operation constitutive of the symbolic and the social to appear in its full truth and for it to be understood by both sexes, it would be just to emphasize its extension to all that is privation of fulfilment and of totality; exclusion of a pleasing, natural and sound state: in short, the break indispensable to the advent of the symbolic.

It can now be seen how women, starting with this theoretical apparatus, might try to understand their sexual and symbolic difference in the framework of social, cultural and professional realization, in order to try, by seeing their position therein, either to fulfil their own experience to a maximum or – but always starting from this point – to go further and call into question the very apparatus itself.

Living the sacrifice

In any case, and for women in Europe today, whether or not they are conscious of the various mutations (socialist and Freudian) which have produced or simply accompanied their coming into their own, the urgent question on our agenda might be formulated as follows: *What can be our place in the symbolic contract?* If the social contract, far from being that of equal men, is based on an essentially sacrificial relationship of separation and articulation of differences which in this way produces communicable meaning, what is our place in this order of sacrifice and/or of language? No longer wishing to be excluded or no longer content with the function which has always been demanded of us (to maintain, arrange and perpetuate this socio-symbolic contract as mothers, wives, nurses, doctors, teachers. . .), how can we reveal our place, first as it is bequeathed to us by tradition, and then as we want to transform it?

It is difficult to evaluate what in the relationship of women to the symbolic as it reveals itself now arises from a socio-historical conjuncture (patriarchal ideology, whether Christian, humanist, socialist or so forth), and what arises from a structure. We can speak only about a structure observed in a socio-historical context, which is that of Christian, Western civilization and its lay ramifications. In this sense of psycho-symbolic structure, women, 'we' (is it necessary to recall the warnings we issued at the beginning of this article concerning the totalizing use of this plural?) seem to feel that they are the casualties, that they have been left out of the socio-symbolic contract, of language as the fundamental social bond. They find no affect there, no more than they find the fluid and infinitesimal significations of their relationships with the nature of their own bodies, that of the child, another woman or a man. This frustration, which to a certain extent belongs to men also, is being voiced today principally by women, to the point of becoming the essence of the new feminist ideology. A therefore difficult, if not impossible, identification with the sacrificial logic of separation and syntactical sequence at the foundation of language and the social code leads to the rejection of the symbolic – lived as the rejection of the paternal function and ultimately generating psychoses.

But this limit, rarely reached as such, produces two types of counter-investment of what we have termed the socio-symbolic contract. On the one hand, there are attempts to take hold of this contract, to possess it in order to enjoy it as such or to subvert it. How? The answer remains difficult to formulate (since, precisely, any formulation is deemed frustrating, mutilating, sacrificial) or else is in fact formulated using stereotypes taken from extremist and often deadly ideologies. On the other hand, another attitude is more lucid from the beginning, more self-analytical which – without refusing or sidestepping this socio-symbolic order – consists in trying to explore the constitution and functioning of this contract, starting less from the knowledge accumulated about it (anthropology, psychoanalysis, linguistics) than from the very personal affect experienced when facing it as subject and as a woman. This leads to the active research,[14] still rare, undoubtedly hesitant but always dissident, being carried out by women in the human sciences; particularly those attempts, in the wake of contemporary art, to break the code, to shatter language, to find a specific discourse closer to the body and emotions, to the unnameable repressed by the social contract. I am not speaking here of a 'woman's language', whose (at least syntactical) existence is highly problematical and whose apparent lexical specificity is perhaps more the product of a social marginality than of a sexual-symbolic difference.[15]

Nor am I speaking of the aesthetic quality of productions by women, most of which – with a few exceptions (but has this not always been the case with both sexes?) – are a reiteration of a more or less euphoric or depressed romanticism and always an explosion of an ego lacking narcissistic gratification.[16] What I should like to retain, none the less, as a mark of collective aspiration, as an undoubtedly vague and un-implemented intention, but one which is intense and which has been deeply revealing these past few years, is this: The new generation of women is showing that its major social concern has become the socio-symbolic contract as a sacrificial contract. If anthropologists and psychologists, for at least a century, have not stopped insisting on this in their attention to 'savage thought', wars, the discourse of dreams or writers, women are today affirming – and we consequently face a mass phenomenon – that they are forced to experience this sacrificial contract against their will.[17] Based on this, they are attempting a revolt which they see as a resurrection but which society as a whole understands as murder. This attempt can lead us to a not less and sometimes more deadly violence. Or to a cultural innovation. Probably to both at once. But that is precisely where the stakes are, and they are of epochal significance.

The terror of power or the power of terrorism

First in socialist countries (such as the USSR and China) and increasingly in Western democracies, under pressure from feminist movements, women are being promoted to leadership positions in government, industry and culture. Inequalities, devalorizations, underestimations, even persecution of women at this level continue to hold sway in vain. The struggle against them is a struggle against archaisms. The cause has none the less been understood, the principle has been accepted.[18] What remains is to break down the resistance to change. In this sense, this struggle, while still one of the main concerns of the new generation, is not, strictly speaking, *its* problem. In relationship to *power*, its problem might rather be summarized as follows: What happens when, on the contrary, they refuse power and create a parallel society, a counter-power which then takes on aspects ranging from a club of ideas to a group of terrorist commandos?

The assumption by women of executive, industrial and cultural power has not, up to the present time, radically changed the nature of this power. This can be clearly seen in the East, where women promoted to decision-making positions suddenly obtain the economic as well as the narcissistic advantages refused them for thousands of years and become the pillars of the existing governments, guardians of the status quo, the most zealous protectors of the established order.[19] This identification by women with the very power structures previously considered as frustrating, oppressive or inaccessible has often been used in modern times by totalitarian regimes: the German National Socialists and the Chilean junta are examples of this.[20] The fact that this is a paranoid type of counter-investment in an initially denied symbolic order can perhaps explain this troubling phenomenon; but an explanation does not prevent its massive propagation around the globe, perhaps in less dramatic forms than the totalitarian ones mentioned above, but all moving towards levelling, stabilization, conformism, at the cost of crushing exceptions, experiments, chance occurrences.

Some will regret that the rise of a libertarian movement such as feminism ends, in some of its aspects, in the consolidation of conformism; others will rejoice and profit from this fact. Electoral campaigns, the very life of political parties, continue to bet on this latter tendency. Experience proves that too quickly even the protest or innovative initiatives on the part of women inhaled by power systems (when they do not submit to them right away) are soon credited to the system's account; and that the long-awaited democratization of institutions as a result of the entry of women most often comes down to fabricating a few 'chiefs' among them. The difficulty presented by this logic of integrating the second sex into a value-system experienced as foreign and therefore counter-invested is how to avoid the centralization of power, how to detach women from it and how then to proceed, through their critical, differential and autonomous interventions, to render decision-making institutions more flexible.

Then there are the more radical feminist currents which, refusing homologation to any role of identification with existing power no matter what the power may be, make of the second sex a *counter-society*. A 'female society' is then constituted as a sort of alter ego of the official society, in which all real or fantasized possibilities for *jouissance* take refuge. Against the socio-symbolic contract, both sacrificial and frustrating, this counter-society is imagined as harmonious, without prohibitions, free and fulfilling. In our modern societies which have no hereafter or, at least, which are caught up in a transcendency either reduced to this side of the world (protestantism) or crumbling (catholicism and its current challenges), the counter-society remains the only refuge for fulfilment since it is precisely an a-topia, a place outside the law, utopia's floodgate.

As with any society, the counter-society is based on the expulsion of an excluded element, a scapegoat charged with the evil of which the community duly constituted can then purge itself;[21] a purge which will finally exonerate that community of any future criticism. Modern protest movements have often reiterated this logic, locating the guilty one – in order to fend off criticism – in the foreign, in capital alone, in the other religion, in the other sex. Does not feminism become a kind of inverted sexism when this logic is followed to its conclusion? The various forms of marginalism – according to sex, age, religion or ideology – represent in the modern world this refuge for *jouissance*, a sort of laicized transcendence. But with women, and in so far as the number of those feeling concerned by this problem has increased, although in less spectacular forms than a few years ago, the problem of the counter-society is becoming massive: It occupies no more and no less than 'half of the sky'.

It has, therefore, become clear, because of the particular radicalization of the second generation, that these protest movements, including feminism, are not 'initially libertarian' movements which only later, through internal deviations or external chance manipulations, fall back into the old ruts of the initially combated archetypes. Rather, the very logic of counter-power and of counter-society necessarily generates, by its very structure, its essence as a simulacrum of the combated society or of power. In this sense and from a viewpoint undoubtedly too Hegelian, modern feminism has only been but a moment in the interminable process of coming to consciousness about the implacable violence (separation, castration, etc.) which constitutes any symbolic contract.

Thus the identification with power in order to consolidate it or the constitution of a fetishist counter-power – restorer of the crises of the self and provider of a *jouissance* which is always already a transgression – seem to be the two social forms which the face-off between the new generation of women and the social contract can take. That one also finds the problem of terrorism there is structurally related.

The large number of women in terrorist groups (Palestinian commandos, the Baader-Meinhoff Gang, Red Brigades, etc.) has already been pointed out, either violently or prudently according to the source of information. The exploitation of women is still too great and the traditional prejudices against them too violent for one to be able to envision this phenomenon with sufficient distance. It can, however, be said from now on that this is the inevitable product of what we have called a denial of the socio-symbolic contract and its counter-investment as the only means of self-defence in the struggle to safeguard an identity. This paranoid-type mechanism is at the base of any political involvement. It may produce different civilizing attitudes in the sense that these attitudes allow a more or less flexible reabsorption of violence and death. But when a subject is too brutally excluded from this socio-symbolic stratum; when, for example, a woman feels her affective life as a woman or her condition as a social being too brutally ignored by existing discourse or power (from her family to social institutions); she may, by counter-investing the violence she has endured, make of herself a 'possessed' agent of this violence in order to combat what was experienced as frustration – with arms which may seem disproportional, but which are not so in comparison with the subjective or more precisely narcissistic suffering from which they originate. Necessarily opposed to the bourgeois democratic regimes in power, this terrorist violence offers as a progamme of liberation an order which is even more oppressive, more sacrificial than those it combats. Strangely enough, it is not against totalitarian regimes that these terrorist groups with women participants unleash themselves but, rather, against liberal systems, whose essence is, of course, exploitative, but whose expanding democratic legality guarantees relative tolerance. Each time, the mobilization takes place in the name of a nation, of an oppressed group, of a human essence imagined as good and sound; in the name, then, of a kind of fantasy of archaic fulfilment which an arbitrary, abstract and thus even bad and ultimately discriminatory order has come to disrupt. While that order is accused of being oppressive, is it not actually being reproached with being too weak, with not measuring up to this pure and good, but henceforth lost, substance? Anthropology has shown that the social order is sacrificial, but sacrifice orders violence, binds it, tames it. Refusal of the social order exposes one to the risk that the so-called good substance, once it is unchained, will explode, without curbs, without law or right, to become an absolute arbitrariness.

Following the crisis of monotheism, the revolutions of the past two centuries, and more recently Fascism and Stalinism, have tragically set in action this logic of the oppressed goodwill which leads to massacres. Are women more apt than other social categories, notably the exploited classes, to invest in this implacable machine of terrorism? No categorical response, either positive or negative, can currently be given to this question. It must be pointed out, however, that since the dawn of feminism, and certainly before, the political activity of exceptional women, and thus in a certain sense of liberated women, has taken the form of murder, conspiracy and crime. Finally, there is also the connivance of the young girl with her mother, her greater difficulty than the boy in detaching herself from the mother in order to accede to the order of signs as invested by the absence and separation constitutive of the paternal function. A girl will never be able to re-establish this contact with her mother – a contact which the boy may possibly rediscover through his relationship with the opposite sex – except by becoming a mother herself, through a child or through a homosexuality which is in itself extremely difficult and judged as suspect by society; and, what is more, why and in the name of what dubious symbolic benefit would she want to make this detachment so as to conform to a symbolic system which remains foreign to her? In sum, all of these considerations – her eternal debt to the woman-mother – make a woman more vulnerable within the symbolic order, more fragile when she suffers within it, more virulent when she protects herself from it. If the archetype of the belief in a good and pure substance, that of utopias, is the belief in the omnipotence of an archaic, full, total englobing mother with no frustration, no separation, with no break-producing symbolism (with no castration, in other words), then it becomes evident that we will never be able to defuse the violences mobilized through the counter-investment necessary to carrying out this phantasm, unless one challenges precisely this myth of the archaic mother. It is in this way that we can understand the warnings against the recent invasion of the women's movements by paranoia,[22] as in Lacan's scandalous sentence 'There is no such thing as Woman'.[23] Indeed, she does *not* exist with a capital 'W', possessor of some mythical unity – a supreme power, on which is based the terror of power and terrorism as the desire for power. But what an unbelievable force for subversion in the modern world! And, at the same time, what playing with fire!

Creatures and creatresses

The desire to be a mother, considered alienating and even reactionary by the preceding generation of feminists, has obviously not become a standard for the present generation. But we have seen in the past few years an increasing number of women who not only consider their maternity compatible with their professional life or their feminist involvement (certain improvements in the quality of life are also at the origin of this: an increase in the number of daycare centres and nursery schools, more active participation of men in child care and domestic life, etc.), but also find it indispensable to their discovery, not of the plenitude, but of the complexity of the female experience, with all that this complexity comprises in joy and pain. This tendency has its extreme: in the refusal of the paternal function by lesbian and single mothers can be seen one of the most violent forms taken by the rejection of the symbolic outlined above, as well as one of the most fervent divinizations of maternal power – all of which cannot help but trouble an entire legal and moral order without, however, proposing an alternative to it. Let us remember here that Hegel distinguished between female right (familial and religious) and male law (civil and political). If our societies know well the uses and abuses of male law, it must also be recognized that female right is designated, for the moment, by a blank. And if these practices of maternity, among others, were to be generalized, women themselves would be responsible for elaborating the appropriate legislation to check the violence to which, otherwise, both their children and men would be subject. But are they capable of doing so? This is one of the important questions that the new generation of women encounters, especially when the members of this new generation refuse to ask those questions seized by the same rage with which the dominant order originally victimized them.

Faced with this situation, it seems obvious – and feminist groups become more aware of this when they attempt to broaden their audience – that the refusal of maternity cannot be a mass policy and that the majority of women today see the possibility for fulfilment, if not entirely at least to a large degree, in bringing a child into the world. What does this desire for motherhood correspond to? This is one of the new questions for the new generation, a question the preceding generation had foreclosed. For want of an answer to this question, feminist ideology leaves the door open to the return of religion, whose discourse, tried and proved over thousands of years, provides the necessary ingredients for satisfying the anguish, the suffering and the hopes of mothers. If Freud's affirmation – that the desire for a child is the desire for a penis and, in this sense, a substitute for phallic and symbolic dominion – can be only partially accepted, what modern women have to say about this experience should none the less be listened to attentively. Pregnancy seems to be experienced as the radical ordeal of the splitting of the subject:[24] redoubling up of the body, separation and coexistence of the self and of an other, of nature and consciousness, of physiology and speech. This fundamental challenge to identity is then accompanied by a fantasy of totality – narcissistic completeness – a sort of instituted, socialized, natural psychosis. The arrival of the child, on the other hand, leads the mother into the labyrinths of an experience that, without the child, she would only rarely encounter: love for an other. Not for herself, nor for an identical being, and still less for another person with whom 'I' fuse (love or sexual passion). But the slow, difficult and delightful apprenticeship in attentiveness, gentleness, forgetting oneself. The ability to succeed in this path without masochism and without annihilating one's affective, intellectual and professional personality – such would seem to be the stakes to be won through guiltless maternity. It then becomes a creation in the strong sense of the term. For this moment, utopian?

On the other hand, it is in the aspiration towards artistic and, in particular, literary creation that woman's desire for affirmation now manifests itself. Why literature?

Is it because, faced with social norms, literature reveals a certain knowledge and sometimes the truth itself about an otherwise repressed, nocturnal, secret and unconscious universe? Because it thus redoubles the social contract by exposing the unsaid, the uncanny? And because it makes a game, a space of fantasy and pleasure, out of the abstract and frustrating order of social signs, the words of everyday communication? Flaubert said, 'Madame Bovary, c'est moi'. Today many women imagine, 'Flaubert, c'est moi'. This identification with the potency of the imaginary is not only an identification, an imaginary potency (a fetish, a belief in the maternal penis maintained at all costs), as a far too normative view of the social and symbolic relationship would have it. This identification also bears witness to women's desire to lift the weight of what is sacrificial in the social contract from their shoulders, to nourish our societies with a more flexible and free discourse, one able to name what has thus far never been an object of circulation in the community: the enigmas of the body, the dreams, secret joys, shames, hatreds of the second sex.

It is understandable from this that women's writing has lately attracted the maximum attention of both 'specialists' and the media.[25] The pitfalls encountered along the way, however, are not to be minimized: for example, does one not read there a relentless belittling of male writers whose books, nevertheless, often serve as 'models' for countless productions by women? Thanks to the feminist label, does one not sell numerous works whose naïve whining or market-place romanticism would otherwise have been rejected as anachronistic? And does one not find the pen of many a female writer being devoted to phantasmic attacks against Language and Sign as the ultimate supports of phallocratic power, in the name of a semi-aphonic corporality whose truth can only be found in that which is 'gestural' or 'tonal'?

And yet, no matter how dubious the results of these recent productions by women, the symptom is there – women are writing, and the air is heavy with expectation: What will they write that is new?

In the Name of the Father, the Son...and the Woman?

These few elements of the manifestations by the new generation of women in Europe seem to me to demonstrate that, beyond the socio-political level where it is generally inscribed (or inscribes itself), the women's movement – in its present stage, less aggressive but more artful – is situated within the very framework of the religious crisis of our civilization.

I call 'religion' this phantasmic necessity on the part of speaking beings to provide themselves with a *representation* (animal, female, male, parental, etc.) in place of what constitutes them as such, in other words, symbolization – the double articulation and syntactic sequence of language, as well as its preconditions or substitutes (thoughts, affects, etc.). The elements of the current practice of feminism that we have just brought to light seem precisely to constitute such a representation which makes up for the frustrations imposed on women by the anterior code (Christianity or its lay humanist variant). The fact that this new ideology has affinities, often revindicated by its creators, with so-called matriarchal beliefs (in other words, those beliefs characterizing matrilinear societies) should not overshadow its radical novelty. This ideology seems to me to be part of the broader anti-sacrificial current which is animating our culture and which, in its protest against the constraints of the socio-symbolic contract, is no less exposed to the risks of violence and terrorism. At this level of radicalism, it is the very principle of sociality which is challenged.

Certain contemporary thinkers consider, as is well known, that modernity is characterized as the first epoch in human history in which human beings attempt to live without religion. In its present form, is not feminism in the process of becoming one?

Or is it, on the contrary and as avant-garde feminists hope, that having started with the idea of difference, feminism will be able to break free of its belief in Woman, Her power, Her writing, so as to channel this demand for difference into each and every element of the female whole, and, finally, to bring out the singularity of each woman, and beyond this, her multiplicities, her plural languages, beyond the horizon, beyond sight, beyond faith itself?

A factor for ultimate mobilization? Or a factor for analysis?

Imaginary support in a technocratic era where all narcissism is frustrated? Or instruments fitted to these times in which the cosmos, atoms and cells – our true contemporaries – call for the constitution of a fluid and free subjectivity?

The question has been posed. Is to pose it already to answer it?

Another generation is another space

If the preceding can be *said* – the question whether all this is *true* belongs to a different register – it is undoubtedly because it is now possible to gain some distance on these two preceding generations of women. This implies, of course, that a *third* generation is now forming, at least in Europe. I am not speaking of a new group of young women (though its importance should not be underestimated) or of another 'mass feminist movement' taking the torch passed on from the second generation. My usage of the word 'generation' implies less a chronology than a *signifying space*, a both corporeal and desiring mental space. So it can be argued that as of now a third attitude is possible, thus a third generation, which does not exclude – quite to the contrary – the *parallel* existence of all three in the same historical time, or even that they be interwoven one with the other.

In this third attitude, which I strongly advocate – which I imagine? – the very dichotomy man/woman as an opposition between two rival entities may be understood as belonging to *metaphysics*. What can 'identity', even 'sexual identity', mean in a new theoretical and scientific space where the very notion of identity is challenged?[26] I am not simply suggesting a very hypothetical bisexuality which, even if it existed, would only, in fact, be the aspiration towards the totality of one of the sexes and thus an effacing of difference. What I mean is, first of all, the demassification of the problematic of *difference*, which would imply, in a first phase, an apparent de-dramatization of the 'fight to the death' between rival groups and thus between the sexes. And this not in the name of some reconciliation – feminism has at least had the merit of showing what is irreducible and even deadly in the social contract – but in order that the struggle, the implacable difference, the violence be conceived in the very place where it operates with the maximum intransigence, in other words, in personal and sexual identity itself, so as to make it disintegrate in its very nucleus.

It necessarily follows that this involves risks not only for what we understand today as 'personal equilibrium' but also for social equilibrium itself, made up as it now is of the counterbalancing of aggressive and murderous forces massed in social, national, religious and political groups. But is it not the insupportable situation of tension and explosive risk that the existing 'equilibrium' presupposes which leads some of those who suffer from it to divest it of its economy, to detach themselves from it and to seek another means of regulating difference?

To restrict myself here to a personal level, as related to the question of women, I see arising, under the cover of a relative indifference towards the militance of the first and second generations, an attitude of retreat from sexism (male as well as female) and, gradually, from any kind of anthropomorphism. The fact that this might quickly become another form of spiritualism turning its back on social problems, or else a form of repression[27] ready to support all status quos, should not hide the radicalness of the process. This process could be summarized as an *interiorization of the founding separation of the socio-symbolic contract*, as an introduction of its cutting edge into the very interior of every identity whether subjective, sexual, ideological, or so forth. This in such a way that the habitual and increasingly explicit attempt to fabricate a scapegoat victim as foundress of a society or a counter-society may be replaced by the analysis of the potentialities of *victim/executioner* which characterize each identity, each subject, each sex.

What discourse, if not that of a religion, would be able to support this adventure which surfaces as a real possibility, after both the achievements and the impasses of the present ideological reworkings, in which feminism has participated? It seems to me that the role of what is usually called 'aesthetic practices' must increase not only to counterbalance the storage and uniformity of information by present-day mass media, data-bank systems and, in particular, modern communications technology, but also to demystify the identity of the symbolic bond itself, to demystify, therefore, the *community* of language as a universal and unifying tool, one which totalizes and equalizes. In order to bring out – along with the *singularity* of each person and, even more, along with the multiplicity of every person's possible identifications (with atoms, e.g., stretching from the family to the stars) – the *relativity of his/her symbolic as well as biological existence*, according to the variation in his/her specific symbolic capacities. And in order to emphasize the *responsibility* which all will immediately face of putting this fluidity into play against the threats of death which are unavoidable whenever an inside and an outside, a self and an other, one group and another, are constituted. At this level of interiorization with its social as well as individual stakes, what I have called 'aesthetic practices' are undoubtedly nothing other than the modern reply to the eternal question of morality. At least, this is how we might understand an ethics which, conscious of the fact that its order is sacrificial, reserves part of the burden for each of its adherents, therefore declaring them guilty while immediately affording them the possibility for *jouissance*, for various productions, for a life made up of both challenges and differences.

Spinoza's question can be taken up again here: Are women subject to ethics? If not to that ethics defined by classical philosophy – in relationship to which the ups and downs of feminist generations seem dangerously precarious – are women not already participating in the rapid dismantling that our age is experiencing at various levels (from wars to drugs to artificial insemination) and which poses the *demand* for a new ethics? The answer to Spinoza's question can be affirmative only at the cost of considering feminism as but a *moment* in the thought of that anthropomorphic identity which currently blocks the horizon of the discursive and scientific adventure of our species.

NOTES

1 Sigmund Freud and Carl G. Jung, *Correspondance* (Paris: Gallimard, 1975), vol. I, p. 87.

2 R. Spitz, *La Première Année de la vie de l'enfant* [First year of life: a psychoanalytic study of normal and deviant development of object relations] (Paris: PUF, 1958); D. Winnicott, *Jeu et réalité* [Playing and reality] (Paris: Gallimard, 1975); Julia Kristeva, 'Noms de lieu', in *Polylogue* (Paris: Seuil, 1977), translated as 'Place names' in Julia Kristeva, *Desire in Language: a semiotic approach to literature and art*, ed. Leon S. Roudiez, tr. Thomas Gora, Alice Jardine and Leon Roudiez (New York: Columbia University Press, 1980).

3 Plato, *Timeus* 52: 'Indefinitely a place; it cannot be destroyed, but provides a ground for all that can come into being; itself being perceptible, outside of all sensation, by means of a sort of bastard reasoning; barely assuming credibility, it is precisely that which makes us dream when we perceive it, and affirm that all that exists must be somewhere, in a determined place...' (author's translation).

4 As most readers of recent French theory in translation know, *le féminin* does not have the same pejorative connotations it has come to have in English. It is a term used to speak about women in general, but, as used most often in this article, it probably comes closest to our 'female' as defined by Elaine Showalter in *A Literature of Their Own* (Princeton, NJ: Princeton University Press, 1977). I have therefore used either 'women' or 'female' according to the context. – AJ.

5 I have retained *jouissance* – that word for pleasure which defies translation – as it is rapidly becoming a 'believable neologism' in English (see the glossary in *Desire in Language*). – AJ.

6 This particular mythology has important implications – equal only to those of the Oedipal myth – for current French thought. – AJ.

7 See Julia Kristeva, 'Stabat Mater' in this volume, first published as 'Héréthique de l'amour', *Tel Quel*, 74 (1977), pp. 30–49.

8 See H. C. Puech, *La Gnose et le temps* (Paris: Gallimard, 1977).

9 The term 'identification' belongs to a wide semantic field ranging from everyday language to philosophy and psychoanalysis. While Kristeva is certainly referring in principle to its elaboration in Freudian and Lacanian psychoanalysis, it can be understood here as a logic, in its most general sense (see the entry on 'identification' in Jean Laplanche and J. B. Pontalis, *Vocabulaire de la psychanalyse* [The language of psychoanalysis], Paris: Presses Universitaires de France, 1967; rev. ed., 1976). – AJ.

10 See D. Desanti, 'L'autre sexe des bolcheviks', *Tel Quel*, 76 (1978); Julia Kristeva, *Des Chinoises* (Paris: des femmes, 1975), translated as *On Chinese Women*, tr. Anita Barrows (London: Marion Boyars, 1977). [See also the excerpts from *About Chinese Women* in this volume.]

11 See Arthur Hertzberg, *The French Enlightenment and the Jews* (New York: Columbia University Press, 1968); *Les Juifs et la révolution française*, ed. B. Blumenkranz and A. Seboul (Paris: Editions Privat, 1976).

12 Here, 'symbolic' is being more strictly used in terms of that function defined by Kristeva in opposition to the semiotic: 'it involves the thetic phase, the identification of subject and its distinction from objects, and the establishment of a sign system'. – AJ.

13 See, in general, Jacques Lacan, *Ecrits* (Paris: Seuil, 1966) and in particular, Jacques Lacan, *Le Séminaire XX: Encore* (Paris: Seuil, 1975). – AJ.

14 This work is periodically published in various academic women's journals, one of the most prestigious being *Signs: Journal of Women in Culture and Society*, University of Chicago Press. Also of note are the special issues: 'Ecriture, féminité, féminisme', *La Revue des Sciences Humaines* (Lille III), no. 4 (1977); and 'Les femmes et la philosophie', *Le Doctrinal de sapience* (Editions Solin), no. 3 (1977).

15 See linguistic research on 'female language': Robin Lakoff, *Language and Women's Place* (New York: Harper & Row, 1974); Mary R. Key, *Male/Female Language* (Metuchen, NJ: Scarecrow Press, 1973); A. M. Houdebine, 'Les femmes et la langue', *Tel Quel*, 74 (1977), pp. 84–95. The contrast between these 'empirical' investigations of women's 'speech acts' and much of the research in France on the conceptual bases for a 'female language' must be emphasized here. It is somewhat helpful, if ultimately inaccurate, to think of the former as an 'external' study of language and the latter as an 'internal' exploration of the process of signification. For further contrast, see, e.g., 'Part II: Contemporary Feminist Thought in France: Translating Difference', in *The Future of Difference*, ed. Hester Eisenstein and Alice Jardine (Boston: G. K. Hall, 1980); the 'Introductions' to *New French Feminisms*, ed. Elaine Marks and Isabelle de Courtivron (Amherst, Mass.: University of Massachusetts Press, 1980); and for a very helpful overview of the problem of 'difference and language' in France, see Stephen Heath, 'Difference', in *Screen*, 19 no. 3 (Autumn 1978), pp. 51–112. – AJ.

16 This is one of the more explicit references to the mass marketing of 'écriture féminine' in Paris over the last ten years. – AJ.

17 The expression *à leur corps défendant* translates as 'against their will', but here the emphasis is on women's bodies: literally, 'against their bodies'. I have retained the

former expression in English, partly because of its obvious intertextuality with Susan Brownmiller's *Against Our Will* (New York: Simon & Schuster, 1975). Women are increasingly describing their experience of the violence of the symbolic contract as a form of rape. – AJ.

18 Many women in the West who are once again finding all doors closed to them above a certain level of employment, especially in the current economic chaos, may find this statement, even qualified, troubling, to say the least. It is accurate, however, *in principle*: whether that of infinite capitalist recuperation or increasing socialist expansion – within both economies, our integration functions as a kind of *operative* illusion. – AJ.

19 See *Des Chinoises*.

20 See M. A. Macciocchi, *Eléments pour une analyse du fascisme* (Paris: 10/18, 1976); Michèle Mattelart, 'Le coup d'état au féminin', *Les Temps Modernes* (January 1975).

21 The principles of a 'sacrificial anthropology' are developed by René Girard in *La Violence et le sacré* [Violence and the sacred] (Paris: Grasset, 1972) and esp. in *Des choses cachées depuis la fondation du monde* (Paris: Grasset, 1978).

22 Cf. Micheline Enriquez, 'Fantasmes paranoiaques: différences des sexes, homosexualité, loi du père', *Topiques*, 13 (1974).

23 See Jacques Lacan, 'Dieu et la jouissance de la femme', in *Encore* (Paris: Seuil, 1975), pp. 61–71, esp. p. 68. This seminar has remained a primary critical and polemical focus for multiple tendencies in the French women's movement. For a brief discussion of the seminar in English, see Heath (n. 15 above). – AJ.

24 The 'split subject' (from *Spaltung* as both 'splitting' and 'cleavage'), as used in Freudian psychoanalysis, here refers directly to Kristeva's 'subject in process/in question/on trial' as opposed to the unity of the transcendental ego. – AJ.

25 Again a reference to *écriture féminine* as generically labelled in France over the past few years and not to women's writing in general. – AJ.

26 See Seminar on *Identity* directed by Lévi-Strauss (Paris: Grasset & Fasquelle, 1977).

27 Repression (*le refoulement* or *Verdrängung*) as distinguished from the foreclosure (*la forclusion* or *Verwerfung*) evoked earlier in the article (see Laplanche and Pontalis). – AJ.

Translated by Alice Jardine and Harry Blake

9

The True-Real

First published as 'Le vréel' in Julia Kristeva and Jean-Michel Ribette (eds), *Folle vérité: vérité et vraisemblance du texte psychotique* (Paris: Seuil, 1979, pp. 11–35), 'The True-Real' was originally written as a paper for Kristeva's seminar at the Service de psychiatrie of the Hôpital de la Cité Universitaire in Paris. The original edition contains a transcript of the discussion among seminar members after the paper, a discussion not translated here, although Kristeva's own references to the specific context of the seminar have been retained.

In this ambitious essay, Kristeva coins the term 'le vréel' in order to account for the modernist revolution in Western thought and art, which she sees as the effort to formulate a truth that would *be* the *real* in the Lacanian sense of the term, or in other words: a 'true-real' or *vréel* (from *le vrai* [the true] and *le réel* [the real]). The speaking subject in search of the 'true-real' no longer distinguishes between the sign and its referent in the usual Saussurian way, but takes the signifier for the real (treats the signifier *as* the real) in a move which leaves no space for the signified. This 'concretization' of the signifier is not only typical of modernist art, it is also a striking feature of the discourse of psychotic patients (such as, among others, the famous French modernist writer Antonin Artaud).

Before exploring the function of the true-real in the discourse of psychosis, Kristeva spends some time situating the term in relation to the history of the concept of truth in Western philosophy and logic. Her account of the Platonic theory of the relation between language and truth presents a particular problem of translation, since Kristeva's original French repeatedly refers to the figure of the *logothète* in Plato's *Cratylus*. The original Greek, however, has *nomothete* (from *nomos* meaning 'law'), and most translators of Plato, whether English or French, have therefore translated the term as 'lawgiver' or *législateur*. The original Greek, however, makes it abundantly clear that it is punning on the similarity of sound between *nomo* (law) and *onoma* (name or noun), thus giving rise to a field of associations around names given as laws, the name as law, etc. Kristeva's *logothète*, which literally means 'word-giver', draws on the name/law pun in order to explicate her own particular argument about the nature of psychotic words. We have decided to translate her *logothète* as 'namegiver', in the hope that this will capture some of the original Platonic flavour as well as Kristeva's specific use of the word.

In the *Cratylus* Plato raises the question of whether names (words) are significant by nature or convention. At an early stage in the dialogue, Socrates introduces the namegiver as a kind of intermediate solution to the problem. A mythical and authoritative creature, the namegiver imposes names on things due to his superior knowledge of the truth (the ideas): a role that would seem to make language both quasi-conventional (words are imposed) and quasi-essentialist (words are imposed as a result of insight into the true nature of things). Kristeva's fascination with this figure seems to stem from the fact that on the one hand he symbolizes the Law that according to Lacanian psychoanalytical theory rules the acquisition of language, while on the other hand he represents that space of uncertainty and ambiguity which, as we shall see, is central to Kristeva's theory of the psychotic origins of any irruption of the true-real, whether as discourse or hallucinations.

According to Lacan, psychosis is characterized by the *foreclosure* of the Name of the Father. *Foreclosure*, a term introduced by Lacan, denotes a primordial expulsion of the fundamental signifier (the phallus) from the subject's symbolic universe. Having foreclosed the castrating phallus, the psychotic subject can thus be said never to have entered the symbolic order. This is why foreclosure differs from *repression*: what has been foreclosed is something that never entered the subject's unconscious in the first place. Unlike repressed signifiers, foreclosed signifiers do not return from the 'inside', they re-emerge in the real, particularly through the phenomenon of hallucination. (For further discussion of foreclosure, psychosis and repression, see J. Laplanche and J.-B. Pontalis, *The Language of Psychoanalysis*, tr. Donald Nicholson-Smith, London: The Hogarth Press, 1980).

Closely linked to the idea of foreclosure is the Freudian term of *Verleugnung*, mostly translated as *disavowal* (more rarely as *denial*). After French usage, *Verleugnung* is now also increasingly translated as *denegation* (French: *dénégation*). *Denegation* or *disavowal* is a specific mode of defence which consists in the subject's refusing to recognize the reality of a traumatic perception. According to Laplanche and Pontalis, Freud invokes this mechanism particularly when accounting for fetishism and the psychoses.

Denegation should be carefully distinguished from *negation*. Although the original German for negation, *Verneinung*, suggests disavowal as well as negation, Kristeva's usage follows post-Lacanian tradition in distinguishing between the two. *Negation* then is simply the act of linguistically or conceptually negating a statement: 'No, I did not say that.' For Freud negation is a sign of the lifting of repression: it is the subject's last-ditch defence against the repressed idea which here is emerging. It is therefore clearly different from *denegation* which, as we have seen, denotes the absolute refusal to perceive a fact imposed by the external world.

Kristeva's argument then is that, as the true-real falls outside the framework of what is considered intelligible or plausible in the socialized space of the symbolic order, it is necessary at once to consider why this is so and what it means when the true-real actually occurs in language. The first question is answered by linking the true-real to the psychotic foreclosure of the phallic signifier representing the Law of the Father. The second question requires further study of the rhetoric of psychosis. Kristeva discovers that even in the discourse of hysterics (who, theoretically speaking, as neurotics should only suffer from symptoms produced by repression, not foreclosure) can be shot through with heterogeneous semiotic spaces (hallucinations, 'meaningless' phrases indicating the insistence of the true-real) which mark the irruption of the real into the discourse of the hysteric. The hallucination, which Kristeva, following C. S. Peirce, labels an icon – i.e., a signifier which *is* or *incarnates* its referent – marks a pre-symbolic space and thereby also a gap or a hole in the hysterical subject. For Kristeva, the psychotic hallucinations occurring in some cases of hysteria are linked to the anal drive which dominates the subject in the period before the recognition of castration and sexual difference. The iconic hallucination (the signifier 'green' becoming a vision of the colour green, for example) marks the unstable point in which the archaic (pre-Oedipal) mother is not yet separated from the paternal (phallic) instance. Consequently the recurrence of the true-real or the iconic hallucination marks the confusion of the sexes, and the reduction of the Other (as the site of the signifier) to a 'pre-object' prefiguring the phallic signifier of the symbolic order, but situated in the Imaginary.

This process of obliteration of sexual difference and destabilization of the paternal signifier is then shown to be a feature of certain linguistic categories often exploited by psychotics (such as Schreber who furnishes some of Kristeva's examples here) for their intrinsic instability and ambiguity: demonstratives (deictics) and proper names.

The True-Real

When we listen to the contemporary forms of discourse that try to expound on its source and development, we recognize that the great disruptive force in present-day speech can be summed up as follows: the *truth* they seek (to say) is the *real*, that is, the 'true-real' [*vréel*].

This obsessive fear, which we have always possessed, has become today a massive (if not mass) burden, all the more so since no common code exists to justify, and so neutralize, it.

Perhaps the Freudian discovery of the unconscious was merely the cautious start of an epistemological and existential revolution which destroyed the whole rational system installed by the classical age and marked out before it by ancient philosophy. We know (and I shall return briefly to this) how logic and ontology have inscribed the question of *truth* within *judgement* (or sentence structure) and *being*, dismissing as *madness, mysticism or poetry* any attempt to articulate that impossible element which henceforth can only be designated by the Lacanian category of the *real*. After the flowering of mysticism, classical rationality, first by embracing Folly with Erasmus, and then by excluding it with Descartes, attempted to enunciate the real as truth by setting limits on Madness; modernity, on the other hand, opens up this enclosure in a search for other forms capable of transforming or rehabilitating the status of *truth*.

The spectacles of mass terror and terrorism, as well as the inquiry into the 'languages' of the unnameable provided by the analysis of psychosis and the new experiences of modern theatre, painting and literature, are just some of the indications of how the *true* has lost its former logical and ontological security, and is now expressed instead as the *true-real*.

However, this irruption immediately raises the problem of socialization. How can this fear of the *true-real* be signified and included in a (social) contrct, however modified? The old question returns: how can the *true-real* be made *plausible*?

Let us not be fooled by words: our perspective goes well beyond the limits of the old problem of rhetoric. The traditional true [*vrai*] and plausible [*vraisemblable*], which will be considered, will be stretched by the 'true-real' [*vréel*] (an area of risk and salvation for the speaking being) and by *semblance* [*semblant*], which is given a social meaning by its own perverse cunning. This gives enunciation a topology constructed by heterogeneous spaces which is completely different from ontological topology.

At all events, this is how I have understood Dr Consoli's suggestion that we concentrate our studies this year on the topic of the 'truth or plausibility of the psychotic text' – a formulation arrived at through his work as an analyst at the university hospital and his attempt to speed up and refine this process with the help of the apparatus of semiology. The suggestion could not fail to interest me, as it seemed to outline with the maximum clarity and the minimum constraint the direction in which we have been moving for several years, both here and at La Borde: a confrontation of the psychotic text by semiology and psycho-analysis that would examine the extreme case of psychosis in order to isolate certain characteristics relevant to any speaking subject.

This means we shall be led to consider how the *foreclosure* that decapitates the Name of the Father and snatches the subject away, in-to the real, is *contained* within different kinds of discourse at the very point at which each speaks its *true-real*. We shall therefore have to envisage certain *kinds* of foreclosure (specific to the limits of each discourse), if we accept that psychosis is the crisis of truth in language.

Beside this typology of foreclosure, another, even more delicate task might consist of envisaging the linguistic and rhetorical *categories* as '*strategies of discourse*' that would allow the subject to articulate abrupt passages between the real, the imaginary and the symbolic: in other words, how the real can be articulated through various linguistic and stylistic categories in order to create a possible distinction betweeen true, false or plausible. This archaeology of enunciation [*énonciation*] would then lead to a consideration of the subjective conditions of production of its elements and operations.

But if the semiological or linguistic description (and critique) of categories is possible and relatively easy, to the extent that its problem is not that of the *true-real*, the reintroduction of the latter, subsequent to this description, adds an analytic dimension to the strategies of discourse. These are as much the morphological or syntactic categories (pronouns, demonstratives, complementation, modalization, etc.) as the construction of large units (the narrative) or intersubjective relations (presupposition, interrogation, etc.) within discourse. To impose a psychoanalytic perspective on those strategies of discourse that are used by a text, especially the psychotic text surrounding us here, means examining in depth a question that has remained unresolved in today's sciences of symbols: what topoi are the subject of enunciation permitted to use, by so-called natural language on the one hand, and by rhetorical operations on the other?

In this session, I shall offer only a few remarks, to be enriched by your fortnightly expositions of your own work in the area of 'strategies of discourse and their relation to truth', which our observations of patients may perhaps illuminate or displace. My remarks take the following form:

- a rapid, historical look at the various philosophico-logical concepts of truth;
- the Freudian concept of truth;
- a humdrum example: hysterical hallucination;
- two linguistic examples, which will help to reveal the true position of the subject of enunciation: demonstratives and proper names;
- a thematic example: truth as murder or castration (Schreber, Artaud).

The artificial truth of the namegiver

To continue, then, let me briefly recall the philosophical tradition from which an analytic concept of enunciation breaks loose.

From Plato on, *Being* is already a *true Being*: *esse verum*, as the scholastics were to put it. The strategy of this formulation gradually becomes clearer: the subject of enunciation has foreclosed his real, 'natural' dependence as well as his symbolic debt to the Other. This subject, who is punctual, atomic, put up simply in order to be denied in terms of volume and dynamics (and who will become, with some supplementary constraints, the subject of science), falls within a register of a visionary *representation* that must be sutured in order to preserve it from psychosis. Once the Heraclitean *Logos* has been transformed into visual images, anything that can be considered external to its order takes on the uncomfortable status, not so much of an *object*, as of an object-spoken-in-a-representing-utterance [*énoncé*]: the status of a *complement*. Since the foreclosure of the real and of the Other brings about the fall of the subject of enunciation, the ensuing gap [*béance*] is elaborated through a process of *subtle suture* between different orders: Being, which has become an *object*, now becomes a *complement* in the linguistic chain of a discourse that can speak the *truth* precisely because of this transformation. This shows why the truth in question has nothing to do with the authenticity of real Being, but is synonymous with the *coherence* of the complement-formation, which *is* what this denied subject is saying. It is a truth of the order of syntax (whoever says 'complement' says 'syntax') that can be linguistic or logical, but that nevertheless governs the conditions of production both of the subject of enunciation and of its potential multiplicity of statements.[1]

Grammar, logic, ontology – sentence, judgement, being – syntax, syllogism, reference: the philosophico-logical debate on truth oscillates between three axes which give rise to different movements and disciplines. Since truth consists of whatever is demonstrable, it either frees itself from the laws of the *sentence* and the order in which elements are given; or it lies in the psychic act of nominating and judging; or else it is to be located in the correspondence between this act and a referent, or to Being in general. The namegiver in Plato's *Cratylus* is undoubtedly the prototype of this master-subject of the law who guarantees the possibility of truth in Platonic discourse, by being presented as complete and untouchable, like a God or a fictional creation.

For all the distinctions I have just recalled are indeed to be found in Plato, with the famous suggestion that there is a 'necessary connection' between the truth of the sentence and the truth of the judgement, between the parts of discourse and thought: the Forms (*eide*), that are neither things nor ideas, but which institute the order of 'universals'. A sentence is true if the arrangement of its parts corresponds to a connection between the eidetic essences: from this we derive the notion of truth as revelation, as the uncovering of its *eide*, as *aletheia* (see the *Theaetetus*, for example, which has been commented on by Heidegger). Aristotle, more formalist, perceives one single class of propositions (logoi), that of declaratives which can be true or false, while prayers and orders have only rhetorical value (*On Interpretation*). But the *Metaphysics* is much more Platonic: a statement is true if it states whatever is. Being is formulated in this way, without any explicit relation to the 'speaking subject' other than that of the internal dependence (resonance, interdiction) between Being and *Logos* revealed later by phenomenology. However, if no economy or subject of enunciation is conceived of, already it is no longer the sentence which is true, but what is expressed by the sentence, namely the *proposition*. This is the direction which medieval philosophy was to take.

But the ongoing subjectivization of truth, the fact that it depends on the namegiver inevitably gives rise to uneasiness in the face of another truth which cannot be determined and which does not even operate in its own field of effects, although it is always evoked, like a phantom, by those who wish to understand: that is to say, the *semblance* of truth which is at work in the discourse of art. This widens the field of the *plausible*, making it decidable but uncertain, making homologous with the truth the discourse of another speaking being, who is no longer a namegiver but a ludic accomplice of the law: the subject of art, and the object of rhetoric.[2]

With Abelard, but also with Peter of Ailly and Gregory of Rimini, the Middle Ages essentially returns to the theory of truth as being something peculiar to the *proposition* (but not to the sentence) and therefore to judgement. At the centre of its preoccupations, therefore, is the relation between the speaking subject and a universe of things which are divine and true to the extent that they refer to the divine Thing (*Una Res*). Consequently, this theory puts forward the most subjective concept of semantics possible: that of *modi significandi*.

Modernity, in the major philosophical movements, relativizes the notion of truth, and, while maintaining it, often presents it to us in an extremely attractive way. Leibniz thus recognizes that truth cannot be solely an affair of *actual* propositions, but that unformulated prior propositions (the pre-supposition?) must be found. He grants truth to *non-existent* but *possible* propositions (envisaging a plurality of worlds, including a non-human one). This truth of the sole signifier is suggested in a startling way in the dialogue *De connexione inter res et verba et veritatis realitate* (*New Essays*, IV, v): truth is a network of signs which can be classed according to their printing ink (although Leibniz does admit that truth all the same belongs only to *certain* signs). The more sombre Hegel stresses the inseparability of truth from falsity in the Spirit's movement as absolute totality, and, alongside assertions about the possibility of attaining truth in ethics, gives this definition which acknowledges the importance of the 'uncanny': '*The truth is thus the bacchanalian revel, where not a member is sober*; and because every member no sooner becomes detached than it *eo ipso* collapses straightaway, the revel is just as much a state of transparent unbroken calm' (my emphasis).[3]

The break between the concept of a truth which we might call theoretical and which acknowledges the place of the real, and a linguistico-logical truth, is from this point on complete. In its rupture with classical philosophy logical positivism draws out all the consequences of such a break. Thus, for Frege, truth is confused with reference. *Über Sinn und Bedeutung* therefore postulates that the distinction between truth and falsity does not hold for fiction since its sentences have no reference; but that it applies to historical discourse since the latter is referential.[4] Tarski is even more rigorous in his use of this distinction: 'true' and 'false' apply only to sentences, not to propositions ('The Concept of Truth in Formalized Languages'); but since the use of a sentence to nominate an existing object is the criterion of its truth, and since this use in natural languages depends on circumstance, then truth, in the strict sense of the term, that is, eternal truth, applies only to formal languages.

This brings us to the end of the chain of development which led the philosophy of logic to exclude the question of its *own* truth as it had originally posed it, from 'natural' discourse. Since the namegiver and his true utterance are shown to be an artifice, thought is left with only one alternative: either to conserve this term (truth) for formalized languages and metaphoric (strong) usage in religious discourse; or else to move towards another notion of truth for so-called natural discourses, that is, for differentiated subjective structures. It is the latter which is the wager of the Freudian undertaking.

Truth as separation

Freud rarely uses the notion of *truth*. In the *New Introductory Lectures on Psycho-Analysis* (1932), truth appears as something belonging to religion, or a *Weltanschauung*. Psychoanalysis can never be such a thing, although there is a scientific truth, despite the scientific relativism (an allusion to Heisenberg) which Freud calls a 'nihilism'. It is obvious, then, why the Freudian text most concerned with 'truth' is one on religion, *Moses and Monotheism*, completed in London in 1938. It is a text, as we know, which has been endlessly discussed, but one that is of prime importance for an understanding of Freud, the real issues at stake in psychoanalysis and perhaps even in monotheism and what remains of it today. Let us re-read a few propositions:

> It has not been possible to demonstrate in other connections that the human intellect has a particularly fine flair for the truth or that the human mind shows any special inclination for recognizing the truth. We have rather found, on the contrary, that our intellect very easily goes astray without any warning, and that nothing is more easily believed by us than what, without reference to the truth, comes to meet our wishful illusions.[5]

This scepticism introduces a distinction between 'historical truth' and 'material truth'.[6] The historical truth is a 'small fragment of truth', 'a core', but always repressed; and it is its *return*, in the form of a neurotic symptom or religion, which the subject takes to be the whole, 'material' truth. *('Historical') truth is therefore merely a part (not The Whole), ('material') truth is merely deformed:*

> We have long understood that a portion of forgotten truth lies hidden in delusional ideas, that when this returns it has to put up with distortions and misunderstandings, and that the compulsive conviction which attaches to the delusion arises from this core of truth and spreads out on to the errors that wrap it round. We must grant an ingredient such as this of what may be called *historical* truth to the dogmas of religion as well.[7]

> To the extent to which it is distorted, it may be described as a *delusion*; in so far as it brings a return of the past, it must be called the *truth*. Psychiatric delusions, too, contain a small fragment of truth and the patient's conviction extends over from this truth on to its delusional wrappings.[8]

These observations do not simply mean that such a delusion or such a religion contains an event that actually *occurred*. The proof of this lies in the fact that, for Freud, the 'historical' event in Moses is the 'existence' of the Egyptian called Moses, an event not based on any real historical document (the texts on which Sellin based his work seem contestable), but on a narrative construction, a story, a fiction created by Freud himself.

On the other hand, what this narrative fiction constructs as material truth, or as a deformation of 'historical truth', is the *plausible evolution*, not of an *event* of historical reality, but of a *process* that creates the ('historical') advent of logic: the process of separation. In fact, the Freudian narrative (whose structuration of plausibility can be analysed à la Propp) exists to give meaning, motivation and plausibility to certain 'universals' that recur throughout this narration: *alterity, strangeness, disavowal of identity, separation and murder.* Moses is not a Jew, the Jews leave Egypt, kill Moses, etc. One can even risk the interpretation that this Freudian narrative is the obsessional's way of rationalizing another, more 'psychotic' Freudian discovery concerning the negativity of the symbolic function. Separation, rejection, displacement, gap [*béance*] – isn't it in this way that language constitutes itself and operates in the radical discoveries of Freud? In this sense, even if one adheres to the

Freudian thesis of the murder of the father as a 'historical' (or the) event that is basic to humanity, one can say that all of psychoanalysis corroborates and in a way demonstrates this theory – albeit through a process of renewal within each speaking subject – through the way in which it reveals the modification, displacement and negativity at work within the symbolic function. The murder of the father is thus inscribed within the linguistic sign, which does not necessarily mean that it never took place. *Moses and Monotheism* is not only the most Christian of all Freud's writings (since he affirms that Christians unknowingly speak the truth about – or truth as – murder: that is, they absolve themselves with this avowal, but need a guilty party, namely the Jews, in order to have something by which to measure the price of guilt, and so institute the Jewish-Christian couple that is intrinsic to monotheism). It also shows that the *psychoanalytic mechanism*, to the extent that it leads the subject into the negation and denegation which structure language, is an *invention* that is *hyper-Catholic*, in the sense of being *post-Catholic*. Not only is truth murder (as the Jewish Golem says: 'emeth – meth'); not only have we killed the father (enacted by Catholicism); but *truth* is nothing more than language as a mechanism of displacement, negation and denegation. Freud's work therefore traces a movement in which *truth* is continually put up and knocked down, a process that confronts it in its safest haven, religion, destroys it as *identity* (Being, correspondence to Being, etc.) and leaves behind only a system of passages, folds, thresholds, catastrophes – in short, negation.

Within Freudian thought, precise operations organize various aspects of this modification by which truth is always already 'falsified': the constitutive negativity (*Negativität*) of the symbol; the repression (*Verdrängung*) of the content of affect; foreclosure (*Verwerfung*); and effacement of perception [*scotomization*], a fall into the blind spot of the retina.

Disavowal (*Verleugnung*) retains our attention, first because of its special status: it is at once *specific* (perverse disavowal) and *general* to every neurotic structure, but is also used to describe psychosis (although working within another topography). It is consequently this type of negation which I feel is coextensive with verbal symbolism (it is employed, moreover, by the article on negativity that in particular deals with the advent and use of the word): it gives a negative, if not perverse, dimension to every verbal usage and, more especially, to every art that plays with it, thus exaggerating its effects.[9]

It would seem to consist of a bivalent process concerning the recognition of castration: the boy notes the mother's lack of a penis, but continues to think that she has one. The first attitude creates fear, the second creates fetishes; hence the coexistence of the two. Disavowal therefore centres on the 'perceptions which bring to knowledge this demand from reality';[10] but it is a 'half-measure' of detachment from reality, none the less accompanied by knowledge. As it represents a 'conflict between the demand by the instinct and the prohibition by reality', it is the very topos of the splitting of the Ego.[11] In such a process of symbolization and knowledge, it is our belief that we are no longer concerned with the truth but with reality, prohibition, drive, demand and the conflict between them which is resolved by disavowal. The result is twofold: hallucination (of the penis where it is lacking) and displacement (another part of the body or an object is cathected with the same drive-related demand).

If the mechanism is true, the decisive, and no doubt risky, step consists in seeing it as coextensive with any symbolic and linguistic function. Isn't the enigmatic acquisition of language, which according to some fulfils an innate programme, achieved when the child is in fact capable of withdrawing cathexis from his imaginary representation of the maternal phallus, in order to cathect with at least the same degree of intensity that which represents it, and even better, *any* representative instance. It is this process that opens up the chain of signifiers and the knowledge of a reality which only now is perceived as such.

It now remains to push these consequences to their conclusion: the fact that disavowal is immanent in the symbolic faculty conditions the permanent feeling of loss of reality in the speaking being: 'New elements, which may give occasion for defensive measures, approach the ego from two directions – from the real external world and from the internal world of thoughts and impulses that emerge in the ego. It is possible that this alternative concides with the choice between derealizations proper and depersonalizations.'[12] Between repression and the 'normal method' of defending oneself against what is distressing or unbearable by means of recognizing it, considering it, making a judgement upon it, etc., 'there lie a whole series of more or less clearly pathological methods of behaviour on the part of the ego'.

The area of disavowal ('I know very well but all the same'), the last-ditch hope and defence of the Ego, is introduced everywhere by the mechanism of language. This seems to dawn on Freud as well, since, when using this notion, he employs it as a synonym of the negativity proper to the symbolic function.[13] Is this an improper use of terms, or an acknowledgement of the universal nature of the process? The various subjective structures ('truths') do differ, however, according to the physical topography supported by the term *disavowal* (*Verleugnung*).[14] On the death of her sister, the *neurotic* woman is overcome with desire for her brother-in-law, but by disavowing this *desire*, she produces her hysteric symptom. The *psychotic* would have disavowed the very *reality* of death.

Thus, we have a choice between disavowing 'historical' *reality* (the only radical one, that of death) which places us in the series of the signifier alone (paranoid delirium or its suturing, which is science), or disavowing *desire* (that is, the transference of one signifier to another), an action which makes our body into a symptom and/or a fight against death. In the first case, we have the 'truth' of the signifier, which eventually can be demonstrated (science), but only at the expense of disavowing reality; the psychotic and the scientist bear witness (tragically for the one, optimistically for the other) to an impossible reality; they fail to articulate reality [*le réel*]. In the second case, we have the truth of the symptom, expressed by a suffering body or by a kind of prompted language; the latter is always a semblance, plausible but never true, and only its accidents (slips, errors of reasoning, etc.) relate it to the first case, that is, to the impossibility of 'truth'.

Neurosis operates through the disavowal of desire and/or of the signifier. It is related to reality via a series of rhetorical strategies producing plausibility (syntactically normative language, classical narrative, etc.): strategies of *semblance*, that help to construct subjective economies of identification and projection, normalized and stabilized by the Oedipus complex. The gaps in this system reveal the bodily symptom or induce 'psychotic' operations.

Psychosis proceeds by the disavowal of reality and demands that the signifier be real in order to be true. An indefinite *combinatoire* of signs ensues, beyond the conditions of truth specified by science: this decodes the expansion of the limits of the Ego and consequently of the percept (the object of perception). This is a lexical, syntactic or narrative modification, whose operations we have begun to isolate, by analysing the discourses and texts collected both here and at La Borde. Consoli's study of psychotic negation is very suggestive in this respect. Only the suture of scientific discourse can create a space for reality in this subjective economy, precisely by defining the conditions of logical truth (peculiar to the proposition or sentence) which guarantee the existence of this reality.

I feel more and more that a separate place must be set aside for so-called artistic discourse. If there is any disavowal, it is introduced in the minutiae of such a practice (in each word, sound, colour, rhythm...) such that these are never 'pure signifiers' but always 'word' and 'flesh' and consequently situate themselves at the very heart of the distinction between these extremes and/or their identity to the extent that they are a microscopic exploration of murder *as* resurrection.

This presents us with a chiasmus: access to reality is in the register of the plausible; access to truth depends on the signifier alone although it is achieved at the expense of an eclipse of reality:

$$\text{Psychosis:} \quad \frac{\text{Signifier T Real}}{\emptyset \text{ Reality}} \diagdown \text{V} \diagup \frac{\text{Signifier } \emptyset \text{ Real}}{\text{Reality; P; (t, f)}} \quad : \text{Neurosis}$$

$\emptyset$ = foreclosure; T = truth; P = plausible; t, f = true, false; V = versus.

Religious discourse is formed in the diagonal corridor 'Signifier T Real = Reality; P; (t, f)'. Initially postulating the impossible as faith, this discourse maintains the existence of the signifier as real but retains the dogmatic and rhetorical conditions which produce plausibility and truthful demonstration.

Scientific discourse is situated in the same corridor but, foreclosing the subject of enunciation, it merely translates its economy into the laws of isolated signs. It misses out on the left-hand side of the diagram. Artistic discourse, in the same corridor, eliminates the operator (t, f), but succeeds in bestowing plausibility on the signifier and the real in each unit and operation in its field: a microscopic expansion of the 'true-real'.

To see the voice or the hallucinatory weft of hysteria

In hysterical discourse, truth, when not weighed down by the symptom, often assumes the obsessive, unsayable and emotionally charged weft of visual representation. Floating in isolation, this vision of an unnamed real rejects all nomination and any possible narrative. Instead it remains enigmatic, setting the field of speech ablaze only to reduce it to cold ashes, fixing in this way an hallucinatory and untouchable *jouissance*.

Without being able to speak of hysterical psychosis (in so far as the term means anything) it is none the less necessary to recognize this as a banal immersion of hysterical discourse in the structures of psychosis: a banality seized upon as a historical provocation in the present feminist dissatisfaction with a language reputed to be too abstract and incapable of rendering the truth of the body: or to put it bluntly, with a language that is phallic. In the hysterical hallucination so current in this discourse, we therefore find ourselves in a border zone where the real, in order to burst on the scene as truth, leaves a hole in the subject's discourse, but is none the less taken up by that very discourse in a repetitive representation that produces meaning (thus allowing life and *jouissance* to continue), without creating signification (thus, by producing a too flimsy barrier against the symptom, this process opens the door to the manic-depressive states).

My first suggestion is that, in spite of being representations, these hallucinations do not have the value of a metaphor (which is always a purely linguistic process), but are composite products of *language* as well as of a more archaic register, the *scopic*, and of the *drive* that founders on the differentiation of the proper body and the recognition of sexual difference: namely the anal drive. I shall then attempt to trace the specific kind of foreclosure whose existence is implied by this type of hallucination: a foreclosure of the name of the Father no doubt, but one that operates in a specific relation to the structure as a whole.[15]

In a case history I have come to know, a young woman, J., with an ease that was perhaps slightly too spectacular, organized and rationalized all her personal and professional activities. Nothing appeared to escape her control (apart from a few trivial somatic expressions and bouts of melancholy) except for the enigmatic recurrence of an image, a word, a sensation that was indefinable but always linked to certain moments of great intensity: the recurrence, in fact, of the colour green [*vert*]. Analysis gradually placed this blinding moment that corresponded to no object, not even to the word green itself ('it's too simple, too weak, it's not that') in a series which could be interpreted once it had been elaborated in the transference. The analysts's first name (*Veronica*) introduced the first name of the paternal sister (*Vera*), a name which J.'s father had wanted her to have, while her dreams revealed the mother carrying a green watering-can. Family history re-emerged and reminded the patient of their early worries over the baby's (green) stools, a problem which was resolved with the birth of J.'s young sister. She then detached herself from her mother who was busy with the new baby, and 'flung' herself at her father ('there was already a linguistic and intellectual affinity'). As a case history, this was all too neat and simple, for the female analyst simply had to behave as the Other without actually renouncing her sex in order to avoid being dragged into this 'green' into which J. would have been delighted to [*jouissait de*] take her.

Between the ages of 2 and 3, the young girl experienced her anal superiority: having already paid attention to defecation and distinguished between faecal matter and her own body, she identified this action with the maternal function of giving birth to a new child. This superiority brought to a climax her primary narcissism, that is, her imaginary identification with her mother, and simultaneously represented an exclusion of the father and a defence against the lack of a penis. The acme of the specular therefore coincided for her with a strong anal investment as a denial [*dénégation*] of sexual difference. This anus was rented out to the *eye*: this accounts for the Chinese wall erected by the hysterical woman, a psychotic partition-wall which enables her not to see or know [*sa-voir*] that the Father exists as Other. Within this enclosure, 'daddy' will still be easily reducible to 'mummy'.

But at the same time the imaginary is lifted into the symbolic: the transitional objects can now be signified, and the imaginary is inscribed as what it is, a function of the Other, through the sublation of the maternal site in the paternal metaphor operated by language. The attention paid to signs – images, forms and colours – culminates, through a process of abstraction, in the signifying sound that creates language. However, this isolation of the symbolic from the imaginary, retraced by Lacan in the ideal Oedipal triangle, is never perfect and, in hysterical hallucination, remains as fundamentally problematic as the process of dissociation of the daddy from the Father. The 'objective' failure of daddy (feminization, social depreciation, absence, etc.) is merely grist to this mill that turns on structure.

A signifier, then, by combining index $\overline{\Phi}$ with index A, can bring about not the *gap* [*écart*] separating the imaginary and symbolic axes in order to ensure a normal perception of the real, but rather their *meeting*: an encounter in which the maternal (specular-anal) instance clings for a timeless moment to the paternal (vocal-phallic) instance. Such a signifier uses the gifts of language to target both sides, and is consequently a hallucinatory signifier: *Green* [*Vert*]. Green of faeces, green of fields, the close comfort of mummy, walks with daddy; the verdure of the anal serpent, and the proper name of the paternal sister. Non-object and sublimation. This vocal signifier often designates the visible for the girl as well as for the boy, devoted as they both are to their mother in a prolonged state of specularization. The paternal voice names, but without transforming anything into a sign; it names by flinging itself wide open to the semiotic material that creates a pre-object which carries a foreseeable *jouissance*.

This heterogeneous semiotic encounter (sound/vision, pre-object/sign) is a hallucination that marks the insistence of the *true-real*, an archaic and salutary attempt to elaborate the irruption of the real that leaves a hole in the symbolical weft of hysterical discourse. This hallucination recurs periodically, in order to indicate, like an icon, an unutterable *jouissance* that endangers the symbolic resources of the speaking being.[16] The hallucinatory icon, which becomes obsessive by virtue of its repetition, challenges what may be structured as a language: it obliterates reality and makes the real loom forth as a jubilant enigma. But, since this hallucinatory icon is neither a (psychotic) hole in which the subject might be lost, nor a phobic object that might bring him an anguish as fatal as it is indispensable to his pleasure, it has a double function:

1   It emerges when the question of the lack of distinction between father and mother crops up again, and stresses the fact that it is from this lack of distinction that the hysteric experiences *jouissance*. Or rather from the confusion of sexes which she represents. For it is in this locus that an effect of subject is produced for the hysteric, an effect which she therefore attains only periodically, and at the expense of an hallucination. This recurrence of the 'true-real' is represented by those points where the sinusoid of the imaginary cuts through the straight line of the symbolic, and remodels the 'normal' tripod of the imaginary, the symbolic and the real: see figure 1.[17]

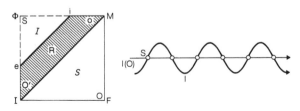

Figure 1

2 It indicates that the Other (like the phallus) as a third term of subjective structure is a universal for the hysteric, but one which can only be included in his or her *I* by being particularized: that is, it can only be postulated by being reduced to that particular point at which *I* encompasses father/mother, male/female, voice/sight. The Other exists, says the hysterical hallucination, as the site of a pure signifier, if, and only if, He speaks to me via a pre-object. The hallucination recognizes the Other only if the father acts as a mother, and vice versa; this is the vice or, if you like, the condition that allows Him to be revealed. Without this revelation, there is no obvious Other for the hysteric, and the denegation of the symbolic reaches its apogee in the psychosomatic symptom. In this sense, hallucination is an artistic elaboration by which a semiotic condensation protects the body from illness.

Symptom ϵ, on the other hand, wishes to fill with the flesh the gap [*béance*] between the two axes (imaginary/symbolic, maternal/paternal), when these axes are separated due to the absence of any signifier that might lead them to cross (as in the case of the hallucinatory icon) or to enter into a triangular relationship (as in the classic Oedipal solution): see figure 2.

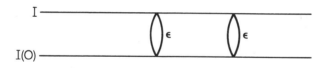

Figure 2

This revelation (that a signifier gives symbolic existence to an archaic *jouissance* not yet cathected to any object), this predilection for vision as a method of sublimation – not as in scoptophilia but, on the contrary, as in painting – guarantees the insistance of the Other in the structure of hysteria. A hysteric, whether male or female, can be devout, provided that God is visible in painting. But this addiction to the visible is merely one more indication of the impasse in which his or her desire finds itself with regard to the other sex.

The icon of sight and speech returns in the form of 'mania': a mania for cleanliness, tidiness, buying, punctuality. Every 'pointillist' or 'tachist' working-out of an anality that can no longer be seen is drifting, not towards obsessionality, but towards a manic symptomatology: the failure of the subject faced with the 'pure' signifier. It is a desire, then, for iconicity, which, in extreme cases, is lost in a gaze that has no object: a blinding field of colour and light.

Let us now turn from the hysteric icon and try to put into linguistic terms this inscription of the real in the symbolic that is postulated for the subject by a verifiable reality.

Two examples of passages between enunciative spaces

Demonstratives

Demonstratives (this, that, this one, that one) mark the passage of discourse within the system of language: they are essentially defined by the use to which they are put by the subject of enunciation. If it is true that they have a referent, it is equally the case that they refer to a sign other than themselves: they are metalinguistic and self-referential. Through the use of the many forms of enunciation which this linguistic category possesses, the subject can straddle several enunciative spaces. This explains the impact of demonstratives in those discourses where the identity of the speaking subject is in question.

In infantile discourse, one notes not only a statistical preponderance of demonstratives ('That's X') prior to their eclipse by the personal pronoun, but above all the contiguity (both spatial and chronological) between the demonstratives and the evocation of the mother or her proper name. The subjective economy underlying the infantile enunciation of demonstratives recalls Winnicott's 'potential space': there is as yet no clear distinction between subject and object.

In psychotic discourse, when the patient is presented with an image, the use of 'this' or 'that' to refer to the same sort of representation varies widely. 'That's me', 'that's a violinist', 'that's a man'. The 'same' imaged referent, introduced into discourse by the 'same' *that*, gives rise to several different positions for the subject of enunciation and creates several different narratives. This 'delirium', however, is merely the realization of the semantic qualities latent in the demonstrative as such, a series of latent possibilities not realized in normal or neurotic discourse. Having denied the latent elements in the signifier, the latter attributes plausibility to a reality (referent), while psychotic discourse forecloses reality and explores the 'truth' (that can be called 'historical', but equally 'linguistic' or 'scientific') of the signifier, notably the potential ability of the demonstrative to place the subject of enunciation in several enunciative spaces.

This capacity of demonstratives to embrace several enunciative spaces has been commented on by Arnauld and Nicole, when considering a use of demonstratives that is famous for not being normative: the words of Christ ('This is my body') where *this* designates both the bread and the body of Christ. The logicians of Port-Royal, true followers of the Cartesian subject, can rationalize the passage from one to the other identity (from bread to body) within the same *this* only through the use of a double justification. They double the demonstrative's space of enunciation by explaining: (a) that it marks 'the confused idea of the present thing'; and (b) that it none the less permits the mind to add ideas that are 'inspired by circumstance'.[18] However, since the *Port-Royal Logic* does not have a plural, or at all events dynamic, conception of the subject of enunciation, it cannot explain the identity of the subject who can assume these remarkably different 'ideas which are inspired by circumstance', to the point of designating the 'same' present thing, that is now 'bread', now 'my body'. Port-Royal therefore has recourse to *time: now* this is bread, *then* this is my body. Reason is saved at the expense of an obsessive use of time that consequently deletes the mystery of transubstantiation. Might transubstantiation then be an indelible thematization of the fold [*pli*] to be found between two spaces (the real space of need, nutrition and survival: bread; and the symbolic space of designation: the signifying body itself)? Such a fold would then be produced in the archaeology of demonstratives (the archaic designation of the mother, the breaking-off of our need for her), as well as in every experience that is at the limits of corporeal identity, that is, an identity of meaning and presence.

Certain religious themes (such as transubstantiation) were no doubt social ways of calling into play the enunciative *true-real* of language (to which, in a more marginalized way, psychosis bears witness). The gradual decline of these religious themes left the task of revealing the enunciative *true-real* proper to language to a literature without such close ties with the community. Beckett's *How It Is* [*Comment c'est*] is a trans-substantiation acting in reverse: no longer from food to body, but from body to refuse. As such it still employs the same demonstrative [*c'est*], engaging discourse in the form of elliptical sentences and mini-narratives (a paragraph, three to four lines), and 'inspiring', around the same 'present thing', the permanent fluctuation in speech between a subject *I*, and an I-object/I-refuse, an *I* referring to objects...

Proper names

Proper names have been compared to demonstratives. For John Stuart Mill, proper names are 'meaningless' (meaning being for him a connotation that implies an attribute). The proper name would then designate a *referent* by a *signifier*, but it would have no *signified*. Does this mean that it has only *signifiance* or, in other words, that it is a potential space for the process of *signifiance*? At all events, a proper name is identified not through intellect but through the senses.[19] For Bertrand Russell, proper names are *abbreviations of descriptions*; they describe not particulars but *systems* of particulars, *classes* or *series*.[20] Are they, in fact, then the least 'proper' and 'individualizing' of names? Russell also compares proper names to demonstratives: as *this one*, the proper name does not designate the same thing for two interlocutors, or at two different moments. Russell therefore has recourse to the subject of enunciation in order to establish the meaning of the proper name. This logical embarrassment is confirmed by Gardiner: 'the operative power of proper names is reflected in, and facilitated by, *our recognition* of them as such'; 'the purely logical view of words is [thus] seriously at fault' (my emphasis). Wittgenstein is even more suggestive:

> Consider this example. If one says 'Moses did not exist', this may mean various things. It may mean: the Israelites did not have a *single* leader when they withdrew from Egypt – or: their leader was not called Moses – or: there cannot have been anyone who accomplished all that the Bible relates of Moses – or: etc. etc. – ...But when I make a statement about Moses, – am I always ready to substitute some *one* of these descriptions for 'Moses'? I shall perhaps say: By 'Moses' I understand the man who did what the Bible relates of Moses, or any any rate a good deal of it. But how much? Have I decided how much must be proved false for me to give up my proposition as false? Has the name 'Moses' got a fixed and unequivocal use for me in all possible cases?[21]

If the *truth* or *falseness* of proper names is problematic, one can speak of their *necessity*, but for *whom?*

From a fairly naïve point of view, Freud's book on Moses is a reply to this concern over the logical truth of proper names. It shows the logicians that any fabulation around a name (as is the case with the great religions) is articulated around a name whose 'historical truth' is undecidable, revealing only the fact that the feature peculiar to every proper name is that it does not have an 'historical truth'. It also shows that the proper name gives rise to fiction as the permanent separation of language from itself. The only basic truth of the name would then be the one we would approach if the speaking being were willing to face up to the most fundamental separation of all: the murder (of the Father) as the basic condition of the symbolic function. For the Jews, isn't baptism a split [*coupure*] which the Christians simply bring about more discretely, by placing its origins in language (in the sign itself)?

The proper name therefore surfaces as an indeterminate elaboration on the separation of a particular sign from the general set of signs, but also of a signifier from its signified and its referent. Logic sutures this indeterminacy by presenting the meaning of the proper name as a family of definitions (the name Moses then 'means' all the possible definitions that the circumstances and the protagonists of discourse can give it). By using it as a starting-point for a narrative, literature bestows plausibility upon it.

The psychotic, lacking any religious or artistic code with which to produce plausibility, once again calls into play the latent enunciative truth of the proper name. When souls invade Shreber's body and, in a move bordering on emasculation, render it voluptuous and female, he sees himself filled with other 'nerves of individual destiny', the 'blackened nerves' of other 'dead men', who are just so many proper names: Bernard Haase, bad boy and murderer; R., traveller and rake; Julius Emile Haase, a wise and respectable man.[22] And one does not have to look too far to see that the numerous Rs are inscribed in 'Schreber' and that these Haase characters bear the maiden name of Schreber's own mother, Pauline Haase.

In this way the fragility of the proper name when it comes to fixing a signified identity is shown first of all in the *multiplication* of proper names. This explosion of identity ultimately confronts that same un-nameable *space of need* which I have called semiotic and which is also bordered by the demonstrative – the site of the archaic mother. Beneath the plausibility of Schreber's narrative lies the 'core' of a truth: the enunciative archaeology of the proper name as a strategy of discourse.

By virtue of his own specific structure (that makes him express the truth of the signifier as a mourning for an impossible real) the psychotic makes explicit this necessity which is repressed in normal verbal communication. Benveniste said that Artaud was the greatest French linguist.

To be sure: such a practice of truth cannot be carried out with impunity. Since the signifier is the (sole) truth, it is the body and vice versa. In this economy, there are no *images* or *semblances* (any more than in the Eucharist): each element is neither real, nor symbolic, nor imaginary, but true. Thus the truth of the signifier, namely its separability, otherness, death, can be seen to be exerted on the flesh itself – as on words. The mutilation of the hands of a female painter is perhaps no more or less painful than the displacement of the language she writes or draws. In a man, Artaud, the fundamental sign/body of enunciative truth can only be castration. In Artaud's texts, Abelard and Heliogabalus are perhaps not mere fantasies, but rather the necessary culmination of the process of 'true' writing. That this is so is corroborated by the *jouissance* of the text describing these bodies, these moments of castration.

Who can prevent this *jouissance*, this truth, and replace it with the plausibility of reasonable discourse? Here medicine and psychoanalysis encounter the old weapon, the proven balm for use against this sort of wound: religion. The latter is a discourse that creates plausibility through fictional devices (projection, introjection, characters, etc.), and economizes on the signifier as truth and/or as death: castration, and rejection or refuse. And apart from these solutions? There still remains that language-practice in which the true is the beautiful. But can one learn to write? And anyway, who can write alone? The mystery remains, but today its backdrop is a void.

NOTES

1 See my 'Object or complement' in *Polylogue* (Paris: Seuil, 1977), pp. 225–62.
2 I shall not repeat here what I have written elsewhere of the plausible. See 'Meaning and fashion' and 'The productivity called text', in *Séméiotiké* (Paris: Seuil, 1969), pp. 60–89 and pp. 208–45 respectively.
3 G. W. F. Hegel, *The Phenomenology of Mind*, tr. J. B. Baillie (London: Allen & Unwin, 1966), p. 105. My emphasis.
4 I have tackled the undecidable nature of the reference in literary discourse in 'Poetry and negativity', in *Séméiotiké*, pp. 246–77. One question: what is the status of reference in psychotic discourse?

5 S. Freud, *Moses and Monotheism, Standard Edition*, vol. XXIII (London: Hogarth Press, 1964), p. 129.

6 Loc. cit. See the article by Louis Beirnaert, '*Moses and Monotheism* in reply to the Nazi persecutions', *SIC, Matériaux pour la psychanalyse*, 6 (Sept. 1976), pp. 14–20.

7 Ibid., p. 85.

8 Ibid., p. 130.

9 S. Freud, 'Negation', *Standard Edition*, vol. XIX (London: Hogarth Press, 1961), p. 235.

10 S. Freud, *An Outline of Psycho-Analysis, Standard Edition*, vol. XXIII (London: Hogarth Press, 1964), p. 204.

11 S. Freud, 'The splitting of the ego in the process of defence', *Standard Edition*, vol. XXIII (London: Hogarth Press, 1964), pp. 275ff.

12 S. Freud, 'A disturbance of memory on the Acropolis', *Standard Edition*, vol. XXII (London: Hogarth Press, 1964), p. 245.

13 S. Freud, 'The loss of reality in neurosis and psychosis', *Standard Edition*, vol. XIX (London: Hogarth Press, 1961), pp. 184–5.

14 Loc. cit.

15 On the subject of hallucination, see the work of W. R. Bion and, in particular, *Attention and Interpretation* (London: Tavistock, 1970). My semiotic/symbolic distinction, as well as the semiological referral of hallucination to the icon, may be read as a clarification of the famous point O and its transformations.

16 In the sense in which it is used by C. S. Peirce, who contrasts it with 'index' and 'symbol'.

17 The figure on the left is taken from Jacques Lacan, 'On a question preliminary to any possible treatment of psychosis', in *Ecrits. A selection*, tr. Alan Sheridan (London: Tavistock, 1977), p. 197.

18 Arnauld and Nicole, *La Logique, ou l'art de penser* (Paris: Presses Universitaires de France, 1965), p. 101.

19 According to A. H. Gardiner, *Theory of Proper Names* (London: Oxford University Press (Humphrey Milford), 1940), pp. 64–5.

20 B. Russell, 'The philosophy of logical Atomism', *The Monist*, 1918.

21 L. Wittgenstein, *Philosophical Investigations* (Oxford: Blackwell, 1958), p. 79.

22 D. P. Schreber, *Denkwurdigkeiten eines Nervenkranken* (Leipzig: Oswald Mutze, 1903) (*Memorabilia of a Nerve Patient*, tr. I. Macalpine and R. A. Hunter, London: William Dawson, 1953).

Translated by Seán Hand

10

Freud and Love:
Treatment and Its Discontents

A rewritten and expanded version of an earlier essay entitled 'L'abjet d'amour' (*Tel Quel*, 91 (Spring 1982), pp. 17–32), 'Freud and Love' was published as the first part of Kristeva's *Histoires d'amour* (Paris: Denoël, 1983, pp. 27–58). This translation is taken from the forthcoming American edition of *Histoires d'amour*, to be published by Columbia University Press. In many ways, the central project of *Histoires d'amour* is to present psychoanalytical discourse as a discourse of *love* (as opposed to *desire*), one that situates itself in the space previously filled by religion. This, I believe, is why Kristeva not only presents this fascinating book as the archaeology of love in the Western world, but pays particular attention to love in its Catholic elaborations (through analysis of the discourse of mystics, saints and theologians). In an accessible and highly readable essay published as a separate pamphlet in 1985 (*Au commencement était l'amour: psychanalyse et foi*, Paris: Hachette), Kristeva returns to the question of the relationship between psychoanalytic theory and practice and Catholic theology and symbolism.

In 'Freud and Love', Kristeva presupposes a certain knowledge of the concept of the *abject* as developed in her *Powers of Horror* (Paris: Seuil, 1980; tr. Léon S. Roudiez, New York: Columbia University Press, 1982). Neither subject nor object, the 'abject' may be defined as a kind of 'pre-object' or, perhaps, as a *fallen* object. Although situated in the Imaginary, it precedes and in no way coincides with the Imaginary Other of the mirror stage. The abject, then, represents the first effort of the future subject to separate itself from the pre-Oedipal mother. Nausea, distaste, horror: these are the signs of a radical revulsion (or *expulsion*) which serves to situate the 'I', or more accurately to *create* a first, fragile sense of 'I' in a space where before there was only emptiness. The abject does not fill the void of the 'pre-subject', it simply throws up a fragile boundary wall around it. In this sense the abject (the 'object' of revulsion) is more a process than a 'thing'. Stressing the fact that the abject is not *per se* linked to dirt or putrefaction, Kristeva insists that it can be represented by any kind of transgressive, ambiguous or intermediary state.

Abjecting the archaic mother, the child tentatively creates its first separate space. This space, however, remains empty: it is simply a screen hiding nothing, an emptiness always present in patients usually called 'borderline cases', that is to say, patients whose problems are situated on the frontier between neurosis and psychosis, and perhaps more specifically, those whose apparently neurotic symptoms serve to mask a latent form of psychosis. In Kristeva's case histories at the end of this essay, these patients emerge as marked by a peculiarly 'post-modern' relationship to language and the sacred. For these patients nothing is taboo because nothing seems to be meaningful: all their utterances lack depth, and their stream of words, far from repressing anything simply seem to be masking a void. For Kristeva, such patients, like other psychotics, have foreclosed the Name of the Father (see also 'The True-Real'), but in their case, it is not so much a question of foreclosing the paternal signifier in its Oedipal and symbolic guise, as an earlier, paternal, pre-object, which Kristeva, quoting Freud, labels the 'father of individual prehistory'.

According to 'Freud and Love', this 'father of individual prehistory' designates an archaic disposition of the paternal function, which must intervene in the child's original auto-eroticism in order to produce primary narcissism, the stage which in its turn provides the necessary grounding of the mirror stage, and thus for the subsequent development of the Ego. Situating this intervention at about four months, Kristeva argues that it is only the hypothesis of such a triangulating instance (the 'archaic father') which can explain the shift from the *paranoid* to the *depressive position* described by Melanie Klein.

The 'father of individual prehistory' serves as an instance of *identification* for the child. Given that the child at this early stage relates exclusively to the mother, what happens is that he or she in fact identifies with the pre-Oedipal mother's desire for the phallus. The point stressed by Kristeva is that the triangulation necessary for the development of primary narcissism will not take place if the *child* is the mother's sole object of desire: in that case the child risks precisely developing into one of the 'borderline cases' described at the end of this essay.

The child's relationship with this early paternal instance is not one of *desire* (Eros), which, according to Lacan, is *metonymical displacement*, but one of *love* (Agape), which Kristeva here defines as a *metaphorical identification*. For Kristeva, transference and counter-transference in analysis is *love* in this sense, a love that repeats or reinforces the child's relationship with the 'father of personal prehistory'.

Freud and Love:
Treatment and Its Discontents

In his journey through the land of love Freud reaches Narcissus only after having travelled over the dissociated space of hysteria. The latter leads him to establish the 'psychic space' that he will explode, first through Narcissus and finally through the death drive, into the impossible spaces of 'lovehate',[1] that is, infinite transference.

Narcissism – a screen for emptiness

The hypothesis of Narcissus is crucial to this Freudian course. Before calling itself 'death', the libido undergoes a first threat to its omnipotence – one that makes the existence of an *other* for the *self* appear problematic. Freud seems to suggest that it is not Eros but narcissistic primacy that sparks and perhaps dominates psychic life; he thus sets up fancy at the basis of one's relationship to reality. Such a perpetuance of illusion, however, finds itself rehabilitated, neutralized, normalized, at the bosom of my loving reality. For Freud, as we know, binds the state of loving to narcissism; the choice of the love object, be it 'narcissistic' or 'anaclitic', proves satisfying in any case if and only if that object relates to the subject's narcissism in one of two ways: either through personal narcissistic reward (where Narcissus is the subject), or there is narcissistic delegation (Narcissus is the other; for Freud, the woman). A narcissistic destiny would in some way underlie all our object choices, but this is a destiny that society on the one hand, and the moral rigour of Freud on the other, tend to thrust aside in favour of a 'true' object choice.[2] And yet on closer examination even the Ego Ideal, which ensures the transference of our claims and desires toward a true object laden with all the pomp of good and beauty as defined by parental and social codes, is a revival of narcissism, its abeyance, its conciliation, its consolation. Freud's text, one might say, imposes an omnipresence of narcissism, which permeates the other realms, to the point that one finds it again in the *object* (where it is reflected) – if we assume that an object can be designated, in other words symbolized and loved as such, outside of chaos, rejection and destruction.

Moreover, the ubiquity of the notion of 'narcissism' goes hand in hand with its being far from originary. It is an accrual, and Freud points out that it is the product of a 'new action', which we should understand as that of a third realm supplementing the auto-eroticism of the mother–child dyad: '*Die autoerotischen Triebe sind aber uhrfanglich; es muss also irgend etwas zum Autoerotismus hinzukommen,* eine neue psychische Aktion, um den *Narzissmus zu gestalten.*' 'The auto-erotic drives, however, are there from the very first; so there must be something added to auto-eroticism – a new physical action – in order to bring about narcissism.'[3]

That observation endows narcissism with an intra-symbolic status, dependent upon a third party, but within a disposition that chronologically and logically precedes that of the Oedipal Ego. It prompts one to conceive of an archaic disposition of the paternal function, preceding the Name, the symbolic, but also the 'mirror stage' whose logical potentiality it would harbour – a disposition that one might call that of the imaginary father (a point I shall return to). Lacan takes up Freud's observation only briefly to emphasize the need to stipulate the 'mirror stage'. He specifies that 'The human ego establishes itself on the basis of the imaginary relation'.[4]

The question prompted by the Freudian notion of narcissism would then be the following: what is this narcissistic 'identity'? How stable are its borders, its relation to the other? Does the 'mirror stage' emerge out of nowhere? What are the conditions of its emergence? A whole *complex structuration* can seemingly be conceived through what is after all a psychiatric term, 'narcissism'; it is an already ternary structuration with a different articulation than the Ego–object–Other triangle that is put together in the shadow of the Oedipus complex.

Furthermore, the ubiquity of Freudian narcissism has caused some to suggest that narcissism is no more than a Freudian fantasy – and that nothing else exists but originary mimetism. Such a thesis is probably a paranoid version of what would lie at the basis of social and symbolic relations: its finds its mechanism in the 'scapegoat' theory, where Melanie Klein's 'projective relationship' unwittingly serves as cornerstone for society and the sacred. Nevertheless, it is still a fact that narcissism, caught in a play of rebounds within the Freudian text, in a first stage seems to be a mimetic play that would establish psychic identities (Ego/object), until that play finally, and in the dizziness of rebounds, reveals itself as a screen over *emptiness*. That notion has been developed in psychoanalysis by André Green, whose reflections I draw upon for this particular point.[5]

Consequently I shall emphasize this notion of emptiness, which is at the root of the human psyche. It does not reveal itself merely because 'psychotic states' have broken forth on psychoanalytic couches or have shown through the low points of many neuroses. One is compelled to note that the aims of psychoanalysis have changed. After psychiatric *semiology*, Freud had discovered the *symptom* as metaphor, that is, condensation, of fantasy. Now, and thanks to Lacan, one analyses the symptom as a screen through which one detects the workings of *signifiance* (the process of formation and de-formation of meaning and the subject); these coextend with the speaking being as such and, consequently, they cut through not only 'normal' and 'pathological' states but also psychoanalytic symptomatology. In this respect, the arbitrariness of the Saussurian sign has placed us in front of a *bar*, or even an *emptiness*, that constitutes the referent/signified/signifier relationship, of which Lacan has merely taken up the 'visible' aspect in the *gaping hole* of the mirror stage. Saussure's *arbitrariness* of the sign and Lacan's *gaping hole* both readily point to what might be understood from the standpoint of representation – given the uneasy uncertainty, ubiquity and inconsistency of 'narcissism' in Freud...

Thus, against the background of linguistic theory and language learning, the *emptiness* that is intrinsic to the beginnings of the symbolic function appears as the first separation between what is not yet an *Ego* and what is not yet an *object*. Might narcissism be a means for protecting that emptiness? But against what? – A protection of emptiness (of 'arbitrariness', of the 'gaping hole') through the display of a decidedly narcissistic parry, so that emptiness can be maintained, lest chaos prevail and borders dissolve. Narcissism protects emptiness, causes it to exist and thus, as lining of that emptiness, ensures an elementary separation. Without that solidarity between emptiness and narcissism, chaos would sweep away any possibility of distinction, trace and symbolization, which would in turn confuse the limits of the body, words, the real and the symbolic. The child, with all due respect to Lacan, not only *needs* the real and the symbolic – it signifies itself as child, in other words as the subject that it is, and neither as a psychotic nor as an adult, precisely in that zone where *emptiness and narcissism*, the one upholding the other, constitute the zero degree of imagination.

We have, however, reached the threshold of another question: what is it that preserves this emptiness – cause for complaint but also absolute necessity of so-called narcissistic structures, fleeting effect of enigmatic as well as creative non-sense – at the heart of childhood narcissism? This is where we need to return to the notion of 'identification'.

Einfühlung – an identification with a metaphorical 'object'

Amatory identification, *Einfühlung* (the assimilation of other people's feelings), appears to be madness when seen in the light of Freud's caustic lucidity: the ferment of collective hysteria in which crowds abdicate their own judgement, a hypnosis that causes us to lose perception of reality since we hand it over to the *Ego Ideal*.[6] The object in hypnosis devours or absorbs the Ego, the voice of consciousness becomes blurred, 'in loving blindness one becomes a criminal without remorse' – *the object has taken the place of what was the Ego Ideal*.[7]

The identification that provides the support for the hypnotic state known as loving madness rests upon a strange object. This archaic identification, which is characteristic of the oral phase of the libido's organization where what I incorporate is what I become, where *having* amounts to *being*, is not, truly speaking, objectal. I identify, not with an object, but with what offers itself to me as a *model*. That enigmatic apprehending of a *pattern* to be imitated, one that is not yet an object to be libidinally cathected, leads us to wonder whether the loving state is a state without object and reminds us of an archaic *reduplication* (rather than imitation), 'possible before any choice of object'.[8] This enigmatic, non-objectal identification might be related to the internal, recursive, redundant logic of discourse, which is accessible within the 'after-speech'; it is an identification that sets up love, the sign and repetition at the heart of the psyche. For the sake of an object to come, later or never?...It does not matter, since I am already in the throes of *Einfühlung*...Later I shall examine the conditions that allow the advent of that unification, that identification, on the basis of auto-eroticism and within the pre-Oedipal triad...

For the moment let me simply note that becoming *as* the One is imagined by Freud as an oral assimilation; indeed he links the possibility of archaic identification to the 'oral phase of the libido's organization',[9] and he then cites Robertson Smith who, in his *Kinship and Marriage* (1885), describes the communal bonds set up through participation in a common meal as resting upon 'the acknowledgement of the possession of a common substance'.[10] Ferenczi and his followers would later develop the notions of *introjection* and *incorporation*.

Nevertheless, one might well wonder about the notional slippage that takes place between the 'incorporation' of an object, or even its 'introjection', and an *Identifizierung* that is not on the level of 'having' but locates itself at once on that of 'being-like'. On what ground, within what material does *having* switch over to *being*? – While seeking an answer to that question it appeared to me that incorporating and introjecting orality's function is the essential substratum of what constitutes man's being, namely *language*. When the object that I incorporate is the speech of the other – precisely a non-object, a pattern, a model – I bind myself to him in a primary fusion, communion, unification. An identification. For me to have been capable of such a process, my libido had to be restrained; my thirst to devour had to be deferred and displaced to a level one may well call 'psychic', provided one adds that if there is repression it is quite primal, and that it lets one hold on to the joys of chewing, swallowing, nourishing oneself. . .with words. In being able to receive the other's words, to assimilate, repeat and reproduce them, I become like him: One. A subject of enunciation. Through psychic osmosis/identification. Through love.

Freud has described the One with whom I fulfil the identification (this 'most primitive aspect of affective binding to an object'[11]) as a father. Although he did not elaborate what he meant by 'primary identification', he made it clear that this father is a 'father of individual prehistory'.

An 'immediate' and objectless identification

A strange father if there ever was one, since for Freud, because there is no awareness of sexual difference during that period (more accurately: within that disposition), such a 'father' is the same as 'both parents'. Identification with that 'father of prehistory', that imaginary father, is called 'immediate', 'direct', and Freud emphasizes again, 'previous to any concentration on any object whatsoever': '*Diese scheint zunächst nicht Erfolg oder Ausgang einer Objektbesetzung zu sein, sie ist eine direkte und unmittelbare und frühzeitiger als jede Objektbesetzung.*' Only with secondary identification does the 'libidinal covetousness that is part of the first sexual period and is directed towards the father and the mother appear, in normal instances, to be resolved in a secondary, mediate identification that would come and reinforce the primary, direct identification'.[12]

The whole symbolic matrix sheltering emptiness is thus set in place in an elaboration that precedes the Oedipus complex. Indeed, if the primary identification constitutive of the Ego Ideal does not involve libidinal cathexis, drives are dissociated from the psychic realm. Simultaneously, what one can only call the *absolute* existence of *transference* is established, a transference laden with libido. It is a transference rather than an 'identification', a transference in the sense of *Verschiebung*, a displacement, as in *The Interpretation of Dreams*, but also and at the same time in the sense of *Übertragung*, as it will show up during treatment and be directed towards the person of the analyst. Finally, such a transference is called *immediate (unmittelbare)* and works in the direction of a complex, composite and, in short, imaginary realm ('the father of individual prehistory').

We know that, *empirically*, the first affections, the first imitations and the first vocalizations as well are directed towards the mother; it is thus hardly necessary to stress that one's pointing to the father as the magnet for primary love, primary identification, is tenable only if one conceives of *identification* as being always already within the symbolic orbit, under the sway of language. Such appears to be, implicitly, the Freudian position, which owes its acuity as much to Freud's sensitivity concerning the dominant place of language in the constitution of *being* as it does to the resurgence of monotheism in his thought. But is there really a difference?

On the contrary, there is Melanie Klein's well-known position, which must be called inexpressible and closer to ordinary common sense. The bold theoretician of the death drive is also a theoretician of gratitude seen as 'an important offshoot of the capacity for love', 'necessary for the acknowledgement of what is "good" in others and in oneself'.[13] Where does this capacity come from? It is innate and leads to the experience of a 'good breast' that states the child's hunger; it is also apt to convey the feeling of a plenitude that would be the prototype of all subsequent experience of *jouissance* and happiness. Melanie Klein's gratitude is nevertheless and at the same time directed towards the maternal object in its entirety: 'I am not saying that for the child the breast simply represents a physical object.'[14]

Yet, along with such innateness, Melanie Klein maintains that the capacity for love is not an activity of the organism (as it would seem to be, according to Klein, for Freud) but rather that it is a 'primordial activity of the ego'. Gratitude would stem from a necessity to confront the forces of death and consist in a 'progressive integration born out of life drive'.[15] Without being identical with the 'good object', the idealized object reinforces it. 'Idealization stems from persecution anguish and constitutes a defence against it', 'the ideal breast is a complement of the devouring breast'.[16] It is as if those who are unable to set up a 'good breast' for themselves naturally manage it by idealizing; now idealization often collapses and reveals its cause, which is the persecution against which it had established itself. But how does one succeed in idealizing? By what miracle is that possible in a Kleinian life where two live without a third party other than a persecuting or fascinating penis?

The problem is not to find an answer to the enigma: who might be the object of primary identification, daddy or mummy? Such an attempt would only open up the impossible quest for the absolute origin of the capacity for love as a psychic and symbolic capacity. The question is rather: of what value would the question be when it actually bears on states existing on the border between the psychic and the somatic, idealization and eroticism, within analytic treatment itself? To emphasize transference, the love that founds the analytic process, implies that one hears the discourse that is performed there starting with that limit of advent-and-loss of the subject – which is *Einfühlung*.

Provided one does not forget that in analysis any discourse complies with the dynamics of identification, with and beyond resistances, this entails at least two consequences for interpretation. First, the analyst situates himself on a ridge where, on the one hand, the 'maternal' position – gratifying needs, 'holding' (Winnicott) – and on the other the 'paternal' position – the differentiation, distance and prohibition that produces both meaning and absurdity – are intermingled and severed, infinitely and without end. Analytic tactfulness – ultimate refuge of an interpretation's relevance – is perhaps no more than the capacity to make use of identification and along with it the imaginal resources of the analyst, in order to accompany the patient as far as the limits and accidents of his object relations. This ability is even more important precisely when the patient has difficulty in establishing, or fails to establish, an object relation.

Metonymic object and metaphorical object

Secondly, the *Einfühlung* gives the language signifier exchanged during treatment a heterogeneous, drive-affected dimension. It loads it with something pre-verbal, or even non-representable that needs to be deciphered while taking into account the more precise articulations of discourse (style, grammar, phonetics), and at the same time while cutting through language, in the direction of the unspeakable, indicated by fantasies and 'insight' narratives as well as by symptomatic misspeech (slips of the tongue, illogical statements, etc.).

Such analytic attentiveness to *Einfühlung* through transference speech imposes another status of the psychic *object* on the analyst's attention, one that is different from the metonymic object of desire called 'object "a" by Lacan.[17]

We are dealing less with a partial object than with a non-object. As magnet of identification constitutive of identity and condition for that unification, which ensures the advent of a subject for an object, the 'object' of *Einfühlung* is a *metaphorical* object. Carrying auto-erotic motility to the unifying image of One Agency that already sets me up *as* an opposite One is the zero degree of subjectivity. *Metaphor* should be understood as movement towards the discernible, a journey towards the visible. *Anaphora, gesture, indication* would probably be more adequate terms for this sundered unity, in the process of being set up, which I am presently conjuring. Aristotle refers to an *epiphora*: a generic term for the metaphorical motility previous to any objectivation of *a* figurative meaning... The object of love is a metaphor for the subject – its constitutive metaphor, its 'unary feature', which, by having it choose an adored part of the loved one, already locates it within the symbolic code of which this feature is a part.[18] Nevertheless, situating this unifying guideline within an objectality in the process of being established rather than in the absolute of the reference to the phallus as such has several advantages. It makes the transference relation dynamic, involves to the utmost the interpretative intervention of the analyst and calls attention to counter-transference as identification, this time of the analyst with the patient, along with the entire aura of imaginary formations germane to the analyst that all this entails. Without those conditions doesn't analysis run the risk of becoming set within the tyranny of idealization, precisely? Of the phallus or of the Superego? A word to wise Lacanians should be enough!

Metonymic object of desire. Metaphorical object of love. The former controls the phantasmatic *narrative*. The latter outlines the *crystallization* of fantasy and rules the poeticalness of the discourse of love...

During treatment, the analyst interprets his desire and his love, and that sets him apart from the perverse position of the seducer and from that of a virtuous Werther as well. But he must display himself sometimes as desiring, other times as loving. By ensuring a loving Other to the patient, the analyst (temporarily) allows the Ego in the throes of drive to take shelter in the following fantasy: the analyst is not a dead Father but a living Father; this non-desiring but loving father reconciles the Ideal Ego with the Ego Ideal and elaborates the psychic space where, possibly and subsequently, an analysis can take place.

Henceforth, the analyst must in addition let it be known – since he is an analyst and neither a good shepherd nor a father-confessor – that he is a fleeting, failing or even abject subject of desire. He will then trigger within the psychic space his love has allowed to exist the tragicomedy of life drives and death drives, knowing in his nescience that if Eros opposes Thanatos they are not evenly matched in their struggle. For Thanatos is pure while Eros has, since the beginning, been permeated with Thanatos, the most deep-seated drive being the death drive (Freud).

To say that the analyst handles *love* as a discourse allowing idealizing distance as a condition for the very existence of psychic space is not to assimilate analytic attitude to that of a *primary love* object, the archaic prototype of the *genital* love, as Balint's work suggests with seductive munificence.[19] Concentrating, *for a while*, one's thoughts on love within analysis actually leads one to scrutinize, in the treatment, not a narcissistic merger with the maternal container but the emergence of a *metaphorical object* – in other words, the very splitting that establishes the psyche and, let us call this 'primal repression', bends the drive towards the symbolic of an other. Only the metaphorical dynamics (in the sense of a *heterogeneous* displacement shattering the isotopy of organic needs) justifies that this other be a Great Other. The analyst thus temporarily stands in the place of the Great Other inasmuch as he is a metaphorical object of idealizing identification. It is in knowing this and doing it that he creates the space of transference. If he represses it, on the other hand, the analyst becomes the *Führer* that Freud already loathed in *Group Psychology* – a loathing that showed to what extent analytic practice was not exempt from such hysterical phenomena.

Hate identification, love identification

'It is easy', Freud believed, 'to translate into a phrase the difference between identification with the father and affection for the father as sexual object (*der Unterschied einer solchen Vateridentifizierung von einer Vaterobjektwahl*): in the first instance the father is what one would want to *be* (*das, was man sein möchte*), in the second he is what one would want to *have* (*das, was man haben möchte*). In the first instance, it is the subject of the *ego* that is concerned, in the second it is its object. That is why identification is possible before any choice of object is made (*Es is also der Unterschied, ob die Bindung am Subjekt oder am Objekt des Ichs angreift. Die erstere ist darum bereits vor jeder sexuellen Objektwahl möglich*).'[20]

It will be noted that the first identification Freud points to in this study is a morbid identification with the mother (for instance, the little girl takes up her mother's cough on account of 'a hostile desire to take the mother's place – *ein feindseliges Ersetzenwollen der Mutter* – in which case the symptom expresses the erotic fondness for the father'). Though conceived within the system of the Oedipus complex (*Entweder ist die Identifizierung dieselbe aus dem Ödipuskomplex*), such an identification nevertheless reminds one of Melanie Klein's projective identification, which is sustained by the 'hostile' as well as guilt-ridden desire to take the place of a persecuting mother out of envy. Object identification because of hatred for one part of the object and fear of persecution. The second type of identification is revealed by a symptom that apes that of the loved one (the daughter, Dora, catches the father's cough). Here, 'identification has taken the place of erotic propensity, and the latter has been changed, through regression, into identification' (*die Identifizierung sei an Stelle der Objektwahl getreten, die Objektwahl sei zur Identifizierung regrediert*). Without hostility in this case, identification coincides with the object of desire through 'a kind of insertion of the object into the ego' (*gleichsam durch Introjektion des Objekts ins Ich*). Love, contrary to the morbid identification mentioned above, would be the merging of the identifying ideal with the object of desire. In the third place, libidinal desires can be completely lacking when identification with another person is made on the basis of some common traits.

One is thus led to conceive of at least two identifications; a primal one, resulting from a sentimental (*Gefühlsbindung an ein Objekt*), archaic and ambivalent affection for the maternal object, more frequently produced by the impetus of guilt-producing hostility; the other, which underlies the introjection into the Ego of an object itself already libidinal (*libidinöse Objektbindung*), providing the dynamics of the pure loving relationship. The former is closer to depersonalization, phobia and psychosis; the second is closer to hysterical lovehate, taking to itself the phallic ideal that it pursues.

Between hysteria and inability to love

The lover is a narcissist with an *object*. Love involves a sizeable 'Aufhebung' of narcissism; consequently, the relationship established by Freud between love and narcissism must not cause us to forget their essential difference. Is it not true that the narcissist, as such, is precisely someone incapable of love?

The lover, in fact, reconciles narcissism and hysteria. As far as he is concerned, there is an idealizable other who returns his own ideal image (that is the narcissistic moment), but he is nevertheless an other. It is essential for the lover to maintain the existence of that ideal other and to be able to imagine himself similar, merging with him and even indistinguishable from him. In amorous hysteria the ideal other is a reality, not a metaphor. The archaeology of such an identifying possibility with an *other* is provided by the huge place taken up within narcissistic structure by the vortex of *primary identification* with what Freud called a 'father of individual prehistory'. Endowed with the sexual attributes of both parents, and by that very token a totalizing, phallic figure, it provides satisfactions that are already psychic and not simply immediate, existential requests; that archaic vortex of idealization is immediately an *other* who gives rise to a powerful, already psychic transference of the previous semiotic body in the process of becoming a narcissistic Ego. Its very existence and my being able to take myself for it – that is what already moves us away from the primal maternal satisfaction and situates us within the hysterical universe of loving idealization.

It is obvious from the behaviour of young children, that the first love object of boys and girls is the mother. Then where does one fit in this 'father of individual prehistory'? Freud's bent perhaps causes him to speak as a Jew, but he speaks foremost as a psychoanalyst. He in fact dissociates idealization (and with it the amatory relationship) from the bodily exchange between mother and child, and he introduces the Third Party as a condition of psychic life, to the extent that it is a loving life. If love stems from narcissistic idealization, it has nothing to do with the protective wrapping over skin and sphincters that maternal care provides for the baby. Worse yet, if that protection continues, if the mother 'clings' to her offspring, laying on it the request that originates in her own request as confused neotenic and hysteric in want of love, the chances are that neither love nor psychic life will ever hatch from such an egg. The loving mother, different from the caring and clinging mother, is someone who has an object of desire; beyond that, she has an Other with relation to whom the child will serve as go-between. She will love her child with respect to that Other, and it is through a discourse aimed at that Third Party that the child will be set up as 'loved' for the mother. 'Isn't he beautiful', or 'I am proud of you', and so forth, are statements of maternal love because they involve a Third Party; it is in the eyes of a Third Party that the baby the mother speaks to becomes a *he*, it is with respect to others that 'I am proud of you', and so forth. Against this verbal backdrop or in the silence that presupposes it the bodily exchange of maternal fondness may take on the imaginary burden of representing love in its most characteristic form. Nevertheless, without the maternal 'diversion' towards a Third Party, the bodily exchange is abjection or devouring; the eventual schizophrene, whether phobic or borderline, will keep its hot-iron brand against which his only recourse will be hatred. Any borderline person ends up finding a mother who is 'loving' for her own sake, but he cannot accept her as loving himself, for she did not love any *other* one. The Oedipal negation of the father is here linked with a complaint against an adhesive maternal wrapping, and it leads the subject towards psychic pain dominated by the inability to love.

If one grants the ternary structure of narcissism and its already harbouring the hysterical beginning of an idealizable object (the object of love germane to primary identification), how can one, to the contrary, understand the inability to love? The cold, set and somewhat false complaint of the borderline person that he is unable to love needs perhaps to be related not to narcissism but to auto-eroticism. Previous to the 'new psychic action' that includes a third party within narcissism, the auto-erotic set-up has neither an other nor an image. All of its figures, all figures disappoint it as much as they fascinate it. The auto-erotic person cannot allow himself to be 'loved' (no more than he can let himself be lovable), except by a maternal substitute who would cling to his body like a poultice – a reassuring balm, asthmogenic perhaps, but nevertheless a permanent wrapping. Such a false mother is the only 'farthering' [*père-manence*] tolerated by one who, henceforth, will indolently be able to enjoy his own organs in polymorphous perversity.

He is undifferentiated, set within the shattered territories of his parcelled body, coiled up about his erogenous zones. He is indifferent to love, withdrawn in the pleasure that a provisionally reassuring diving-suit gives him. The auto-erotic person is not, however, autistic: he discovers objects, but they are objects of hatred. Nevertheless, during those moments that have no saving grace and when the subject is deprived of durability, the hatred that an opposite object projects before him works indeed more strongly upon himself, threatening him with decomposition or petrifaction. The auto-erotic person who complains or boasts of being unable to love is afraid of going mad – schizophrenia or catatonia...

Dynamics of the ideal

The subject exists only inasmuch as it identifies with an ideal other who is the speaking other, the other in so far as he speaks. A ghost,[21] a symbolic formation beyond the mirror, this Other, who is indeed the size of a Master, is a magnet for identification because he is neither an object of need nor one of desire. The Ego Ideal includes the Ego on account of the love that this Ego has for it and thus unifies it, restrains its drives, turns it into a *Subject*. An Ego is a body to be put to death, or at least to be deferred, for the love of the Other and so that Myself can be. Love is a death sentence that causes me to be. When death, which is intrinsic to amorous passion, takes place in reality and carries away the body of one of the lovers, it is at its most unbearable; the surviving lover then realizes the abyss that separates the imaginary death that he experienced in his passion from the relentless reality from which love had forever set him apart: saved...

The subject's identification with the symbolic Other, with its Ego Ideal, goes through a narcissistic absorption of the mother as object of need, an absorption that sets up the Ideal Ego. The lover is cognizant of the regression that leads him from adoring an ideal ghost to the ecstatic or painful inflating of his own image, his own body.

Such a logic of idealizing identification leads one to posit, as lining of the visual, specular structure of the fantasy ($ \diamond$ a) in search of the ever inadequate image of a desired other, the existence of a preliminary condition. If the object of fantasy is receding, metonymical, it is because it does not correspond to the preliminary ideal that the identification process, $\varnothing \epsilon A$, has constructed. The subject exists because it belongs to the Other, and it is in proceeding from that symbolic belonging that causes him to be subject to love and death that he will be able to set up for himself imaginary objects of desire. Transferred to the Other (SeA) as to the very place from which he is seen and heard, the loving subject does not have access to that Other as to an object, but as to the very possibility of the perception, distinction and differentiation that allows one to see. That ideal is nevertheless a blinding, non-representable power – sun or ghost. Romeo says, '. . . Juliet is the sun', and that loving metaphor transfers on to Juliet the glare Romeo experiences in the state of love, dedicating his body to death, in order to become immortal within the symbolic community of others restored by his love precisely.

The ideal identification with the symbolic upheld by the Other thus activates speech more than image. Doesn't the signifying voice, in the final analysis, shape the visible, hence fantasy? Whenever we observe how young children learn forms we are led to understand to what extent 'sensorimotor spontaneity' is of little avail without the help of language. Poets have known from time immemorial that music is the language of love, and it has led them to suggest that the yearning captured by the loved beauty is nevertheless transcended – preceded and guided – by the ideal signifier: a sound on the fringe of my being, which transfers me to the place of the Other, astray, beyond meaning, out of sight.[22] In short, identification causes the subject to exist within the signifier of the Other. Archaically, primitively, it is not object-oriented but carried out as transference to the place of a captivating and unifying feature, a 'unary feature'. The analyst is an object (necessarily a partial one) but he also exerts the drawing power of a 'unary feature', of a non-object: the actual drifting of a possible metaphoricality.

Here the term metaphor should not bring to mind the classic rhetorical trope (*figurative* v. *plain*) but instead, on the one hand, the modern theories of metaphor that decipher within it an indefinite jamming of semantic features one in to the other, a meaning being acted out; and, on the other, the drifting of heterogeneity within a heterogeneous psychic apparatus, going from drives and sensations to signifier and conversely.[23]

Since it is not object-oriented, identification reveals how the subject that ventures there can finally find himself a hypnotized slave of his master; how he can turn out to be a non-subject, the shadow of a non-object. Nevertheless, it is because identification is not object-oriented, that the signifier's non-object-oriented underlying layer of drives becomes activated during the treatment that is carried out without the *Einfühlung* being repressed. In such a case, therefore, it is possible for transference to gain a hold on non-object-oriented psychic states such as 'false selves', borderline cases and even psychosomatic symptoms. It is indeed true that one is ill when not loved; this means that a psychic structure that lacks an identifying metaphor or idealization tends to realize it in that embodied non-object called somatic symptom – illness. Somatic persons are not those who do not verbalize, they are subjects who lack or miscarry the dynamics of metaphoricity, which constitute idealization as a complex process.

Finally, being the magnet for loving identification causes the *Other* to be understood not as a 'pure signifier' but as the very space of metaphorical shifting: a condensation of semantic features as well as non-representable drive heterogeneity that subtends them, goes beyond them and slips away. Actually, by stressing the partiality of the 'unary feature' during idealizing identification, Lacan located idealization solely within the field of the signifier and of desire; he clearly if not drastically separated it from narcissism as well as from drive heterogeneity and its archaic hold on the maternal vessel. To the contrary, by emphasizing the *metaphoricality* of the identifying idealization movement, we can attempt to restore to the analytic bond located there (transference and counter-transference) its complex dynamics, which includes the narcissistic, drive-animated pre-object-orientation and allows it to be tied down to signifying ideals. From this standpoint, there would be no analytical idealization that did not rest upon sublimation. In other words, psychoanalysis skirts religious faith in order to expend it in the form of literary discourse.

Immediate and absolute

Freud's definition of 'primary identification' as 'direct and immediate' (*direkte und unmittelbare*)[24] has not, as far as I know, aroused the attention of analysts. In light of that phrase, let us reflect for a moment on the value that speculative philosophy, particularly that of Hegel, assigns to such *immediacy*.

The immanent presence of the Absolute in Knowing is *immediately* revealed to the Subject as the recognition of that which never left him. More specifically, the Hegelian *immediate* (*Unmittelbare*) is the ultimate disengagement of consistency for the sake of form, the internal overthrow of reflection-in-itself, matter being removed from the self, without yet being for itself and hence for the other. Hegel notes in his *Science of Logic* 'Immediacy, which, as reflection-in-itself, is *consistency* (*Bestehen*) as well as form, reflection on something else, reflection *doing away with itself*.'[25] Heidegger, in his text on Hegel's Introduction to the *Phenomenology of the Spirit* entitled 'Hegel and His Concept of Experience' wished to investigate that immediate presence of the Absolute in order to show the a priori or arbitrariness of the 'immediate' and reveal, on both its far and near sides, the 'blossoming of the Logos', dear to Heideggerian discourse.[26] Within the scope of these reflections, one might maintain that the *immediate*, being the auto-severance of certainty in the self, is at the same time that which severs it from object-relation and bestows on it its power of acquittance (*Absolvenz*) without mediation, without object, but keeping and containing both; hence the immediate is the very logic of *parousia*, that is, the presence of the subject for the object. 'It behoves him to keep any relation that merely pertains to the object...' is Heidegger's comment. As the most basic indication of parousia, the immediate also presents itself as the logic of *Absolvenz*, as severance outside of relationship, and constitutes the absoluteness of the Absolute. 'It is there, in auto-representation, that the parousia of the absolute is displayed' (ibid.).

In other words, the presence of the Absolute in Knowing is *immediately* revealed to the subject; consequently, any other 'means' of knowledge is no more than a recognition. 'The absolute is from the outset in and for itself beside us and wants to be beside us', Hegel states in his introduction to the *Phenomenology*. Such a *being-beside-us* would be 'the manner in which the light of the truth of the absolute itself enlightens us', as Heidegger says in his commentary. We are immediately within parousia, 'always-already', before producing a 'relationship' to it.

Let us put aside the visual aspect, be it imagined or imaginary, of that immediacy of the Absolute, which Heidegger enabled us to hear when he unfolded the word for knowledge [*Wissenschaft*] in its sonorousness [*novisse*, to have a knowledge of, *viso*, to look at], and which Lacan emphasized when he placed the *mirror* at the core of the Ego's formation. Let me first stress that specular fascination is a belated phenomenon in the genesis of the Ego. And let us try to think through the philosophical investigation against the backdrop of what the analyst might see in the appearance of the term 'immediate' at the heart of primary identification.

With Freud, the arbitrariness of paternal emergence seems undeniable, at any rate absolutely necessary to the interpretative analytic construction. Nevertheless, clinical experience has led us to ascertain that the advent of the *Vater der persönlichen Vorzeit* takes place thanks to the assistance of the so-called pre-Oedipal mother, to the extent that she can indicate to her child that her desire is not limited to responding to her offspring's request (or simply turning it down). This assistance is none other than maternal desire for the father's phallus.

Which father? The child's father or her own? For 'primary identification' the question is not relevant. If there is an *immediacy* of the child's identification with *that desire* (of the father's phallus), it probably comes from the child's not having to elaborate it; rather, he receives it, mimics it or even sustains it through the mother who offers it to him (or refuses it) as a gift. In a way, such an identification with the father-mother conglomerate, as Freud would have it, or with what we just called the maternal desire for the phallus, comes as a godsend. And for a very good reason, since without that disposition of the psyche, the child and the mother do not yet constitute 'two'...

As for the image making up this 'imagination', it should not be conceived as simply visual but as a representation activating various facilitations corresponding to the entire gamut of perceptions, especially the *sonorous* ones; this because of their precocious appearance in the domain of neuro-psychological maturation, but also because of their dominant function in speech.

Nevertheless, let us not be mistaken about the ease of such an *immediacy*. It entails an important consequence: within that logic, the word 'object', just like the word 'identification', becomes *improper*. A not-yet-identity (of the child) is transferred or rather displaced to the site of an Other who is not libidinally cathexed as an object but remains an Ego Ideal.

Not I

Let me now point out that the most archaic unity that we thus retrieve – an identity so autonomous that it calls forth displacements – is that of the phallus desired by the mother. It is the unity of the imaginary father, a coagulation of the mother and her desire. The imaginary father would thus be the indication that the mother is not complete but that she wants...Who? What? The question has no answer other than the one that uncovers narcissistic emptiness; 'At any rate, not I.' Freud's famous 'What does a woman want' is perhaps only the echo of the more fundamental 'What does a mother want?' It runs up against the same impossibility, bordered on one side by the imaginary father, on the other by a 'not I'. And it is out of this 'not I' (see Beckett's play with that title) that an Ego painfully attempts to come into being...

In order to maintain himself in that place, to assume the *leap* that will definitely anchor him in the imaginary father and in language or even in art, the speaking being must engage in a struggle with the imaginary mother, for whom it will eventually constitute an object separated from the Ego. But we are not at that stage yet. The immediate transference towards the imaginary father, who is such a godsend that you have the impression that it is he who is transferred into you, withstands a process of rejection involving what may have been chaos and is about to become an *abject*. The maternal space can come into being as such, before becoming an object correlative to the Ego's desire, only as an *abject*.

In short, primary identification appears to be a transference to (from) the imaginary father, correlative to the establishment of the mother as 'ab-jected'. Narcissism would be that correlation (with the imaginary father and the 'ab-jected' mother) enacted around the central emptiness of that transference. This emptiness, which is apparently the primer of symbolic function, is precisely encompassed in linguistics by the bar separating signifier from signified and by the 'arbitrariness' of the sign, or in psychoanalysis by the 'gaping' of the mirror.

If narcissism is a defence against the emptiness of separation, then the whole contrivance of imagery, representations, identifications and projections that accompany it on the way towards strengthening the Ego and the Subject is a means of exorcising that emptiness. Separation is our opportunity to become narcissists or narcissistic, at any rate subjects of representation. The emptiness it opens up is nevertheless also the barely covered abyss where our identities, images and words run the risk of being engulfed.

The mythical Narcissus would heroically lean over that emptiness to seek in the maternal watery element the possibility of representing the self or the other – someone to love. Beginning with Plotinus at least,[27] theoretical thought has forgotten that it rumbled along over emptiness before lovingly springing towards the solar source of representation, the light that enables us to see and with which we aspire to become equal, idealization following upon idealization, perfecting upon perfecting: *In lumine tuo videbimus lumen.* Psychotic persons, however, remind us, in case we had forgotten, that the representational contrivances that cause us to speak, elaborate or believe rest upon emptiness. Possibly the most radical atheists are those who, not knowing what the ability to represent owes to a Third Party, remain prisoners of the archaic mother, for whom they mourn in the suffering of emptiness.

Within sight of that Third Party I elaborate the narcissistic parry that allows me to block up that emptiness, to calm it and turn it into a producer of signs, representations and meanings. I elaborate it within sight of the Third Party. I seduce this 'father of individual prehistory' because he has already caught me, for he is simple virtuality, a potential presence, a form to be cathected. Always already there, the forming presence that none the less satisfies none of my auto-erotic needs draws me into the imaginary exchange, the specular seduction. He or I – who is the agent? Or even, is it he or is it she? The immanence of its transcendence, as well as the instability of our borders before the setting of my image as 'my own', turn the murky source (*eine neue psychische Aktion*) from which narcissism will flow into a dynamics of confusion and delight. Secrets of our loves.

The Ideal Ego sated with the Ego Ideal will take over from that alchemy and strengthen the defences of the narcissistic Ego. Consciousness, along with moral conscience (that stern and precious paternal inheritance), will not truly lead us, under the tyrannical protection of the Superego, to forget the narcissistic emptiness and its surface composed of imaginary recognitions and cathexes. At least it will help us block them up; they always remain as more or less painful wounds at the heart of our functions, successes or failures. Beneath homosexual libido, which our social objectives catch and maintain captive, the chasms of narcissistic emptiness spread out; although the latter can be a powerful motive for ideal or superegotic cathexis, it is also the primary source of inhibition.

In being narcissistic one has already throttled the suffering of emptiness. The fragility, however, of the narcissistic elaboration, underpinning the ego image as well as ideal cathexes, is such that it cracks immediately reveal the negative of our image films to those that others consider to be 'narcissistic'. More than insane, empty, that lining of our projection and representation devices is yet another defence of the living being. When he succeeds in eroticizing it, when he allows the non-object-oriented, pre-narcissistic violence of the drive directed towards an abject to run wild, then death triumphs in that strange path. Death drive and its psychological equivalent, hatred, is what Freud discovers after stopping off at Narcissus. Narcissism and its lining, emptiness, are in short our most intimate, brittle and archaic elaborations of death drive. The most advanced, courageous and threatened sentries of primal repression.

In contrast with Melanie Klein's 'projective identification', the proposition I am offering here has the advantage of pointing to, even before the Oedipal triangle and within a specific disposition, the place of the Third Party; without the latter the phase Melanie Klein calls 'schizo-paranoid' could not become a 'depressive' phase and thus could not carry the 'symbolic equivalences' to the level of linguistic 'signs'. The archaic inscription of the father seems to me a way of modifying the fantasy of a phallic mother playing at the phallus game all by herself, alone and complete, in the back room of Kleinism and post-Kleinism.

As for language, the notion outlined here differs, furthermore, from innatist theories concerning linguistic competence (Chomsky) as well as from Lacanian notions of an always-already-there of language that would be revealed as such in the subject of the unconscious. I of course assume, with respect to the *infans*, that the symbolic function pre-exists, but also maintain an evolutionary postulate that leads me to seek to elaborate *various dispositions* giving access to that function, and this corresponds as well to various psychic structures.

In the light of what precedes, what I have called a 'narcissistic structuration' appears to be the earliest juncture (chronologically and logically) whose spoors we might detect in the unconscious. Conversely, understanding narcissism as origin or as undecomposable, unanalysable screen leads the analyst (and no matter what theoretical warnings might be given in other respects) to present his interpretative discourse as a haven, either comforting or confrontingly aggressive, for a narcissism that thus finds itself recognized and renewed. Whether comforting or authenticating (by rational criticism, for instance, in interpretations of the 'mental process' sort), such a welcome falls into the trap of narcissism and seldom succeeds in leading it through the Oedipal procession on to the topology of a complex subject.

In fact, clinical practicians like Winnicot protected themselves against such a danger, if only by always advocating a mixture of 'narcissistic' and 'Oedipal' interpretations in so-called psychotic states. Nevertheless, if the dead end that has just been noted can be encountered by others, the reason for it must probably be located in a basic omission – that of the agency of the imaginary father from the start of primary identification, an agency of which 'projective identification' is a more belated consequence (logically and chronologically). One may still reach that dead end, by the same token, if one ignores the very concrete and specific structuration required by psychicism within that very elementary disposition, which the term 'narcissism' threatens to reduce to a fascination for what is nothing else than the mother's phallus.

Persian or Christian

The dynamics of primary identification, which structures *emptiness* and *object* as what may have appeared as a 'narcissistic screen', will allow us to examine another enigmatic juncture on the Freudian path.

Freud's uneasiness concerning Christianity is well known, and his rationality would not let him put it into words with respect to revealed religion, but, dazzled and prudent, he did express it when faced with Persian religion. 'The sun-drenched face of the young Persian god has remained incomprehensible to us.'[28] It is indeed possible to interpret that refulgent *jouissance* as 'direct and immediate' primary identification with the phallus desired by the mother; this amounts neither to being the mother's phallus nor entering the Oedipal drama. A certain phantasmatic incestuous potentiality is thus set aside; it works from the place of the imaginary father and constitutes the basis of imagination itself. Moreover, the subsequent naming of that relationship perhaps represents the conditions of sublimation.

In Freud's text, the 'refulgent and incomprehensible' face, lacking an Oedipal feeling of fault or guilt, would be that of the leader of the horde of brothers who kills the father and boasts of his feat (as Ernest Jones suggests).[29] One might, on the other hand, consider a pre- or non-Oedipal disposition of that *jouissance*; a position of symbolicity that stems from primary identification, coupled with what the latter infers as to sexual non-differentiation (father-and-mother, man-and-woman) and immediate transference to the site of *maternal desire*. That would constitute a fragile inscription of subjecthood, one which, under the subsequent Oedipal sway, would retain no more than a phantasmatic status. In addition, such a warm but dazzling, domesticated paternity includes imaginary exultation as well as a risk of dissolving identities that only the Freudian Oedipal process ends up strengthening, in the ideal hypothesis of course.

Maintaining against the winds and high tides of our modern civilization the requirement of a stern father who, through his Name, brings about separation, judgement and identity, constitutes a necessity, a more or less pious wish. But we can only note that if this sternness is shaken, far from leaving us orphaned or inexorably psychotic, such an unsettling action will reveal multiple and varied destinies for paternity – notably of archaic, imaginary paternity. Those destinies could or can be manifested by the clan as a whole, by the priest or by the therapist. In all cases, however, we are dealing with a function that guarantees the subject's entry into a disposition, a fragile one to be sure, of an ulterior, unavoidable Oedipal destiny, but one that can also be playful and sublimational.

Seducer or ideal father

The tragical dynamics of the father's idealization is taken up again in *Moses and Monotheism* through the theme of the election of the Jewish people by its God and through the story of Moses. There is nothing to make one conceive this election as a revival of the old idea, subsequently abandoned by Freud, of the father as the hysterical person's first seducer. The father who brings a people into being through his love is perhaps indeed closer to the 'father of individual prehistory', and, at any rate, to the idealizing agency that drains early identifications, not as object but as 'unary feature'. One might nevertheless interpret Freudian thought with respect to this loving father in the following fashion. The hysterical structure of the horde of brothers construes him as a seducer, an agent of the libido, of Eros, and puts him to death; this is Moses' murdered body. Yet there is also a structural necessity for his unique love as symbolic choice; it appears later on as a pressing need to lay down moral rules or a right to the tribe. The father will then be recognized not as seducer but as Law, as an abstract agency of the One that selects our identifying and idealizing power. The Christian trinity, for its part, reconciles the seducer and the legislator by inventing another form of love – *Agapē*, symbolic (nominal, spiritual) from the very start *and* corporeal, absorbing the acknowledged murder of the erotic body into the universalist profusion of the symbolist distinction for everyone (brother or stranger, faithful or sinner).[30]

What is opposed to the recognition of the imaginary father? What is it that produces its repression, or even its burial? Freud drops the word 'character', with its well-known anal connotations. 'Whatever resistance character might later be able to bring to bear against the influence of abandoned sexual objects, the effects of earlier identifications, carried out in the most precocious stages of life, will always keep their general, lasting features.'[31]

Character is one of the limits to what is analysable, and that is confirmed by the difficulties encountered in the region we are now investigating. Furthermore, because of the anal character's resistance against primary identification, the advent of the abject during treatment can clearly be seen as the first breach in resistance...Nevertheless and above all it is Oedipal rivalry, which creates mediations, that tragically darkens the dazzlement of primary identification. Within the Oedipus complex, the question is no longer 'Who *is* it?' but 'Who *has* it?'; the narcissistic question 'Am I?' becomes a possessive or attributive question, 'Have I?' It is none the less true that by starting from Oedipal dramas and their failures – backwards, in other words – one will be able to detect the particulars of primary identification. It is to be noted, however, that 'boundary states' lead us there directly, locating the Oedipal conflict as ulterior or secondary.

A boy will have difficulty tearing himself away from the petrifying situation of being his mother's phallus; or if he succeeds, through the maternal grandfather (among others) who has come in between, he will never cease waging war against his brothers in the shadow of an inaccessible father. Only in poetic enunciation will it be possible for him to be son-and-father within the immediate and direct disposition of primary identification, and bypassing sexual difference – witness the troubadours and Joyce. As for the girl she will retain the traces of that primary transference only if assisted by a father having a maternal character, who nevertheless will not be of much help in her breaking away from the mother and finding a heterosexual object. She will thus tend to bury that primary identification under the disappointed feverishness of the homosexual, or else in abstraction, which, as it flies away from the body, fully constitutes itself as 'soul' or fuses with an Idea, a Love, a Self-sacrifice...If ever a *jouissance* remains, it still seems to partake of that archaic differentiation that Freud so delicately and elliptically touched on under the heading of 'primary identification'.

'Narcissistic structure' thus remains a permanent fixture in the threnodies of love that beckon to us . . .

John, the ferryman, and emptiness

John comes into analysis with the complaints of borderline cases, which have been fully catalogued by Winnicot, Fairbairn and Rosenfeld – false self, sexual impotence, professional dissatisfaction. His discourse seems to pay tribute to fashion, of which he is yet largely unaware, when he plays with signifiers, deals with words as if they were objects or proceeds by fragmentary, illogical, chaotic sentence concatenations; thus, after having lived and talked so much, he gives the impression of being *empty*. The theme of emptiness, explicit during the treatment of this man, generates multiple metaphors and configurations, all centred in the mother, for which he never uses the possessive adjective. As if repression were problematic, all incestuous as well as murderous contents are present in his discourse. Nevertheless, if they have a *meaning*, they have no signification for this patient. Within the empty enclosure of his narcissism, contents (drives and representations) could not find an *other* (an addressee) who, alone, might have given a signification to their weighty meaning that is still felt as empty because it is deprived of love. Transference caused two elements to surface out of the void, and they allowed the long walk around the Oedipal problematics.

First there was the outbreak of abjection.[32] Desired or to be killed, the mother was embodied only as abject, repulsive, decked out with all the details of a previously frozen anality. In the same way, and still protected by an explicitly idealizing transference, the patient transforms the uncertain boundaries between what is not yet an Ego and what is not yet an Other by filling this not-yet-an-Ego with 'abjects', thus bringing it out of emptiness, and then giving it only a narcissistic consistency. 'I am repulsive, therefore I can be.' Neither subject nor object, both ab-jects each in his or her turn, mother and son painfully separate all through the initial stage of the treatment, necessarily activating the body's boundaries (skin or sphincters), fluids and ejections, so that passing symptoms might find a place in them. I saw that elementary structuration of narcissism as preceding any possibility of 'projective identification', which, although diffuse during the first phase of the treatment, did not appear essential (it had a *meaning* but no *signification*); only later could it be elaborated and interpreted.

Meanwhile, and this is the second noteworthy element corresponding to the advent of the abject, the patient has a dream. In order to shield himself from his mother's lover who attracts his Oedipal identifications, John races away frantically, but he is losing ground when an old man, who resembles a saint, miraculously shows up. 'It is Christopher, I think, the one who carries the child Jesus, who lifts me upon his shoulders and takes me across the bridge. He carries me, but my own feet are doing the walking...' The following sessions evoke John's father, who died when he was very young, but also the maternal uncle and grandfather, with whom he had spent his early years. The father, who had been disparaged up to now, averred absent or of no account, is shyly silhouetted in the patient's talk as an 'unassuming intellectual', 'movie buff', 'reader of James' ('strange for an unpretentious clerk, reading works like that'); this to uphold him in his struggle against the abject, thus giving him stabler boundaries, selves that last a little longer before appearing to be false, conflictual landmarks that blaze out the whiteness of a narcissism whose emptiness he initially deplored.

Unlike Freud's patients, the *borderline speaks of Eros but dreams of Agape*. What was interpreted as a 'problematic repression', or even as a 'lack of repression' in such patients appears to be rather *another position* of repression. With the borderline patient, a negation weighs above all and heavily on primary identification. To say that this indicates a 'repudiation of the Name of the Father' is too sweeping and inaccurate, if only because of the existence of transference and, following upon the treatment, the emergence of the Oedipus complex, which can be more or less analysed. But that repression reminds one if anything of a negation of Agape (I shall use this term as synonymous to primary identification), with everything this implies concerning repression of homosexuality when a man is involved; it modifies the status of those representations linked to repressed erotic drives and mainly to erotic relation-ships within the dual relationship (including 'projective identification'). Consequently, affect representatives pass through the censorship of repression and appear within discourse as empty, without signification. Discourse itself undergoes an analogous process; laden with drives, it is nevertheless experi-enced as 'castrated', John says, without consistency, empty, too, for want of that elementary, archaic Third Party who could have been its addressee and, by receiving it, could have authenticated it. If all that remains is an Oedipal father, a symbolic father, no struggle against the 'abject', no becoming autonomous with respect to the phallic mother, could be inscribed in the body of language.

The analyst, along this route, is summoned in place of the imaginary father, especially (and this is what the borderline patient dreams of) in order for him or her, apprehensively, to serve as a support for abjection.

Marie and the absence of the mother

Marie exhibits all the delightful throes of hysteria: demand following upon demand, affirmation upon affirmation, until she encounters 'total failure', which yet leaves her 'cold', although dramatically restless, apprehensive, distressed... 'It's amazing, I'm constantly struck by the futility of it all.' This does not, however, spare her the symptom that prompts her to come into analysis – a suffocation that grips her as soon as she sits at the wheel of her car. Marie's story is not an ordinary one. Abandoned by her mother who disappeared during the war, she was first taken care of by her father's family and then put out to nurse. The father remarries and, 'completely terrorized by his wife', Marie says, sees his daughter only rarely; to him she is the burden of a youthful error whom he is ready to support but not to love. The mother's real absence raises to the highest pitch idealization and hatred towards her, with nothing left but the latter when, at age 25, Marie meets with and is disappointed by the family of the one who never ceases not to have room for her. Marie's relationships with women are frequent, conflictive and 'insignificant': 'That doesn't interest me', she says, after having hundreds of times duplicated her 'symptom', as she puts it, when going to visit those women. But she holds back, expresses nothing, raises no objection – 'totally masochistic, you can say that again'. Concern for an essential narcissistic protection makes her 'obliging, friendly, kind', whereas her two ('never fewer than two', Marie specifies) sexual partners with whom she maintains alternating separate and conflictive relationships allow her to lose nothing of either the structure or the bounties of her childhood, and they restore to her a completion that is sometimes 'suffocating' but very satisfying, above all during the quarrels of the threesome.

Out of the central emptiness of narcissism that the story of Marie outlines perhaps too straightforwardly (but how many actual, adored or hated, mothers of hysterical persons undergo the same occultation behind the screen of a winded narcissistic quest in the infinite mirror of hysteria?), measure herself or project herself. What was abjection for John is for Marie pure and simple inanity, restless, feverish and hollow; she is on an impossible search for a 'real job', a 'true love', which would bring an end to 'nobody loves me'. Such a logic dooms her to be a victim, but she realizes it only when a friend tells her, lost as she is within a space without boundaries, punctuated only by her symptoms (the 'suffocations' – a boundary, barrier or buttress?) and the *jouissance* of her fits of anger.

On the occasion of her father's serious illness when she thought she might lose him, Marie had a dream. There is a death notice, a man has died, but the name on the notice is that of a woman. It is soon clear that it is the name of Marie's half-sister, her father's favorite. Marie subsequently discovers that the two men in her life also had other women, hence she is not unique. She becomes jealous, flares up against those women, against the analyst...

The hysteric *speaks of Agape and dreams of Eros Thanatos*. But whether in this or that disposition of her love, she sustains her narcissistic infinite by jumbling the boundaries with her mother, and they both founder there in the delights of absence. Absence in relation to what? In relation to the elementary shift effected by primary identification, which allows for the existence of a potentially symbolic Other. For if it is transferred to the place of the imaginary father, inasmuch as he guarantees entrance into language and thwarts the phobic and psychotic potentiality of fusion hysteria, it is transferred along with the kit of representation but without the caboodle of drive.

The caboodle remained in the emptiness of maternal fusion and/or maternal absence. I do mean *and/or*, for at this juncture, provided needs are satisfied (by a wet-nurse, nurse or mother who is only a care-giver without an *other desire*), having a mother or not makes no difference: they are the same, she is the same. The being that satisfies needs (that is, the mother without desire for the Other) can leave no other spoor than that of not being, of non-being. What endows the mother with existence is primary identification, on the basis of which the hysterical person's mother will not assume the outlines of an *abject* but those of a stranger, an absentee, an indifferent one, before becoming, thanks to the incipient Oedipus complex, a conflictive object of projective identification.

Such a hysteria will then experience its Eros with women, while waiting for a symbolic, idealizing Agape on the part of a man who will never, just the same, correspond to its design. That is what mortgages the Oedipus complex of hysteria and explains why it will have the greatest difficulty in choosing a loving object of the paternal kind. For, in that structure, the imaginary father does not exist – he gave out before allowing it to have an object finally capable of love and hate emerge out of maternal emptiness, an erotic object necessarily in the mother's likeness (for the man and for the woman).

Caught between derealization (blurring of boundaries, somatic symptoms), where a narcissism without boundaries unfolds in self-satisfied fashion, and settling scores with women – scores that are necessarily anal but repressed and for that reason not at all abject – hysteria seeks its identity under the stern attention of the symbolic father, a ruthless father. The way towards Oedipal identification with the father is either blocked or impeded by repression of the imaginary father who is fully transferred to the mother's account. The hysterical person, man or woman, is not the mother's phallus but does not want to know this. Negation of primary identification endows him or her with that perverse plasticity, coyness, feigned susceptibility . . . pretending that she does not exist since she is . . . the mother, in other words, nothing . . . or an inaccessible *totality*.

It is possible to discern in the narcissistic hollowing out of the mother and in the anal economizing (in the sense of thrift) of abjection concerning her (the hysterical person spares itself maternal abjection, allowing, with respect to this proto-object, only emptiness or hatred, a 'lovehatred'), one of the conditions permitting the violence characteristic of projective identifications within this structure. Still more pronounced with women, these features, as I see it, shed light on the feminine paranoia that lies dormant in so many cases of hysteria.

Matthew or the walkman against Saturn

Matthew is one of those youngsters equipped with *walkmen* who have recently invaded the streets of Paris and, I suppose, are rarely seen on couches. He comes in wearing his headphones steeped in music that is 'classical, of course', as he specifies; he removes them only when he sees me, putting them back on upon leaving my office. A university graduate, an 'expert and bored' mathematician, as he puts it, he devotes himself to singing, which, however, he is no longer able to do, hence his entry into analysis. Gifted for computer languages, Matthew was no longer able to speak with his friends, nor could he utter a single word during a previous attempt at analysis that supposedly lasted three months. During several months of face-to-face therapy Matthew did not so much analyse as learn to put together a discourse for an other. Afterwards, reclining, he retraced a family history that was interrupted by brief sequences during which he said he was the victim of aggression – on the street, subway or bus. Music isolates him from such violence, but now he believes that it also brings it about. An elliptic, allusive language, as if fastened to abstraction, serves him more to *delineate* space than to *signify* something for me. For him, speaking is painful and tiring, either too diffusive or too intrusive. Music alone harmonizes that bipolarity (abstraction – intrusion), which, without the headphones, becomes petrified and ties Matthew to his bed, without a phone, cut off from others, as if 'surrounded with a chalk circle, invisible and impassable'.

This phobo-obsessional equipment began to thaw when treatment caused the image of a devouring father to appear – eating, voracious, insatiable. A father-Saturn who took the place of the 'poor guy' and induced a whole series of masculine and feminine figures, educators-persecutors-seducers; starting from there, Matthew began to examine the role of his walkman and his retreat into music.

Basing myself on this stage of his analysis, punctuated for me by Matthew's arrival with the headphones, I still have the feeling that he fears paternal seduction; is this phantasmatic or real? Appended to his mother, described as the key figure in the family, Matthew has not ceased being her phallus. Within their dual economy, which the father did not broach, it seemed apparently inconceivable that she might have a desire other than her child. The voracity of the dual symbiosis, accompanied by denial of the imaginary father and, consequently, an outpouring of withheld anal sadism, came back to Matthew from outside, projected – and this as soon as an object appeared, as masculine one preferably (for the mother blended with the patient).

Music was the father-again, the landmark, the intermediary between confusion on the one hand and the invisible chalk circle, besieged by onslaughts, on the other. It allowed Matthew to set up a mobile identity for himself and to reject out of it, as abject, whatever did not belong (especially the Oedipal array to which were added the more archaic oral loathing and sadism). Matthew was gleeful, ecstatic and amorous but only as walkman. The headphones were a spot that included all other spots, an organized, differentiated infinity that filled him with consistency and allowed him to face Saturn's devouring but also to have his own destructiveness towards him recognized. Matthew's maternal uncle was a well-known pianist. Analysis made use of the walkman; identifying the shell that the headphones were destined to become, it turned it into a premise of autonomy, of demarcation.

Obsessional neurosis, in the vault of its rituals, shelters a drifting, an instability that reveals the failure or fragility of primary identification, and that is what Matthew's walkman helped me to hear...

'O God, I could be bounded in a nut-shell and count myself a king of infinite space, were it not that I have bad dreams', Hamlet said (II, 2), and Borges quotes those lines at the outset of his *Aleph*. 'The place where all the places of the universe can be located, without intermingling', the Aleph is a 'privilege' granted the child in order that 'the man, some day, might engrave a poem'.

Could what is thus being considered be the condition, and for some the sublimational possibility, for remaking an imaginary father, taking his place, creating his place within language? Such an economy takes nomination closest to that spot without object, both point and infinity, blocked identity and immediate identification. It is the place where narcissism is said to hold sway only in the painful manner of Hamlet, surrounded by abjectness, emptiness, ghostliness and quest for paternal love. For before killing him in Oedipal fashion, the speaking being, in order to speak, loves the 'father of personal prehistory'. Suffering, he beguiles himself with the sound of his cross, an acrobat walking a tightrope: should he let himself be walled in alive or make a poem out of it?

NOTES

1 This corresponds to, although it does not fully render, Kristeva's coinage, *hainamoration*. It was suggested by Margaret Waller (who translated *Revolution in Poetic Language*) to replace one of my own less fortunate neologisms – and I am indebted to her for many other suggestions and corrections as well.

2 See *On Narcissism: an introduction* (1914) in volume XIV of the *Standard Edition*;

this text is doubtless very bound up with the war, Freud's insecurity and Jung.

Nevertheless, from the time of his earliest works, Freud insisted on a *resistance* that would have been imbedded in the very structure of neurons as well as on *inhibition* as master faculty of the Ego (*Project for a scientific psychology*, 1895, in volume I of the *Standard Edition*). 'We must reckon with the possibility that something in the nature of the sexual drive itself is unfavorable to the realization of complete satisfaction', he notes in 'The tendency to debasement in love', in *The Psychology of Love, Standard Edition*, vol. XI, pp. 188–9, before discovering narcissism at the same time as the illusion present at the outset of psychicism, as it is at the heart of amatory experience. Next comes what Freud himself called the 'strange' postulate of death drive, posited towards the end of an exposition on the impossible in love, on loving hatred and primary masochism ('Beyond the pleasure principle', *Standard Edition*, vol. XVIII, pp. 51–61). See also chapter V of *Histoires d'amour* (Paris: Denoël, 1983), the section on Romeo and Juliet.

3 *Standard Edition*, vol. XIV, p. 77.

4 Jacques Lacan, *Le Séminaire, Livre I, Les Ecrits techniques de Freud* (Paris: Seuil, 1975), p. 133.

5 André Green, *Narcissisme de vie, narcissisme de mort* (Paris: Minuit, 1983).

6 See 'Being in love and hypnosis', in *Group Psychology and the Analysis of the Ego* (1921), *Standard Edition*, vol. XVIII, pp. 111ff.

7 Ibid., p. 112.

8 'Identification', in *Group Psychology and the Analysis of the Ego*, p. 105.

9 Ibid., p. 105.

10 Ibid., p. 110.

11 Ibid., p. 107.

12 *The Ego and the Id* (1923), *Standard Edition*, vol. XIX, p. 31. One of the main ideas of Freud's breviary of love amounts to positing that the Oedipus complex's decline (which he calls 'natural' but is in fact enigmatic) during the latency period favours the inhibition of partial drives and strengthens ideals – thus making the erotico-ideal cathexis of the love object possible during puberty. 'I am in love' is a fact of adolescence when the teenager is capable of partial repression because of difficulties in realizing Oedipal fantasies and can project his idealizing capabilities on to a person towards whom erotic desire can be deferred (see Christian David, *L'Etat amoureux*, Paris: Payot, 1971). Nevertheless, the premises for such a state of love go back to *primary identification* and, before they constitute a lover, they shape psychic space itself.

13 Melanie Klein, *Envy and Gratitude* (London: Hogarth Press, 1957), p. 187. See also Melanie Klein and Jean Rivière, *Love, hate, and Reparation* (London: Hogarth Press, 1967). On Melanie Klein see Jean-Michel Petot, *Melanie Klein, le moi et le bon objet (1932–1960)* (Paris: Dunot, 1982).

14 Klein, *Envy and Gratitude*, p. 180.

15 Ibid., p. 191.

16 Ibid., p. 193.

17 Recalling that in analytical literature the object is in most instances a partial object (mammilla, scybalum, phallus, urine), Lacan specifies: 'This feature, this partial feature, rightly emphasized in objects, is applicable not because these objects are

part of a total object, the body, but because they represent only partially the function that produces them.' Being a function of separation and of want that found the signifying relationship, these objects, designated by a lower case 'a', will be called 'objects of want': 'These objects have one common feature in my elaboration of them – they have no specular image, or, in other words, alterity. It is what enables them to be the 'stuff', or rather the lining, though not in any sense the reverse, of the very subject that one takes to be the subject of consciousness...It is to this object that cannot be grasped in the mirror that the specular image lends its clothes' ('Subversion of the subject and dialectic of desire', in *Ecrits. A selection*, tr. Alan Sheridan [New York: Norton, 1977], pp. 315–16. Lacan discovered in *fantasy* the exemplary efficacy of the object 'a' since in his view the structure of fantasy is linked 'to the condition of an object...the moment of a "fading" or eclipse of the subject that is closely bound up with the *Spaltung* or splitting that it suffers from its subordination to the signifier' (ibid., p. 313). That is what is symbolized by the formula ($ \lozenge $ a) where $\lozenge$ indicates desire. Finally, the *metonymical* structure defines the Lacanian object relation to the extent that 'it is the connection between signifier and signifier that permits the elision in which the signifier installs the want-of-being in the object relation, using the value of "reference back" possessed by signification in order to invest it with the desire aimed at the very want it supports' ('The agency of the letter in the unconscious', ibid., p. 164).

18 'Take just one signifier as an emblem of this omnipotence [of the other's authority], that is to say of this wholly potential power (*ce pouvoir tout en puissance*), this birth of possibility, and you have the unary feature (*trait unaire*), which, by filling in the invisible mark that that the subject derives from the signifier, alienates this subject in the primary identification that forms the ego ideal' ('Subversion of the subject and dialectic of desire', in *Ecrits*, p. 306). The unary feature of Lacan goes back to the 'unique feature' (*einziger Zug*), to which would be limited the identification that is only partial, according to Freud in *Identification* (*das beide Male die Identifizierung eine partielle, höchst beschränkte ist*) – see the *Seminars on Transference* (1960–61) and on *Identification* (1961–2). Lacan takes advantage of that partial status, on the whole rather imprecise with Freud, in order to insist upon the *unique feature* (*einziger Zug*) that establishes identification as intrinsically symbolic, hence subjected to the distinctiveness of signifying traits, and finally ruled by the benchmark of One feature, of the Unique – foundation of my very own unicity...This unary feature is not 'in the first field of narcissistic identification' where we have witnessed the emergence of the imaginary father; Lacan sees it straight off 'in the field of desire...in the reign of the signifier' (*The Four Fundamental Concepts of Psychoanalysis*, New York: Norton, 1978, p. 256).

19 See Michael Balint, *Amour primaire et technique psychanalytique* (Paris: Payot, 1972).

20 See 'Identification', in *Group Psychology and the Analysis of the Ego*, p. 105.

21 'Therefore the subject becomes conscious of his desire in the other, by means of the other's image, which presents him with the spectre of his own mastery' (Jacques Lacan, *Séminaire I, Les Ecrits techniques de Freud*, Paris: Seuil, 1975, p. 178).

22 '[The imaginary position of desire] is conceivable only to the extent that a guide may be found beyond the imaginary, at the level of the symbolic plane, the legal exchange that can be embodied only on the basis of verbal exchange among human

beings. The guide that rules the subject is the ego ideal' (ibid., p. 162). And this is true even if 'love is a phenomenon taking place on the level of the imaginary and provoking a real subduction of the symbolic, a kind of annulment or perturbation of the ego ideal' (loc. cit.).

23 I shall return to the metaphor; see chapter VI of *Histoires d'amour*.
24 *The Ego and the Id*, p. 31.
25 G. W. F. Hegel, *Science de la logique* (Paris: Vrin, 1970), pp. 385–6.
26 See Martin Heidegger, *Holzwege*, Frankfurt: Klostermann, 1950; French translation *Chemins qui ne mènent nulle part*, Paris: Gallimard, 1962. (There is no collected English translation of the essays in this book.)
27 See chapter V of *Histoires d'amour*.
28 *Totem and Taboo* in *Standard Edition*, vol. XIII, p. 153.
29 See *Moses and Monotheism*, in *Standard Edition*, vol. XXIII, p. 110.
30 See *Histoires d'amour*, Chapter IV, 1, 'Dieu est Agapê'.
31 *The Ego and the Id*, in *Standard Edition*, vol. XIX, p. 31.
32 See my *Powers of Horror: an essay on abjection* (New York: Columbia University Press, 1982).

Translated by Léon S. Roudiez

11

Why the United States?

This discussion between Julia Kristeva, Marcelin Pleynet and Philippe Sollers was originally published in 1977 as the introduction to a special issue of *Tel Quel* (no. 71/73) on the United States, and first translated as 'The U.S. Now: a Conversation' in *October*, 6 (Fall 1978). A few references to this 'American' issue of *Tel Quel* have been cut from the new translation published here.

Like the following essay on dissidence, 'Why the United States?' is reprinted here as an example of Kristeva's more directly political discourse. Marking as it does the shift away from the *Tel Quel* group's fascination with China and their tentative turn towards the USA as a possible symbol of the post-modern era, this text has become extremely controversial, at least among English-speaking readers of Kristeva. Some have accused her of abdicating her left-wing politics when confronted with the glamour of monopoly-capitalism, while others, such as Jacqueline Rose, have stressed the fact that Kristeva's description of the USA as a 'non-verbal' society is not to be taken as an uncritical celebration of a 'semiotic' culture: it is after all Kristeva who in her final intervention warns against the psychotic violence which may lurk under this surface of 'non-verbalization'. (See Jacqueline Rose, 'Julia Kristeva: Take Two' in her *Sexuality in the Field of Vision*, London: NLB/Verso, 1986.)

To a non-French European reader, the most striking aspect of this text may well be its extreme ethnocentrism: throughout the conversation, the words 'France' (and even 'Paris') and 'Europe' seem to be used more or less as synonyms. The American reader, on the other hand, may well feel scandalized at the Parisian trio's somewhat condescending description of the non-verbalized American void, which supposedly is crying out to be filled with the discourse of European (French?) intellectuals. In spite of these misgivings, or perhaps because of them, the essay throws much light on the mode of political thought dominant in the *Tel Quel* group in 1977, a mode striking for its insistence on the *textual* (linguistic) nature of political and historical change.

The opening reference to Kristeva's previously published essay 'From Ithaca to New York' refers to a text which first appeared in *Promesse* (no. 36–7) in the spring of 1974 (i.e., at the time of Kristeva's visit to China), and which was reprinted (with some changes) in *Polylogue* (Paris: Seuil, 1977, pp. 495–515). Already containing many of the observations Kristeva makes in 'Why the United States?', the earlier essay is more deeply involved in the burning issues of its day such as the Yom Kippur war and Watergate. Presenting as it does a series of reflections on the growing women's movement in the USA and the situation of intellectual women in that country, 'From Ithaca to New York' is of special interest to feminists.

Why the United States?

MP   Since Julia is the only one here who has already written and published something about one of her visits to the United States, perhaps she could begin by telling us how she re-reads her text 'From Ithaca to New York', reprinted in *Polylogue*. That is, how does she read it today, after several other trips to New York and the United States?

JK   I feel that my vision of the United States isn't entirely French and may consequently appear too idiosyncratic. In fact, I went to the United States with almost the same desire for discovery and change that took me from Bulgaria to Paris ten years ago. More and more I had the impression that what was happening in France – due to the various developments of a Gaullism in its death-throes on the one hand and the growing power of the so-called masses or petit-bourgeois masses on the other – was making the history of the European continent predictable, so that if one were interested in the breaks within history, culture and time, one had to change continents. I also tried to experience such a change through my interest in China, which I viewed as an anarchist outbreak within Marxism. But the trip to China finally made me realize that this was really a re-run, somewhat revised perhaps, but a re-run none the less, of the same Stalinist or let's say Marxist-Stalinist model. It was therefore out of curiosity and the desire to discover some other solution to the impasse of the West that made me fly off twice to the United States, and then finally a third time for a longer stay. It was a *journey*, but not necessarily 'to the end of night'. That is, it was not necessarily accompanied by an apocalyptic or desperate vision, but was rather made in an attempt to understand, perhaps also from a particular and subjective point of view.

Two things struck me during my first brief visits, and these became accentuated during the semester I spent at Columbia University. First, I feel that American capitalism – which everyone agrees is the most advanced and totalizing in the world today – far from undergoing a crisis (and yet this was during crisis periods, notably that of the Yom Kippur war, the energy crisis, the Watergate crisis, the crisis of the presidential election last autumn) is a system of permanent recuperation, of patching-up of crisis. Here I don't mean to be pejorative, but rather want to convey a sense of the most livable possibility of survival. I seemed to perceive in the economic and political logic of America a new way of dealing with the law, with the increasingly brutal economic and political constraints which are inevitable in any society, and all the more so in a technocratic system. The question is to know 'how to deal with' this economic or political constraint. In both Western and Eastern Europe, our way of doing things, which is perhaps the result of a certain religious or state tradition, consists of 'dealing with' a constraint by confronting it with its antithesis. But, to invert Spinoza's phrase, as everyone knows every negation is a definition. An 'opposing' position is therefore determined by what is being opposed. And in this way we arrive at two antithetical systems which internalize and reflect one another's qualities: on the one hand, a government, the conservative and established System; and on the other hand, an opposition which ultimately has the same statist, collectivist and totalitarian flaws. All this has culminated in the twentieth-century dramas of Fascism and Stalinism, which work together like the well-oiled routine of an old couple.

In America, though, it seems to me that opposition to constraint is not unique, isolated and centralized, but is *polyvalent* in a way that undermines the law without attacking it head-on.

It can be said that this polyvalence, that is, the multiplicity of social, ethnic, cultural and sexual groups, of discourse – in brief, the multiplicity of subdivisions that are economic, cultural, political, artistic, and so on – ends up 'ghettoizing' the opposition, since for each opposition an enclave is created where it stagnates. There is in fact the risk of encountering the enormous difficulties and considerable repression which this type of system can generate. But there is also a positive aspect, which is precisely that it avoids developing into paranoia and the confrontation of two laws, each equally sure of itself but fascinated by, and internalizing, the other.

The second striking feature of the United States which seems interesting to me in relation to European culture and society is the place of *artistic practice*. It is a place that is by definition marginal, as in every society. But it concerns a marginality that is also *polyvalent*: 'aesthetic' experiments are more frequent and more varied than in Europe. There are many more enclaves of painting, music, dance, etc. Obviously, this numerical factor would be insignificant if one did not bear in mind the peculiar nature of these aesthetic practices.

For they are *non-verbal*. The Americans today seem to me to excel in any research into gesture, colour and sound, which they pursue in great depth and scope and much more radically than is done in Europe. I attended several exhibitions or performances, both of the recognized avant-garde and of the underground in the lofts and cellars of the Village which attract many young people, and I felt as though I were in the catacombs of the early Christians. This metaphor means first of all that there is a passionate search, and a feeling of discovery, even if it sometimes involves discovering the bicycle a century late. One senses the passage of Surrealism or of Artaud in these discoveries, but it's done with a great deal of passion and commitment. It is none the less a metaphor because this American art does not correspond exactly to the historical reality to which I'm referring. For in the beginning is not the Word, at any rate not in this particular beginning. They know what they do: they don't have a verbal, that is to say, conscious and analytical (in the naïve sense of analysis) connection to what they are doing. When they do say something in these performances, it does not correspond to what is done in gesture, colour and sound.

Two results are produced by this non-correspondence. On the one hand, there is an interest in all the more-or-less avant-garde or modernist forms of discourse to be found in Europe, including those in philosophy and the social sciences. I sometimes felt, especially in my classes, that even though I was using a specialized language, I was speaking to people who knew what it was about, even if they found it difficult. It corresponded to a lived experience, whether pictorial, gestural or sexual. Thus, despite their naïvety, the American audience gives the European intellectual the impression that there is something he can do on the other side of the Atlantic, namely that he can speak in a place where it [ça] doesn't speak. This entails, of course, speaking like a psycho-analytic patient: into a void which returns little more than a dim presence and the punctuations of sounds, colours and gestures. It is very stimulating, I think, for any intellectual work; in any case, it was for mine.

The second consequence of the fact that the most radical practices are non-verbal is that there is no great American literature today, apart from a few exceptions, which are in any case of English origins, and nostalgically oriented towards a Kafkaesque Jewish humour. American literature is perhaps Cage, perhaps Bob Wilson, or even – why not? – Wolfson's *The Schizo and Language*; it is therefore something which opens up the word to the unspeakable, with all the risks of psychosis that this breakthrough implies.

In fact the American culture that interests me (which in its own way is not Catholic, but more Protestant, and for that very reason interesting to the ethnologist that one becomes as soon as one sets foot on another continent) is the culture that confronts psychosis and sublates it. I think this is the fundamental problem for twentieth-century culture, one that will only become more pronounced here in Catholic Western Europe and will force us to think of other forms. They may not necessarily be the American ones, but I'm convinced that these new forms can't develop in ignorance of the response that America has given to the crises of identity and rationality.

A great deal can also be said about the American sense of *time*, the American notion of history which seems to question the linearity of our contemporary history. European societies obviously have an evolutionary perspective: since there are elections certain changes in historical cycles will take place. I don't think the late nineteenth-century historical view has ever been more influential, even if it is contested by some philosophical schemes, and in some areas of research. We've had the bourgeoisie, now it's the turn of 'socialism' and 'progress'. Well, I think that American time short-circuits this evolutionist vision because it entails a *split history*: on the one hand, there is in fact the evolutionism dictated by the development of the links between production and reproduction; but on the other hand, this evolutionism has as its underlying base a conjunction of several temporalities. Since this country is made up of emigrants (Jews, English, French, Central Europeans, Blacks, Indians, etc.), various individual ways of experiencing time and history intersect. The linearity dictated by the economic development seems never to correspond exactly to this religious and cultural base, and it is this non-correspondence that produces flashes that challenge the evolutionism and faith in a progress that none the less exists. For this faith does indeed exist, all the more so since, through the development both of economic and cultural exchange, American thought and culture is contaminated by European culture and, in particular, by Marxism. One sometimes feels that a Marxist discourse of the sort experienced in Europe in the 1950s is returning in the American university. And, in a sense, this is quite logical. The two great powers inevitably influence each other. In Russia this produces Bukovsky, and in America, the Marxist academic, though the gifts are not of equal value. However, even in these communicating vessels, I feel that this linear rationality, with its over-dogmatic Marxism, is confined to a limited context, thanks to the split American temporality I have mentioned. The cultural, technical and religious base is so riotous and multi-faceted that the non-truth that may obtain in a linearizing evolutionism or in the gratifying populism of dogmatic Marxism doesn't seem to be able to increase its influence.

Finally, I was very aware of the problem of the intellectuals. The United States, as it were, does not accord the status to the intellectual that exists in Europe where, if we go back very far, it probably derives from a kind of clergy, but where it essentially comes from the French Revolution's idea of the intellectual as a mediator between the different political parties and thought. In fact, we can deplore the absence of this type of intellectual in the United States, since ideas consequently remain confined to universities or to areas set aside for them, but don't seem to reach the political class. A very sharp clevage exists, in which the intellectuals, apart from the Marxists, don't have ideas that can be politicized. Instead, it is positivism which is the prerogative of the academic intellectual, for he doesn't see himself as entrusted with a political mission, and when he does, it's under the auspices of Marxism, which is a recent trend, a return of everything McCarthyism repressed.

But on the other hand, this sort of American intellectual, by the very limitation of his positivism, brings out certain problems of the belief in politics or in the kind of politics espoused by the European intellectual. Today in particular, due to a sort of permanent feeling of guilt in relation to politics, the latter is abandoning his specificity and transforming every debate into a kind of anti-intellectual witch-hunt, or into coffee-house chitchat, reducing every discussion to the level of electoral politics.

The limitations of the intellectual's role in the United States, which I incidentally consider unsatisfactory, therefore serve to foregound some of the problems in the overexpansion of the 'intellectual vocation' of the Europeans which now is sinking its own ship, as it were.

MP   I feel that the American scene is always a lot more unsettled and complex than is assumed when one tries to understand it. Don't you think that precisely the relationship between the American intellectual and political classes entails exchanges and links of a different order from those found in France, of a completely different order but which as such are far from insignificant? I'm thinking particularly of the fact that the American intellectual class, the academic bigwigs, are for the most part specialists. Universities turn out specialists, and very frequently the link between the intellectual and political classes passes through this type of specialization, which is totally unknown here. That is, over here intellectuals are called upon to argue about ideas; they can't produce real, objective knowledge and take concrete action. I feel that when the political class in the United States calls upon intellectuals – which it does constantly – it calls upon them as specialists, which implies a completely different relation to the intellectual and political functions. This ought to be examined from a European point of view!

JK   The role of the intellectual is defined differently in each case. The intellectual you describe is in fact the technician, the specialist in foreign affairs, the Sinologist or economist, etc. That does exist, and in fact this sort of collaboration between the government and the intellectuals would be the actual equivalent of a graduate of the Ecole Nationale d'Administration or of the Ecole Polytechnique working for the French government. But in the United States the intellectual doesn't cook up ideas, or act as a go-between for the masses, the media, the political parties and learning, as in Europe. Another example of the gap between research and politics in the United States, this time from the Left: a linguist can develop the most Cartesian ideas in his own scholarship, but once he becomes politically involved, he doesn't work for the government in a technical capacity, but commits himself to the Left. He even considers himself an anarchist, although that doesn't affect his thought. Whereas the European intellectual, at least in recent years, will try to question his own theory if his political practice is already out of line with certain kinds of rationality. We've seen notions of truth, knowledge, identity, etc. challenged as a result of socio-political experience. In the United States, on the contrary, I have the impression that notions of Truth, law and the University have remained sacrosanct.

They remain the law or the laws remain there. If nevertheless they are weaker than here it's because there are so many of them. It's not because they're attacked head-on and pursued in depth as, for example, would be done by any French intellectual shaken up in May 68. It's because they're multiplied. It's another way, not necessarily more radical in terms of thought, but more efficient in terms of society as a whole. Their system therefore even accords a place to European intellectuals, including all their radicalism.

PhS Can one hypothesize about the future of psychoanalysis in the United States?

JK I don't want to hypothesize. I can only give my impressions of the current state of affairs.

I shall say a few words about psychoanalysis since you've asked the question. I think that psychoanalysis has quite simply fallen through over there. What does that mean? It has become normative, and the different psychoanalytical factions I could observe and listen to, even if they're now becoming interdisciplinary and beginning to pay more attention to sociology as well as psychoanalysis, to linguistics as well as to psychoanalysis, etc., have an outlook that is still dominated by classical, scientific and superegotistic rationalism, when they aren't spiritualist. I wonder if psychoanalysis hasn't escaped them because of Protestantism on the one hand and, on the other hand, because they have no language, since English, in America, is a code. Can psychoanalysis be implanted in a code? It's a shame, in fact it's a great disaster, the 'plague' as Freud said. At the same time one may wonder whether this failure doesn't prepare the way for certain paths which go beyond psychoanalysis. Obviously there's no 'beyond' if there hasn't already been psychoanalysis; it can't be traversed without first being entered. But the eruption of pornography, the various forms of mysticism, the proliferation of trans-psychotic aesthetic experiments, etc., which, while troubling and while perhaps being so many dead ends, may also be ways of dealing with sublimation in a manner different from that of psychoanalysis, which, as we've all too frequently seen, produces its own particular chapels and dead ends.

PhS The United States is 1776, something that doesn't belong to the Jacobin model of the French Revolution. If we look at what was happening in the nineteenth century, if we re-read Baudelaire's important text on Edgar Poe, it's very clear that the adventure of thought, the literary adventure, the adventure of the American avant-garde at that time was not so different from what in the nineteenth century was to affect all of Europe: that is to say, that the discovery or manifestation of an 'abnormal' and particularly critical subjectivity was to be rejected by this American progressive, positivist nineteenth century, in full expansion. Now, what happened in the twentieth century with the First and Second World Wars? Strangely, we witnessed a completely spectacular grafting of the different subjective liberations which had erupted in Europe as dissidence or marginality. Naturally, I see the main graft at the time of the Second World War as being the draining of marginalized European personalities into an American exile. Let's call it the grafting of the European avant-garde on to the United States, even though the problem is complex, involving Schoenberg and a great many others. I think this is very important and we must return to it. Let's also call it the grafting of Surrealism on to the United States during the war.

This grafting, it seems to me, is at the source of what we call American art. Like it or not, the very rapid development of an American art dates from this point, whether we're talking about painting or gesture, or the creation of an atmosphere bordering on something like the materialization of an unconscious which might have been experienced in Europe.

This situation seems to me to have been rapid and explosive, and to have gone unperceived in Europe, in France, before, say, the 1960s. We had the cold war, a kind of politico-military planetary freeze, and gradually, around 1960, this memory grafted on to the United States resurfaced, and has ever since posed a question for Europe. Now the problem is whether the kind of delegation, or extensive breeding-ground exported to the United States as the result of Fascism and Stalinism can be re-examined in the light of what may emerge in Europe as the archaeology of our twentieth-century history. And here again no doubt we face some burning questions: the question of Freud in 1909; the introduction of Jungian ideas; the multivalent resistance of religious attitudes which, despite their decentralizing and polymorphic aspects, remain resistant. And there is also the problem of knowing what American intellectuals and academics now accept as the archaeology of the history of this graft which in a way has been indirectly made on them and which presupposes a loss at some point. That is, what kind of philosophy or theory of language, or method of reading or interpretation are they interested in today? And what interests them on the level of a deep understanding of the great avant-garde phenomena of the twentieth century, such as Joyce, for example, or Artaud, or whoever you wish. That's my question. At the moment, we're at a very important turning-point, such that this possibility of creative non-verbalization, that is, this passage through colour, sound, gesture, etc. based on an absence of verbalization, makes it necessary to ask one question: Why is there this gap in verbalization? Is it still productive? It has been in the past, and still is today. And who's going to be able to begin to speak within it, or not?

JK   It's difficult to make an indictment. That's not our aim. We ought to find out what it is we are looking for in them. It's not so much 'why do they do this and not that?', as 'why do they interest us?'. Isn't it because they make an appeal to us by their gap in verbalization? And when facing this void we feel we are being called, perhaps not exactly chosen, but at least called.

PhS   In questioning the meaning of this graft we address a displaced memory. We live among the ruins of Stalinism and Fascism, among the ruins of a Europe ravaged by them.

JK   I completely agree. As for the graft, it undoubtedly took place, but it produced something entirely different from what was to be expected. They took Artaud and Duchamp but produced Pollock, which couldn't have happened in either France or Moscow. So there's something specific and interesting in America. They may be getting bogged down today now they take anything and everything from Parisian intellectual cuisine, but in fact there's no mainstream in their choice. Obviously in so far as there are institutions, they're tempted to choose what is valued in French institutions, and it then goes out of fashion in the analogous American institution. A philosopher who's in fashion at the rue d'Ulm will be in fashion at Yale for two years, and that will upset his colleagues. But these phenomena get lost in such a variety that in the end they don't involve the same diktat of styles as they do in Paris. And then they borrow from intellectual masters to make ideologies as ephemeral as they are unrecognizable. It is an immense machine turning Western discourse into refuse. This refuse may generate a new burst of energy. But for the moment I see this energy only in sounds, colours and gestures, not words. If something other than waste is to be produced on the verbal level, it obviously must be a two-way operation. I think it's important not to exalt or condemn New York, but to appreciate the reciprocal benefits of the exchange. New York and Paris are specific places, and we shouldn't criticize one in the name of the other. The way in which one reciprocally illuminates the other will perhaps get round those problems which are too great. I think that our aim here is therefore precisely to indicate how a graft can flourish in different soils.

MP   The question is perhaps precisely the kind of vision we offer of America. Obviously, I think our view isn't a French one, nor undoubtedly is it American, because it isn't a national view. I'm very much interested in the fact that the exile of artists and intellectuals to the United States is not only that of the Surrealists; I mean it's not only the exile of the French, it's the exile of all of Europe. It's the exile of Austria, Germany, Italy, France, and it's also the exile of certain English intellectuals. I think something extremely significant is happening in that respect, at all events for me.

It's certainly no accident that those who were chased out of Europe by Stalinist and Hitlerian Fascism and those who were chased out of other parts of the world by dictatorial regimes found a home in the United States, and I think one might perhaps try to explain how this came about.

There are obviously several points to raise. There is the point that, as a state and as a country, the United States is actually completely new, composed of many ethnic groups and languages, whose very multiplicity does not manage to provide the state with the same repressive structures it can have elsewhere in the world. I don't mean that the American state isn't repressive, but that its form is constantly eroded and divided by the various forms it must assume. That is, everyone knows that there are more Poles in Chicago than in Warsaw; that the Chinese colony in the United States is enormous; that in New York, Jews occupy an important place in the artistic and intellectual milieux and even in politics; that around the Village, the Italian colony is very important; and that politically, all these different European, extra-American references must survive and find a place. I think it's in this context that what I would be tempted to define as modern art can survive. I know that when I first went to the United States in 1966, I left behind a French situation which seemed completely closed and blocked from a cultural point of view. That is, it was academic, or at best attempting to struggle not with its real history, the history of the twentieth century, but with a completely academic cultural anachronism. And when I arrived in the United States I saw that what was happening there corresponded to an experience of modernity that Europe didn't suspect at all then.

JK   Was it unknown here for political reasons?

MP   For many reasons. It was unknown for political reasons, or for historical reasons; that is, if one considers Europe up until 1960, it was both economically and intellectually ruined. If I think about what was becoming most lively around 1955, say in literature, in Europe, I should be forced to say the New Novel. Now it's pretty obvious that if I situate the New Novel in the history of modern culture, it's something progressive in 1955, something completely reactive to an academic fabric established in France after the war. There are economic and political reasons, precise historical and precise cultural reasons for that.

PhS   One mustn't forget in all this that the propaganda internalized from the various European fascisms from the 1930s on had an enormous effect in preparing the violently anti-modern climate, a modernity which the United States could represent at the time. One only has to re-examine the texts, the declarations of everything then that professed to be ever more French, ever more traditional, ever more anti-jazz, anti-whatever, anti-black. One must also keep in mind the close alliance and osmosis between Stalinism and Fascism regarding anything that could be considered, once again, degenerate, cosmopolitan, Jewish, etc. One thing Europeans don't realize, fail to consider in their biography and evaluate very badly within themselves, then, is the extent to which they have internalized and countersigned these archaisms – in the beginning, more or less through their families, and later, more or less through the social fabric itself. Even if these people think, quite wrongly, that they haven't swallowed the values of Fascisim and Stalinism, they have totally ingested them, they have physically assimilated them. I can certify that, for a French intellectual, the discovery of jazz after the war at the age of 14, for example, or blond tobacco, something that came practically from another planet since we were born under the boot of the Germans, or Pétain, or the castrated Pétainist body as it continues to function in French society with its castrated Stalinist alter ego – that sort of postwar flavour in France, that kind of sensuality...Again, I come back to the trumpet of Armstrong or Miles Davis...jazz was a determining factor in my decision to write...The spirituals...And afterwards, what did we experience? We witnessed the attempt to resume this constant effect of anti-modern propaganda in Europe. That is, we've all lost a great deal of time considering problems about world revolution, the unification of thought relative to this revolution, and in our interminable debates on socialism: It is more barbarous? Is it less so here? Will it be less so there? etc. And so it goes on...We must see that European intellectuals misjudge the possibility that a completely different planet can exist on the basis of the underground, non-philosophic, non-Greek history which was grafted there and began to flicker in their biography from the 1960s on. The truth is that many felt guilty, and still feel guilty, about going the 'American' way: caught in their language...inherited centralist pretensions...clanishness, factionalism...'social' worries ...terror or sanctity of knowledge...persistent somnambulistic 'Communist Partyism', etc.

JK　The cold war in culture has lasted a long time.

PhS　The 'cold war', in fact, is a war that doesn't necessarily take the hard, visible forms one might suspect. It's a fabric of propaganda and constant resistance organized by generations who wished at any price to disguise or justify the nationalist or 'socialist' cancer and their Fascist or populist-Stalinist bullshit. They wanted, and continue to want, to impose their artisanal, occultish-rustic stupidity – the remains, in France, for example, of the result of the degeneration of the 'Enlightenment' into a profoundly regressive provincial irrationalism. European intellectuals, with a few rare exceptions, have failed to grasp the new *rhythm* of the planet as it developed in the USA. They were philosophers, rationalists, Mediterraneans, humanists with a big thesis, Aristotelian-Platonists, post-Proustians, aphorists, shameful Zhdanovites, refurbished Stendhalians, children of the Third Republic – institutionalized, universalized, normalized. In short, lagging very much beind the Germans or the Russians *in exile*. *Arcane 17* brings back *nothing* from the United States, and Céline would have done better, after the *Voyage*, to stay in New York. Duchamp should have brought Artaud there by force; that way, we wouldn't be reduced to reading exegeses of what happened at Rodez, etc. I mean that everything great in Europe had to be delirious, to struggle under the weight of atrocious misunderstandings, as Poe had done earlier, over there...there was of course the inhuman composure of Joyce...Perhaps one had to be Irish...

JK It is always difficult to be on the Left and to be interested in American culture; one becomes suspect. The 'cold war' of the superstructures isn't over. American friends have given me Simone de Beauvoir's trip as an example of it. She went to look for the exploited workers and the slums she had read about in a novel. She was told that this didn't exist any longer, but she didn't believe it. She wanted to witness it, to visit it, etc. There's a naïve image of America which isn't always false, but which can hide the forest.

MP My perception of America and, to return to what Julia was saying before, my perception even of China is based, I think, on a certain type of relationship with language, and which I'd define as determined by what one could generally call art. That is, during the trip to China I constantly experienced two things: what I would call the discourse on China, even within China; and what I, as poet and writer, could perceive of the flashes and remains of the life of another culture and another language. It's more or less the same with the USA for me. What finally interests me is the way I can experience things there as more compelling, alive, risky and intense than elsewhere. If you start with the observation that the French artist has internalized Pétainism, which is more or less undeniable, then in my view it's grounded in what I should call a subjective economy in which, in a way, art is shocking. In Europe, art, and in a certain way modern art, is completely intolerable. It is intolerable because it's a luxury, because it's not destined for the masses; because it's a demand that supports no system, state, nation or law other than its own. And I think that there are in modern art certain extremely significant symptoms that could actually be called 'drifting'; during the twentieth century there's a drifting of artists and intellectuals throughout the world. And this symptom begins to create meaning and a vision. When one arrives in the United States one drifts around very easily, with a liberty found absolutely nowhere else, simply because, as you were saying, there are so many discourses and their subjects are multiple. You can always leave a milieu, abandon a discourse to enter another...The resulting impression is one of waste, of useless expense, of marginality, all of which are always extremely positive for artistic creation, for the life of languages and ideas...

JK   ...if one is a foreigner, that is: it may not be the case for many people who live there. If it's true that a person of the twentieth century can exist honestly only as a foreigner, then America provides us with an example. Those who are established there can live as in any form of Pétainist state: there certainly exists a Pétainism of the Middle West.

MP   On this point I don't think you get anywhere through generalities, but only through our relationship to the real, through concrete practices, which is itself foreign. I must say, as a poet, I feel just as foreign in France.

JK   I'd be curious to know how you saw this country in terms of your own novel, *Paradis*. What did the United States give to the writing of a text like that?

PhS   The fact that I myself was not lagging as far 'behind' my own writing as usual. In France, in Europe, I always feel my language is ahead of me; it gets less 'bored' than I do. New York, from this point of view, means a change of scenery, a completely different syntax, a shift from the horizontal to the vertical. In Paris, for example, you have to follow a flatter prose, that is, one must use a syllogistic and appropriative style. What struck me the most in New York was the information stacked up on the ocean. I didn't feel 'sea' or 'river'. The very clear sky, the flashing, high-tech architecture, the gaps 'in negative space' in the air, the cold water sweeping away the well-stacked electronics ...There's an obviously strong sense of non-sense you can decode in details...it's not 'expanding', not going anywhere, it's starting from minute elements with a blow of the brain, a wash of water...I rediscovered my preference for Bordeaux, Amsterdam, London, Venice to the thousandth power...New Rochelle...a stimulation of energy, while here you must always excuse yourself if you're a little too rhythmic... Here I often tell myself that *Paradis* is 'too much'; over there it's obviously not enough, never enough, accumulation and expense...it makes you modest. Modest in relation to everything that could still be said. Nothing is said, always too much inhibition, too much false modesty...Much more liberty, it's simple, many fewer cops, in uniform or plain clothes. Less on record, less oriented, less centred, less identifies...A land of foreigners as one is or ought to be oneself in relation to all language...As *Paradis* is an ensemble of limits of discourse set to music, a mix of populations of sentences...As I don't particularly write in French but in 'translation'...OK, I felt silently at home, that's it.

MP   Don't you think we've been talking around the problem of having to redefine a place, if indeed it is a question of place, for the artist and intellectual which would be neither what one might want to establish in France nor what one can see in the United States?

JK   We begin from the experience of dissident intellectuals. To speak of this America means making one more sign indicating the difference and the multiplicity each feels in his practice, but it in no ways means soliciting identification with a model.

MP   I've been thinking a bit about that. I'm not so interested in synthesizing, but I was thinking about that when Sollers raised the question of psychoanalysis in the United States and in France, or when you referred to the absence of literature in the United States...

JK   It's perhaps wrong...

MP   No, I don't think it's wrong...not in that sense, in any case. I thought your remarks about the development of particularly silent arts as opposed to verbal ones were absolutely true; that is, American psychoanalysis was in a certain way rather regressive: literature seemed very anachronistic compared to the great cultural and literary effects of the twentieth century and to what can happen in France today. And at the same time I was thinking that the forms taken by this non-assimilation of psychoanalysis, or of discourse, or the new languages of the modern in the United States were, for the moment anyway, extremely anarchic and rather difficult to define. (These forms, moreover, seem to me to be found most often in a quasi-religious domain.) But they seemed at the same time to offer experiments from which no conclusions could have been, or can yet be drawn. We don't know whether these experiments may not lead to a completely surprising modernity tomorrow. In any case, for me they are still rich in potentiality and meaning.

PhS   For me, a tolerable society is one where the sexual fix [*impasse*] is the most visible. And the sexual fix is nowhere more visible than in the United States. Everywhere else the great art of power and its pleasures consists of hiding the sexual fix as much as possible. In the United States, through multiple channels, through this effervescence, you clearly see the same old sexual fix being trotted out. It ranges from the perfectly traditional little puritan family to desperate efforts to explore the limits of perversion or psychosis involving an impossible relation to perversion. You get a spectacle of the sexual fix. This spectacle immediately produces religious substitutions aimed at warding it off, which means this sexual fix unquestionably coexists with the different forms of religion. I don't think any American can imagine the *reason* for this state of affairs. It is a society that experiences this fix by demonstrating it, while others enjoy demonstrating it as little as possible and behave as though there were some way out of it. It is a country that lives on the edge of the new Reason and can't realize it.

JK   Isn't there in all that a deep pessimism with regard to the 'sexual relationship'? It's plausible in literature. If you don't have 'formal' experiments which explore the word and rediscover its nothingness, creating, if possible, a new impetus in the process, you do have a common discourse haunted by the demonic. This has produced not only Faulkner, but also a writer in many respects American, namely Céline. The New York subway is *London Bridge* plus the 'emotional subway' of Céline. A certain experience of fragmentation and of the sexual fix is spoken and enacted in reality. 'Literature' seems weak in the face of this urban, social space which is already that of apocalyptic literature. The United States is a supermodern society which leaves great areas where reality becomes the real, as in the Middle Ages or the Orient...

PhS   Outside the United States we usually hear a load of rubbish designed to *conceal* sexual rubbish. In the United States we hear an awful load of rubbish that is overtly sexual...I prefer to hear sexual rubbish rather than rubbish designed to conceal sexual rubbish (I don't know if I'm making myself clearly understood). Perhaps it's just a foreigner's fleeting impression but since it did strike me I'll mention it. It's very obvious that in American society, signifiers of money and sexual signifiers have a presence and a capacity for repetition that is far greater than elsewhere. There's certainly what must be seen as a link, a deep connection, between exposing the banknote, making it a meaningful signifier, and sexual ideas. I tried to explain this by saying there was an American ideology which, contrary to general opinion, reveals itself as fundamentally matriarchal. I think it's something completely visible, and actually linked to the banknote, to its front and back, if I may put it that way. Having said that, it seems to involve a very hesitant stand on sexual difference.

JK   Yes, but I'm going to play devil's advocate...It is precisely the fact that the unconscious becomes currency and circulates that makes it far less sacrosanct than the Holy Catholic mother.

MP   There are extremely different kinds of repression. There's surely the Catholic, and the Protestant in a certain way, and I'd say that the Protestant gives me the feeling now of being more religious than the Catholic. I feel that repression in the United States feels closer to the religious now than in Europe; the religious element isn't so much denied in the United States, even among the intellectuals – much, much less so than it is in Europe.

PhS   ...and with good reason.

MP   And for me, in this affair, this business of the relationship between sexuality and money seems rather to declare something that is completely and obviously true, and (like all truths) wholly understandable, and which may even function effectively the day it becomes conscious.

PhS   Certainly, I said that it was positive, and that it demonstrated the limits of the social phenomenon itself. That's where it can best be observed. You asked me what relationship that has with *Paradis*, assuming that *Paradis* is the systematic description of all expressible limits, of the fact that, after all, one always writes from the immeasurable weakness of wanting to be read some day by someone, which is absurd ...Well, assuming that this is indeed an effort to describe all possible limits of statements, whether in the form of parody, comedy or in serious form, it's clear that this is best represented in the American society of today, of which we experience only an archaic subgroup. When we say, and rightly, that socialism is unsuccessful capitalism, we always risk getting stuck within petty limits and failing to see society as an adventure that's both multiple and absurd. We can wonder why this self-justification of society and the existence of the species can't be perceived critically from the United States. I have this rapid view, but I believe they have a real block in not perceiving gratuitousness. By gratuitousness I mean the moment where some aspect of sexual difference would be touched on in depth and where a banknote could thus be destroyed because it no longer meant anything from that point on. This doesn't mean that they don't do apparently gratuitous things.

JK   There's a belief in non-gratuitousness best shown, although weakly, by the profusion of religions.

PhS   Religious elements perceptible in the United States are particularly weak. I mean you do see that the different sorts of religious, 'mystic' investments are rather flat, when it comes to the consistency of the experience or of the discourse which articulates it.

JK   Do they seem weak to you because they're not illuminated by criticism, because they're presented as they are, with reference only to the texts?

PhS   No, I find them weak in that they have no language, as it were, no relief, no deep, subjective penetration. It is here that I immediately see something that I find parodic and naïve. One doesn't transcend Catholicism as easily as all that.

JK   But aren't you asking statistically large groups to have an experience of language which is available only to a few? Is middle-class American spiritualism any more inane than the Auvergnats at church and at the healer's? Moreover, even the modern spiritualism which is making a revival here can be considered an American graft. . .this spiritualism also remains extremely naïve.

PhS   My remarks were insidiously directed towards the American mother. This raises a question that seems important to me if you want to assess the involvement of intellectuals and artists in the non-verbal, as we've said. That remains, as everywhere, no doubt, infantile and exhibitionistic.

MP   Don't you think that this naïvety and the ultimate simplicity of the legislative structure in the United States, and in a certain way the fact that these subjective and objective structures are so simple, don't you think that this is also what allows to a certain extent for the place of marginality? Namely, that structures are so simple and classic that they cannot control the entire social body, that they allow part of it to keep control and autonomy, and that this autonomous, non-institutionalized sector will ultimately produce interesting developments, though not necessarily the most interesting ones.

JK   Nothing proves that everything there is right. I wonder about the distress I feel, faced with this weakness and naïvety. You begin by judging it, and then you wonder if this naïvety is not precisely a way of showing the futility of sexual relationships, the emptiness of these relationships and the lack of deep convictions.

PhS   I think that what you're presenting as a conscience of humanity, and therefore as a sort of lucidity, is in fact resistance. One shouldn't be in too much of a hurry to say: 'there is no sexual relationship'. That can be the form used by someone who's defending himself against what he might actually discover through an illusion. Sometimes you learn more from an illusion than from knowing in advance that it won't get you anywhere.

There is thus the very strong and consistent impulse to exhibitionism, to act out the exhibitionist impulse. It seems to be situated between the levels of religious discourse, which I call weak, and of sexual discourse, which I call naïve. Between these two poles an enormously exhibitionistic discourse emerges as a form of sublimation. But we seem to agree that it's characterized at the same time by a kind of relative aphasia. These are discourses of exhibitionism which cannot explain themselves through verbal articulation and which, therefore, cannot be judged in language. It's a very interesting phenomenon, I feel, but it clearly points to a *lack* of perspective on this exposure as a form of spectacle. This doesn't at all mean that the spectacle isn't interesting.

JK   We're making two types of observations here, one analytic, the other sociological. On the analytic level, it's obvious that this lack of verbalization can be resistance. The proof lies in its silence, in its expenditure of exuberant activity. It is a society where people are always on the move, getting from one place to another, working. Skyscrapers are constructed, satellites are built, they are ceaselessly rising up higher, and all crises are digested. There's a kind of immediate acting out of the drive which can also be psychotic (hence the violence, the murders). One question: doesn't this weakened verbalization open up other ways towards *other sublimations*? In fact, although originating in European society and thought, America poses problems for our religions and sense of reason precisely in those areas where we experience our own crises. Perhaps it also gives us some different answers.

Translated by Seán Hand

12

A New Type of Intellectual: The Dissident

Originally published as an editorial in *Tel Quel* in 1977 (no. 74, Winter 1977, pp. 3–8) under the title 'Un nouveau type d'intellectuel: le dissident', this article is almost contemporary with 'Why the United States?'.

In this short essay Kristeva puts the case for a new form of political engagement among intellectuals, an engagement that would escape the old master-slave dialectics outlined by Hegel. In her description of the new politics of marginality, she indicates how a move away from the purely verbal level of politics (mentioning colour, sound and gesture as alternatives) would mobilize the forces necessary to break up the symbolic order and its law. The article, however, does not reject law and society; rather it hopes for a new law and a different society. Drawing on the experience of marginality and exile, whether physical or cultural, the intellectual can still spearhead a certain kind of subversion of Western bourgeois society. For Kristeva, there are three groups of intellectual dissidents (the word is chosen with direct reference to the dissident movements in the Soviet bloc): the intellectual who attacks political power directly (thus inevitably remaining within the very discourse of power that he is out to undo); the psychoanalyst whose major counterpart is religion; and the experimental writer who is out to undermine the law of symbolic language. In addition to these three groups, there is the subversive potential of women. Kristeva here gives a brief and lucid outline of her analysis of the position of women within the symbolic order. This article provides a valuable example of Kristeva's political thought in the late 1970s.

A New Type of Intellectual: The Dissident

Whether seen from the point of view of the Gramscian 'organic intellectual', our portrayal of the intellectual in the modern world is dependent on an insuperable opposition between the masses and the individual, an opposition which is governed by the master–slave dialectic and which generates pity and guilt. Whether or not the master is the Greatest Number and Everyone's Idea of Good, this cannot hide the fact that this dichotomy induces a kind of pro-slavery mentality in the intellectual, who represents the supreme product of the systematic conjunction of Christianity and capitalist production. The intellectual perceiving himself as the guardian of supposedly universal thought, private property and private goods poured back into public resources – these are just some of the stages marking the rocky road from the library to the political party.

The prominent events of the twentieth century do not seem to have shaken the intellectual. So far, only bitterness and regret have been felt over the crisis in social groups, the decline of the family and the nation, or religion and the State (as seen in the difficulties faced by the paternal function), or the codes of sublimation and law, and the ensuing advent of Fascism and Stalinism. There has been no radical analysis of the symbolic and political causes of these phenomena, let alone a *fundamental* questioning of the relationship of the individual to the masses, and, *a fortiori*, of the intellectual to society. Precisely because of this lack of analysis and questioning, we can see that the role of the Western intellectual has been reduced to that of patching up the social groups. The intellectuals (a separate sociological entity made necessary by the present development of productive forces) have used their superior historical perspective inherited from the nineteenth century to devote themselves to a cause whose ideal of social and economic equality is evident but which serves both to swallow up the particular characteristics of intellectual work and to perpetuate the myth of a successful society whose messianism, when not Utopian, has turned out to border on totalitarianism. Whether euro-communist or not, the future of Western society will greatly depend on a re-evaluation of the relationship of the masses to the individual or intellectual, and on our ability to break out of the dialectical trap between these oppositions and to recast the whole relationship.

This recasting had already been outlined by Nietzsche, when he traced the genealogy of morals and located the roots of modern revolt in the Antichrist. But it surfaces above all in the eruption of the languages of modernity. In the wake of a Christianity in a state of terminal crisis, one sees only too well how modern art, whether painting, music or literature, is an attempt to achieve sublimation even when it inevitably borders on psychosis or mental disorder. But the *modern community* is given a new status by the practice of this independent avant-garde, and above all by the spread of underground culture to the masses. There is a new synthesis between sense, sound, gesture and colour, the master discourses begin to drift and the simple rational coherence of cultural and institutional codes breaks down. It is on this background that we can perceive a new status of the *modern community*. In place of the mass meeting or the walkabout whose most 'successful' manifestations are fascist meetings or socialist realism, these new languages use the group to question particular forms of subjectivity or the unconscious. What has emerged in our postwar culture, after the wave of totalitarianism, is these peculiar kinds of speeches and *jouissance* directed against the equalizing Word, even when it is secular or militant. This is something ignored by the machinery of politics, including that on the left, which has been caught up in a large history that excludes the specific histories of speech, dreams and *jouissance*. Communal but particular, addressed to all and yet carried out by each individual: such is the culture of our age, that is, when it is not only an echo-chamber of the past. From this point on, another society, another community, another body start to emerge.

It is the task of the intellectual, who has inherited those 'unproductive' elements of our modern technocratic society which used to be called the 'humanities', not just to produce this right to speak and behave in an individual way in our culture, but to assert its *political value*. Failing this, the function of the intellectual strangely enough turns into one of coercion. In the wake of the priest, it is the Marxist and the Freudian who today have become these manufacturers of an all-embracing rationality. When taken out of their own time and space (when no longer considered in terms of economic struggle or transference) Marxism and Freudianism fill in the gaps and stem all escape, and often become the magic password that closes the door and reinforces the belief in a society shaped by constraint, thus justifying the obsessional dialectic of the slave.

It was perhaps inevitable, then, that the *dissident function* of the intellectual should have been asserted by the unemployed of the future, those intellectuals without a job or students with no prospects of being taken on by any restrictive and bankrupt social 'formations'. If it had not been for this situation, the Western intellectual would still have too many 'reception facilities' that allow him to feel at home, including and perhaps even above all when he is 'in opposition'.

A spectre haunts Europe: the dissident.

Give voice to each individual form of the unconscious, to every desire and need. Call into play the identity and/or the language of the individual and the group. Become the analyst of every kind of speech and institution considered socially impossible. Proclaim that we reveal the Impossible.

Perhaps the Paris Commune, as the first and only post-bourgeois revolution, displayed this degree of anarchist enthusiasm in its fight against all power, beliefs and institutions.

But an eruption of languages, like that of our own age, has rarely produced such a clear awareness of the closed nature of society and its safety mechanisms, which range from the group (the Family, the Nation, the State, the Party) to its rational technological forms of discourse. The intellectual, who is the instrument of this discursive rationality, is the first to feel the effects of its break-up: his own identity is called into question, his dissidence becomes more radical.

It is possible to distinguish three types of dissident today. First, there is the rebel who attacks political power. He transforms the dialectic of law-and-desire into a war waged between *Power and Resentment*. His paranoia, however, means that he still remains within the limits of the old master–slave couple. Secondly, there is the psychoanalyst, who transforms the dialectic of law-and-desire into a contest between *death and discourse*. His archetypal rival from whom he tries to distance himself is religion. For in the endless process by which death and discourse beget one another, psychoanalysis sustains itself with a perverse belief in limits, and the necessity of a positive attitude: in short, the community. Though it may resemble Judaism when it seeks to transcribe this social limit as the split, wound or truth in every speaking being, or Christianity when it articulates the *jouissance* arising from the ability to transcend this limit in a resurrection that is as imaginary as it is symbolic or real, psychoanalysis and its spiritual spin-offs none the less still remain today a site of active dissidence in the face of an all-embracing rationality. Thirdly, there is the writer who experiments with the limits of identity, producing texts where the law does not exist outside language. A playful language therefore gives rise to a law that is over-turned, violated and pluralized, a law upheld only to allow a polyvalent, polylogical sense of play that sets the being of the law ablaze in a peaceful, relaxing void. As for desire, it is stripped down to its basic structure: rhythm, the conjunction of body and music, which is precisely what is put into play when the linguistic *I* takes hold of this law.

And sexual difference, women: isn't that another form of dissidence?

When he spoke of law, Hegel distinguished between Human Law (that of man, governments and ethics) and Divine Law (that of women, families, the worship of the dead and religion). On the side of men, the clear laws of conscious existence; on the side of women, the dark right of the nether world. We can criticize the old 'master thinker', who has already been bombarded from all sides, for this pre-Freudian and no doubt highly phallic vision. Let us none the less retain the point that ultimate law (Divine Law) becomes instituted through Death. There is no law but the law of death. To acknowledge this may help us to cause fewer deaths with the law. Freud knew this, since he worked from the principle that any society, and consequently the law, is 'founded on a common crime'. Even more fundamentally, though, and this is a point feminism does not make, it is women who are least afraid of death or the law, which is why they administer both. In more modern terms, they administer the affairs of that nether world of political law represented by the laws of reproduction. Does this mean, then, that mothers, at the opposite extreme of dissidence, are the last guarantee of sociality, since they ultimately ensure the continuation of the species?

In this way a woman never participates as such in the consensual law of politics and society but, like a slave promoted to the rank of master, she gains admission to it only if she becomes man's homologous equal. A woman is trapped within the frontiers of her body and even of her species, and consequently always feels *exiled* both by the general clichés that make up a common consensus and by the very powers of generalization intrinsic to language. This female exile in relation to the General and to Meaning is such that a woman is always singular, to the point where she comes to represent the singularity of the singular – the fragmentation, the drive, the unnameable. This is why philosophy has always placed her on the side of that singularity – that fragmentation prior to name or to meaning which one calls the Daemon – she is demonic, a witch. But this fiendish force exiled from meaning can also aspire to recognition in another diabolical way: this is why women have been swallowed up by the machinery of institutionalized power to the extent that today they represent its best hopes (cf. the rise of women within the political parties).

As for the laws of reproduction of the species, here we touch on the most difficult and perhaps most risky point raised by the problem of women. To query the stability of the female role in the reproduction of the species is an act that affects the child and therefore ultimately calls into question the species itself. But, in fact, are not the great problems of our age (from 'madness' to the extreme language of the avant-garde or of psychedelic experience) precisely those that question the limits of the species? For in this 'right of the nether world' (as Hegel described the law of the family and reproduction), a woman or mother is a conflict – the incarnation of the split of the complete subject, a passion. We still cannot reply to Mallarmé's question: *What is there to say concerning childbirth?*, which is probably just as poignant if not more so than the famous *Che vuoi?* which Freud once addressed to a woman. After the Virgin, what do we know of a mother's (introspective) speech? In this domain, desire (of the child) lays down the law – and here I have described a tendency towards paranoia that may well constitute the repressed basis of any feminine specificity. But simply through being pregnant and then becoming a mother, a woman finds a way that is both natural and cultural (it is possibly banal, but it certainly works) not to live out this temptation towards paranoia, but to spread it over the social body to alleviate the strain. Pregnancy is first of all an institutionalized form of psychosis: me or it, my own body or another body. It is an identity that splits, turns in on itself and changes without becoming other: the threshold between nature and culture, biology and language. Subsequently, with the arrival of the child and the start of love (perhaps the only true love of a woman for another person, embracing the complete range, from Lady Macbeth to self-sacrifice), the woman gains the chance to form that relationship with the symbolic and ethic Other so difficult to achieve for a woman. If pregnancy is a threshold between nature and culture, maternity is a bridge between singularity and ethics. Through the events of her life, a woman thus finds herself at the pivot of sociality – she is at once the guarantee and a threat to its stability.

Under these conditions, female 'creation' cannot be taken for granted. It can be said that artistic creation always feeds on an identification, or rivalry, with what is presumed to be the mother's *jouissance* (which has nothing agreeable about it). This is why one of the most accurate representations of creation, that is, of artistic practice, is the series of paintings by De Kooning entitled *Women*: savage, explosive, funny and inaccessible creatures in spite of the fact that they have been massacred by the artist. But what if they had been created by a woman? Obviously she would have had to deal with her own mother, and therefore with herself, which is a lot less funny. That is why there is not a lot of female laughter to be found (no female Aristophanes or Nietzsche). In any case, far from contradicting creativity (as the existentialist myth would still have us believe), maternity as such can favour a certain kind of female creation, provided the economic constraints are not too heavy, at least in so far as it lifts fixations, and circulates passion between life and death, self and other, culture and nature, singularity and ethics, narcissism and self-denial. Maternity may thus well be called Penelope's tapestry or Leibniz's network, depending on whether it follows the logic of gestures or of thought, but it always succeeds in connecting up heterogeneous sites.

While a certain feminism continues to mistake its own sulking isolation for political protest or even dissidence, real female innovation (in whatever social field) will only come about when maternity, female creation and the link between them are better understood. But for that to happen we must stop making feminism into a new religion, undertaking or sect and begin the work of specific and detailed analysis which will take us beyond romantic melodrama and beyond complacency.

You will have understood that I am speaking the language of exile. The language of the exile muffles a cry, it doesn't ever shout. No doubt it is for this reason that it produces symptoms which, when written by me (as either signifier or signified), are of course, personal, but also inevitably become symptoms of the French language. Our present age is one of exile. How can one avoid sinking into the mire of common sense, if not by becoming a stranger to one's own country, language, sex and identity? Writing is impossible without some kind of exile.

Exile is already in itself a form of *dissidence*, since it involves uprooting oneself from a family, a country or a language. More importantly, it is an irreligious act that cuts all ties, for religion is nothing more than membership of a real or symbolic community which may or may not be transcendental, but which always constitutes a link, a homology, an understanding. The exile cuts all links, including those that bind him to the belief that the thing called life has A Meaning guaranteed by the dead father. For if meaning exists in the state of exile, it nevertheless finds no incarnation, and is ceaselessly produced and destroyed in geographical or discursive transformations. Exile is a way of surviving in the face of the *dead father*, of gambling with death, which is the meaning of life, of stubbornly refusing to give in to the law of death. Throughout history, there have been several great generations of non-religious exiles:

- The diaspora of the Jews, up until Spinoza, who mistrusted their religion and opened up the way to a Reason that had not yet become an object of worship. As Spinoza said: 'The desire born of Reason cannot be excessive' (the French Revolution gave the lie to this); or 'The knowledge of evil is an inadequate knowledge' (Freud disagreed). This was before they joined wholeheartedly in the new religion of the Enlightenment, whose universalism began by sweeping away all differences and ended up trying to conceal the anti-Semitism of the twentieth century.
- The diaspora of those languages that pluralize meaning and cross all national and linguistic barriers, represented by the literature of Kafka, Joyce and Beckett, who were in turn prefigured by Mallarmé, in spite of his more restrained, more isolated and less strident French style.
- The exiles from the Gulags: some of them retain a certain nostalgia for community and law, and find a substitute in orthodox religion (Solzhenitsyn); while others are even more desperate and take refuge in an irony designed to undermine all law (Bukovsky).
- Finally, the more Western and better-informed exiles who have not experienced the Gulags, and among whom I count myself. I am an exile from socialism and Marxist rationality, but far from seeing socialism as an impossible hypothesis for the West, as those from the Gulag think, I believe on the contrary that it is inevitable and consequently something that one can speak to. We must therefore attack the very premises of this rationality and this society, as well as the notion of a complete historical cycle, and dismantle them patiently and meticulously, starting with language and working right up to culture and institutions. This ruthless and irreverent dismantling of the workings of discourse, thought, and existence, is therefore the work of a dissident. Such dissidence requires ceaseless analysis, vigilance and will to subversion, and therefore necessarily enters into complicity with other dissident practices in the modern Western world.

For true dissidence today is perhaps simply what it has always been: *thought*. Now that Reason has become absorbed by technology, thought is tenable only as an 'analytic position' that affirms dissolution and works through differences. It is an analytic position in the face of conceptual, subjective, sexual and linguistic identity. From this, modern philosophy only retains either the notion of a *position*, in order to offer a specialist or totalizing point of view (as in Marxism, Freudianism, Phenomenology and various forms of empiricism); or else it retains only the notion of analysis as *dissolution*, and writes in a style similar to that of an outmoded avant-garde such as symbolism. Torn between being the guardian of the law and that instance which disavows the law, hasn't philosophy turned away from thought?

If it is true that the sudden surge of women and children in discourse poses insoluble questions for Reason and Right, it is because this surge is also yet another symptom of the Death of Man (with all the intolerable consequences that this entails for classical rationality and individuality). So the sole sublation of this Death is perhaps not a Resurrection: what form could the Transcendence take, if the Beyond has already become incarnate in Madness? And it is even less a Renaissance: since the enlightened Prince has ended up working for the Politbureau or the Corporation. But through the efforts of thought in language, or precisely through the excesses of the languages whose very multitude is the only sign of life, one can attempt to bring about multiple sublations of the unnameable, the unrepresentable, the void. This is the real cutting edge of dissidence.

Translated by Seán Hand

13

Psychoanalysis and the Polis

First given as a paper at 'The Politics of Interpretation' symposium sponsored by *Critical Inquiry* and held at the University of Chicago's Center for Continuing Education in the autumn of 1981, this essay was published in *Critical Inquiry*, 9, no. 1 (September 1982), and reprinted in an expanded edition of that issue edited by W. J. T. Mitchell, entitled *The Politics of Interpretation* (Chicago: University of Chicago Press, 1983, pp. 83–98). References to the original context of publication have been retained.

In this essay, Kristeva distinguishes between two forms of interpretation: psychoanalytic and political, the latter apparently used in its original Greek sense of 'popular' (*politikos*) discourse, or discourse for and of the citizens (*politēs*) of the city-state (*polis*). Claiming that psychoanalytic interpretation is at once more unsettling and more radical in its implications than the Marxist and deconstructive modes of interpretation currently dominant among American academic professionals, Kristeva chooses to stress the political implications of the act of interpretation itself. The very fact of positing oneself as an interpreter, regardless of the actual meaning one finds in one's object, she argues, is rooted in the subject's need for reassurance as to the stability of his or her identity.

Threatened both by delirium and by the totalitarian pleasures of the belief in One Meaning, the analyst takes up a position, at once necessary and untenable, midway between the classical method of interpretation (where the stability of the interpretive position itself was not questioned) and the modern deconstruction or eradication of the presumed subject–object relationship between interpreter and interpretant. For Kristeva, interpretation is to make connections in a way which opens up the field of subjectivity (the subject as producer of the field of interpretation). This in itself is not a radically new position: Marx and Freud, however, further transformed our understanding of the nature of interpretation by turning it into an *action*: revolution or cure.

Political and analytical interpretation both seek to read the desires of the subject, although the 'political man' focuses on the desire of the masses, and the analyst deals with the individual. In so far as the politician catches the real desire of the masses, his (or her) interpretation is *true*, while nevertheless remaining ideological and utopian. Only the dynamic of the analytic interpretation, however, goes on to demonstrate the erosion of meaning in the discourse of the analysand, pointing to the pressure of heterogeneous forces which are essential constituents of language, the meaningless and the unnameable. In the same way, the discourse of the analyst will also eventually be perceived as language constructed around a void. While political interpretation remains caught in the syndrome of the One Meaning, according to Kristeva, analysis deflates the fantasies of the subject, showing how they founder on the *absence* of meaning. This is not to say that analytic interpretation turns into non-meaning. On the contrary: while indicating the *void* situated precisely at the point where the politician sees the World, it nevertheless weaves its own interpretive discourse, designed to provide support for the transference without which analysis cannot take place. The purpose of transference, however, is eventually to dissolve itself.

Turning to the works of Céline, well known for his extreme anti-Semitism, Kristeva shows how his discourse turns the abject (here defined as the 'locus of needs, of attraction and repulsion, from which an object of forbidden desire arises'; but see also the introduction to 'Freud and Love') into the object of a unifying discourse from which he derives both his own identity and *jouissance* as well as his paranoid urge to exterminate the very object that allows him to speak in the first place. The case of Céline shows how such a delirium of interpretation can arise from a fascination with the enigma of that which is beyond discourse (the abject, desire). This, however, is precisely the terrain on which the analyst must place herself: analytic interpretation is only truly psychoanalytic when it avoids masking the *dangers* of interpretation. Instead it must open for a series of 'free associations' which allows the analytic interpreter to affirm that the crisis of interpretation is inherent in the symbolic function itself. The analyst thus perceives as symptoms all constructions which seek to deny this crisis.

Quoting as she does both Marx and Freud as epigraphs and 'fathers' of a new form of interpretation, Kristeva here raises, but does not pursue, the question of the relationship between a revolutionary Marxist mode of interpretation and the therapeutic Freudian mode described in her essay.

Psychoanalysis and the Polis

Up until now philosophers have only interpreted the world. The point now is to change it.

Karl Marx and Friedrich Engels, *Theses on Feuerbach*

The delusions [*Wahnbildungen*] of patients appear to me to be the equivalents of the [interpretive] constructions which we build up in the course of an analytic treatment – attempts at explanation and cure.

Sigmund Freud, 'Constructions in Analysis'

The essays in this volume convince me of something which, until now, was only a hypothesis of mine. Academic discourse, and perhaps American university discourse in particular, possesses an extraordinary ability to absorb, digest and neutralize all of the key, radical or dramatic moments of thought, particularly a fortiori, of contemporary thought. Marxism in the United States, though marginalized, remains deafly dominant and exercizes a fascination that we have not seen in Europe since the Russian *Proletkult* on the 1930s. Post-Heideggerian 'deconstructivism', though esoteric, is welcomed in the United States as an antidote to analytic philosophy or, rather, as a way to valorize, through contrast, that philosophy. Only one theoretical breakthrough seems consistently to *mobilize* resistances, rejections and deafness; psychoanalysis – not as the 'plague' allowed by Freud to implant itself in America as a 'commerce in couches' but rather as that which, with Freud and after him, has led the psychoanalytic decentring of the speaking subject to the very foundations of language. It is this latter direction that I will be exploring here, with no other hope than to awaken the resistances and, perhaps, the attention of a concerned few, after the event [*après coup*].

For I have the impression that the 'professionalism' discussed throughout the 'Politics of Interpretation' conference is never as strong as when profesionals denounce it. In fact, the same pre-analytic rationality unites them all, 'conservatives', and 'revolutionaries' – in all cases, jealous guardians of their academic 'chairs' whose very existence, I am sure, is thrown into question and put into jeopardy by psychoanalytic discourse. I would therefore schematically summarize what is to follow in this way:

1 There are political implications inherent in the act of interpretation itself, whatever meaning that interpretation bestows. What is the meaning, interest and benefit of the interpretive position itself, a position from which I wish to give meaning to an enigma? To give a political meaning to something is perhaps only the ultimate consequence of the epistemological attitude which consists, simply, of the desire

to give meaning. This attitude is not innocent but, rather, is rooted in the speaking subject's need to reassure himself of his image and his identity faced with an object. Political interpretation is thus the apogee of the obsessive quest for A Meaning.

2   The psychoanalytic intervention within Western knowledge has a fundamentally deceptive effect. Psychoanalysis, critical and dissolvant, cuts through political illusions, fantasies and beliefs to the extent that they consist in providing only one meaning, an uncriticizable ultimate Meaning, to human behaviour. If such a situation can lead to despair within the polis, we must not forget that it is also a source of lucidity and ethics. The psychoanalytic intervention is, from this point of view, a counterweight, an antidote, to political discourse which, without it, is free to become our modern religion: the final explanation.

3   The political interpretations of our century have produced two powerful and totalitarian results: Fascism and Stalinism. Parallel to the socio-economic reasons for these phenomena, there exists as well another, more intrinsic reason: the simple desire to give a meaning, to explain, to provide the answer, to interpret. In that context I will briefly discuss Louis Ferdinand Céline's texts in so far as the ideological interpretations given by him are an example of political delirium in avant-garde writing.

I would say that interpretation as an epistemological and ethical attitude began with the Stoics. In other words, it should not be confused with *theory* in the Platonic sense, which assumes a prior knowledge of the ideal Forms to which all action or creation is subordinate. Man, says Epictetus, is 'born to contemplate God and his works, and not only to contemplate them but also interpret them [kai ou monon teatin, ala kai exegetin auton]'. 'To interpret' in this context, and I think always, means 'to make a connection'. Thus the birth of interpretation is considered the birth of semiology, since the semiological sciences relate a sign (an event-sign) to a signified in order to *act* accordingly, consistently, consequently.[1]

Much has been made of the circularity of this connection which, throughout the history of interpretive disciplines up to hermeneutics, consists in enclosing the enigmatic (interpretable) object within the interpretive theory's pre-existent system. Instead of creating an object, however, this process merely produces what the interpretive theory had pre-selected as an object within the enclosure of its own system. Thus it seems that one does not interpret something outside theory but rather that theory harbours its object within its own logic. Theory merely projects that object on to a theoretical place at a distance, outside its grasp, thereby eliciting the very possibility of interrogation (Heidegger's *Sachverhalt*).

We could argue at length about whether interpretation is a circle or a spiral: in other words, whether the interpretable object it assigns itself is simply constituted by the interpretation's own logic or whether it is recreated, enriched and thus raised to a higher level of knowledge through the unfolding of interpretive discourse. Prestigious work in philosophy and logic is engaged in this investigation. I will not pursue it here. Such a question, finally, seems to me closer to a Platonic idea of interpretation (i.e., theorization) than it does to the true innovation of the Stoics' undertaking. This innovation is the reduction, indeed the elimination, of the distance between theory and action as well as between model and copy. What permits this elimination of the distance between nature (which the Stoics considered interpretable) and the interpreter is the extraordinary opening of the field of subjectivity. The person who does the interpretation, the subject who makes the connection between the sign and the signified, is the Stoic sage displaying, on the one hand, the extraordinary architectonics of his *will* and, on the other, his mastery of *time* (both momentary and infinite).

I merely want to allude to this Stoic notion of the primordial interdependence of *interpretation*, subjective *will* and mastery of *time*. For my own interest is in contemporary thought which has rediscovered, in its own way, that even if interpretation does no more than establish a simple logical connection, it is netvertheles played out on the scene of speaking subjectivity and the moment of speech. Two great intellectual ventures of our time, those of Marx and Freud, have broken through the hermeneutic tautology to make of it a *revolution* in one instance and, in the other, a *cure*. We must recognize that all contemporary political thought which does not deal with technocratic administration – although technocratic purity is perhaps only a dream – uses interpretation in Marx's and Freud's sense: as transformation and as cure. Whatever *object* one selects (a patient's discourse, a literary or journalistic text or certain socio-political behaviour), its interpretation reaches its full power, so as to tip the object towards the *unknown* of the interpretive theory or, more simply, toward the theory's *intentions*, only when the interpreter *confronts* the interpretable object.

It is within this field of confrontation between the object and the subject of interpretation that I want to pursue my investigation. I assume that at its resolution there are two major outcomes. First, the object may succumb to the interpretive intentions of the interpreter, and then we have the whole range of domination from suggestion to propaganda to revolution. Or second, the object may reveal to the interpreter the unknown of his theory and permit the constitution of a new theory. Discourse in this case is renewed; it can begin again: it forms a new object and a new interpretation in this reciprocal transference.

Before going any further, however, I would like to suggest that another path, post-hermeneutic and perhaps even post-interpretive, opens up for us within the lucidity of contemporary discourse. Not satisfied to stay within the interpretive place which is, essentially, that of the Stoic sage, the contemporary interpreter renounces the game of *indebtedness*, *proximity* and *presence* hidden within the connotations of the concept of interpretation. (*Interpretare* means 'to be mutually indebted'; *prêt*: from popular Latin *praestus*, from the classical adverb *praesto*, meaning 'close at hand', 'nearby'; *praesto esse*: 'to be present, attend' *praestare*: 'to furnish, to present [as an object, e.g., money]'.) The modern interpreter avoids the presentness of subjects to themselves and to things. For in this presentness a strange object appears to speaking subjects, a kind of currency they grant themselves – interpretation – to make certain that they are really there, close by, within reach. Breaking out of the enclosure of the presentness of meaning, the *new* 'interpreter' no longer interprets: he speaks, he 'associates', because there is no longer an object to interpret; there is, instead, the setting-off of semantic, logical, phantasmatic and indeterminable sequences. As a result, a fiction, an uncentred discourse, a subjective polytopia come about, cancelling the metalinguistic status of the discourses currently governing the post-analytic fate of interpretation.

The Freudian position on interpretation has the immense advantage of being midway between a classic interpretive attitude – that of providing meaning through the connection of two terms from a stable place and theory – and the questioning of the subjective and theoretical stability of the interpretant which, in the act of interpretation itself, establishes the theory and the interpreter himself as interpretable objects. The dimension of *desire*, appearing for the first time in the citadel of interpretive will, steals the platform from the Stoic sage, but at the same time it opens up time, suspends Stoic suicide and confers not only an interpretive power but also a transforming power to these new, unpredictable signifying effects which must be called *an imaginary*. I would suggest that the wise interpreter give way to delirium so that, out of his desire, the imaginary may join interpretive closure, thus producing a perpetual interpretive creative force.

1 What is delirium?

Delirium is a discourse which has supposedly strayed from a presumed reality. The speaking subject is presumed to have known an object, a relationship, an experience that he is henceforth incapable of reconstituting accurately. Why? Because the knowing subject is also a *desiring* subject, and the paths of desire ensnarl the paths of knowledge.

Repressed desire pushes against the repression barrier in order to impose its contents on consciousness. Yet the resistance offered by consciousness, on the one hand, and the pressure of desire, on the other, leads to a displacement and deformation of that which otherwise could be reconstituted unaltered. This dynamic of delirium recalls the constitution of the dream or the phantasm. Two of its most important moments are especially noteworthy here.

First, we normally assume the opposite of delirium to be an objective reality, objectively perceptible and objectively knowable, as if the speaking subject were only a simple knowing subject. Yet we must admit that, given the cleavage of the subject (conscious/unconscious) and given that the subject is also a subject of desire, perceptual and knowing apprehension of the original object is only a theoretical, albeit undoubtedly indispensable, hypothesis. More importantly, the system Freud calls perception-knowledge (subsequently an object of interpretation or delirium) is always already marked by a *lack*: for it shelters within its very being the non-signifiable, the non-symbolized. This 'minus factor', by which, even in perception-knowledge, the subject signifies himself as subject of the desire of the Other, is what provokes, through its insistence on acceding to further significations, those deformations and displacements which characterize delirium. Within the nucleus of delirious construction, we must retain this hollow, this void, this 'minus 1', as the instinctual drive's insistence, as the unsymbolizable condition of the desire to speak and to know.

Yet delirium holds; it asserts itself to the point of procuring for the subject both *jouissance* and stability which, without that adhesive of delirium, would disintegrate rapidly into a somatic symptom, indeed, into the unleashing of the death drive. It can do so, however, only because the discourse of delirium 'owes its convincing power to the element of historical truth which it inserts in the place of the rejected reality'.[2] In other words, delirium masks reality or spares itself from a reality while at the same time saying a truth about it. More true? Less true? Does delirium know a truth which is true in a different way than objective reality because it speaks a certain subjective truth, instead of a presumed objective truth? Because it presents the state of the subject's desire? This 'mad truth' (*folle vérité*) of delirium is not evoked here to introduce some kind of relativism or epistemological skepticism.[3] I am insisting on the part played by truth in delirium to indicate, rather, that since the displacement and deformation peculiar to delirium are moved by desire, they are not foreign to the passion for knowledge, that is, the subject's subjugation to the desire to know. Desire and the desire to know are not strangers to each other, up to a certain point. What is that point?

Desire, the discourse of desire, moves towards its object through a connection, by displacement and deformation. The discourse of desire becomes a discourse of delirium when it forecloses its object, which is always already marked by that 'minus factor' mentioned earlier, and when it establishes itself as the complete locus of *jouissance* (full and without exteriority). In other words, no other exists, no object survives in its irreducible alterity. On the contrary, he who speaks, Daniel Schreber, for example, identifies himself with the very place of alterity, he merges with the Other, experiencing *jouissance* in and through the place of otherness. Thus in delirium the subject himself is so to speak the Phallus, which implies that he has obliterated the primordial object of desire – the mother – either because he has foreclosed the mother, whom he finds lacking, or because he has submerged himself in her, exaggerating the totality thus formed, as if it were the Phallus. Delirium's structure thus constitutes the foreclosure of the paternal function because of the place it reserves for the maternal – but also feminine – object which serves to exclude, moreover, any other consideration of objectality.

By contrast, if it is true that the discourse of knowledge leads its enigmatic pre-object, that which solicits interpretation – its *Sachverhalt* – inside its own circle and as such brings about a certain hesitation of objectness, it does not take itself for the Phallus but rather places the

Phallus outside itself in what is to be known: object, nature, destiny. That is why the person through whom knowledge comes about is not mad, but (as the Stoics have indicated) he is (subject to) death. The time of accurate interpretation, that is, an interpretation in accordance with destiny (or the Other's Phallus), is a moment that includes and completes eternity; interpretation is consequently both happiness and death of time and of the subject: suicide. The transformation of sexual desire into the desire to know an object deprives the subject of this desire and abandons him or reveals him as subject to death. Interpretation, in its felicitous accuracy, expurgating passion and desire, reveals the interpreter as master of his will but at the same time as slave of death. Stoicism is, and I'll return to this point, the last great pagan ideology, tributary of nature as mother, raised to the phallic rank of Destiny to be interpreted.

2 Analytic interpretation

Like the delirious subject, the psychoanalyst builds, by way of interpretation, a construction which is true only if it triggers other associations on the part of the analysand, thus expanding the boundaries of the analysable. In other words, this analytic interpretation is only, in the best of cases, *partially true*, and its truth, even though it operates with the past, is demonstrable only by its *effects in the present*.

In a strictly Stoic sense, analytic interpretation aims to correspond to a (repressed) event or sign in order to *act*. In the same sense, it is a *connection* between disparate terms of the patient's discourse, thereby re-establishing the causes and effects of desire; but it is especially a connection of the signifiers peculiar to the analyst with those of the analysand. This second circulation, dependent on the analyst's desire and operative only with him, departs from interpretive mastery and opens the field to suggestion as well as to projection and indeterminable drifts. In this way, the analyst approaches the vertigo of delirium and, with it, the phallic *jouissance* of a subject subsumed in the dyadic, narcissistic construction of a discourse in which the *Same* mistakes itself for the *Other*. It is, however, only by detaching himself from such a vertigo that the analyst derives both his *jouissance* and his efficacy.

Thus far, we have seen that analytic interpretation resembles delirium in that it introduces desire into discourse. It does so by giving narcissistic satisfaction to the subject (the analyst or the analysand), who, at the risk of foreclosing any true object, derives phallic jubilation from being the author/actor of a connection that leaves room for desire or for death in discourse.

Yet the analytic position also has counterweights that make delirium work on behalf of analytic truth. The most obvious, the most often cited, of these is the *suspension* of interpretation: silence as frustration of meaning reveals the ex-centricity of desire with regard to meaning. Madness/meaninglessness *exists* – that is what interpretive silence suggests. Secondly, the analyst, constantly tracking his own desire, never stops analysing not only his patients' discourse but also his own attitude towards it which is his own counter-transference. He is not fixed in the position of the classical interpreter, who interprets by virtue of stable meanings derived from a solid system or morality or who at least tries to restrict the range of his delirium through a stable theoretical counterweight. This is not to say that analytic theory does not exist but rather that, all things considered, its consistency is rudimentary when compared to the counter-transferential operation which is always specific and which sets the interpretive machine in motion differently every time. If I know that my desire can make me delirious in my interpretive constructions, my return to this delirium allows me to dissolve its meaning, to displace by one or more notches the quest for meaning which I suppose to be *one* and *one only* but which I can *only* indefinitely approach. *There is meaning, and I am supposed to know it to the extent that it escapes me.*

Finally, there is what I will call the *unnameable*: that which is necessarily enclosed in every questionable, interpretable, enigmatic object. The analyst does not exclude the unnameable. He knows that every interpretation will float over that shadowy point which Freud in *The Interpretation of Dreams* calls the dreams' 'umbilical'. The analyst knows that delirium, in its phallic ambition, consists precisely in the belief that light can rule everywhere, without a shadow. Yet the analyst can sight and hear the unnameable, which he preserves as the condition of interpretation, *only if he sees it as a phantasm.* As origin and condition of the interpretable, the unnameable is, perhaps, the primordial phantasm. What analysis reveals is that the human being does not speak and that, a fortiori, he does not interpret *without* the phantasm of a return to the origin, without the hypothesis of an unnameable, of a *Sachverhalt.*

Furthermore, analysis reveals that interpretive speech, like all speech which is concerned with an object, is acted upon by the desire to return to the archaic mother who is resistant to meaning. Interpretive speech does this so as to place the archaic mother within the order of language – where the subject of desire, in so far as he is a speaking subject, is immediately displaced and yet, henceforth, situated. The return to the unnameable mother may take the form of narcissistic and masochistic delirium, in which the subject merely confronts an idealized petrification of himself in the form of an interpretive Verb, interpretation becoming, in this case, Everything, subject and object. This is what analytic interpretation confronts, undergoes and, also, displaces.

For, in short, the analyst-interpreter or the interpreter turned analyst derives the originality of his position from his capacity for displacement, from his mobility, from his polytopia. From past to present, from frustration to desire, from the parameter of pleasure to the parameter of death, and so on – he dazes the analysand with the unexpectedness of his interpretation; even so, however, the unexpectedness of the analysis is in any case sustained by a constant: the desire for the Other. ('If you want me to interpret, you are bound in my desire').

Since Edward Glover's *Technique of Psychoanalysis* (1928), a highly regarded work in its time, analytic theory has appreciably refined its notion of interpretation.[4] The criteria for sound interpretation may undoubtedly vary: 'good adaptation' of the analysand, 'progress', appearance of remote childhood memories, encounter with the analyst's transference, and so on. Or criteria for a sound interpretation may even disappear, leaving only the need for a temporary sanction (which may be on the order of the parameters already outlined) within an essentially open interpretive process. In this process, *one* meaning and *one meaning alone* is always specifiable for a particular moment of transference; but, given the vast storehouse of the unknown from which analytic interpretation proceeds, this meaning must be transformed.

If it seems that analytic interpretation, like all interpretation in the strong sense of the word, is therefore an action, can we say that this interpretation aims to change the analysand? Two extreme practices exist. In one, the analysis suggests interpretations; in the other, it assumes a purist attitude: by refusing to interpret, the analysis leaves the patient, faced with the absolute silence of the interpreter, dependent on his own capacity for listening, interpreting and eventually changing. Faced with these excesses, one could argue that in the vast majority of analyses a psychotherapeutic moment occurs which consists in compensating for previous traumatic situations and allowing the analysand to construct another transference, another meaning of his relationship to the Other, the analyst. In the analytic interpretation, however, such a therapeutic moment has, ultimately, no other function than to effect a transference which would otherwise remain doubtful. Only from that moment does true analytic work (i.e., *dissolving*) begin. Basically, this work involves removing obvious, immediate, realistic meaning from discourse so that the meaninglessness/madness of desire may appear and, beyond that, so that every phantasm is revealed as an attempt to return to the unnameable.

I interpret, the analyst seems to say, because Meaning exists. But my interpretation is infinite because Meaning is made infinite by desire. I am not therefore a dead subject, a wise interpreter, happy and self-annihilated in a uniform totality. I am subject to Meaning, a non-Total Meaning, which escapes me.

Analytic interpretation finally leads the analyst to a fundamental problem which I believe underlies all theory and practice of interpretation: the heterogeneous in meaning, the limitation of meaning, its incompleteness. Psychoanalysis, the only modern interpretive theory to hypothesize the heterogeneous in meaning, nevertheless makes that heterogeneity so interdependent with language and thought as to be its very condition, indeed, its driving force. Furthermore, psychoanalysis gives heterogeneity an operative and analysable status by designating it as sexual desire and/or as death wish.

3 Can political interpretation be true?

The efficacy of interpretation is a function of its transferential truth: this is what political man learns from the analyst, or in any case shares with him. Consider, for example, those political discourses which are said to reflect the desires of a social group or even of large masses. There is always a moment in history when those discourses obtain a general consensus not so much because they interpret the situation correctly (i.e., in accordance with the exigencies of the moment and developments dictated by the needs of the majority) but rather because they correspond to the essentially utopian desires of that majority. Such political interpretation interprets *desires*; even if it lacks reality, it contains the truth of desires. It is, for that very reason, utopian and ideological.

Yet, as in analysis, such an interpretation can be a powerful factor in the mobilization of energies that can lead social groups and masses beyond a sado-masochistic ascesis to change real conditions. Such a mobilizing interpretation can be called revolution or demagogy. By contrast, a more objective, neutral and technocratic interpretation would only solidify or very slowly modify the real conditions.

All political discourse that wants to be and is efficacious shares that dynamic. Unlike the analytic dynamic, however, the dynamic of political interpretation does not lead its subjects to an elucidation of their own (and its own) truth. For, as I pointed out earlier, analytic interpretation uses desire and transference, but only to lead the subject, faced with the erosion of meaning, to the economy of his own speaking. It does so by deflating the subject's phantasms and by showing that all phantasms, like any attempt to give meaning, come from the phallic *jouissance* obtained by usurping that unnameable object, that *Sacherverhalt*, which is the archaic mother.

Of course, no political discourse can pass into non-meaning. Its goal, Marx stated explicitly, is to reach the goal of interpretation: interpreting the world in order to transform it according to our needs and desires. Now, from the position of the post-Freudian, post-phenomenological analyst – a position which is really an untenable locus of rationality, a close proximity of meaning and non-meaning – it is clear that there is no World (or that the World is not all there is) and that *to transform* it is only one of the circles of the interpretation – be it Marxist – which refuses to perceive that it winds around a *void*.

Given this constant factor of the human psyche confirmed by the semiotician and the psychoanalyst when they analyse that ordeal of discourse which is the discourse of delirium, what becomes of interpretive discourse? Indeed, what happens to interpretive discourse in view of the void which is integral to meaning and which we find, for example, in the 'arbitrariness of the sign' (the unmotivated relation between signifier and signified in Saussure), in the 'mirror stage' (where the subject perceives his own image as essentially split, foreign, other), or in the various forms of psychic alienation? Clearly, interpretive discourse cannot be merely a hermeneutics or a politics. Different variants of sacred discourse assume the function of interpretation at this point.

Our cultural orb is centred around the axiom that 'the Word became flesh'. Two thousand years after a tireless exploration of the comings and goings between discourse and the object to be named or interpreted, an object which is the solicitor of interrogation, we have finally achieved a discourse on discourse, an interpretation of interpretation. For the psychoanalyst, this vertigo in abstraction is, nevertheless, a means of protecting us from a masochistic and jubilatory fall into nature, into the full and pagan mother, a fall which is a tempting and crushing enigma for anyone who has not gained some distance from it with the help of an interpretive device. However, and this is the second step post-phenomenological analytic rationality has taken, we have also perceived the incompleteness of interpretation itself, the incompleteness charac-teristic of all language, sign, discourse. This perception prevents the closure of our interpretation as a self-sufficient totality, which resembles delirium, and at the same time this perception of the interpretation constitutes the true life of interpretation*s* (in the plural).

4   Literature as interpretation: the text

Philosophical interpretation as well as literary criticism therefore and henceforth both have a tendency to be written as *texts*. They openly assume their status as fiction without, however, abandoning their goal of stating One Meaning, The True Meaning, of the discourse they interpret.

The fate of interpretation has allowed it to leave behind the protective enclosure of a metalanguage and to approach the imaginary, without necessarily confusing the two. I would now like to evoke some specifics and some dangers of openly fictional interpretation in literary discourse itself. So as not to simplify the task, I will take as my example a modern French novelist, Louis Ferdinand Céline (1894–1961), whose popular and musical style represents the height of twentieth-century French literature and whose anti-Semitic and para-Nazi pamphlets reveal one of the blackest aspects of contemporary history.

I consider all fiction (poetic language or narrative) already an inter-pretation in the broad sense of the speaking subject's implication in a transposition (connection) of a presupposed object. If it is impossible to assign to a literary text a pre-existing 'objective reality', the critic (the interpreter) can nevertheless find the mark of the interpretive function of writing in the transformation which that writing inflicts on the language of everyday communication. In other words, *style* is the mark of interpretation in literature. To quote Céline, 'I am not a man of ideas. I am a man of style... This involves taking sentences, I was telling you, and unhinging them.'[5] Such an interpretive strategy is clearly an enunciative strategy, and, in Célinian language, it uses two fundamental techniques: *segmentation* of the sentence, characteristic of the first novels; and the more or less recuperable *syntactical ellipses* which appear in the late novels.

The peculiar segmentation of the Célinian phrase, which is considered colloquial, is a cutting up of the syntactic unit by the projected or rejected displacement of one of its components. As a result, the normally descending modulation of the phrasal melody becomes an intonation with two centres. Thus: 'I had just discovered war in its entirety... Have to be almost in front of it, like I was then, to really see it, the bitch, face on and in profile.'[6]

An analysis of this utterance, not as a syntactic structure but as a *message* in the process of enunciation between a speaking subject and his addressee, would show that the aim of this ejection is to *thematize* the displaced element, which then acquires the status not merely of a theme but of an emphatic theme. 'La vache' ('the bitch') is the vehicle for the primary information, the essential message which the speaker emphasizes. From this perspective, the ejected element is desyntacticized, but it is charged with supplementary semantic value, bearing the speaker's emotive attitude and his moral judgement. Thus, the ejection emphasizes the informative kernel at the expense of the syntactic structure and makes the logic of the message (theme/rheme, support/apart, topic/comment, presupposed/posed) dominate over the logic of syntax (verb-object); in other words, the logic of enunciation dominates over that of the enunciated. In fact, the terminal intonational contour of the rheme (along two modalities: assertive and interrogative) indicates the very point at which the modality of enunciation is most profoundly revealed. The notable preponderance of this contour with the bipartition theme/rheme in children's acquisition of syntax or in the emotive or relaxed speech of popular or everyday discourse is added proof that it is a *deeper* organizer of the utterance than syntactic structures.

This 'binary shape' in Céline's first novels has been interpreted as an indication of his uncertainty about self-narration in front of the Other. Awareness of the Other's existence would be what determines the phenomena of recall and excessive clarity, which then produces segmentation. In this type of sentence, then, the speaking subject would occupy two places: that of his own identity (when he goes straight to the information, to the rheme) and that of objective expression, for the Other (when he goes back, recalls, clarifies). Given the prevalence of this type of construction in the first phases of children's acquisition of syntax, we can state that this binomial, which is both intonational and logical, coincides with a fundamental stage in the constitution of the speaking subject: his autonomization with respect to the Other, the constitution of his own identity.

To Freud's and René Spitz's insistence that 'no' is the mark of man's access to the symbolic and the founding of a distinction between the pleasure principle and the reality principle, one could add that the 'binarism' of the message (theme/rheme and vice versa) is another step, a fundamental step, in the symbolic integration of negativism, rejection and the death drive. It is even a decisive step: with the binarism of the message and before the constitution of syntax, the subject not only differentiates pleasure from reality – a painful and ultimately impossible distinction – but he also distinguishes between the statements: 'I say by presupposing' and 'I say by making explicit', that is, 'I say what matters to me' versus 'I say to be clear' or even, 'I say what I like' versus 'I say for you, for us, so that we can understand each other'. In this way, the binary message effects a slippage from the *I* as the pole of pleasure to the *you* as addressee and to the impersonal *one*, he, which is necessary to establish a true universal syntax. This is how the subject of enunciation is born. And it is in remembering this path that the subject rediscovers, if not his origin, at least his originality. The 'spoken' writing of Céline achieves just such a remembering.

In addition, in Céline's last novels, *D'un château l'autre*, *Nord* and *Rigodon*, he repeatedly uses the famous 'three dots' (suspension points) and the exclamations which sometimes indicate an ellipsis in the clause but serve more fundamentally to make the clause overflow into the larger whole of the message. This technique produces a kind of long syntactic period, covering a half-page, a full page or more. In contrast to Proustian fluctuation, it avoid subordinations, is not given as a logical-syntactic unit and proceeds by brief utterances: clauses pronounceable in one breath which cut, chop and give rhythm. Laconism (nominal sentences), exclamations and the predominance of intonation over syntax re-echo (like segmentation but in another way) the archaic phases of the subject of enunciation. On the one hand, these techniques, because of the influx of non-meaning, arouse the non-semanticized emotion of the reader. On the other hand, they give an infra-syntactical, intonational inscription of that same emotion which transverses syntax but integrates the message (theme/rheme and subject-addressee).[7]

From this brief linguistico-stylistic discussion, I would like to stress the following: style is interpretation in the sense that it is a connection between the logic of utterance and the logic of enunciation, between syntax and message and their two corresponding subjective structures. The unobjectifiable, unnameable 'object' which is thereby caught in the text is what Céline calls an *emotion*. 'Drive', and its most radical component, the death drive, is perhaps an even better term for it. 'You know, in Scriptures, it is written: "In the beginning was the Word." No! In the beginning was emotion. The Word came afterwards to replace emotion as the trot replaced the gallop.'[8] And again: 'Slang is a language of hatred that knocks the reader over for you...annihilates him!...at your mercy!...he sits there like an ass.'[9]

It is as if Céline's stylistic adventure were an aspect of the eternal return to a place which escapes naming and which can be named only if one plays on the whole register of language (syntax, but also message, intonation, etc.). This locus of emotion, of instinctual drive, of non-semanticized hatred, resistant to logico-syntactic naming, appears in Céline's work, as in other great literary texts, as a locus of the ab-ject. The abject, not yet object, is anterior to the distinction between subject and object in normative language. But the abject is also the non-objectality of the archaic mother, the locus of needs, of attraction and repulsion, from which an object of forbidden desire arises. And finally, abject can be understood in the sense of the horrible and fascinating abomination which is connoted in all cultures by the feminine or, more indirectly, by every partial object which is related to the state of abjection (in the sense of the non-separation subject/object). It becomes what culture, the *sacred* must purge, separate and banish so that it may establish itself as such in the universal logic of catharsis.

Is the abject, the ultimate object of style, the archetype of the *Sachverhalt*, of what solicits interpretation? Is it the archi-interpretable? This is, as I said earlier, something analytic interpretation can argue. Meaning, and the interpretation which both posits and lives off meaning, are sustained by that *elsewhere* which goes beyond them and which fiction, style (other variants of interpretation), never stops approaching – and dissolving.

For this is in fact the central issue in Céline as in the great writers of all times. By their themes (evil, idiocy, infamy, the feminine, etc.)

and their styles, they immerse us in the ab-ject (the unnameable, the *Sachverhalt*), not in order to name, reify or objectify them once and for all but to dissolve them and to displace us. In what direction? Into the harmony of the Word and into the fundamental incompleteness of discourse constituted by a cleavage, a void: an effervescent and dangerous beauty, the fragile obverse of a radical nihilism that can only fade away in 'those sparkling depths which [say] that nothing exists any more'.[10]

Yet this pulverization of the abject, the ultimate case of interpretation by style, remains fragile. Because it does not always satisfy desire, the writer is tempted to give one interpretation and one only to the outer limit of the nameable. The *Sacherverhalt*, the abject, is then embodied in the figure of a maleficent agent, both feminine and phallic, miserable and all-powerful, victim and satrap, idiot and genius, bestial and wily. What once defied discourse now becomes the ultimate object of one and only one interpretation, the source and acme of a polymorphous *jouissance* in which the interpreter, this time in his delirium, is finally reunited with what denies, exceeds and excites him. He blends into this abject and its feminine-maternal resonance which threatens identity itself. This interpretive delirium – writing's weak moment – found in Céline the Jew as its privileged object in the context of Hitlerism. The historical and social causes of Céline's anti-Semitism can be sought in monotheism, or, rather, in its denials, and in the history of France and the reality of the Second World War. His anti-Semitism also has a more subtle foundation, more intrinsically linked to the psychic instability of the writer and the speaking subject in general: it is the fascination with the wandering and elusive other, who attracts, repels, puts one literally beside oneself. This other, before being another subject, is an object of discourse, a non-object, an abject. This abject awakens in the one who speaks archaic conflicts with his own improper objects, his ab-jects, at the edge of meaning, at the limits of the interpretable. And it arouses the paranoid rage to dominate those objects, to transform them, to exterminate them.

I do not presume to elucidate in this brief presentation the many causes and aspects of Céline's anti-Semitism. A lengthier consideration of the subject can be found in my *Pouvoirs de l'horreur*. I have broached this difficult and complex subject here to indicate by a *paroxysm*, which we could take as a *hyperbole*, the dangerous paths of interpretive passion, fascinated by an enigma that is beyond discourse. For the psychoanalyst, it recalls a desiring indebtedness to the maternal continent.

I would like the above remarks to be taken both as a 'free association' and as the consequence of a certain position. I would want them to be considered not only an epistemological discussion but also a personal involvement (need I say one of desire?) in the dramas of thought, personality and contemporary politics. Such a vast theme ('the politics of interpretation') cannot help but involve a multiplicity of questions. If their conjunction in my paper seems chaotic, inelegant and non-scientific to a positivist rationality, this conjunction is precisely what defines for me the originality and the difficulty of psychoanalytic interpretation. The task is not to make an interpretive summa in the name of a system of truths – for that attitude has always made interpretation a rather poor cousin of theology. The task is, instead, to record the *crisis* of modern interpretive systems without smoothing it over, to affirm that this crisis is inherent in the symbolic function itself and to perceive as symptoms all constructions, including totalizing interpretation, which try to deny this crisis: to dissolve, to displace indefinitely, in Kafka's words, 'temporarily and for a lifetime'.

Perhaps nothing of the wise Stoic interpreter remains in the analyst except his function as *actor*: he accepts the text and puts all his effort and desire, his passion and personal virtuosity, into reciting it, while remaining indifferent to the events that he enacts. This 'indifference', called 'benevolent neutrality', is the modest toga with which we cover our interpretive desire. Yet by shedding it, by implicating ourselves, we bring to life, to meaning, the dead discourses of patients which summon us. The ambiguity of such an interpretive position is both untenable and pleasurable. Knowing this, knowing that he is constantly in abjection and in neutrality, in desire and in indifference, the analyst builds a strong ethics, not normative but directed, which no transcendence guarantees. That is where, it seems to me, the modern version of liberty is being played out, threatened as much by a single, total and totalitarian Meaning as it is by delirium.

NOTES

1 See Victor Goldschmidt, *Le Système stoïcien et l'idée du temps* (Paris, 1953).
2 Sigmund Freud, 'Construction in analysis', *The Standard Edition of the Complete Psychological Works of Sigmund Freud*, tr. and ed. James Strachey (24 vols, London. 1953–74), vol. XXIII, p. 268.
3 See in my *Folle vérité* (Paris, 1979) the texts presented in my seminar at l'Hôpital de la Cité Universitaire, Service de psychiatrie. [*Editor's note*: Kristeva's main contribution to this book, 'Le vréel', is translated in this volume under the title 'The true-real'.]

4 See esp. Jacques Lacan, 'De l'interprétation au transfert', *Le Séminaire de Jacques Lacan*, vol. XI, *Les Quatre concepts fondamentaux de la psychanalyse* (Paris, 1973), pp. 221ff.

5 Louis Ferdinand Céline, 'Louis Ferdinand Céline vous parle', *Oeuvres complètes* (2 vols, Paris, 1966–9), vol. II, p. 934.

6 'Je venais de découvrir la guerre toute entière. . . Faut être à peu près devant elle comme je l'étais à ce moment-là pour bien la voir, *la vache*, en face et de profil' (Céline, *Voyage au bout de la nuit, Oeuvres complètes*, vol. I, p. 8).

7 For a lengthier discussion of Céline's style and its interpretation, see my *Pouvoirs de l'horreur: essai sur l'abjection* (Paris, 1980). [*Editor's note*: Translated by Léon Roudiez as *Powers of Horror: an essay on abjection*, New York: Columbia University Press, 1982.]

8 Céline, 'Céline vous parle', p. 933.

9 Céline, *Entretiens avec le professeur Y*, 1955; (Paris, 1976), p. 72.

10 Céline, *Rigodon, Oeuvres complètes*, vol. II, p. 927.

[*Translator's note*: I would like to thank Domna Stanton and Alice Jardine for their help on an earlier version of this translation.]

Translated by Margaret Waller

Index